Across
the
SPECTRUM

Across
the
SPECTRUM

Understanding Issues in Evangelical Theology

Second Edition

GREGORY A. BOYD
AND PAUL R. EDDY

BakerAcademic

a division of Baker Publishing Group
Grand Rapids, Michigan

Published by Baker Academic
a division of Baker Publishing Group
P.O. Box 6287, Grand Rapids, MI 49516-6287
www.bakeracademic.com

Second edition published in 2009

Printed in the United States of America

Library of Congress Cataloging-in-Publication Data
Boyd, Gregory A., 1957–
    Across the spectrum : understanding issues in evangelical theology / Gregory A. Boyd &
Paul R. Eddy. — 2nd ed.
      p. cm.
    Includes bibliographical references and index.
    ISBN 978-0-8010-3793-1 (pbk.)
    1. Evangelicalism. 2. Theology, Doctrinal. I. Eddy, Paul R. II. Title.
BR1640.B69 2009
230'.04624—dc22   2009010396

18   19   20   21   22   23   24   14   13   12   11   10   9   8

In keeping with biblical principles of creation stewardship, Baker Publishing Group advocates the responsible use of our natural resources. As a member of the Green Press Initiative, our company uses recycled paper when possible. The text paper of this book is composed in part of post-consumer waste.

green press INITIATIVE

To
our children,
Denay, Alisha, and Nathan,
and Jordan, Juston, and Rachel,

and to
our grandchildren,
Soel and Sage,
and Rylie

Contents

Acknowledgments

We would like to acknowledge several people for their support of this project. A distinct word of appreciation goes to our friend and colleague Don Alexander for contributing the bulk of the chapter on the sanctification debate. We also want to thank our good friend (and Paul's mentor) David K. Clark for contributing the section on speech act theory in the chapter on the inerrancy debate. Our appreciation also goes to our Bethel University colleagues Jim Beilby and Dan Kent for using an early draft of this text and supplying valuable feedback. To our friend and acquisitions editor at Baker Academic Robert N. Hosack, we offer our gratefulness for his encouragement and oversight of this project from conception through a second edition.

Our final word of appreciation goes to our families. Our wives, Shelley Boyd and Kelly Eddy, have offered their unfailing support throughout our various theological endeavors. Our children—Denay, Alisha, and Nathan (Greg's), and Jordan, Juston, and Rachel (Paul's)—remind us daily of the true gifts of God in this lifetime. Our grandchildren—Soel and Sage (Greg's), and Rylie (Paul's)—remind us that there *are* precious blessings to growing older! It is to our children and grandchildren that we dedicate this book.

Preface to the Second Edition

We are grateful for the many students, professors, pastors, and other readers who have made use of our book over the last few years, a number of whom provided feedback and suggestions for a second edition. The primary changes in this new edition include:

- rewriting "The Foreknowledge Debate" chapter to include three views on the topic
- reducing the former "Human Constitution Debate" chapter to one of the issues covered in the appendix
- updating the "Further Reading" sections at the end of each chapter
- including in the book itself the appendix that was formerly online

It is our hope that this second edition will continue to serve our readers as we all, within the body of Christ, seek to live out that ancient piece of Christian wisdom: "In the essential things, unity. In the nonessential things, liberty. And in all things, charity."

Introduction

While this book will appeal to all people interested in the diversity of views that comprise evangelicalism, we have written it specifically for evangelical college students. Its purpose is to introduce these students to the range of positions evangelicals take on various disputed topics. Each position is argued from the perspective of one defending the position and is therefore presented as persuasively as possible (given the introductory nature and space limitations of this book).

This book clearly assumes a distinctly liberal arts approach to the study of theology. It presupposes that the goal of teaching is not for a teacher simply to persuade students of his or her own perspective. Rather, the goal is to broaden students' minds by helping them empathetically understand a variety of perspectives while training them to think critically for themselves. The goal is not indoctrination, in other words, but the development of people who are able to arrive at their own convictions in a prayerful, critically informed manner—whether they agree with the teacher or not.

This approach does not imply that the teacher cannot or should not be passionately committed to particular theological views, nor that he or she should altogether refrain from trying to persuade students of his or her views. But a liberal arts approach to theology does require that all views be presented in as fair and compelling a manner as possible. Students must be allowed to appreciate *why* sincere, godly, biblically-oriented people assume differing positions on various topics. They must be encouraged and empowered to develop a respect and appreciation even for positions with which they and/or their teachers strongly disagree. The purpose of this book is to facilitate teachers in achieving these objectives.

The nature and presuppositions of this work are as follows.

1. The goal of this book is not to present a balanced overview of Christian doctrine. Doctrines are not considered in terms of their historic or existential importance to the evangelical faith but strictly in terms of the differing interpretations contemporary evangelicals have of these doctrines. Hence, for example, the doctrine of the Trinity, which is by most accounts the centerpiece of historic, orthodox Christianity, is relegated to the appendix, and is considered only in terms of the two primary interpretations evangelicals have of this doctrine. The reason is that, while this doctrine is extremely important, the disagreements evangelicals have over how to understand it are not. For courses in theology that offer a well-rounded overview of basic Christian doctrine, we recommend supplementing this book with a standard introductory survey of Christian doctrine.

2. This book considers only options that are discussed and embraced *within evangelicalism.* There is, of course, no universally accepted definition of "evangelicalism." Evangelicals themselves express strong disagreements over this matter. There is, therefore, an unavoidable element of subjectivity in our decisions as to (1) what issues and positions fall within the parameters of evangelicalism, and (2) which issues are major (found in the body of the text) and which are not (found in the appendix or omitted altogether). Our perspective is that for all evangelicalism's diversity, evangelicals are united in their commitment to the core beliefs of historic, orthodox Christianity as expressed in the **ecumenical** creeds and to the primacy of Scripture in all matters of faith and practice. Hence, positions that are distinctly Catholic (e.g., **transubstantiation**) and positions that are distinctly liberal (e.g., revisioning God as Gaia) are not included in this work. Our decisions as to what constituted "major" and "minor" issues were governed mostly by our assessment of how widespread and lively a particular debate was or is within evangelicalism, broadly considered.

Some readers will undoubtedly feel that we have drawn the circle too large, including, for example, the annihilationist position as an evangelical option. Others may feel we have drawn the circle too small, omitting, for example, "evangelical" versions of **universalism.** We make no claim that our particular delineation of the parameters of evangelicalism is *the* correct one. Still less do we claim that our assessment of what constitutes a major and minor issue is infallible. We take some consolation in the awareness that disagreement over these matters would arise no matter where we drew the parameters and how we assessed the topics. We can only encourage teachers to make these issues part of classroom discussions as they deem appropriate.

3. This is an *introductory* book on different positions within evangelicalism. We hope to present to students with no prior background in theology the theological positions evangelicals take on various issues and to do so in a clear and compelling manner. For this reason, as well as space limitations,

the essays in this book are intentionally basic and general in nature. We have at points omitted more technical academic discussions that could perhaps help nuance and sometimes strengthen various positions. Such omissions were deemed necessary to keep this work accessible to students with no prior background in theology, as well as to keep the size manageable and the price affordable. We encourage teachers to consider the essays in this book as springboards from which they can facilitate lively discussions and/ or deeper, more nuanced presentations of various views.

4. The theological criteria assumed in these essays are those suggested by John Wesley's quadrilateral: Scripture, tradition, reason, and experience. However, because this book is designed for an evangelical audience, which in principle holds that Scripture is the final arbiter of theological truth (*sola scriptura*), and because these essays are brief and introductory in nature, the emphasis in most essays is on defending each position biblically. We encourage teachers and students to integrate more thoroughly considerations of tradition, reason, and experience as they critically evaluate various positions.

5. Each chapter follows a basic outline: First, a brief section introduces each topic. The section entitled "Posing the Question" helps students appreciate the real-life relevance of the topic. "The Center and Its Contrasts" follows, which outlines the common ground evangelicals share on the topic over against non-evangelical and/or non-Christian perspectives. Each introduction concludes with a brief survey of the different views evangelicals embrace concerning the topic. Next, these perspectives are presented and defended. The biblical case is presented first, followed by arguments from tradition, reason, and experience when appropriate. Each essay concludes by refuting objections to the position under discussion. A further reading list ends each chapter and helps interested students explore the various positions more thoroughly and/or facilitates research assignments as the teacher sees fit. A glossary of terms that may be unfamiliar to students is found at the end of the book. Terms found in this glossary are in boldface type the first time they appear in the text. Finally, an appendix containing thirteen other issues complements this book.

Our hope and prayer is that this textbook will aid students in arriving at their own informed theological convictions and in developing an understanding of and appreciation for the views of those with whom they disagree.

1

The Inerrancy Debate

Without Error of Any Kind (The Inerrantist View)
Infallible in Matters of Faith and Practice (The Infallibilist View)

Posing the Question

Rachel, a sophomore social work major at a state university, has been building a relationship with her roommate, Molly. As the relationship has developed, she has found opportunities to share her **faith** in Jesus. Molly, a history major, has been showing interest in spiritual things. One day, things take a challenging turn. After listening to a lecture on ancient historiography, in which the New Testament Gospels were used as an example, Molly returned to their room and posed a series of troubling questions to Rachel. Why is the fourth Gospel's record of Jesus' words and deeds so unlike that of the other three? Why do the various Gospel accounts of Jesus' resurrection differ in some of their details? Is the Bible really historically reliable? Historic Christianity has always claimed that the Bible is the trustworthy written Word of God, but how can we be sure of this?

The Center and Its Contrasts

One of the core distinctives of evangelical theology is the conviction that the Bible is the inspired Word of God. With the apostle Paul, evangelicals affirm that "all scripture is inspired by God and is useful for teaching, for reproof, for correction, and for training in righteousness, so that everyone who belongs to God may be proficient, equipped for every good work" (2 Tim. 3:16–17; see also 2 Pet. 1:20–21). Following from this conviction of biblical *inspiration* is the equally important and universally shared evangelical claim of the *authority* of the Bible—that is, the Bible is recognized as the final authority on all matters of Christian faith and practice. Thus, with the Protestant Reformers, evangelicals hold to the principle of *sola scriptura*, that "Scripture alone" is the final authority on religious matters.

The evangelical position stands in contrast to a number of other stances people have adopted toward the Bible. Many non-Christians regard portions of the Bible as "inspiring," but they do not believe the Bible was "inspired by God" (literally, "breathed by God"). Some non-Christians and even some non-evangelical Christians believe the Bible was in some sense divinely inspired, but they do not believe it is unique in this regard. Other religious writings may be equally inspired. Some liberal Christians, for example, suggest that the **Qur'an** or **Bhagavad Gita** were divinely inspired (even though they embody teachings that contradict the Bible). Mormons affirm that the Bible was inspired by God, but they believe the same is true of the **Book of Mormon** and other religious writings. They deny the principle of *sola scriptura*. Catholics deny the principle of *sola scriptura* as well, for they also regard the pope and church tradition as sources of religious authority.

In addition, non-evangelical theologians have proposed a number of views regarding biblical inspiration. For example, Karl Barth, founder of **neo-orthodoxy,** maintained that the Bible *becomes* the Word of God when God sovereignly chooses to make it so, but we cannot claim that this book is inspired in and of itself. Others who follow the *Heilsgeschichte* ("salvation history") school of theology argue that God's revelation is found in events, not writings. The Bible thus witnesses to the revelatory events of God in history but cannot itself be regarded as a divinely inspired book.

Against all such perspectives, evangelicals affirm that the Bible, and the Bible alone, is inspired by God and is the final authority on matters of faith and practice. At the same time, there is some disagreement among evangelicals concerning the question of factual errors in parts of the Bible that touch on things other than Christian faith and practice.

In the 1970s, what has come to be known as the "inerrancy debate" erupted in evangelical circles. The gauntlet was thrown down by the more conservative evangelical perspective with the publication of Harold Lindsell's *The Battle for the Bible* (1976). He maintained that evangelicals have always affirmed that the Bible is absolutely inerrant on all matters that it addresses. Jack Rogers and Donald McKim responded in a work entitled *The Authority and Interpretation of the Bible* (1979). They defended the view that, while the Bible is **infallible** in that it does not fail believers when trusted to do what God inspired it to do, believers need not and should not claim that it is absolutely *inerrant* in all matters it addresses. More specifically, believers should not claim that the Bible is inerrant in some of its tangential scientific and historical statements.

In more recent years, many who hold to the "inerrancy" view have distanced themselves from Lindsell's approach (and more simplistic "Fundamentalist" approaches), and have offered much more sophisticated, nuanced, and hermeneutically sensitive articulations of the inerrancy of the Bible. From the 1978 *Chicago Statement on Biblical Inerrancy* to more recent expressions grounded in "speech act" theory, many evangelicals today acknowledge the complex realities of the biblical texts, while still affirming that, in its original form, the Bible is entirely without error in all of the various matters that it addresses.

The two essays that follow will provide defenses of each of these two perspectives—first, a more nuanced expression of the inerrantist view, followed by an articulation of the infallibilist view.

Without Error of Any Kind (The Inerrantist View)

While the technical term **inerrancy** is of recent origin, the conviction that the Bible is "without error" is not. One cannot find a Christian theologian before the modern period (seventeenth century) who claimed that the Bible makes mistakes (assuming its meaning is properly understood). This is evidence that Christians throughout history have assumed the Bible is without error of any kind. It is "inerrant."

According to the inerrantist view, the Bible is not simply without error in matters of faith and practice, as some evangelicals today teach. It is without error in all matters it addresses, including history and even science. The health, vibrancy, and stability of the church is greatly affected by whether or not this traditional perspective is affirmed.

Having said this, it is important to note several qualifications. First, inerrantists do not claim that the Bible is without any *apparent* errors, only that it is without any *real* errors. They readily admit that there are things about the Bible our finite minds cannot explain. It is incorrect and arrogant, however, to locate the problem in the Bible itself rather than in our limited understanding of the Bible.

Second, the inerrancy of the Bible applies only to the original manuscripts (see **autographs**), not to later copies of these manuscripts. **Textual criticism** has revealed that many minor errors crept into later copies of the biblical documents. The scribes were not divinely inspired in making their copies, so we have no reason to expect their copies to be without error. The Bible we possess today is very close to the originals—the Bible is, in fact, the best attested work in all of history—but it is not identical to the originals.

Third, the inerrancy of the Bible relates to the authors' original intent, not necessarily to our interpretation of a passage. Moreover, the inerrancy of an author's writing must be understood in accordance with the genre of literature the author was using and the culture the author was writing within. For example, we cannot say that an ancient author was incorrect in what he said just because he did not employ the same standard of precision we employ in our culture. Nor can we charge an author with error for using expressions that are not literally true unless their intention was to communicate literal truth. When David speaks of God riding on clouds, blowing smoke out of his nostrils, and throwing thunderbolts (Ps. 18:8–15), for example, he is using metaphors to communicate God's majesty. The expressions are not literally true, of course, but they nevertheless communicate profound truth.

The Biblical Argument

Since all evangelical Christians affirm that the Bible is the inspired foundation of all we believe, we must consult it to determine what we should believe about its nature. The Bible clearly teaches that it is without error. For example, throughout the Bible we learn the truth that God cannot lie or deceive (Num. 23:19; 1 Sam. 15:29; Titus 1:2). When God promises something, it *must* come to pass (e.g., Isa. 46:8–10). When he speaks, it must be true. If someone speaks in the name of God and what he said fails to come to pass, this is proof that the person was not a true prophet of God (Deut. 13:1–5; 18:20–22). The assumption, obviously, is that God cannot err, and all who are inspired to speak on his behalf cannot err. In the words of the psalmist, God's "word is firmly fixed in heaven" (Ps. 119:89). And again, God's "word is truth" and "every one of [his] righteous ordinances endures forever" (Ps. 119:160).

Jesus held this view. In fact, it is impossible to overemphasize Jesus' trust in Scripture. He customarily used the phrases "Scripture says" and "God says" interchangably. He taught that "until heaven and earth pass away, not one letter, not one stroke of a letter, will pass from the law until all is accomplished" (Matt. 5:18). He reiterated the point in even stronger terms when he claimed that "it is easier for heaven and earth to pass away, than for one stroke of a letter in the law to be dropped" (Luke 16:17). In simplest terms, Jesus believed that "scripture cannot be annulled" (John 10:35). When people were in error regarding theological matters, Jesus believed it was most fundamentally because they did not know Scripture well enough (Matt. 22:29). He assumed that if a person knew Scripture properly, that person would know truth. Scripture is true, through and through. It is impossible to imagine a stronger affirmation of the inerrancy of Scripture than that which Jesus gave. If we conclude that Scripture contains errors, we must also conclude that Jesus, the Son of God, was in error.

This same view is found throughout the New Testament. Paul taught that "all scripture is inspired by God" (2 Tim. 3:16). The term *inspired* literally means "God-breathed." For Paul, as well as for Jesus and other New Testament authors, the words of the Bible came directly from the mouth of God. It would be as inconceivable to them that Scripture could err as it would that God could err. If it is indeed "impossible that God would prove false" (Heb. 6:18), it is impossible that Scripture would prove false. This level of confidence extends to the smallest details of Scripture. For example, Jesus wagers an entire argument on the single word "God" found in Psalms (John 10:34–36; cf. Ps. 82:6). And Paul bases an entire argument on the singular form of one word in Genesis (Gal. 3:16; cf. Gen. 13:16).

The only reasonable conclusion is that the Word of God itself supports the inerrantist view.

Supporting Arguments

1. *Church tradition.* As noted earlier, theologians throughout history have assumed that the Bible is without error. Augustine reflected the universal conviction when he wrote, "Only to those books which are called canonical have I learned to give honor so that I believe most firmly that no author in these books made any error in writing."[1] Similarly, Martin Luther insisted that "Scripture cannot err,"[2] and John Calvin referred to the Bible as "the inerring standard."[3]

2. *A logical argument.* Consider the following argument:

  a. God is perfect and thus cannot err.
  b. Scripture is God-breathed (inspired).
  c. What God breathes retains his perfect character.
  d. Scripture cannot err.

The argument is logically sound. The question is, are all the premises valid? With few exceptions, evangelicals generally embrace a and b. Some do not embrace c, however. Yes, Scripture is "inspired," they say, but this does not mean it is inerrant. Consider how paradoxical this position is, however. It is like saying that a certain person never lies but that this characteristic does not necessarily apply to what he says! What is the force of claiming that God cannot err if this does not apply to what comes out of his mouth? Premise c should be accepted, therefore, and this leads directly to the conclusion that Scripture cannot err.

3. *An argument from epistemology.* If we do not accept the view that the Bible is inerrant, then we must accept that the decision as to when the Bible is and is not speaking correctly is in our court. But this means that we have authority over the Bible instead of the other way around. When the Bible agrees with us, we accept its authority. When it does not, we don't. This is an impotent authority.

Some may respond that we may assume the Bible is inerrant in all matters of faith and practice but not in so-called irrelevant matters of history or science. There are two problems with this suggestion, however.

First, what inerrant authority did we use to develop this criterion of what is and is not inerrant in the Bible? There is no such authority. This is simply a convenient thing to believe, so some choose to believe it. As shown, it certainly is not rooted in Scripture, tradition, or the teaching of Jesus.

Second, how are we to decide what is and is not irrelevant? For example, what is to prevent someone from concluding that Paul was simply reflecting an irrelevant aspect of his historically conditioned culture when he denounced fornication or homosexuality (Rom. 1:21–32; 1 Cor. 6:9–10)? Indeed, how are we to decide what is "history" as opposed to a "matter of faith"? Does the story of the flood belong in the category of inerrant teaching relevant to faith or in the category of irrelevant history?

The point is that if we do not have an unassailable foundation for our faith, everything is in principle up for grabs.

4. *A historical argument.* The Bible tells us that the heart is desperately wicked (Jer. 17:9). There is a side of fallen humanity that consistently wants to run away from God. This is why it is so dangerous to deny the inerrancy of Scripture. We cannot trust our own fallen hearts and minds to decide what is true. Invariably, our perception is skewed. As fallen rebels, we will always be inclined to conclude that those aspects of Scripture we do not like are in error, while those aspects we do like are true.

An honest assessment of the recent history of the church in the West bears this out. While it is true that heretical groups have at times affirmed the inerrancy of Scripture (e.g., the early Unitarians, Jehovah's Witnesses), it is also true that the denial of inerrancy has almost always led to some form of heresy if not total unbelief. To illustrate, consider that until the twentieth century the majority of college campuses in America were founded as evangelical Christian institutions. Today, there is no distinctive Christian presence at an institutional level in the vast majority of them. The major shift toward secularism occurred toward the end of the nineteenth century, when professors of theology began to accept **higher biblical criticism** and deny the inerrancy of Scripture. It is with good reason that many evangelical leaders today worry about evangelical teachers and institutions that are equivocating in regard to this foundational Christian doctrine.

5. *Insights from speech act theory.* One contemporary philosophical theory can greatly enhance the doctrine of inerrancy. It's called speech act theory.[4] Its central idea is this: language *does* many things. Normally people think the main task of language is to *say* things (to describe). But according to speech act theory, the purpose of language is broader: its purpose is to *do* things. Saying things (describing the world) is *one* thing that language does, but it's not the *only* valid thing language does.

Take an example: "Abraham Lincoln was our sixteenth president." This sentence describes a part of reality. And so it can be either true or false. But language can rightly do other things besides describe. Take another example: a teenager yells "Yeeow" as he rides the world's wildest roller coaster. This utterance doesn't say something about the world. (It doesn't describe.) So it can't be true or false. But it does communicate; it's a normal communicative act. Speech act says we should view language as doing many things, including both saying true things about the world and expressing someone's feelings.

What else does language do? (1) Statements tell people what is true. (2) Commands try to get people to do things. (3) Promises commit the speaker to doing certain things. (4) Exclamations express feelings or attitudes. (5) Performatives create new realities. Only the first is descriptive, but all five are proper linguistic acts.

How can we apply this insight to inerrancy? Some perfectly proper speech acts in the Bible don't describe the world, so they aren't true or false. But they are legitimate linguistic speech acts. Utterances that don't describe can't be true (inerrant) or false (errant). But the purpose of these utterances is not to describe; it wouldn't make sense to ask whether they're inerrant or errant. Now that shouldn't trouble us. They're still important and meaningful linguistic acts. They're just doing something other than telling us truths about the world.

The Bible is a vehicle, not just for stating truths, but also for creating spiritual connection and growth. The words of Scripture inform the mind and create spiritual response. They create proper feelings that lead us to God. The Psalms, for instance, aren't merely truthful statements. They express deep emotions and love commitments, and they invite us personally to enter into similar emotions and commitments to God. God inspired the Psalms so that they would draw out certain kinds of beliefs, passions, commitments, attitudes, experiences, and actions. The Psalms use many linguistic features to create these responses. So God intended that the Bible go beyond *truthful information* to achieve *spiritual transformation*. God's purpose in the Bible is that we not only connect with *ideas* about him but also *connect with him*. This means that *some* of Scripture's utterances are descriptive. Inerrancy says these descriptions are true. And that's extremely important. But *some* of the Bible's purposes go beyond description. In these instances, asking the inerrancy question simply isn't relevant.

The truth-telling role of the Bible and the other functions of Scripture support one another. On the one hand, true information without spiritual transformation is dead. On the other hand, radical transformation without true information is rudderless. The *informational* assertions of the Bible that tell us about God the Father, the work of Christ, and the presence of the Spirit are proper and *true*! The *formational* utterances that ignite passionate worship, spiritual growth, inner healing, godly community, and sacrificial service are proper and good. So inerrancy is important because it declares that the Bible is true. But speech act theory enhances inerrancy because it shows how God intends for the truths of the Bible not only to describe the world and inform our minds but also to grow us spiritually, personally, and communally.

Responding to Objections

1. *Dealing with alleged errors.* The major objection to the inerrantist view is that it does not square with the facts. Whatever theory we hold about inspiration must square with the facts, and the fact is that the Bible contains errors that cannot be explained away. In reply, while it may be true that certain apparent errors cannot be explained away, they do not constitute sufficient grounds for overturning the belief in biblical inerrancy. Several observations support this response.

First, it is extremely important to pay attention to our starting point as we discuss the nature of the Bible. Do we start with the alleged errors in the Bible and then draw conclusions about the errant nature of the Bible? Or do we start with the teaching about the inerrant nature of the Bible found in the Bible itself and then try to explain the alleged errors? Faith must assume the second starting point. This was the posture of both Jesus and the early church.

In this light, whether we can adequately explain any particular alleged error in the Bible is actually of little consequence. Given the limitations of human rationality, knowledge, and experience, we should expect anomalies, regardless of what we believe. Indeed, every well-established scientific theory conflicts with the relevant data at points. Scientists do not thereby reject these theories. Rather, they patiently wait for the data to be explained. This is precisely the inerrantist posture toward the alleged errors in the Bible.

Nonetheless, inerrantists agree that we should try to account for alleged errors in Scripture. Most can be adequately accounted for in one of four ways.

First, we can explain some errors by supposing that they crept into the text as it was transmitted by scribes throughout history. Most apparent contradictions regarding numbers in the Bible can be explained in this way. In some instances, more significant discrepancies can be explained in this way as well.

For example, Mark and Luke say that Jesus sent demons into swine at Gerasa, while Matthew says it was in Gadara (Mark 5:1; Luke 8:26; Matt. 8:28). Not only is there a discrepancy between the places, but the town of Gerasa was not near the Sea of Galilea, where this episode is said to have taken place. One plausible explanation of this apparent contradiction is that the original town was an obscure village named Khersa. This town, known today only through archaeology, was in the province of Gadara and was located on the Sea of Galilee. Perhaps later manuscript copiers who did not have firsthand knowledge of the geography of this region mistook the obscure village of Khersa for the better known village of Gerasa.

Second, we can account for some alleged errors by noting that the language of Scripture is often phenomenological. (See **phenomenology.**) For example, the Bible is not erroneous in saying that the sun stood still when Joshua prayed (Josh. 10:12–14), for it is describing how things appeared from Joshua's perspective. While scientifically inaccurate, this language cannot be labeled erroneous. No one accuses anyone today of scientific error simply because he or she talks about the "rising" or "setting" of the sun.

Third, some alleged errors can be explained by considering the standard of accuracy of the culture in which the author was writing. For example, people frequently point out that the wording of Jesus is often different from one Gospel to the next. Indeed, the style of Jesus' language in the Gospel of John is significantly different from his style in the other three Gospels. These differences might be troublesome if they occurred in four modern biographies concerning someone who lived in the recent past. Our standard of accuracy has increased because of modern technology (e.g., tape recorders, video cameras) and lawsuits. Ancient people were much looser about such matters. As long as the gist of what a person said was accurately conveyed, no one worried about exact wording and minute details. We must judge the Gospel authors by the standards of their time, not by the standards of the twenty-first century.

Finally, we can explain some alleged errors by developing scenarios that harmonize the apparently discrepant data. For example, at first glance the Gospel resurrection narratives seem to contradict each other on several accounts. However, scholars have demonstrated that the accounts can be harmonized as long as we see the individual Gospel accounts as *part* of a story, not the entire story itself. While some object to this process, believing it contrived, historians, detectives, and reporters do the same thing all the time. Rarely do witnesses of the same event agree on every detail.

Consider, for example, the conflicting reports of the sinking of the *Titanic* or John F. Kennedy's assassination.

Again, inerrantists do not pretend to have solved every alleged error in the Bible. Enough errors have been solved, however, to give confidence that more will be solved in the future. In the meantime, people are not irrational for accepting the inerrancy of Scripture on the authority of Scripture, church tradition, and Jesus himself.

2. *The inerrancy of the original manuscripts.* A second objection is that belief in the inerrancy of Scripture is irrelevant if not meaningless because Scripture's inerrancy relates only to the original manuscripts. Unfortunately, these manuscripts no longer exist. We have only copies of the originals. So, some argue, what is the point of this debate? We are arguing about the nature of a nonexistent book!

In response, the claim that the original documents alone are inerrant, not the copies, is no more problematic than the claim, made by all evangelicals, that the original documents alone are inspired, not the copies. If the former is meaningless and irrelevant, so is the latter. In truth, however, neither view is problematic. Through textual criticism we are able to discern what was part of the original Word of God with a remarkably high degree of accuracy. As a result, the fact that we do not possess the original manuscripts is completely irrelevant in regard to the inspiration and/or inerrancy of the Bible.

Infallible in Matters of Faith and Practice (The Infallibilist View)

This essay defends the view that the Bible can and should be trusted as unfailing (infallible) in all matters that pertain to Christian faith and living. It cannot be considered inerrant, however, especially in regard to minor matters of history or science.

The Biblical Argument

Throughout the Gospels, Jesus expressed an unqualified confidence that Scripture infallibly communicates the will of God (Luke 16:17; John 10:35). He consistently referred to it when deciding matters related to faith. This attitude of trust was adopted by Jesus' disciples and has characterized the church throughout history (2 Pet. 1:20–21).

Two points regarding this attitude of trust need to be made. First, as it is found in Jesus and the earliest disciples, this unswerving attitude of trust in Scripture always relates to what Christians are to believe and how they are to live. Paul expressed the general attitude well when he argued that because Scripture is "inspired," it is "useful for teaching, for reproof, for correction, and for training in righteousness." The ultimate goal of Scripture and the teaching that arises from it is to make "everyone who belongs to God . . . proficient, equipped for every good work" (2 Tim. 3:16–17). The focus of inspiration is exclusively on faith and practice. Neither Paul nor any other biblical author was concerned with resolving whether the Bible represents history or the cosmos in a way that would qualify as "inerrant" by modern standards. This was not their concern, and we misuse their expressions of trust in Scripture when we try to make them address these concerns.

Second, it is important to realize that this attitude of trust toward Scripture is not a *theory* about *how* God inspired Scripture. God simply has not given us an inspired theory of inspiration. Scripture goes so far as to tell us that God moved humans to communicate his Word (2 Pet. 1:21). But it does not resolve many of the questions we may have about this teaching—questions that a theory of inspiration would presumably be designed to answer. For example, nowhere do scriptural authors demonstrate any concern with the issue of how much control God exerted over the authors he used and how much of their limited, culturally bound perspectives he left intact.

To address this issue we would have to do more than simply cite the attitude of trust demonstrated by people in the Bible toward the Bible. This is the mistake many who advocate an inerrantist view of the Bible make. Rather, to surmise how much limited and fallible humanity God left intact in the people he used to write the Bible, we must take a comprehensive and honest look at the Bible itself. An honest examination of Scripture leads to the conclusion that the Bible is thoroughly inspired but also *thoroughly human*. The human element in Scripture reflects the limitations and fallibility that are a part of all human perspectives and all human thinking. This human element can be clearly seen in at least three areas of Scripture.

First, without exception, biblical authors presupposed a premodern view of the world. To illustrate, as with all people in the ancient Near East, the Hebrews believed that the sky was "hard as a molten mirror" (Job 37:18). It had to be hard, in their view, for it was a "dome" that "separated the waters that were under the dome from the waters that were above the dome" (Gen. 1:7). This dome rested on "pillars," as did the earth as it sat upon the "waters" that encircled it (Ps. 75:3; 104:2–3, 5–6; cf. Job 9:6; 26:11). "Windows" in the solid dome were opened when Yahweh wanted it to rain, allowing the waters "above the dome" to fall to the ground (Gen. 7:11). The sun, moon, and stars were all "lights in the dome" that were placed there to function as "signs and for seasons and for days and years" (Gen. 1:14). The Lord, along with other heavenly beings, sat in a chamber above the dome. From this location God threw lightning bolts (Ps. 18:12–14), shook the pillars (earthquakes? Job 9:6), and caused the wind to blow (Ps. 107:25).

We modern people routinely assume this language is merely poetic, but at the time it was the way people really understood the world.

It is completely understandable that God would leave the primitive world-view of ancient authors intact as he used ancient authors to communicate his Word. How else could he effectively communicate to the people of the time? Had God attempted to communicate a scientifically accurate view of the world, the theological truth he wanted to convey would not have been communicated. At the same time, we must frankly admit that given what we know about the world today, the view of the cosmos presupposed in the Bible is inaccurate. The earth does not rest on pillars, and the sky is not hard! The Bible's theological message is unfailing though its view of the cosmos is scientifically incorrect.

A second and closely related culturally bound aspect of Scripture concerns the primordial belief that the earth was engulfed by cosmic forces and surrounded by cosmic monsters. At times the people of the ancient Near East (as well as other primordial people) depicted the mythological waters that surrounded the earth as hostile to the intention of various good gods who were in charge of preserving order in the world. According to these ancient views, humans needed the good gods to keep these hostile waters in check.

Old Testament authors accepted this view but insisted that it was Yahweh, not any other deity, who kept the rebel waters in check. For example, the psalmist declares that it is Yahweh's "rebuke," no one else's, that causes the hostile waters to "flee." It is "at the sound of [his] thunder" that "they take to flight" (Ps. 104:7). Indeed, these hostile waters take flight at the very sight of Yahweh (Ps. 77:16). Moreover, it is the Lord who assigns these rebel waters a "boundary that they may not pass" (Ps. 104:9; cf. Job 38:6–11; Prov. 8:27–29). It is the Lord and none other who defeats these enemies, who tramples on the sea with his warring horses (Hab. 3:15), and who sits enthroned above "the mighty waters" (Ps. 29:3–4, 10; cf. Nah. 1:4; Hab. 3:12–13).

Old Testament authors also accepted the ancient Near Eastern view that the earth was surrounded by threatening cosmic monsters. The two most frequently mentioned cosmic beasts in the Old Testament are **Leviathan** and **Rahab.** As in the mythology of other ancient Near Eastern people, Leviathan is depicted in Scripture as a ferocious, twisting serpent of the sea, encircling the earth (his name means "coiling one"). He had (on some accounts) many heads (Ps. 74:14) and could blow smoke out of his nose(s) and fire out of his mouth(s) (Job 41:18–21). Human weapons were useless against a creature of such ferocious might. Indeed, this monster could eat iron like straw and crush bronze as if it were decayed timber (Job 41:26–27)! Only God could subdue such a creature (cf. Isa. 27:1).

Rahab is portrayed in similar terms. This cosmic creature, which inhabited the waters that encircled the earth, was a threat to the entire earth. He was no match for Yahweh, however. When Yahweh expressed his wrath against evil, "the helpers of Rahab bowed beneath him" (Job 9:13). In the primordial past, Yahweh's power "stilled the Sea," his understanding "struck down Rahab," and his hand "pierced the fleeing serpent" (Job 26:12–13). The psalmist also celebrated Yahweh's sovereignty over "the raging sea" by announcing that he had "crushed Rahab like a carcass" and "scattered [his] enemies with [his] mighty arm" (Ps. 89:9–10). In similar fashion, Isaiah reassured himself that Yahweh would "awake" to deliver Israel by remembering that in the primordial past he had "cut Rahab to pieces" and "pierced the dragon" (Isa. 51:9; cf. Ps. 87:4; Isa. 30:7; Jer. 51:34; Ezek. 29:3; 32:2).

Again, we can readily understand why God would leave intact this mythological view of hostile waters and cosmic monsters when he inspired ancient people to communicate his Word. This mythology communicated the reality of spiritual warfare to ancient people in vivid terms they could readily understand. At the same time, we must frankly admit that this view of the world is scientifically inaccurate. Though the ancient biblical authors believed otherwise, there are in fact no hostile waters or cosmic sea dragons threatening the earth. These illustrations teach an infallible spiritual truth about spiritual warfare, even though their view of the cosmos is scientifically erroneous.

Yet a third way in which we see the fallible humanity of biblical authors is found in the way they contradict each other on minor matters. Space allows for just one example. Compare the following Synoptic (see **Synoptic Gospels**) accounts of Jesus' command to his seventy missionaries.

- "Take . . . no bag for your journey, or two tunics, or sandals, or a staff; for laborers deserve their food" (Matt. 10:9–10).
- "Take nothing for [your] journey except a staff; no bread, no bag, no money in [your] belts; but to wear sandals and not to put on two tunics" (Mark 6:8–9).
- "Take nothing for your journey, no staff, nor bag, nor bread, nor money—not even an extra tunic" (Luke 9:3).

The three accounts obviously do not completely agree. Did Jesus say to take a staff, as Mark reports, or not to take a staff, as Matthew and Luke report? Did Jesus say to wear sandals, as Mark's account says, or not to wear sandals, as Matthew's account suggests? Such disagreements clearly do not affect the basic teaching all three accounts seek to relay—namely, that disciples were to trust God the Father, not their own provisions, as they carried out the work of expanding God's kingdom. But just as clearly, the three accounts do disagree and thus cannot in any literal sense be labeled "inerrant."

As a matter of fact, minor inconsistencies such as these occur throughout the Bible. Sometimes they can be explained away; other times they cannot. Even when they cannot be explained, however, they never affect anything important. Minor contradictions in the Bible become a concern only when someone embraces a theory of inspiration that stipulates that such contradictions should not occur—namely, that the Bible is inerrant. If we focus our attention on the infallible teaching of Scripture on matters of faith and practice, however, rather than on whether the Bible is meticulously accurate and consistent in matters of history or science, we are free to see that these inconsistencies and scientific or historical inaccuracies are irrelevant to our faith.

Supporting Arguments

1. *Church history.* Inerrantists routinely assume that church tradition is unequivocally on their side in this debate. As noted earlier, theologians throughout history have assumed Jesus' attitude of complete trust in Scripture on matters of faith and practice. But it must also be noted that throughout church history, going back at least to Augustine in the fifth century, many theologians insisted that the Bible should not be used to settle "scientific" disputes. This point was driven home in the sixteenth century when the church embarrassed itself by locking horns with the scientific establishment over whether the earth or the sun was the center of the solar system. To avoid further embarrassment, the evangelical church should reaffirm the view that the Bible is infallible in matters of faith and practice but that it never claimed to be free from errors in regard to scientific matters.

2. *Apologetic and evangelistic advantages.* If the Bible must be inerrant in order to be inspired, as inerrantists teach, then the credibility of the Bible hangs on one's ability to resolve every error in the Bible. This is an unfortunate posture to assume, especially in our post-Christian age, for most people readily see that the contradictions and premodern aspects of the Bible are difficult, if not impossible, to account for adequately. This inerrantist view of inspiration thus hinders effective apologetics and evangelism.

Indeed, beyond making it difficult to win believers, the inerrantist theory of inspiration sometimes makes it difficult to keep believers. More than a few college students have abandoned the faith because they had been taught that believing in the Bible meant believing it is inerrant in every respect. When confronted in college classrooms with indisputable evidence that the Bible is not inerrant in this way, their faith in the inspiration of the Bible and (for some) Christianity as a whole is undermined. Those who embrace infallibility rather than inerrancy are not faced with this unfortunate and unnecessary dilemma.

3. *Bibliolatry.* The inerrancy theory tends to shift the focus of faith away from Jesus Christ and toward the accuracy of the Bible. This is **bibliolatry.** According to the Bible itself, faith should rest on Jesus Christ, not on one's opinion about the degree of accuracy of the Bible.

Responding to Objections

1. *The epistemological objection.* One of the strongest driving forces behind the theory of inerrancy is the worry that if we admit that the Bible can be mistaken on any point, then we cannot be certain of the Bible on any point. If we must judge what is and is not true in Scripture, then we are *its* authority rather than it being *our* authority. Three things may be said in response to this objection.

First, even if this objection were valid, it would not address the issue of whether the Bible is inerrant. A person cannot reject facts simply because they place the person in an epistemologically awkward situation. So, too, a person cannot legitimately argue that the Bible must be inerrant on the grounds that it would cause epistemological difficulties for his or her theology if it were not so. The issue of whether the Bible is inerrant must be settled by an honest investigation into whether the Bible in fact contains any errors. The above investigation suggests that it does.

Second, if this objection were valid, it would adversely affect the inerrantist position as much as the infallibilist position, for, in the light of textual criticism, the inerrantist admits that the Bible we possess today contains errors. Despite some acknowledged textual errors, however, they continue to be confident that they possess an *adequately accurate* version of the Bible. If they were consistent with the logic of their objection, however, they should conclude that we cannot trust *any* passage in the Bible unless we can trust *every* passage in the Bible. The argument regarding how one can trust the Bible despite its occasional scientific or historical errors directly parallels the inerrantist's ability to trust the Bible despite its occasional textual errors. Inerrantists cannot object to this stance unless they are willing to apply their objection to their own position.

Third, having said all this, we must now insist that the objection is simply not valid. On what basis can we demand that a source be without error *in all respects* before we give it credence *in some respects*. We customarily accept a source to the extent that we have reasons for accepting it, and we reject it to the extent that we have reasons for rejecting it. This essay has supplied good reasons for rejecting some of what the Bible says about the natural world and history. At the same time, though they cannot be addressed in this essay, there are good reasons for accepting what the Bible says about faith and practice. Among other things, all the historical and personal reasons to accept Jesus as the Son of God are reasons to accept that the Bible is infallible on the matters he himself trusted it for. Thankfully, this does not require that we pretend that the errors in the Bible are not there.

2. *This view creates an implicit contradiction.* Some argue that there is a contradiction involved in admitting that God cannot err while denying that what he inspires cannot err. This argument does not work on at least two counts.

First, we do not know enough about divine inspiration to stipulate in an **a priori** fashion what it does and does not logically entail. The only way we can learn what divine inspiration entails is by observing how God in fact divinely inspires a work. In other words, we must examine the phenomenon of the Bible. What we learn when we do is that divine inspiration does not logically imply inerrancy, for, as a matter of fact, the Bible contains errors. Divine inspiration requires only that the Bible is unfailing in all that God intends to use it for.

Second, evangelicals often refer to preachers as inspired when they give certain messages. Whether or not minor mistakes about incidental matters were made during the delivery is inconsequential to this assessment. We routinely understand that the "inspiration" concerns the power of the central point(s) the preacher intended to make, not to the message's meticulous accuracy. This is enough to show that the concept of "inspiration" does not entail inerrancy. Though Scripture is more perfectly inspired than any preacher, if it is not contradictory to claim that the message of an inspired preacher could contain incidental errors, it cannot be contradictory to claim that a divinely inspired collection of writings could contain incidental errors.

Further Reading

Beale, G. K. *The Erosion of Inerrancy in Evangelicalism: Responding to New Challenges to Biblical Authority*. Wheaton: Crossway, 2008.

Bovell, Carlos R. *Inerrancy and the Spiritual Formation of Younger Evangelicals*. Eugene, OR: Wipf and Stock, 2007.

Conference on Biblical Inerrancy. *The Proceedings of the Conference on Biblical Inerrancy, 1987*. Nashville: Broadman, 1987.

Clark, David K. "Beyond Inerrancy: Speech Acts and an Evangelical View of Scripture." In *For Faith and Clarity: Philosophical Contributions to Christian Theology*, edited by James Beilby, 113–31. Grand Rapids: Baker Academic, 2006.

Dockery, David S. *Christian Scripture: An Evangelical Perspective on Inspiration, Authority, and Interpretation*. Nashville: Broadman and Holman, 1995.

Geisler, Norman L., ed. *Inerrancy*. Grand Rapids: Zondervan, 1979.

Lightner, Robert P. *A Biblical Case for Total Inerrancy: How Jesus Viewed the Old Testament*. Reprint ed. Paris, AR: Baptist Standard Bearer, 2007.

McGowan, A. T. B. *The Divine Authenticity of Scripture: Retrieving an Evangelical Heritage*. Downers Grove, IL: InterVarsity, 2007.

Nicole, Roger R., and J. Ramsey Michaels, eds. *Inerrancy and Common Sense*. Grand Rapids: Baker Academic, 1980.

Pinnock, Clark H. *The Scripture Principle*. San Francisco: Harper & Row, 1984.

Radmacher, Earl D., and Robert D. Preus, eds. *Hermeneutics, Inerrancy, and the Bible: Papers from ICBI Summit II*. Grand Rapids: Academie/Zondervan, 1984.

Rogers, Jack B., ed. *Biblical Authority*. Waco: Word, 1977.

Rogers, Jack B., and Donald K. McKim. *The Authority and Interpretation of the Bible: An Historical Approach*. New York: Harper & Row, 1979.

Wright, N. T. *The Last Word: Beyond the Bible Wars to a New Understanding of the Authority of Scripture*. San Francisco: HarperOne, 2005.

Youngblood, Ronald, ed. *Evangelicals and Inerrancy: Selections from the Journal of the Evangelical Theological Society*. Nashville: Nelson, 1984.

2

The Providence Debate

*All Things Happen according to God's Sovereign Will
(The Calvinist View)
God Limits His Control by Granting Freedom
(The Arminian View)*

Posing the Question

While driving drunk, a person hits and kills a little girl. A Christian friend
of the girl's parents tries to comfort them by reassuring them that "God
is in control" and that somehow "all things work together for good." The
mother is comforted by these words, but the father becomes enraged. "If
God is behind my little girl's death," he insists, "he's not all-loving and
all-good. Any God who would purposely snuff out our little girl's life and
leave us in this nightmare is cruel!" A second friend of the family agrees
with the father and insists that God was not behind the tragedy. "The
drunk driver alone is to blame for your girl's tragic death," he tells the
father. "God is as saddened by this event as you are. Now he just wants to
comfort the two of you."

Which of the friends do you think was right? If you were the parents of
this young girl, how would you respond to each friend's advice? Do you
think God controls everything? Or do you think that decisions such as
whether a person will drive while intoxicated are outside of his control?

If you believe God controlled this event, how can you avoid blaming God for this girl's tragic death? If you believe God did not control this event, how can you avoid the conclusion that God's power is limited? These are the kinds of questions addressed by the doctrine of God's providence.

The Center and Its Contrasts

"God's providence" refers to the way God governs the world. Though Christians disagree as to whether God meticulously controls free decisions, they have always agreed that God is in some sense "in control" of the world. They have always confessed that God created all that is, that all power exercised by agents comes from him, and thus that God's ultimate objectives for the world and for human beings will certainly be achieved. This belief sets them apart from those who hold a variety of non-Christian views about the world and its destiny.

Many people throughout history (and many Two-Thirds World people today) believed that the course of history was determined by a multitude of spiritual beings ("gods"). The belief in many gods is called **polytheism.** According to this view, there is no single, all-powerful being who is steering world history toward an ultimate goal. Rather, the (often capricious) decisions of the gods, and the conflicts that occur between them, affect our lives and alter the course of history in haphazard ways. The most humans can hope for is to court the favor of certain gods and thus enjoy temporary blessings from them.

Some people in the past and many people today believe that the only thing that exists is matter. These people are usually labeled materialists. (See **materialism.**) They do not believe that God exists and thus do not believe that anyone or anything is guiding the world. Things just happen by natural cause and effect, and the final destiny of the universe is determined by the laws that govern matter. Most materialists today conclude that all the energy in the universe will eventually be used up and everything will dissipate into a state of utter darkness.

Others, both past and present, believe in **fate.** There have been many varieties of this belief, but all adherents agree that everything that happens has to happen in a certain way. For example, a seventeenth-century philosopher named Spinoza believed that all of history moves forward with the necessity of a mathematical equation. If we could view all of history at once and understand it in its entirety, he argued, we would see that the idea that anything could have been different is as illogical as saying $2+2=5$.

Some people believe in God but nevertheless deny the Christian understanding of God's providence. Deists (see **Deism**) believe that God created the world but then left it alone to run on its own. God is not involved in the affairs of people and does not lovingly steer history toward a certain goal. Process theologians (see **process theology**) believe in God but deny that he created the world or that he is **omnipotent** (meaning all-powerful). In their view, God forever influences the world and does the best he can to bring about good and avoid evil, but he is limited in what he can accomplish. Moreover, since the world has always existed and will always exist, it is not headed toward an ultimate goal.

The Christian view is distinct from all these views. It affirms that God created the world, that God is omnipotent, and that he is personally and intimately involved in the world as he steers it toward a final destiny. But there have been several conflicting understandings of the extent of God's control of the world. In the first few centuries of church history, theologians reacted strongly against the prevalent opinion that things happen by fate. As a result, they emphasized human freedom and tended to believe that God did not control everything that happened.

Augustine altered this in the late fourth and early fifth centuries. In reaction against a popular view that lives are determined by either a good god or an evil god who are equal or nearly equal in power (**Manichaeism**), Augustine insisted that things occur in accordance with the will of one God alone: the Creator God of the Bible. Augustine's views have been extremely influential throughout church history. Some theologians pushed his view of **providence** so far that they denied that humans are free (e.g., Gottshalk in the ninth century), but most continued to affirm human freedom while also insisting that God controls all things. This position is called **compatibilism,** for it insists that belief in human freedom is compatible with the belief that God controls everything.

The present debate surrounding the providence of God began in the early sixteenth century. A French Reformer named John Calvin strongly emphasized Augustine's view that God controls all things, including who will and will not be saved. Shortly after Calvin died, a theologian named Jacob Arminius argued that this emphasis on divine control is incompatible with human freedom and undermines the biblical teaching that God wants everyone to be saved. (This view is sometimes called **incompatibilism,** for it asserts that human freedom is not compatible with God's control.) Arminius still believed that God "controls the world" in the sense that God is sure to achieve his overall objectives. But he believed that God has purposely decided not to control some things so that a person's decision to believe or not believe in Christ is free. According to this view, God foreknows who will and will not believe, but he does not control who will and will not believe.

A multitude of positions and arguments have been put forward both on the side of Calvinists, who affirm God's exhaustive control of the world, and on the side of Arminians, who deny it. The fundamental debate continues to be between these two schools of thought. Hence, the two essays that follow offer arguments from both the Calvinist and the Arminian perspectives.

All Things Happen According to God's Sovereign Will (The Calvinist View)

The Biblical Argument

At the foundation of the biblical portrayal of God is the stunning truth that he is the omnipotent Creator of all things who is therefore the sovereign Lord over all events. In the majestic words of the apostle Paul, "From him [God] and through him and to him are all things" (Rom. 11:36). Not "all things" except human free will. Not "all things" except evil things. Not "all things" on a general scale but not on a small scale. *All things* come from him, exist through him, and ultimately exist for his glory.

This message is troubling to those who have uncritically accepted the modern humanistic notion that humans possess self-determining free will. (See **self-determination**.) And it invariably raises philosophical issues that are difficult for our finite minds to figure out. Yet, the message of the complete sovereignty of God runs throughout Scripture, and this message forms an awe-inspiring portrait of God whose infinite power and glory are beyond comprehension and who is worthy of worship for this very reason.

Biblical authors consistently depict God as being able to do "whatever he pleases" (Ps. 135:6). As Job confesses to the Lord after going through his terrible trials, "I know that you can do all things, and that no purpose of yours can be thwarted" (Job 42:2). In the words of the prophet Daniel:

> All the inhabitants of the earth are accounted as nothing,
>   and he does what he wills with the host of heaven
>   and the inhabitants of the earth.
> There is no one who can stay his hand
>   or say to him, "What are you doing?" (4:35)

Whatever the Lord plans, he does. His plan cannot be annulled (Isa. 14:24, 27). He determines the precise "times" and "boundaries" of all nations (Acts 17:26). He determines "the days," the "number of months," and the "bounds" of every person he creates (Job 14:5; Ps. 139:16). He "accomplishes all things according to his counsel and will" (Eph. 1:11). When an accident occurs, it is because he willed it (Exod. 21:12–13). When dice are tossed, they land according to God's will (Prov. 16:33). All things come from God, exist for God, and end up glorifying God (Rom. 11:36).

God's sovereign will encompasses even the decisions people make. People may attempt to devise their own plans, but it is the Lord who ultimately determines what they shall and shall not do (Prov. 16:9; cf. 19:21; 20:24). Hence, he controls the hearts of kings, turning them "wherever he wills" (Prov. 21:1). It is for this reason that Scripture credits God and God alone with people's decisions to accept the gospel. For example, Scripture says that "the Lord opened [Lydia's] heart to listen eagerly to what was said by Paul" (Acts 16:14), and therefore, she became a believer. Indeed, no one can confess Jesus Christ as Lord unless the Spirit of God empowers that person to do so (1 Cor. 12:3). Consistent with this, Jesus teaches that "no one can come to me unless drawn by the Father who sent me" (John 6:44). Salvation is, therefore, completely a matter of God's sovereign **grace** (Eph. 2:8).

In fact, those whom the Father "draws" were picked out before the world began. Paul celebrates the fact that God "saved us and called us . . . not according to our works but according to his own purpose and grace." This grace, he continues, "was given to us in Christ Jesus before the ages began" (2 Tim. 1:9). "[God] chose us," Paul says, "before the foundation of the world. . . . He destined us for adoption" (Eph. 1:4–5). We were "destined according to the purpose of him who accomplishes all things according to his counsel and will" (Eph. 1:11). This is why Luke summarizes his account of the preaching of Paul and Barnabas to the Gentiles by noting that "as many as had been destined for eternal life became believers" (Acts 13:48). All who are believers are so not because of *their* choice but because of *God's* choice (John 15:16).

Does God's sovereign will encompass even evil events? Though it may not fit neatly into our preconceptions, the Bible teaches that it does. Of course, Scripture unequivocally affirms that God is perfectly holy and righteous. At the same time, however, we must affirm along with Scripture that it is God who ultimately decides to use evil to suit his sovereign purpose. Through Isaiah the Lord proclaims:

> I form light and create darkness,
>   I make weal and create woe;
>   I the LORD do all these things. (45:7)

Similarly, the prophet Jeremiah announces:

> Who can command and have it done,
>   if the Lord has not ordained it?
> Is it not from the mouth of the Most High
>   that good and bad come? (Lam. 3:37–38)

God is not evil, but his sovereign will encompasses evil. When disaster comes upon a city, the Bible says, it is the Lord's doing (Amos 3:6). It is the Lord who "makes [people] mute or deaf, seeing or blind" (Exod. 4:11). If a woman has lost her husband and two sons, it is "because the hand of the LORD has turned against [her]" (Ruth 1:13). If judges in a city have ceased administering justice, it is because the Lord has covered their eyes (Job 9:24). When Job loses all that he has, he can only confess, "The LORD gave, and the LORD has taken away; blessed be the name of the LORD" (Job 1:21). After his ordeal, Job's friends and family came by and "comforted him for all the evil that the LORD had brought upon him" (Job 42:11).

We see that the sovereign Creator is sovereign over evil. On a moral level, of course, he opposes evil, for he is all-holy. Yet at the level of his sovereign will he decrees that evil events take place for a higher good. Even evil people fit into his divine plan. "The LORD has made everything for its purpose," Scripture says, "even the wicked for the day of trouble" (Prov. 16:4). No one develops this truth more clearly than the apostle Paul: "What if God, desiring to show his wrath and to make known his power, has endured with much patience the objects of wrath that are made for destruction; and what if he has done so in order to make known the riches of his glory for the objects of mercy, which he has prepared beforehand for glory" (Rom. 9:22–23).

In his sovereignty, God has the right to fashion "objects of wrath . . . made for destruction" and "objects of mercy . . . prepared beforehand for glory." He "has mercy on whomever he chooses, and he hardens the heart of whomever he chooses" (Rom. 9:18). We find the Lord exercising this sovereign right throughout the biblical narrative. For example, he hardens the heart of Pharoah "so that he will not let the people go" (Exod. 4:21), thus incurring God's wrath upon him. The Lord said he did this "for the very purpose of showing my power in you, so that my name may be proclaimed in all the earth" (Rom. 9:17; cf. Exod. 7:3–5; 10:1; 14:4). Similarly, God "hardened [the] spirit" of the king of Heshbon and "made his heart defiant" so that he was "not willing to let [the Israelites] pass through" because it was God's plan for Israel to conquer him (Deut. 2:30). So, too, when Joshua entered the Promised Land: "There was not a town that made peace with the Israelites. . . . All were taken in battle. For it was the LORD's doing to harden their hearts so that they would come against Israel in battle, in order that they might be utterly destroyed" (Josh. 11:19–20).

When it suits his purposes, God orchestrates attitudes and behaviors that actually conflict with his moral will but that do so for the greater good of displaying his glory throughout history. Augustine captured this insight when he taught that even events that go against God's [moral] will take place within God's [sovereign] will.[1] Indeed, Scripture asserts that even the activity of evil spirits is controlled by God (Judg. 9:23; 1 Sam. 16:14; 1 Kings 22:19–23; 2 Thess. 2:11–12).

God's sovereign control of humans and spirits does not absolve them of their own moral responsibility, however. There is no incompatibility between the sovereignty of God and the moral responsibility of free agents. When Eli's sons stubbornly resisted their father's advice, Scripture did not excuse them even though it stipulated that they did not listen because "it was the will of the LORD to kill them" (1 Sam. 2:25). When Joseph's brothers sold him into slavery, Scripture does not excuse the brothers, even though Joseph says that it was "God [who] sent me before you to preserve life" (Gen. 45:5). "You intended to do harm to me," Joseph says, but "God intended it for good" (Gen. 50:20). Similarly, Absalom was held morally responsible for following ungodly counsel instead of godly wisdom (the advice of Ahithophel), even though Scripture says that Absalom decided the way he did because "the LORD had ordained to defeat the good counsel of Ahithophel, so that the LORD might bring ruin on Absalom" (2 Sam. 17:14).

As a final example, consider how Scripture speaks of the crucifixion of Jesus Christ. It states that Jesus was "handed over . . . according to the definite plan and foreknowledge of God" and was "crucified and killed by the hands of those outside the law" (Acts 2:23). Again, all who were against Christ "gathered together against . . . Jesus . . . to do whatever [God's] hand and [God's] plan had predestined to take place" (Acts 4:27–28). The fact that these people acted in accordance with God's plan does not in any way alleviate their wickedness in carrying out their deed. Yet what they intended for evil, God intended for good. They were evil in carrying out the deed, for their intentions were wicked. But God was good in ordaining that the deed take place, for he ordained it for a greater good. Through Christ multitudes of sinners would receive forgiveness and enter into eternal glory with the Father.

People are responsible for their decisions. Scripture thus emphasizes the need for people to choose to follow God, resist sin, and so on. Yet how people choose, as with everything else that occurs in world history, is in accordance with the eternal plan of the sovereign God who controls all things and orchestrates them for his glory.

Supporting Arguments

1. *Sovereignty is necessarily all-encompassing.* The absolute sovereignty of God is implied in the very concept of God. If anything can thwart God's will, then that thing is more powerful than God. It is, in effect, god over God. But this, clearly, is a contradiction. Logic dictates that we adhere to Scripture's teaching that all things come from God and exist for God (Rom. 11:36).

What is more, it is difficult to see how God could control anything if he did not control everything. Consider how single decisions produce history-changing results. For example, imagine how history would be different if the father of Alexander the Great had made decisions earlier in life that would have prevented him from meeting Alexander's mother. What would have happened if Adolf Hitler had decided to pursue his youthful aspirations to be an artist? What would have happened if Pilate had decided to pardon Jesus?

The point is that all of history is woven together by the thread of billions of individual decisions. If the decisions are not under the sovereign control of God, neither is the flow of history. Since all Christians agree that God controls the flow of history—at the very least, he wins in the end—all should agree that he controls all the decisions that determine that flow.

2. *Salvation by grace.* If humans must choose to accept or reject salvation, then we cannot affirm with Scripture that we are "dead" in sin (Eph. 2:1) and "by nature children of wrath" (Eph. 2:3). How can dead people choose life? How can people choose what is contrary to their nature? Nor can we affirm with Paul that we are saved solely by God's grace (Eph. 2:8–9). If a self-determining decision is required for us to be saved, faith is a work that we perform. We cannot give God all the credit for our salvation. Rather, we must congratulate ourselves for being at least good enough or smart enough to accept God's offer of salvation. If we agree that this conclusion is unacceptable, we must affirm that the explanation for a person's salvation is found in God, not the person.

3. *The impossibility of self-determining freedom.* A final argument in favor of the view that God controls all things is that the entire case for the Arminian view of providence is rooted in an incoherent concept. Arminians deny that God controls all things because they maintain that humans possess self-determining freedom. But this notion of self-determining freedom is an incoherent notion.

This point can best be made by asking the question, Is a self-determining act caused or uncaused? If the Arminian replies that it is caused, then it cannot be free. But if he replies that it is uncaused, it still cannot be free, for what is uncaused is capricious, sheer chance. It is no more free than, say, the random twitch of an eyebrow. The Arminian view of freedom, therefore, is simply unintelligible.

Responding to an Objection

The problem of evil. Undoubtedly, the most frequent objection against the view that God controls all things is that it creates the **problem of evil**. If

God controls all things, it is argued, then he is responsible for the evil in the world. Three things may be said in response to this objection.

First, since Scripture affirms that God is all-holy, while also teaching that God is sovereign over everything, as we have seen, we must conclude that God ordains all things in such a way that he is not responsible for the evil that occurs in the world. The way God does this may be largely hidden from us, but we must resist the presumptuous conclusion that because something does not square with our finite and fallen reason, it cannot be so.

Second, God is justified in creating a world in which evil occurs if it contributes to a greater good that could not be achieved without it. No Arminian would disagree with this, for they hold that God created a world in which evil occurs for the greater good of freedom. We rather hold that the greater good that explains evil is God's own glory. A world without evil would be a world in which God's justice, goodness, and mercy were not displayed (see Rom. 9:22–23).

Finally, what makes an act evil is not the suffering it produces but the intention a person has in inflicting it. A doctor may inflict suffering on another, but it is not considered evil because it contributes to a greater good, namely, the person's health. This helps us understand how God ordains evil without becoming blameworthy for the evil he ordains. What people intend for evil, God intends for good. The difference is in the intention. As noted above, God predestined that Christ would be crucified for a greater good. Multitudes would be saved by his death. Yet those who crucified him did not have this noble intention in mind when they crucified him. Their motives did not go beyond their desire to unjustly crucify a person who threatened their ungodly position of power. Hence, God was good in predestining Christ to die, while those who carried out his plan were wicked in doing so (Acts 2:23).

God Limits His Control by Granting Freedom (The Arminian View)

The Biblical Argument

The Bible exalts God as the Creator of all that exists and as the sovereign Lord of history (e.g., Gen. 1:1; Deut. 10:14; Ps. 135:6ff.; Dan. 4:34–35; John 1:3; Acts 17:24–27; Eph. 1:11; Col. 1:16–17). He is omnipotent and thus able to do whatever he wills (Ps. 135:6; cf. Job 23:13–14; Ps. 115:3; Dan. 4:35). He controls whatever he wants to control. He predestines whatever he wants to predestine (e.g., Isa. 46:10–11; Acts 2:23; 4:28). His goal of acquiring a people for himself will certainly be achieved (e.g., 1 Cor. 15:25–28; Eph. 1:16–23; Col. 1:18–20). In one way or another, all things are "from him and through him and to him" (Rom. 11:36). He is the omnipotent, sovereign Lord who is in control of the world's destiny.

At the same time, it is also clear from Scripture that God sovereignly chooses not to meticulously control *everything*. He wants people to love him by choice, not necessity, and so he limits the scope of his sovereign control. Three features of the biblical narrative highlight this dimension of God's providential design.

First, the biblical narrative reveals that God gives people the choice of whether to follow him. Thus, for example, the Lord says to Israel:

> I have set before you today life and prosperity, death and adversity. If you obey the commandments of the LORD your God . . . then you shall live . . . and the LORD your God will bless you. . . . But if your heart turns away and you do not hear . . . I declare to you today that you shall perish. . . . I have set before you life and death, blessings and curses. Choose life so that you and your descendants may live. (Deut. 30:15–19; cf. 11:26–28)

This is a theme we find over and over again throughout Scripture (e.g., Josh. 24:15; Jer. 7:1–15; 17:9–27; 21:8; 22:1–5; Rom. 10:13). Beginning in the Garden of Eden and extending through the New Testament, we find that God gives people the ability and the obligation to make morally responsible choices (e.g., Gen. 2:16–17; John 3:16–18). People are free, which is why Scripture consistently holds them responsible for what they do.

For example, when Solomon did "evil in the sight of the LORD," it was because "his heart had turned away from the LORD" (1 Kings 11:6, 9; cf. 2 Chron. 12:14). If the Lord was himself the cause of Solomon's turning from him, this passage makes no sense. Similarly, Zedekiah "did what was evil in the sight of the LORD" and "did not humble himself before the prophet Jeremiah" because he "stiffened his neck and hardened his heart against turning to the LORD" (2 Chron. 36:12–13). The explanation as to why Zedekiah did evil is found in his own heart, not in God.

This leads to a second point. Because God does not control everything humans do, God is often disappointed and frustrated by their choices. The Lord was deeply grieved over the low moral state to which humanity had sunk prior to the flood (Gen. 6:6). He grieved over Israel's persistent resistance to his loving Spirit (e.g., Isa. 63:10; Heb. 3:8, 15; 4:7). The Lord is frequently saddened and sometimes even amazed at how "stiff necked" people are in resisting him (e.g., Exod. 33:3, 5; 34:9; Deut. 9:6, 13; 10:16; 31:27; Judg. 2:19; 2 Kings 17:14; 2 Chron. 30:8; 36:13; Neh. 9:16; Isa. 46:12; 48:4; Jer. 7:26; Hosea 4:16). Like that of a husband of an unfaithful wife, God's heart breaks when his people choose to reject him (Hosea 11). Clearly, people can and do reject "God's purpose for themselves" (Luke 7:30). These passages do not make sense if in fact God secretly controls everything people do. A person cannot grieve, frustrate, or resist you if you exercise exhaustive control over that person.

All of this is especially true in regard to people's eternal destiny. The Lord does not want any human being to perish (Ezek. 18:32; 2 Pet. 3:9). He wants all to choose a relationship with him and be saved (1 Tim. 2:4). He "does not willingly afflict or grieve anyone" (Lam. 3:33). He rather "longs to be gracious" to sinners (Isa. 30:18) and pleads with everyone to turn to him (Isa. 65:2; Ezek. 18:30–32; 33:11; Hosea 11:7ff.; Rom. 10:21). Yet many reject the Lord and end up going to hell. Clearly, it is not God who ordains that this happen. People choose this destiny for themselves (John 3:18–19). Such a situation grieves God deeply, but he prefers this possibility over controlling people to ensure that they do not perish.

Third, the Lord's choice not to control everything is clearly manifested in the ministry of Jesus Christ. Throughout his ministry, Jesus treated infirmities and cases of demonization as things that his Father did not will. Indeed, the purpose of his ministry was to carry out the Father's will—to spread his Father's kingdom—by *opposing* such things. If God's sovereign will was behind the infirmities and cases of demonization that Jesus confronted, we would have to conclude that God's kingdom was "divided against itself" and thus could not stand.

Supporting Arguments

1. *Love requires choice.* If God controlled everything in detail, love would not be possible. Consider this analogy: Suppose I was able to invent a computer chip that could interact with a human brain in a deterministic fashion, causing the person who carried the chip to do exactly what the chip dictated without knowing it. Suppose I programmed this chip to produce the perfect wife and inserted it into my wife's brain while she was sleeping. The next morning she would wake up as "the perfect wife." She would feel, behave, and speak in a perfectly loving fashion. Owing to the sophistication of this chip, she would believe that she was voluntarily choosing to love me, though in truth she could not do otherwise.

Would my wife be genuinely loving me? I think we can all agree that she would not. Any emotionally healthy person would quickly find this "love" unfulfilling. I would know that my wife was not feeling these loving feelings or engaging in this loving behavior on her own. My wife's behavior would not be chosen by *her*, so *she* would not really be loving me at all. She would be the equivalent of a puppet. If I want love from *her*, she must personally possess the capacity to choose *not* to love me.

How would it be different if God controlled whether we loved him? If God wants people to genuinely love him—not just *act* lovingly toward him—he must create people who have the capacity to reject him. They, not he, must determine whether they love him.

2. *The problem of evil.* The Bible teaches that "all [God's] ways are just" for he is "without deceit" (Deut. 32:4). "God is light and in him there is no darkness" (1 John 1:5). Indeed, God's "eyes are too pure to behold evil" (Hab. 1:13). How are these verses consistent with the view that everything—including all the evil that people have experienced throughout history—is part of God's sovereign will?

Some theologians attempt to get around this problem by maintaining that people (and spirits, such as Satan) are responsible for the evil they do, even though God determines what they do. Calvinists admit this is a mystery. From the Arminian perspective, it is a contradiction. No Calvinist has succeeded in providing an explanation that renders this view meaningful. If we acknowledge that humans and spirits are free, however, the problem of evil largely disappears. (See **freewill defense**.) We can acknowledge that while all good things in creation come from God (James 1:17), all evil in creation comes from wills other than that of God. God allows evil to take place because he desires humans to have the potential to love, and for this they must be free. But in no sense does he will their evil.

3. *Motivation for prayer.* A final argument in favor of the view that God does not control all things is that it reveals why the Bible places such an emphasis on prayer. According to Scripture, a great deal of what God does in the world is influenced by whether his people pray (2 Chron. 7:14; Ezek. 22:30; James 5:16–18). If people are free, we can understand why God conditions what he does on whether his people interact with him. If God always controls everything, however, then it is difficult to avoid the dire conclusion that nothing is really influenced by what we do. We may continue to pray simply out of obedience to God's Word, but we may not pray as passionately as we would if we believed that whether God's will is done in a particular situation is genuinely up to us.

Responding to Objections

1. *This view denies God's sovereignty.* Calvinists often argue that if God does not control everything, then he is not truly sovereign. This would be true if God wanted to control everything but could not. But it is not correct if God himself relinquishes his own control. Indeed, with C. S. Lewis we submit that the greatest miracle of omnipotence was in creating beings who had the potential to resist it.[2]

2. *This view reveals the impossibility of freedom.* Some have argued that the very notion of a self-determining being is contradictory. If human actions are not the result of prior causes, including God, then they must

be uncaused. This renders them capricious, not free. Three things may be said in response.

First, if we accept this argument, we must conclude either that God had to create the world or that God's creation of the world was a capricious act. If the concept of a free, self-determining being is truly unintelligible, it does not become intelligible simply because we apply it to God. Yet Christians have always believed that God created the world freely. Nothing caused him to do it, and it was not a capricious act.

Second, it is difficult to maintain that self-determining freedom is unintelligible when we experience it every day. When we deliberate between choices, we assume that we are not wholly determined by previous causes but also that our choices are not random.

Third, the argument against self-determining freedom assumes that causes *determine* effects. Only on this basis can it be maintained that either human actions are caused and determined or uncaused and capricious. But there is no reason to assume this. Something can be caused without being determined. The same causes can produce a variety of possible effects. In this light, human behavior is neither uncaused nor determined. It is free.

3. *The Bible argues against self-determining freedom.* The main objection against the view that God chooses not to control all things is that some passages of Scripture seem to suggest that God *does* control all things. Most of these passages can be explained in one of four ways.

First, what "pleases" the Lord? A number of passages declare that "whatever the LORD pleases he does, in heaven and on earth" (Ps. 135:6; cf. Job 23:13–14; Ps. 115:3; Dan. 4:35). These passages certainly celebrate God's sovereignty, but they imply that God controls all things only if we *assume* that it pleases the Lord to control all things. But why should we assume this? Since other passages tell us that God's will is sometimes thwarted (e.g., Isa. 63:10; Luke 7:30; Acts 7:51; Eph. 4:30; Heb. 3:8, 15; 4:7), it seems more reasonable to conclude that it "pleased" the Lord to create a world in which free agents have the potential to thwart his will.

Second, God responds to people. Many of the passages that depict God controlling what people do are not about God's original plan for these people but about how God *responds* to people's sin. For example, whenever the Bible speaks of God hardening people's hearts, it is speaking of God *judging* people (e.g., Exod. 7:3–4; 10:1; 14:4; Deut. 2:30; Josh. 11:19–20; Rom. 9:18; cf. 1 Sam. 2:25; 2 Sam. 17:14; Isa. 6:10). God ensures that the evil in people's hearts is fully manifested in order to demonstrate his justice in judging them. The passages do not suggest that God hardened people arbitrarily. This would make God the author of their evil.

This is also how we should understand most of the passages that speak of evil as coming from the Lord (Isa. 45:7; Lam. 3:37–38; Amos 3:6). Some cite these passages as evidence that all evil is ordained by God, but if read in context, these passages do not suggest this. In these passages, the word "evil" (*ra'*) does not refer to moral evil. The term rather means "destruction" or "disaster." The "destruction" spoken of in these passages refers specifically to God's righteous *judgment* on people who have freely chosen a lifestyle that deserves it. The passages, therefore, do not teach that every disaster in history is caused by God, only that God can sovereignly bring about disasters to punish people if he so chooses.

Another way God responds to people's sin is by working to bring good out of it (Rom. 8:28). This does not mean that God ordained the evil so that he could bring about a greater good. It simply means that God is able to wisely bring good out of evil that free agents bring about. When Joseph tells his malicious brothers that what they intended for evil "God intended . . . for good" (Gen. 50:20), for example, he is not suggesting that their evil actions were controlled by God. He is simply saying that God foresaw their evil hearts and devised a wise plan to bring good out of their evil plan.

Third, some of the texts that seem to support the view that God meticulously controls the world are easily understood as statements made in unqualified and/or exaggerated terms for emphasis. For example, in Proverbs we read that "the king's heart is a stream of water in the hand of the LORD; he turns it wherever he will" (Prov. 21:1). Does this mean that everything Adolf Hitler or Joseph Stalin dreamed up in their sick and evil minds was actually the Lord's doing? Not at all.

Ancient Jews often stated general principles in unequivocal terms for emphasis. We misinterpret them if we understand them as literal, universal laws. For example, Proverbs 12:21 states, "No harm happens to the righteous, but the wicked are filled with trouble" (cf. Prov. 13:21, 25). If read as an absolute universal law, this passage is obvious nonsense. History and our own experience demonstrate that righteous people frequently suffer great harm, while wicked people often live in peace and prosperity. Indeed, Scripture itself repeatedly makes this observation (Job; Ps. 73). As a *general principle*, however, righteous living helps one avoid harm, while wicked living will lead to trouble. In Proverbs 21:1, therefore, the author is not suggesting that every decision made by every king throughout history was orchestrated by God. He is simply emphasizing God's general sovereignty over kings.

Fourth, some passages cited in support of the view that God controls everything simply teach that God controls some things, not all things. For example, Acts 4:27–28 tells us that "Herod and Pontius Pilate, with the Gentiles and the peoples of Israel, gathered together against [God's] holy servant Jesus . . . to do whatever [God's] hand and [God's] plan had predestined to take place." Some conclude from this that all the individuals who crucified Christ were predestined to do so. The passage does not say this, however. It says only that *Christ's crucifixion* was predestined. Those who freely carried out this deed carried out what God "had predestined to take place," but they were not individually predestined to act a certain way. God could have easily used other people to carry out his predestined plan.

In a similar fashion, the New Testament sometimes refers to the church as being predestined by God (Eph. 1:4–5, 11; 2 Tim. 1:9). This does not mean that the individuals who comprise the church were predestined to believe (while others were predestined not to believe). God wants everyone to believe in Christ and be saved (2 Pet. 3:9). Rather, it means that God decided ahead of time that he would have a group of people ("the church") who would believe in him. Whether an individual becomes part of this predestined group is up to him or her.

Calvinists sometimes argue that God cannot control anything if he does not control everything. God could not have ensured that Christ would be crucified, for example, unless he could ensure that certain individuals would carry out the crucifixion. The argument does not work, however. God can foreknow the decisions of people without determining them. He can, therefore, determine that an event take place without determining who will carry out the event.

Further Reading

Basinger, David, and Randall Basinger, eds. *Predestination and Free Will: Four Views on Divine Sovereignty and Human Freedom*. Downers Grove, IL: InterVarsity, 1985.

Boyd, Gregory A. *Satan and the Problem of Evil*. Downers Grove, IL: InterVarsity, 2001.

Forster, Roger T., and V. Paul Marston. *God's Strategy in Human History*. Minneapolis: Bethany, 1973; Eugene, OR: Wipf and Stock, 2000.

Helm, Paul. *The Providence of God*. Downers Grove, IL: InterVarsity, 1993.

Packer, J. I. *Evangelism and the Sovereignty of God*. Downers Grove, IL: InterVarsity, 1961.

Pinnock, Clark, ed. *The Grace of God and the Will of Man*. Minneapolis: Bethany, 1989.

———, ed. *Grace Unlimited*. Minneapolis: Bethany, 1976.

Poythress, Vern. *Philosophy, Science, and the Sovereignty of God*. Nutley, NJ: Presbyterian and Reformed, 1976.

Sanders, John. *The God Who Risks: A Theology of Providence*. Downers Grove, IL: InterVarsity, 1998.

Schreiner, Thomas R., and Bruce A. Ware, eds. *The Grace of God, the Bondage of the Will*. 2 vols. Grand Rapids: Baker Academic, 1995.

Sproul, R. C. *The Invisible Hand: Do All Things Really Work for Good?* Dallas: Word, 1996.

Ware, Bruce A., ed. *Perspectives on the Doctrine of God: Four Views*. Nashville: Broadman and Holman, 2008.

3

The Foreknowledge Debate

God Foreknows Future Free Actions (The Arminian View)
God Foreknows by Sovereignly Ordaining the Future (The Calvinist View)
God Foreknows All That Shall Be and All That May Be (The Open View)

Posing the Question

Does God already know *if* you're going to marry and, if so, *who* your spouse will be? If this were known with certainty by God before you were even born, do you and your future spouse actually choose each other of your own free will? And what if your spouse tragically ends up cheating on you or turns out to be physically abusive? Did God foreknow this as well? If he did, why didn't he warn you and steer you toward a spouse with whom he knew you'd "live happily ever after"? In fact, if God foreknows everything ahead of time, why does he create people he knows will abuse others and even people he is certain will go to hell? Doesn't he want everyone to go to heaven?

If, however, God doesn't foreknow everything ahead of time, you've got to wonder if you can really trust him with your future. In fact, if God doesn't foreknow all that's going to come to pass, nobody does, leading one to wonder if anybody is in control. Is anyone steering this ship in any particular direction? Is the future just a "wide open sea" to God? Is God waiting to find out where this ship—your life and the entire history of the world—is going and how it will get there, just like we are? And if

God doesn't know everything ahead of time, why is Scripture filled with prophecies that come true and clear promises about the future that God, with absolute certainty, says will come to pass?

The Center and Its Contrasts

Christians have always agreed that God is **omniscient** ("all knowing"). And, though some don't believe the future is entirely settled in God's mind, all have always agreed that God knows "the end from the beginning" (Isa. 46:10). The future is not a "wide open sea" to him. The ship has a captain, and the captain knows where he is going!

This agrees with what Jews, **Muslims,** and most other **theists** throughout history have believed about God. But it contrasts sharply with what many other non-Christian worldviews hold. Many people today believe that the future is entirely up to us. Humans have the sole power and sole responsibility to determine the future for themselves and life on the earth. **Secular humanists** are an example of people who hold this view. Yet others believe in fate: "whatever will be will be." Some of these people think that the future is settled on the grounds that everything, including human choices, is physically determined. These people are usually identified as materialists, for they believe that every event, including every human action, is the result of material cause and effect. Hence, the last effect of the universe was already determined by the first cause, if there was one. Others today think that fate is the result of spiritual laws that have always been in operation. For example, some Eastern teachers and advocates of **New Age** philosophies think that every event is part of one, single, timeless, divine reality. Nothing could be different than it is. This is often labeled **monism.**

The Christian view disagrees with all these beliefs. Christians hold that humans are responsible for their actions but deny that the future is entirely up to us to settle. God knows where history is leading. But he doesn't know this because everything is determined by physical laws or because everything is part of one timeless, divine reality. He knows it because he is the sovereign Lord and Creator of the world.

Most Christians throughout history have believed that God knows everything that is to come. This is often referred to as the "classical" view of divine **foreknowledge,** and it is still what the majority of evangelicals believe. There are, however, a number of variations within the classical view. Some, called Calvinists, believe that God foreknows all that shall come to pass because he has predestined it. Others, called Arminians, believe God foreknows all things simply because they shall come to pass, though humans to some extent determine it by their free will. Some Arminians hold that

God knows not only what will happen but also what would have happened under different circumstances. This is an Arminian subview known as Molinism (after its sixteenth-century originator Luis de Molina) or "Middle Knowledge" (referring to God's knowledge of what free agents would do in every particular circumstance). "Simple Foreknowledge," another form of the Arminian view, claims that God somehow simply knows the future in exhaustive definite detail but that people are still free in the decisions they make. Other subforms of the Arminian view exist as well.

Some, however, have questioned whether God has exhaustive definite foreknowledge of the future on both biblical and philosophical grounds. They believe that while God knows the broad outlines of world history as well as whatever he has predestined to take place, some of the definite details of the future are not known by God until humans decide them by the exercise of their free will. This theology, which has in recent times come to be known as Open Theism or the open view of the future, has had few representatives in the orthodox Christian tradition, though it became more prevalent in the eighteenth and nineteenth centuries. Yet an increasing number of evangelicals have embraced this view in the last several decades, making the debate over foreknowledge one of the liveliest debates within evangelicalism today.

Terminology in this debate can become a bit confusing. With regard to the well-known "Calvinist-Arminian" debate about salvation, Open Theists are Arminian in their perspective (see chap. 8, "The Salvation Debate"). But when it comes to the question of God's foreknowledge, Arminians, as we have seen, can hold differing subviews. The three essays contained in this chapter represent (1) the most common and broad Arminian view, which holds that God knows the future in exhaustive definite detail even though humans have libertarian free will (we are calling this the "Arminian" view), (2) the Calvinist view, and finally (3) the less-common view held by some Arminians, known as "Open Theism," which holds that the future is only partially settled so that God knows this part only in terms of possibilities.

God Foreknows Future Free Actions
(The Arminian View)

All orthodox Christians throughout history have affirmed that God is omniscient. He knows *everything* perfectly. For both Calvinism and Arminianism, the "everything" that God perfectly knows includes all that shall come to pass. Arminians and Calvinists disagree, however, on *how* God possesses this knowledge. Calvinists contend that God knows what shall come to pass because he predestines it. Arminians believe that, while God predetermines certain aspects of the future, he leaves other aspects for free agents to determine. Yet, in contrast to Open Theism, Arminians believe God still possesses the ability to foreknow with certainty how these free agents will choose. God thus foreknows all that will come to pass without predetermining all that will come to pass.

Biblical Arguments

Scripture repeatedly confirms that God possesses foreknowledge of future free-will decisions made by human beings. To begin, the Lord told Abraham he would become the "father of many nations" and would be given a great land (Gen. 17:5–8 NIV). This prophecy and promise depended on Abraham's free choice to have faith and on Abraham proving himself to be a faithful covenant partner with God (e.g., Gen. 17:9; cf. 22:12). So too, the Lord told Abraham that his offspring would be slaves in Egypt "for four hundred years" but afterward would "come out with great possessions" (Gen. 15:13–15). There were a multitude of free decisions involved in Abraham's descendants going into Egypt, including the wicked decisions of Joseph's jealous brothers to sell him into slavery (Gen. 37:18–28). And there were a multitude of free decisions involved in his descendants coming out of Egypt, including the reluctant decision of Moses to obey God and face Pharaoh (Exod. 3:18–4:17).

There is nothing in Scripture to indicate that God controlled these decisions. Indeed, God has to argue with Moses for some time to get him to go along with his plan! Yet God clearly foreknew how the decisions would eventually play themselves out, which is how he could tell Abraham about the captivity and liberation of his descendants four hundred years ahead of time.

Along the same lines, a number of times the Lord reveals that certain things were going to happen to various nations or cities as a result of free decisions people would make. For example, God foretells the succession of four kingdoms through Nebuchadnezzar's dream (Dan. 2:31–45). This was brought about by a multitude of free decisions made by kings and military leaders, yet God foreknew them. So too, the Lord reveals a number of details about the fate of Tyre (Ezek. 26:7–21). The fulfillment of this prophecy largely involved the activity of one ruler, Alexander the Great, centuries after it was given. Alexander did these things freely, but they were foreknown by God centuries before he did them.

Twice in Scripture the Lord actually names individuals long before they are born and provides some detail about choices they'll make. Josiah would tear down the pagan altars and destroy the pagan priesthood that plagued

Israel (1 Kings 13:2–3; cf. 2 Kings 22:1; 23:15–16), while Cyrus would let God's people return to Jerusalem and help rebuild the city (Isa. 45:1–14). Yet there's no indication that either the parents of Josiah and Cyrus or the specific actions these two would engage in once they grew up was controlled by God. In his great omniscience, God simply foreknew how things would turn out.

Similarly, Jesus told Peter he would deny him three times before the next morning (Matt. 26:34) and foretold Judas' betrayal of him (John 6:64, 70–71; 13:18–19; cf. 17:12), despite the fact that these two made their decisions freely. He also prophesied that Peter would follow his example and die a martyr's death (John 21:18–19), which presupposes specific foreknowledge of the free actions of certain future persecutors of the faith.

Some of the most impressive passages of Scripture related to divine foreknowledge concern Jesus' ministry and death. Scripture tells us that "[Christ] was destined before the foundation of the world" (1 Pet. 1:20) and was "the Lamb slain from the creation of the world" (Rev. 13:8 NIV). In Zechariah the Lord says that the Jews would someday "look on the one whom they have pierced [and] . . . mourn for him" (Zech. 12:10), an apparent reference to Christ's crucifixion, centuries before crucifixion had been invented as a form of execution. Similarly, in Isaiah we read that the "suffering servant" would die "with the wicked" though he would be buried "with the rich" (Isa. 53:9). Jesus, of course, was crucified as a common criminal but was buried in the tomb of the wealthy Joseph of Arimathea (Matt. 27:57–60). Jesus also foretold what would happen to him several times throughout his own ministry. He would suffer "at the hands of the elders and chief priests and scribes, and be killed, and on the third day be raised" (Matt. 16:21; cf. 20:17–19). When this actually happened, Scripture says it was "according to the definite plan and foreknowledge of God" (Acts 2:23; 4:28).

Open Theists sometimes claim that God foreordained and therefore foreknew *that* Jesus would be crucified without foreknowing or foreordaining *who* specifically would do it. But consider the vast number of free decisions that were involved in the crucifixion of Christ. Had any of them chosen differently, the entire event might have turned out differently, thus thwarting God's plan. What if Judas had decided not to betray Jesus? What if Pilate had decided to listen to his wife and set Jesus free (Matt. 27:19)? And what if Joseph of Arimathea had decided not to offer up his tomb? For the specific prophecies about Christ to be fulfilled, God had to possess foreknowledge of these and an incalculable number of other free decisions.

The same could be said about a multitude of specific prophecies fulfilled in Christ's ministry. For example, Herod's decision to massacre all the male infants in Bethlehem, which led to Mary and Joseph's flight to Egypt, fulfilled Old Testament prophecies (Matt. 2:16–18). So did the guards' decision to cast lots for Jesus' garments (John 19:24); to pierce his side while refraining from breaking his legs, as was customary with crucifixions (John 19:33–37); and to give Jesus vinegar for water (John 19:28–29). The fulfillment of these and other specific prophecies presupposes that God foreknows what specific people will freely choose to do long before they make these decisions or before they even exist.

Finally, we must mention end-time prophecies in the Bible. While far too much is sometimes made of these on a popular level, it's hard to deny that scriptural authors make predictions about specific things certain people will do at the end of history. For example, Paul says that "in later times some will renounce the faith by paying attention to deceitful spirits and teachings of demons." Among other things, these people "forbid marriage and demand abstinence from foods" (1 Tim. 4:1, 3). He also informs his readers at Thessalonica that before the final day, a great "rebellion" will come and a certain "lawless one" will "[exalt] himself above every so-called god or object of worship" and will "[take] his seat in the temple of God, declaring himself to be God" (2 Thess. 2:3–4). There is no suggestion that these actions by certain people at the end of the age are controlled by God. They are done of people's own free volition. And yet they are foreknown by God centuries before they come to pass. Arminians thus conclude that God foreknows the future free actions of human beings.

Supporting Arguments

1. *Foreknowledge of future free actions is implied in omniscience.* Many theologians and philosophers define omniscience as the ability to know the truth value of all meaningful propositions. God knows all true propositions as true and all false propositions as false. In light of this, Arminians point out that propositions concerning future events, including future free decisions, are either true or false and God must therefore know this. For example, the proposition "In the year 2075 the president of the United States will declare war" is either true or false and God, being omniscient, must know which it is. God must therefore know the future free decisions of the future president and every other free agent that will ever exist. We may not be able to specify *how* God can know this, but *that* he knows it is part of what it means to be omniscient.

2. *Foreknowledge is implied in divine sovereignty.* If God faces an open future, as Open Theism asserts, he cannot guarantee that his will shall be accomplished in any given instance or for world history as a whole. Yet the Bible clearly asserts that God can guarantee the accomplishment of his will (Job 42:2; Rom. 8:28; Eph. 1:11). Along with Calvinists, Arminians

believe that only a God who knows with certainty all that shall come to pass can remain sovereign over creation.

Against Calvinism, however, Arminians deny that foreknowledge implies meticulous divine *control*. The Bible consistently depicts humans (and even, to some degree, angels) as possessing the God-given ability to choose good or evil. Because God foreknows these decisions, he is able to *use* evil decisions to achieve his sovereign purposes. But this does not mean evil decisions *come about* as part of God's sovereign purpose. Failing to distinguish between the sovereign use God makes of evil decisions on the basis of his foreknowledge, on the one hand, and the foreknown occurrence of evil decisions as part of God's sovereign purpose, on the other, lands Calvinism in the deepest ditch of the notorious problem of evil. Because of this, Calvinists must accept that God in some sense wills everything he foreknows, including his foreknowledge of who will end up eternally suffering in hell.

3. *Foreknowledge and foreordination are two different things.* While God certainly foreknows all that he foreordains, there's no reason to conclude that God foreordains all that he foreknows, as Calvinism maintains. To know something and to bring about something are two very different things. Knowledge is about having a capacity to experience reality in a certain way. It is a passive activity. By contrast, bringing about things requires a capacity to actively impact reality in a certain way. Consider that most of what we know—whether this be about the past, present, or future—concerns matters that are wholly outside our control.

While God certainly controls a great deal of what comes to pass, there's simply no reason to think God's knowledge of the past, present, and future is categorically different from ours. It concerns God's ability to experience reality in a certain way. In the Arminian view, God knows all that *shall* occur in the same way he knows all that is *now* occurring and all that *has* occurred. He simply sees it, but doesn't necessarily bring it about. Much of what is brought about is the result of decisions made by free agents. Yet God knows it—past, present, and future—in exhaustive, definite detail.

Responding to Objections

1. *Scripture doesn't teach exhaustive definite foreknowledge.* Open Theists object that none of the passages that Arminians (or Calvinists) cite in support of their view *explicitly say* that God foreknows *all* that shall come to pass. Three considerations refute this objection, however.

First, the Lord specifies in Isaiah that he declares "the end from the beginning" (Isa. 46:10). It seems difficult to avoid the conclusion that this concept encompasses the whole of the future. Second, as we have already argued, it is hard to see how God could foreknow what he explicitly says he foreknows in Scripture without foreknowing everything. The world is an interwoven tapestry of decisions. To know with certainty any part of the future presupposes certain knowledge of all of the future. And third, since God must necessarily know the truth value of all future-tensed propositions, God must know the truth value of all propositions that assert what will and what will not come to pass in the future. Along with Calvinists, Arminians therefore affirm that omniscience implies exhaustive, definite foreknowledge of all that shall come to pass.

2. *But Scripture teaches an open future.* Open Theists argue that while some passages show that God foreknows as settled much of the future, other passages suggest that the future is partly open. Hence, they point out that God speaks about the future in conditional terms ("if," "perhaps," "maybe"); that he sometimes regrets decisions he's made; that he sometimes expresses surprise or disappointment over what happens; that he "tests" his covenant partners to find out what decisions they'll make; and that he sometimes changes his mind in response to new circumstances.

If we take these passages literally, they suggest that the future is partly open. As many theologians (Calvinist and Arminian alike) have always argued, however, there is no reason we should take these passages literally. The Bible often depicts God in human terms, using **anthropomorphisms**. If we were to take these anthropomorphic passages literally we'd have to conclude not only that God doesn't know the future perfectly but also that God doesn't know *the present* perfectly. Several times the Bible depicts God as needing to "go down" to a city (e.g., Babel, Sodom, and Gomorrah) to find out what is going on (Gen. 11:7; 18:20–21). Indeed, we'd have to conclude that God literally "remembers" (Gen. 8:1), and has "eyes" (2 Chron. 16:9) and "arms" (Ps. 44:3). Open Theists, of course, don't want to go this far with their literal reading of the Bible, but their hesitancy undermines their literalistic reading of the "openness" passages.

3. *But what "grounds" God's knowledge of future free decisions?* Calvinists and Open Theists both argue that the Arminian concept of God foreknowing from all eternity what not-yet-existing free agents will choose is incoherent. Knowledge is grounded in reality, they argue. If agents are the ultimate determiners of their own decisions, as Arminians (and Open Theists) hold, then there is no reality to ground God's knowledge of what free agents will choose an eternity before the agents themselves exist to make these decisions. Calvinists avoid this problem by grounding God's knowledge of the future in his own will, while Open Theists avoid it by denying God possesses eternal definite foreknowledge of what free agents will decide.

Arminians have offered two responses to this objection. First, some Arminians have argued that God's foreknowledge of future free decisions doesn't need to be grounded in anything other than God's own omniscience. As mentioned above, an omniscient God must know the truth value of all propositions, including propositions about what future free agents will decide once they exist and make these decisions. There is nothing more that need be said about the matter. Second, many Arminians have held that God is above time. He only *foreknows* the future *from our perspective*. From his own eternal perspective, however, he knows the future in the same timeless moment he knows the present and the past. There is, therefore, no problem of grounding God's knowledge of free decisions *before* agents exist and make these decisions. God knows everything *as it occurs* and *because it occurs*, yet from an eternal, timeless perspective.

God Foreknows by Sovereignly Ordaining the Future (The Calvinist View)

Over and against Open Theism, Calvinists agree with Arminians in affirming that God possesses exhaustively definite and eternal foreknowledge of all that shall come to pass. But while Arminians hold that God's foreknowledge is based on how the future will unfold, Calvinists hold that God's foreknowledge is based on how God wills the future to unfold. In the Calvinist view, this is both a clear teaching of Scripture and an unavoidable inference of reason.

Biblical Arguments

Arminians, Open Theists, and Calvinists agree in affirming that, if God has decided to bring about a future state of affairs, he foreknows with certainty that this state of affairs will come to pass. Calvinism differs from Arminianism and Open Theism in affirming that *every* detail of history is just such a state of affairs, for *nothing* takes place outside the will of God.

In the Calvinist view, God leaves nothing to chance. He "accomplishes all things according to his counsel and will" (Eph. 1:11). For example, the scope and duration of empires may seem to depend on the decisions of kings and military generals. Yet Scripture informs us that it is God who determines these matters (Acts 17:26). If God is able (as he surely is) to inspire prophecies about the future succession of nations (e.g., Dan. 2:31–45) and even provide details of a particular nation's future destruction (Ezek. 26:7–21), this is because when it comes to achieving his will, "the inhabitants of the earth are accounted as nothing" and no king or general "can stay his hand or say to him, 'What are you doing?'" (Dan. 4:35; cf.

Isa. 40:15, 17). God alone is "sovereign over the kingdoms of men" and he "gives them to anyone he wishes" (Dan. 4:17 NIV). God "sets up kings and deposes them" (Dan. 2:21 NIV) and directs the king's heart "like a watercourse wherever he pleases" (Prov. 21:1 NIV).

So it is with every event in world history. God brings about national disasters (Amos 3:6) yet also decides something as small as how dice will land when tossed (Prov. 16:33). When what we call "accidents" happen, God's will is behind them (Exod. 21:12–13) as much as when blessings come a person's way (James 1:17; cf. Job 1:21). If a woman is barren, it is because God made her so (Gen. 20:18) as much as when a woman conceives a child (Ruth 4:11–12; Ps. 113:9; 127:3). The time and circumstances of a person's death are controlled by God as much as a person's birth (Job 14:5; Ps. 139:16). God's sovereign purpose encompasses the activity of the wicked (Prov. 16:4) as much as the activity of the righteous, for God "has mercy on whomever he chooses, and he hardens the heart of whomever he chooses" (Rom. 9:18; cf. vv. 22–23). There are, of course, myriad decisions people make that affect accidents or blessings, infertility or fertility, birth and death, and wickedness or righteousness. Yet Scripture teaches that God's will ultimately decides these matters.

In short, *everything* that comes to pass is ultimately "from him and through him and to him" (Rom. 11:36). And since God's decisions are rooted in his eternal purposes, God foreknows every event that shall ever come to pass from the foundation of the world (Eph. 1:4–13; 3:11).

Many of the passages that are most frequently cited in defense of divine foreknowledge explicitly connect this knowledge with God's will. Undoubtedly the clearest, most-compelling, and most-frequently cited passages defending divine foreknowledge are found in Isaiah. In Isaiah 46:9–10 the Lord says:

> I am God, and there is none other;
>   I am God, and there is no one like me,
> declaring the end from the beginning
>   and from ancient times things not yet done.

Similarly, in Isaiah 48:3–5 the Lord says:

> The former things I declared long ago,
>   they went out from my mouth and I made them known;
>   then suddenly I did them and they came to pass.
> Because I know that you are obstinate,
>   and your neck is an iron sinew
>   and your forehead brass,
> I declared them to you from long ago,
>   before they came to pass I announced them to you,

so that you would not say, "My idol did them,
  my carved image and my cast image commanded them."

Both Calvinists and Arminians affirm that these passages support belief in God's exhaustive, definite foreknowledge. What Arminians do not notice, however, is that these passages are equally clear in teaching us *how* God possesses such amazing foreknowledge. God *declares* the end from the beginning; he doesn't *passively observe* it. And then God himself ensures that what he declares will come to pass. "I made them known," the Lord says, "then suddenly *I did them* and they came to pass" (Isa. 48:3, emphasis added). God foreknows the end from the beginning because God decrees and then brings about every event that moves history from beginning to end.

Along these same lines, it is important to notice why God demonstrated his foreknowledge in these passages. He was doing this to convince the Israelites that he alone is the Lord of history, not the idols they were tempted to worship. He declared events before they came to pass "so that you [Israelites] would not say, 'My idol did them, my carved image and my cast image commanded them'" (Isa. 48:5). Notice that the question answered in these passages is not "What does God happen to foreknow?" but "Who *commands* and *brings about* the events of world history?" In other words, God demonstrates his all-encompassing foreknowledge in order to prove his all-encompassing sovereignty and thus free the Israelites from their idolatry.

The same holds true for a number of other classic texts supporting divine foreknowledge. For example, God tells Abraham that his descendants would remain in Egypt "for four hundred years" before coming out "with great possessions" to inherit the land of Canaan (Gen. 15:13–18). As the narrative unfolds, however, it becomes clear that God didn't merely foreknow that things would happen to turn out this way. He foreknew these matters because he had decided *to actively bring them about*.

For example, when Joseph's brothers sold him into slavery, Scripture informs us that it was God who was sending Joseph to Egypt, which ultimately resulted in all Abraham's descendants ending up there (Gen. 45:5). The brothers intended this action for evil, but "God intended it for good" (Gen. 50:20). As the narrative unfolds it becomes clear that God is directly involved at every turn. From the hardening of Pharaoh's heart (e.g., Exod. 9:12; 11:10) to the sending of the plagues (e.g., Exod. 9:14), and from the unexpected favor the Egyptians showed the Israelites (Exod. 12:35–36) to the responses of kings as the Israelites invaded Canaan (e.g., Judg. 11:20), God was ensuring that his promise to Abraham would be precisely fulfilled. God doesn't merely know how things will happen to turn out; he *determines* how things will turn out, which is why he knows how things will turn out.

In the same fashion, when God demonstrates his foreknowledge that the captivity of the Israelites would end after seventy years, he tells his people it's because "I will come to you and fulfill my gracious promise to bring you back" (Jer. 29:10 NIV). God foreknows their future because he knows his own plans for them, "plans for your welfare and not for harm, to give you a future with hope" (Jer. 29:11). So too, God foreknows that a king will be named Cyrus who will let God's people go because God himself determined to raise up a man by that name and use that man as his servant, turning Cyrus' heart to let God's people go (Isa. 44:28; 45:1, 13; cf. Prov. 21:1).

Many other classic foreknowledge texts also make explicit the connection with God's will. If God foreknows the exact duration of David's life, it's because "all the days ordained for [him] were written in [God's] book before one of them came to be" (Ps. 139:16 NIV). If God foreknows that Jeremiah will be a great "prophet to the nations" and that Paul will be a great messenger to the Gentiles, it's because God himself set these two apart for this purpose when they were still in the wombs of their mothers (Jer. 1:5; cf. Gal. 1:15–16). And if Jesus foreknows that Judas is going to betray him, it's because Judas was not among "the chosen" but rather was "doomed to destruction so that Scripture would be fulfilled" (John 17:12 NIV; cf. John 6:64, 70–71; 13:18–19).

The connection between God's foreknowledge and will is remarkably clear in the crucifixion of Jesus. Scripture states that Jesus was "handed over . . . according to the definite plan and foreknowledge of God" and was "crucified and killed by the hands of those outside the law" (Acts 2:23). Herod and the people "gathered together against . . . Jesus . . . to do whatever [God's] hand and [God's] plan had predestined to take place" (Acts 4:27–28). Clearly, Jesus wasn't just crucified the way God foreknew he would be; he was crucified according to the *definite plan* and foreknowledge of God, just as God *predestined* him to be. God didn't devise a plan based on his foreknowledge. His foreknowledge was based on his plan.

Finally, perhaps the clearest and most important passages that associate God's foreknowledge with God's will are those that address God's foreknowledge of who will be saved. God foreknows who his people will be because "[God] chose us in Christ before the foundation of the world" (Eph. 1:4) and "predestined us to be adopted as his sons" (Eph. 1:5 NIV). We were "destined for eternal life" (Acts 13:48) and given grace "in Christ Jesus before the ages began" (2 Tim. 1:9). We were "chosen, having been predestined according to the plan of him who works out everything in conformity with the purpose of his will" (Eph. 1:11 NIV). Hence, believers are referred to in the New Testament as "the elect" or "chosen ones" (*eklectos*; see Matt. 24:22, 24, 31; Luke 18:7; Rom. 8:33), which means we were preselected from the masses "in accordance with the riches of God's grace" and "for the praise of his glory" (Eph. 1:7, 12 NIV).

Yet God foreknows who his people will be not only because he chooses them but also because he himself ensures that they will come to him. No one can come to the Father unless God himself opens their hearts to believe and unless he himself draws them into a relationship with Christ (John 6:44; Acts 16:14). All who the Father draws come to Christ, and Christ loses none of those who are so drawn (John 6:37, 39).

It is true that in several places the New Testament seems to reverse this order. Paul says that "those whom [God] foreknew he also predestined to be conformed to the image of his Son" (Rom. 8:29), and Peter refers to those who are "God's elect" as those "who have been chosen according to the foreknowledge of God" (1 Pet. 1:1–2 NIV). But it's important to note that neither passage says God chooses people *according to his foreknowledge of their faith*, as Arminianism contends. The foreknowledge referred to in Romans 8:29 can easily be interpreted as referring to God's eternal love for his people, just as the concept is used in Romans 11:2. And the foreknowledge referred in 1 Peter 1:1–2 can easily be interpreted as referring to God's foreknowledge of his plan of salvation, for Peter adds that the elect were saved "through the sanctifying work of the Spirit, for obedience to Jesus Christ and sprinkling by his blood" (1 Pet. 1:2 NIV).

The whole of Scripture, Calvinists believe, supports the conclusion that God foreknows all that shall come to pass because God foreordains all that shall come to pass.

Supporting Arguments

1. *The believer's confidence implies foreknowledge and foreordination.* If God does not know with certainty all that will come to pass, as Open Theism argues, believers cannot have the assurance that God has a purpose for every event of their life. Tragedies may occur that God did not specifically ordain or allow, for he did not even know for certain that they would come about. Against such a notion, Scripture encourages believers to look for the hand of God in the midst of their hardships (Exod. 4:11; Heb. 12:3–13).

2. *A clear answer to the question: "What basis is there for God's foreknowledge of the future?"* The Arminian view requires us to conceive of God knowing all the facts about what future free agents will choose an eternity before the agents themselves, or anything else in creation, actually exist. But where do these eternally existing facts about what free agents will choose come from? What "grounds" these facts? In the Arminian view, they cannot be grounded in God, for this would undermine their

libertarian view of freedom. But neither does it seem that these facts can be grounded in the agents themselves, for prior to the creation of the world only God exists.

Some Arminians try to get around this problem by contending that it is simply an attribute of omniscience to eternally know the truth value of all propositions, including propositions about future free actions. But this response is inadequate, for it simply pushes the question back one step. We must now ask, "What eternally grounds the truth value of propositions regarding future free actions?"

Other Arminians try to get around the problem by appealing to the traditional view of God as timeless, but this too is problematic. Even if one grants that God exists in an "eternal now" (a point that is increasingly questioned by contemporary theologians), God's knowledge of what agents will freely do *logically* precedes the agents' free actions. Prior to the creation of the world (whether "prior" is understood chronologically or logically), only God exists. Hence, if we are going to claim God foreknows all that agents will do throughout history prior to the creation of the world, we must accept that this knowledge is grounded in God's knowledge *of himself*. He foreknows what agents will do because he knows what he is going to do through these agents.

3. *Mere foreknowledge doesn't increase God's providential control.* In Scripture and throughout church history, people have appealed to God's knowledge of the future as a means of increasing believers' confidence that the future is in God's hands. Yet if God's knowledge of the future is based on how the future *happens to* unfold rather than in how God *wills it* to unfold, how does God's foreknowledge increase this confidence? Thus, in the Arminian view the future is as much dependent on the chance decisions of free agents as it is in the open view. The mere fact that God happens to foreknow something changes nothing. Only a God who not only foreknows what will happen but is in control of what happens can give believers confidence that the future is in God's hands.

As we noted earlier, some Arminians known as Molinists respond to this objection by arguing that God knows not only what agents *will do* but also what agents *would have done* in every other possible circumstance in which they might have been placed. Molinism holds that God chooses which future he desires to bring about based on his "middle knowledge." In this way they believe that we can affirm, with Calvinism, that God controls the future while still affirming, with Arminianism, real libertarian freedom.

This view is problematic on a number of counts. First, it's debatable that anything like the Molinist view is espoused in Scripture. Second, Molinism has great difficulty answering the question of what grounds God's supposed middle knowledge. On what is God's knowledge of what free agents would do in every conceivable situation based, since the free agents themselves don't yet exist? And third, while there's no question that this view gives God more control over what comes to pass than the standard Arminian view, Molinism still undermines believers' confidence that the future is entirely in God's hands. For God's knowledge of what agents would do in every possible circumstance is still knowledge of libertarianly free human choices, many of which may not be choices that God would have wanted humans to make. Hence, while Molinism gives God the power to choose which "set" of free human choices (called "feasible worlds") will make up our one actual world, God still has to put up with some choices in our world that are outside of his perfect will. To this extent, the future is not in God's hands.

Responding to an Objection

How are humans free and morally responsible if their actions are predetermined? Arminians and Open Theists argue that if God predetermines what humans choose to do, then they aren't free and morally responsible for their actions. Calvinists offer three responses to this.

First, while Calvinists grant that there is an element of mystery here, Scripture teaches both that God determines all that comes to pass *and* that humans are free and morally responsible. For example, Pilate, Herod, and many others are judged to be "wicked" for crucifying Jesus, yet everything they did was according to "the definite plan and foreknowledge of God" (Acts 2:23; cf. 4:27–28). Mystery or not, therefore, out of fidelity to Scripture Calvinists feel compelled to affirm that God predetermines the actions of agents in such a way that the agents themselves remain free and are morally responsible for their actions (this view is called "compatibilistic freedom," in that human freedom is seen as "compatible" with the claim that God ordains all things that shall happen, including all "free" human choices).

Second, this objection is a curious one for Arminians to raise, for the belief that agents are free and morally responsible while nevertheless conforming to God's eternal decrees is hardly more mysterious than the belief that agents are free and morally responsible while nevertheless conforming to God's eternal foreknowledge. In both views we must accept that agents are free and morally responsible even though the fact of what they will choose is settled an eternity before they choose it. Whether their future choices are eternally settled merely in God's mind (foreknowledge) or also in God's will (predestination) does not substantially increase or decrease this mystery.

Third, the libertarian view of freedom presupposed in this objection, a view held by both Arminians and Open Theists, is at least as mysterious as the Calvinist view that actions are free and the actors morally responsible even though they're predetermined by God. Arminians and Open Theists insist that agents must originate their own choices for them to be free and morally responsible. No prior cause or set of causes is allowed to determine an agent's choices. But an action that isn't brought about by prior causes is capricious, which is neither intelligible nor morally responsible. Calvinists thus see no advantage to embracing the mystery of libertarian free will, which is not taught in Scripture, while rejecting the mystery of a free will that is nevertheless determined and foreknown by God, which is taught in Scripture.

God Foreknows All That Shall Be and All That May Be (The Open View)

Again, while they disagree about how God knows the future, both Arminians and Calvinists agree that an omniscient God must know the future exclusively in terms of what will certainly come to pass. For biblical as well as philosophical reasons, Open Theists depart from this view of foreknowledge and hold instead that the future is not just about what *will* come to pass but also about what *may* or *may not* come to pass. Since Open Theists agree with Arminians and Calvinists that God is omniscient and knows all of reality perfectly, they believe that God knows the future partly in terms of what will come to pass but also partly in terms of what *may* or *may not* come to pass. In other words, while Arminians and Calvinists both hold that the future is exhaustively known by God in an eternal and definite manner, Open Theists hold that the future, since it is partly unsettled or "open," is known by God as such.

Biblical Arguments

Open Theists hold that the future is partly settled and partly unsettled primarily because they find this view reflected in Scripture. Certainly there are many passages that characterize the future as settled, such as when God inspires prophesies about what will come to pass in the future (though Open Theists argue that most prophecies are conditional warnings, not unconditional predictions). They affirm that God is the sovereign Lord of history who can predestine, and therefore foreknow, as much of the future as he chooses. Open Theists part with the classical tradition, however, in their denial that these settled passages tell the whole story. For there are also many other passages that depict the future as unsettled, and Open

Theists believe that these passages must be taken just as seriously as the settled passages.

For example, the Lord often speaks about the future in terms of what may or may not occur. To illustrate, the Lord told Moses that the leaders of Israel "*may* believe" that he sent Moses after the first or second or perhaps third miracle he performed (Exod. 3:18–4:9, emphasis added). Scripture tells us the Lord decided against leading Israel along the shortest route to Canaan because he thought that *if* they faced the Philistines they *might* want to return to Egypt (Exod. 13:17). Similarly, the Lord instructed Ezekiel to symbolically enact Israel's exile as a warning, telling him, "*Perhaps* they will understand, though they are a rebellious house" (Ezek. 12:3, emphasis added). The Lord also told Jeremiah to preach to the Israelites, telling him, "It *may* be that they will listen . . . I *may* change my mind about the disaster I intend to bring" (Jer. 26:3, emphasis added; cf. v. 19). Interestingly enough, the Israelites did *not* understand Ezekiel's warning. If God was certain of this all along, was he not deceiving Ezekiel when he promised him that the people might understand and then using this as the motivation for him to enact the prophecy?

One final example of the Lord treating the future as a "maybe" must suffice. In the Garden of Gethsemane Jesus "threw himself on the ground and prayed, 'My Father, *if it is possible*, let this cup pass from me'" (Matt. 26:39, emphasis added). If anything was predestined and foreknown from the creation of the world it was that the Son of God was going to be killed (Acts 2:23; 4:28; Rev. 13:8 NIV). Indeed, Jesus himself had been teaching this very truth to his disciples (Matt. 12:40; 16:21; John 2:19). Yet here we find Jesus making one last attempt to change his Father's plan, "if it is possible." Does this prayer not reveal Jesus' conviction that there was at least a theoretical possibility that another course of action could be taken at the last moment? Of course, in this instance it was not possible. There were other times in Scripture when God was unwilling to change his mind (cf. Num. 23:19; 1 Sam. 15:29; Ezek. 24:14; Zech. 8:14). Yet this doesn't negate the fact that Jesus' prayer presupposes that divine plans and possible future events are *in principle* alterable. And this means that the future is partly open, even if in this instance Jesus' own fate was not.

Other aspects of the way God talks about the future also suggest that it is partly open. For example, the Lord often expresses surprise or disappointment when events he considered improbable occur (Isa. 5:1–5; cf. Jer. 3:7, 19; 7:31; 19:5; 32:35). Similarly, the Lord tells us he sometimes regrets the way decisions turn out that even he himself made (Gen. 6:6; 1 Sam. 15:11, 35). One can only experience surprise, disappointment, and regret when things turn out differently than one originally expected or hoped. But this is impossible if God is eternally certain of how everything will turn out.

Moreover, God often expresses frustration as he strives with people to get them to align themselves with his will (e.g., Isa. 63:10; cf. Acts 7:51; Eph. 4:30; Heb. 3:8, 15; 4:7). Why would God earnestly try to get people to do things he's eternally certain they will never do? And how could God genuinely grow frustrated with people's stubbornness if he was eternally certain they'd remain stubborn? Similarly, at one point the Lord says, "I *sought* for anyone among [the Israelites] who would repair the wall and stand in the breach before me on behalf of the land, so that I would not destroy it; but I found no one" (Ezek. 22:30, emphasis added). Can one genuinely seek for something they are *certain* is not there to be found? Of course not. Hence, Open Theists conclude it could not have been a settled fact that the Lord would not find an intercessor before he went earnestly searching for one.

Furthermore, Scripture frequently describes God as testing people *to find out* what they will decide to do (e.g., Gen. 22:12; Deut. 8:2; 13:1–3; Judg. 3:4; 2 Chron. 32:31). If God eternally foreknows exactly what people are going to do, how can he—and why would he—test them to find this out? And Scripture often says that God changes his mind in response to new circumstances or the prayers of his people (e.g., Exod. 32:14; Num. 11:1–2; 14:12–20; 16:20–35, 41–48; Deut. 9:13–14, 18–20, 25; Judg. 10:13–15; 2 Sam. 24:17–25; 1 Kings 21:27–29; 2 Kings 13:3–5; 20:1–6; 1 Chron. 21:15; Jer. 18:7–10; 26:2–3, 19). Indeed, God's willingness to adjust his plans in light of new circumstances is described as one of God's attributes of greatness (Joel 2:12–13; Jon. 3:10). It's hard to understand what these passages mean if God faces an exhaustively settled future.

The only one who knows the nature of the future with certainty is God and, as shown, he speaks about it both in terms of what *will* come to pass and in terms of what *may* or *may not* come to pass. Open Theists thus conclude that the future is partly settled and partly open—and God knows it as such.

Supporting Arguments

1. *The nature of freedom.* How can we be free and morally responsible for what we do if our future has been settled in God's mind from all eternity, as both Arminians and Calvinists teach? No one holds that we are morally responsible for events that occurred before we were born, for we have no power to influence the past, and we can't be morally responsible for events we cannot influence. If God has known from all eternity everything I shall choose to do in the future, however, then *the fact* that I shall choose something in the future has been settled in God's mind at every moment in the past. Hence, it seems I have no more power to alter the past-settled fact

of what I shall choose than I have to alter any past fact. And it therefore seems I cannot be free to make, or morally responsible for, choices God has eternally known I shall make. For me to be free and morally responsible, the possibility of my choosing otherwise must be *real*. And since God is omniscient and knows reality exactly as it is, God must know my free future choice as a possibility, not as an eternally settled fact.

2. *The problem of evil.* One has to wonder why God would create beings like Satan and Hitler if he was certain they'd turn out as evil as they did and certain they would end up in hell. We can easily understand why God must allow free agents to do evil and eventually go to hell *once he gives them free will*, for to revoke this gift once it is given is disingenuous. But why would God give this gift in the first place if he were *certain ahead of time* that the agent would misuse it to destroy themselves and others?

3. *The urgency of prayer.* If one accepts that the future is not exhaustively settled, prayer and godly living become extremely important. We are not just waiting for the future to be revealed; we are partnering with God to help determine what the future will be. Because the future is not exhaustively settled, things really hang on the decisions we make, including the decision to pray or not pray. The open view thus infuses the Christian life with a sense of passion, significance, and urgency.

4. *Practical living.* The open view of the future is the most plausible view because it squares with our everyday life. Whatever philosophy we might embrace, *we all live as though the open view were true*. With every decision we make we assume that much of our immediate future is settled (e.g., we take for granted the ongoing reality of our world and the laws of physics) but that *some* of it is up to us to decide. The open view simply says that this common-sense assumption is accurate.

Responding to Objections

1. *The open view denies omniscience.* It is often argued that the open view denies the omniscience of God. This is a misunderstanding. Along with Arminians and Calvinists, Open Theists unequivocally affirm that God is omniscient—that is, God perfectly knows everything there is to know! The disagreement is not about the scope or perfection of God's knowledge but rather about the content of reality that God perfectly knows. Open Theists simply believe that possibilities are real and that God knows them as such.

Some philosophers and theologians object that an omniscient God must know the truth value of all future-tensed propositions, including propositions about what future free agents will choose. In response, some Open Theists argue that future-tensed propositions about what free agents will choose to do have no definite truth value until agents resolve their decisions one way or another. Other Open Theists, however, grant that God must know the truth value of all future-tensed propositions but go on to point out that future-tensed propositions regarding what agents *may* or *may not* do also have truth values that an omniscient God must know.

2. *The open view undermines confidence in God's sovereignty.* If God doesn't foreknow all that shall come to pass, some argue, the future is largely left to chance; people's suffering may be meaningless and God can't assure us he can bring good out of evil or triumph over evil in the end. How can you trust a God who faces a partly open future?

It is true that Open Theists reject the Calvinist belief that God ordains or even "allows" every specific thing that happens for a specific divine reason. Not everything happens "for a divine purpose" in the open view (and many Arminians agree). Far from being an objection to this view, however, Open Theists see this as one advantage of their view. If a person believes every specific thing happens for a specific divine reason, they must accept that every horror in world history—from the raping of children to the gas chambers of Auschwitz to specific individuals going to hell—takes place "for a divine purpose."

At the same time, Open Theism offers at least as much assurance to believers as the Arminian view, which allows for the free will of agents while affirming exhaustively definite foreknowledge. If God has unlimited intelligence, as Christians have always affirmed, then he can anticipate and plan a response to *possible* future events as effectively as he can to *certain* future events. The only reason we humans can more effectively anticipate a certain future event than we can a number of possible future events is because we have a limited amount of intelligence. The more possibilities we have to anticipate, therefore, the thinner we have to spread our limited intelligence to anticipate each possibility. So of course we're less effective at anticipating possibilities than we are certainties.

Open Theists submit, however, that any view that thinks God is more in control of the future merely because he knows it entirely as a certainty rather than partly as a domain of possibilities is bringing God down to a human level by *limiting his intelligence.* A God of unlimited intelligence doesn't have to spread thin his intelligence to cover possibilities the way we do. Rather, a God of unlimited intelligence is able to anticipate each and every one of a gazillion possibilities as effectively as he does a single certainty. In fact, he can anticipate each and every one of these possibilities *as though* each one were an absolute certainty. Only a God of limited intelligence would gain an advantage by foreknowing certainties rather than possibilities.

Thus, if we trust in God's unlimited intelligence, it should not affect our confidence in God in the least, whether we believe God anticipates one certain future story line, as classical theism holds, or a multitude of possible future story lines, as Open Theism holds. Whatever comes to pass, the Open Theists can affirm as confidently as the Arminians and Calvinists that God was preparing a perfect response to *this very event* from the foundation of the world. It's just that Open Theists are so confident of God's infinite wisdom that they deny that God had to be certain the event was going to take place for this to be true. Any number of other things could have happened, and if they had, the Open Theists would be saying the exact same thing about them.

In the open view, not everything happens *for* a divine purpose, but everything does happen *with* a divine purpose, for God *brings to* every event that comes to pass a wise purpose and plan he's been preparing from the foundation of the world *in case this event takes place.* And this plan and purpose is exactly what it would have been had God known with certainty that this event was going to happen.

In this respect, the open view arguably gives God *more* power to control the future than the common Arminian view. For if God faces an eternally settled future, there's nothing God or anyone else can do to change it. If God faces a partly open future, however, then God can intervene to influence agents toward the best possible outcomes.

3. *God cannot foreknow only some of the future.* It is often argued that for God to be certain of *anything* about the future, he must be certain of *everything* about the future. This is an unfounded assumption. Sociologists, biologists, advertisers, and insurance agents accurately predict group behavior all the time without predicting what specific individuals will do. Moreover, quantum physics, chaos theory, complexity theory, non-equilibrium thermodynamics, and other branches of science are now revealing that all of reality is structured as an interplay between determinism and spontaneity. Our own experience reveals the same thing. With every decision we make we reflect a deep conviction that some of the future is settled while some of it is unsettled, left up to us to decide. Far from being problematic, therefore, the balance Open Theists find in Scripture between predestined and foreknown aspects of the future, on the one hand, and open aspects of the future, on the other, is consistent with both modern science and our own experience.

In this light, we should have little trouble accepting that the sovereign God is able to foreordain and foreknow *that* Jesus would be crucified, for example, without having to foreordain or foreknow exactly *who* would carry this out (Acts 2:23; 4:27). Nor should we find it hard to accept that God can predestine and foreknow *that* he will have a beloved church without predestining or foreknowing *which individuals* will and will not choose to belong to his church (Rom. 8:29; Eph. 1:4–5).

4. *The supposed "openness passages" in the Bible are merely examples of anthropomorphic language.* Many have argued that the passages to which

Open Theists appeal for support can be explained as anthropomorphisms (i.e., depicting God in human terms). There is, however, nothing in any of these passages that suggests they are merely anthropomorphic. None of the texts suggest it is *as though* God changes his mind, regrets previous decisions, is surprised or disappointed, and so on. Nor is there anything in the rest of Scripture that requires or even warrants that we interpret all passages that depict a partly open future as anthropomorphic. Scripture describes God's *character* as unchanging (Mal. 3:6), but it never teaches that God is unable to change in *any* respect (e.g., his intentions, experiences). It teaches that the future is settled *to the extent* God wills it, but it never teaches that the future is *exhaustively* settled. And it teaches that God sometimes *chooses* not to change his mind (Num. 23:19; 1 Sam. 15:29; Ezek. 24:14; Zech. 8:14) but never that he *cannot* change his mind. Indeed, passages that reveal God choosing not to change his mind only make sense if God can change his mind when he chooses.

Further, the passages cited in support of the open view do not readily lend themselves to an anthropomorphic interpretation. Like all figures of speech, anthropomorphisms must connect with reality at some point if they are to communicate anything truthful. Expressions like "the right hand of God" or "the eyes of the Lord," for example, communicate something true about God's strength and knowledge. But what does the concept of God "changing" his mind communicate if indeed it is merely an anthropomorphism? If God in fact never changes his mind, saying he does change his mind doesn't communicate anything truthful: *it is simply inaccurate.* This observation is especially important when we consider that some passages of Scripture were written for the expressed purpose of encouraging us to believe God is capable of changing his mind (Jer. 18:1–10; 26:2–3, 13) while others depict God's willingness to change as one of his praiseworthy attributes (Joel 2:13–14; Jon. 4:2).

Finally, interpreting openness passages as anthropomorphisms sometimes results in undermining the integrity of Scripture. For example, Scripture says that because of Moses' intercession, "the Lord changed his mind about the disaster that *he planned to* bring on his people" (Exod. 32:14, emphasis added; cf. Deut. 9:13–14, 18–20; Ps. 106:23). If the Lord didn't really change his mind, then neither did he really plan to bring disaster on his people. If this is merely anthropomorphic, then Scripture misleads us when it explicitly tells us what the Lord was planning before he changed his mind. Similarly, 1 Chronicles 21:15 tells us that the Lord in righteous anger dispatched "an angel to Jerusalem *to destroy it*" (emphasis added). But "when he was about to destroy it, the Lord . . . relented." If God never really changes his mind, the explanation Scripture explicitly offers as to why the Lord sent the angel in the first place cannot be correct, for God never really intended to destroy Jerusalem. For all these reasons, Open

Theists do not find the anthropomorphic interpretation of openness passages to be compelling.

Further Reading

Basinger, David. *The Case for Freewill Theism: A Philosophical Assessment.* Downers Grove, IL: InterVarsity, 1996.

Beilby, James, and Paul R. Eddy, eds. *Divine Foreknowledge: Four Views.* Downers Grove, IL: InterVarsity, 2001.

Boyd, Gregory A. *God of the Possible: A Biblical Introduction to the Open View of God.* Grand Rapids: Baker Books, 2000.

————. *Satan and the Problem of Evil: Constructing a Trinitarian Warfare Theodicy.* Downers Grove, IL: InterVarsity, 2001.

Craig, William Lane. *The Only Wise God: The Compatibility of Divine Foreknowledge and Human Freedom.* Grand Rapids: Baker Academic, 1987.

Erickson, Millard. *What Does God Know and When Does He Know It? The Current Controversy over Divine Foreknowledge.* Grand Rapids: Zondervan, 2006.

Frame, John M. *No Other God: A Response to Open Theism.* Phillipsburg, NJ: Presbyterian and Reformed, 2001.

Geisler, Norman. *Creating God in the Image of Man? The New "Open" View of God: Neotheism's Dangerous Drift.* Minneapolis: Bethany, 1997.

Hall, Christopher A., and John Sanders. *Does God Have a Future? A Debate on Divine Providence.* Grand Rapids: Baker Academic, 2003.

Helm, Paul. "The Philosophical Issue of Divine Foreknowledge." In *The Grace of God, the Bondage of the Will,* edited by Thomas R. Schreiner and Bruce A. Ware, vol. 2, 485–97. Grand Rapids: Baker Academic, 1995.

Hunt, David. "Divine Providence and Simple Foreknowledge." *Faith and Philosophy* 10 (July 1993): 394–414.

Pinnock, Clark, et al. *The Openness of God.* Downers Grove, IL: InterVarsity, 1992.

Roy, Steven C. *How Much Does God Foreknow? A Comprehensive Biblical Study.* Downers Grove, IL: InterVarsity, 2006.

Sanders, John. *The God Who Risks: A Theology of Providence.* 2nd ed. Downers Grove, IL: InterVarsity, 2007.

Ware, Bruce. *God's Lesser Glory: The Diminished God of Open Theism.* Westchester, IL: Crossway, 2001.

4

The Genesis Debate

Created in the Recent Past (The Young Earth View)
A Very Old Work of Art (The Day-Age View)
Restoring a Destroyed Creation (The Restoration View)
Literary Theme over Literal Chronology (The Literary Framework View)

Posing the Question

Juston was excited about his new direction in life. Over the summer he had recommitted his life to Christ, and he had a new passion for pursuing his dream of becoming a medical doctor. Now, instead of joining a practice in his hometown, Juston felt certain that he was being called to the mission field to assist in God's work of healing people's souls and bodies in a Two-Thirds World context. What he hadn't expected was the challenge to his faith that came with his evolutionary biology course. According to his professor, **evolution** was an undisputed fact, and the age of the earth was over four billion years.

After class, Juston approached the professor. His question was simple and straightforward: How, as a Christian, can I reconcile the claims of modern science with the book of Genesis? His professor's response was abrupt and blunt: These two perspectives cannot be squared, because science is based on fact while the first chapter of Genesis is simply religious myth. As

Juston left class that day, he wondered if it were truly possible to be both a Bible-believing Christian and a contemporary-minded scientist.

The Center and Its Contrasts

With all orthodox Christians, evangelicals hold to theism as a worldview. More specifically, they uphold the biblical claim that the Triune God alone is the sovereign Creator of all that is and that he is active in his creation (Gen. 1–2; Col. 1:15–17; Heb. 1:3). Evangelicals, therefore, stand against secular understandings of reality, such as materialism and **naturalism,** which deny that the cosmos was created by a personal Creator. The evangelical view also stands against alternative spiritual worldviews such as **pantheism,** which denies that there is a distinction between God and the world, **panentheism,** which holds that God and the world are both eternal, and polytheism, which denies the existence of one sole Creator. While evangelicals are united in their belief that God created the world, they disagree as to how and when God created the world. More specifically, they disagree over how to interpret Genesis 1 and how it is related to the views of modern science.

Disagreements over the interpretation of Genesis 1 are not new. Early church fathers such as Justin Martyr, Irenaeus, Clement of Alexandria, Origen, and Augustine wrestled with this issue hundreds of years ago. However, the debate within Christian circles over the age of creation has intensified during the last 150 years, largely in response to the Darwinian theory of evolution. While the debate over the age of creation and the debate over whether God created by means of evolution are related, they are, in fact, two different issues. The four essays in this chapter address the former issue alone.

There are at least a dozen theories concerning the nature of "days" in Genesis 1, but four primary views are currently debated within evangelicalism. First, the **young earth view** holds that the "days" refer to literal successive twenty-four-hour periods. According to this view, the creation is no more than ten thousand years old.

The **day-age** (or old earth) **view** argues that the "days" in Genesis 1 are best understood as indefinite periods of time. According to this view, creation is as old as contemporary science claims it is: billions of years.

The third view, the **restoration view** (or **gap theory**) claims that a large gap of time occurred between the first and second verses of Genesis 1. Thus, while the original creation is very old, it is possible to correlate the re-creation phase with an understanding of the "days" of Genesis 1 as six literal twenty-four-hour days.

Finally, the **literary framework view** suggests that adherents of each of the previous views, while well intentioned, are fundamentally off-base, because they fail to realize that they are asking the wrong question of the text. According to this view, the author of Genesis never intended to describe how God created the world, let alone how long it took. Rather, the purpose of this text is to proclaim monotheism in a polytheistic context. It is illegitimate, therefore, to force modern scientific questions on an ancient text.

The four essays in this chapter argue for each of these views.

Created in the Recent Past (The Young Earth View)

The Biblical Argument

The notion that the earth is several billions of years old and that its life-forms have been evolving for millions of years is an integral part of our age's naturalistic worldview. Though it is a highly speculative and unproven theory, it is customarily accepted as unquestionable fact. It feeds into the general sense of modern people that humans are a minute and momentary aspect of a cosmos that extends almost to infinity in time and space. Not coincidentally, it also flatly contradicts the biblical understanding of creation.

The Bible begins by proclaiming that God created the entire cosmos in a mere six days (Gen. 1:1–31). The ordinary meaning of "day" is a twenty-four-hour period. Young earth creationists find no good reason to interpret this word in an extraordinary way. Five biblical arguments defend this view.

First, in its singular noun form, such as is found in Genesis 1, the Hebrew word *yom* ("day") always refers to a twenty-four-hour period. Any period of time referred to by *yom*, in other words, is twenty-four hours in length. Advocates of the day-age interpretation of Genesis 1 dispute this, but the passages they offer as counterexamples to this claim do not prove their case. For instance, day-age theorists often cite Genesis 2:4, which says, "In the day [*yom*] that the LORD God made the earth and the heavens." They argue that here *yom* refers to the entire course of creation, not a twenty-four-hour period. In this case, however, *yom* is part of an adverbial construction that is best translated "when" or "after." Similarly, some cite Psalm 90:4 to support their position: "For a thousand years in [God's] sight are like yesterday when it is past, or like a watch in the night." This passage does not disprove the young earth creation view, however. In this passage, *yom* functions as part of an analogy that emphasizes God's eternity. God's experience of a thousand years is *like* a day for us—namely, like one of our regular twenty-four-hour periods. Far from suggesting that a "day" can literally be a thousand years, as day-age theorists suggest, the biblical author is using the ordinary definition of "day" to make his analogy. Finally, some cite Zechariah 14:7, which speaks of a "continuous day," to support the day-age position. The point of this passage, however, is not to suggest that a day is longer than twenty-four hours. The author is simply declaring that in heaven there shall be neither "day" nor "night," for in "the even time there shall be light." In other words, "day" is used as a synonym for "daylight." The verse does not support the notion that a "day" can refer to a period of time longer than twenty-four hours.

Second, it is crucial to note that whenever "day" (*yom*) is used with a specific number before it, such as in Genesis 1, it always refers to a normal twenty-four-hour day (e.g., Gen. 8:14; Num. 29:1). Some try to argue that Hosea 6:2 provides a counterexample. This passage reads: "After two days he will revive us; on the third day he will raise us up, that we may live before him." Nothing in this text suggests that the author is referring to something other than normal days. His meaning is opaque, to say the least, if he is referring to ages. After two "ages" the Lord will revive Israel, and then on the third "age" raise him up. What could this possibly refer to? What seals the case that the author is referring to normal days, according to most evangelical scholars, is that Paul cites this passage to show that the Old Testament predicted Jesus would rise "on the third day" (1 Cor. 15:4). Paul clearly thought Hosea was referring to literal twenty-four-hour periods.

Third, the fact that the author uses "evening" and "morning" when describing each creation "day" is further evidence that he intended his audience to see these as normal days. It would be unnatural for the author to speak of ages having an "evening" and a "morning." Elsewhere in Scripture this parallel use of "evening" and "morning" clearly refers to normal days (e.g., 1 Sam. 17:16; 1 Chron. 16:40; 2 Chron. 2:4; Ps. 55:17).

Fourth, in Genesis 1:14 we read, "And God said, 'Let there be lights in the dome of the sky to separate the day from the night; and let them be for signs and for seasons and for days and years.'" No one questions that the "days" and "years" referred to in this passage are literal. It is unnatural to suppose that the author suddenly shifted from speaking about ages to normal days while using the same word for each. The most natural conclusion is that the author is using ordinary language throughout Genesis 1. "Year" refers to what we understand as a 365-day time period, and "day" refers to what we understand as a twenty-four-hour time period.

Finally, one of the strongest arguments in favor of the young earth creation interpretation of Genesis 1 is the fact that God commanded Israel to imitate the pattern he set in Genesis 1 by working six days out of the week and resting on the seventh. In Exodus we read:

> Remember the sabbath day, and keep it holy. Six days you shall labor and do all your work. But the seventh day is a sabbath to the LORD your God; you shall not do any work. . . . For in six days the LORD made heaven and earth, the sea, and all that is in them, but rested the seventh day; therefore the LORD blessed the sabbath day and consecrated it. (20:8–11; cf. 31:12–17)

Day-age theorists must suppose that the original hearers of this command would have recognized two different meanings for the word "day" in this passage. God's "day" refers to "ages" while *our* "day" refers to normal twenty-four-hour time periods. This is an extremely implausible suggestion. If this were indeed what the author wanted to communicate, he could have easily done so by using a different word for God's "ages" (e.g., 'olam) than he used for our "day." Instead, the author uses the same word (yom), apparently with the same meaning throughout. The author is not drawing an *analogy* between God and the Israelites; rather, he is expressing a *precedent* set by God for the Israelites. As God worked six days and rested on the seventh, we must work six days and rest on the seventh. The duration of the periods of work and the period of rest is identical.

These arguments provide good reason to accept the normal understanding of "day" in Genesis 1. And this means that the earth is not billions of years old and that evolution has not taken place on it for millions of years, as most Western intellectuals today believe. It means humans are not latecomers on the scene, a sort of footnote to the evolutionary process. If we follow Scripture, we must conclude that the age of the earth is several thousand years and that its history is centered on human beings. We were placed here as stewards of the earth at the very beginning (Gen. 1:26–31).

Supporting Arguments

1. *Revelation and modern science.* The real question involved in this debate is, Do we accept the plainest meaning of the Bible, or do we insist on a reinterpretation in light of the prevailing opinion of scientists? Christians are called to place God's Word and the plainest reading of God's Word above the authority of science. It is puzzling why many evangelical Christians today find this difficult to do. After all, on the authority of God's Word they believe that God created the world from nothing (*ex nihilo*), yet this flies in the face of one of the most fundamental laws of science (namely, matter is neither created nor destroyed). On the authority of God's Word

they believe in miracles, yet this flies in the face of the scientific view that the world is governed by natural laws. Why then do these Christians balk at the notion that God created the world in six literal days? This requires far *less* a miracle than bringing matter into existence from nothing and *no more* of a miracle than raising Jesus from the dead.

2. *The pattern of supernatural work.* Throughout Scripture God's supernatural work (see **supernaturalism**) is typically sudden and instantaneous, not involving long drawn-out periods of time. For example, this pattern is found throughout Jesus' ministry. The healing of people was sudden; the stilling of the sea was instantaneous; the raising of people from the dead was immediate. Genesis 1 fits this pattern. Each day God spoke and what he commanded was instantaneously so. Conversely, the view that God brought creation about over billions of years fits no pattern in Scripture.

3. *Death came through Adam.* The Bible teaches that death had its origin in the world through Adam's disobedience. Death was not intended for either humans or animals. In their originally created state, humans and animals were to live on vegetation. Hence, the Lord says to Adam:

> See, I have given you every plant yielding seed that is upon the face of all the earth, and every tree with seed in its fruit; you shall have *them* for food. And to every beast of the earth, and to every bird of the air, and to everything that creeps on the earth, everything that has the breath of life, I have given *every green plant* for food. (Gen. 1:29–30, emphasis added)

In God's original design, there was to be no pain, no bloodshed, and no death. This is in part why God concluded that his entire creation was "good" (Gen. 1:31). Insentient vegetation was to be the food of humans and animals, and this state shall be restored when God's kingdom is fully established (Isa. 11:6–11; 65:25). How can one reconcile this teaching with the view, espoused by day-age theorists, that animals have been devouring other animals for millions of years? Relatedly, how can we accept that the present state of nature, "red in tooth and claw" as Alfred Tennyson describes it, was the best the all-powerful Creator could come up with? Why would an all-powerful Creator have to use a process of natural selection in which animals prey on other animals to arrive at his goal of human beings? And how could the all-good Creator, whom Scripture depicts as caring about the welfare of animals (Ps. 36:6; Jon. 4:11; cf. Luke 12:6), pronounce this bloody, pain-filled state of affairs to be "good"?

Day-age theorists have no good answer. In our view, nature was designed to be "good." Adam and Eve, along with their descendants, were given authority and responsibility for the earth. When they fell under Satan's power, the entire domain they were responsible for came under Satan's authority and was corrupted (Rom. 8:19–22). Death entered the world because the lord of death had gained power over the world (Heb. 2:14; cf. 2 Cor. 4:4; Eph. 2:2; 1 John 5:19). This is why the entire creation is now in the travail it is in. This perspective is not available to any who hold that death had been exercising its tyranny for millions of years before humans arrived on the scene.

4. *The precariousness of modern science.* This essay cannot explore all the reasons that can be given for questioning the scientific enterprise. Suffice it to say, a good number of learned scientists believe that the entire old earth/evolutionary paradigm with which modern science works is based on weak evidence and supported by inconclusive arguments.

For example, a number of geologists and paleontologists have rejected on scientific grounds many of the dating techniques routinely employed today (e.g., radiometric dating). These techniques have been shown to be notoriously unreliable, often circular in method, and dependent on certain presuppositions that are themselves unproven. Similarly, a number of scientists have raised serious challenges to big bang cosmology. Some have wondered how a supposedly uniform initial explosion could have produced the type of unevenly distributed matter that we find in our universe. Other scientists have convincingly argued that the supposed geological evidence for an old earth can be better accounted for by postulating the occurrence of a universal flood several thousand years ago.

The secular scientific community is a tightly controlled community. To belong to this community requires that one agree substantially with its authoritative paradigms. People who reject these paradigms are simply not taken seriously, regardless of how cogent their arguments are. Hence, the evidence, arguments, and alternative paradigms of young earth creationists are rarely given serious attention by the scientific community. They are no less compelling for this reason, however. But one must be willing to swim against the present academic current of accepted truth in order to consider them. Evangelical Christians who place Scripture above all other authorities should be willing to go against the flow when necessary.

Responding to Objections

1. *The sun was not created until the fourth day.* Critics of the young earth creation perspective often argue that because the sun was not created until the fourth day, the "days" of Genesis 1 are not normal twenty-four-hour days. We should note, however, that the first thing God did on day one was create "light" (Gen. 1:3). We are not told what the source of this light was, but we are told that it allowed for a pattern of "morning" and "evening" to begin and end each day—the same pattern, we must note, that occurred *after* the sun was created as a special source of light for the earth. In other

words, the source of light for the earth was modified on the fourth day, but the fact that light existed that measured each day was not. There is, therefore, nothing significant about the fact that the sun was not created until the fourth day.

2. *The seventh day of rest is still in progress.* Hebrews 4:1–11 suggests that the seventh day is still in progress, for it encourages us to join in the "rest" God has been enjoying since he completed creation (v. 10). Since God's seventh-day rest has been continuing throughout history, day-age theorists argue, we may assume that the previous six days of creation were also long periods of time. Three things may be said in response to this argument.

First, this text does not say that the seventh *day* is still in progress. It simply implies that the Sabbath rest that God began on the seventh day is, in some sense, continuing.

Second, the author is drawing an analogy in this text, rooted in a theological conclusion drawn from Psalm 95, which speaks of the Israelites' rebellion in the desert. The author notes that the Israelites in the desert were not able to enter (namely, rest in) the Promised Land because of their disobedience. The author encourages the Hebrew Christians not to repeat this mistake, for they too have a promised land—a "rest"—that God wants them to enter. However, their rest does not concern simply a piece of land. It is the rest that God has in some sense been enjoying since he ceased from his labors on the first Sabbath. We are going beyond the point of the text if we read anything about the length of God's seventh day into this passage.

Third, this last point is confirmed in that Jesus states that he and his Father are "still working" (John 5:17). Clearly, God is not still literally ceasing from all work, which is what the Sabbath requires (Exod. 31:14–17). The "rest" spoken of in Hebrews should not be pressed too far.

3. *Too much activity took place on the sixth day.* Day-age advocates sometimes argue that too many activities took place on the sixth day for it to be a normal twenty-four-hour day. Among other things, on that one day God had Adam name "every living creature" (Gen. 2:19). This alone would have taken weeks, they argue. This is not a convincing argument for two reasons.

First, Adam at this point had an unfallen mind. It is entirely possible that such a mind would have been capable of performing mental functions at a much faster speed than we are capable of in our fallen condition. Even if his innate capacities were not capable of this, God could have supernaturally assisted him in this task.

Second, it is possible that the animals Adam named were a special class of animals God formed for the express purpose of seeing what Adam would name them (Gen. 2:19). In support of this, Genesis 2 suggests that

God formed these animals *after* he made Adam, while Genesis 1 says that God made all the animals before he made humans. Perhaps the number of animals Adam named was not that great after all.

4. *Is God deceptive?* Some day-age theorists argue that if God created the world with the "appearance of age," he is deceptive. Three replies are in order.

First, we do not accept much of what scientists argue is "the appearance" of old age. When the evidence is examined apart from the prevailing assumption that the earth is billions of years old, it does not "appear" billions of years old. It appears thousands of years old.

Second, anything that God created *ex nihilo* would have the appearance of age. People often facetiously ask, What came first, the chicken or the egg? The biblical answer is decidely "the chicken." God did not create human embryos: He created a developed man and woman. He did not first create animal seeds or eggs: He created developed animals. He did not first create various seeds for vegetation: He created the vegetation. Hence, plants, animals, and humans are going to look aged, though in fact they are not.

Third, the day-age theorist might respond that creating something with the appearance of *some* age is one thing. Creating it with the appearance of being *billions of years old*, however, is deceptive. As stated above, we do not accept that the earth appears to be billions of years old. The dating techniques that are used are faulty. But what about starlight? If this light originated from a star in its present location and traveled to us, it is argued, it would have taken millions or even billions of years to reach us. True enough. But why should we assume that the light had to originate in this fashion? If we allow Scripture to teach us, we find that the purposes of stars are to give light and to measure seasons *for us on the earth* (Gen. 1:14–19). If that is the case, God would of course have created the stars in such a way that their light already reached us.

A Very Old Work of Art (The Day-Age View)

The Biblical Argument

Genesis 1 says that the cosmos was created in six "days." Some Christians interpret these days as six twenty-four-hour periods and thus conclude that the earth is roughly only ten thousand years old. As we shall see, this view runs into difficulties with both Scripture and science. According to the day-age view, the word *day* (*yom*) in this passage actually refers to an "age" of unspecified duration. Thus, the cosmos is a very old work of art, a view that is consistent with both Scripture and science, as the following four points reveal.

First, while the word *day* in Hebrew can of course refer to a twenty-four-hour period, it also often refers to an age. Perhaps the most important example of this latter usage is in the Genesis account itself. Immediately after depicting the six "days" of creation, the author introduces a more detailed human-oriented creation account by saying, "In the day [*yom*] that the LORD God made the earth and the heavens" (Gen. 2:4). The author is clearly referring to "the period of time" or "the epoch" when God created the cosmos. If "day" can refer to an entire epoch here, there is no good reason to insist on a literal twenty-four-hour interpretation in the preceding verses.

Examples of this epochal use of *yom* abound in Scripture. For example, the author of Proverbs says, "Like the cold of snow in the time [*yom*] of harvest are faithful messengers to those who send them" (Prov. 25:13). Here *yom* refers to an entire season. Similarly, Isaiah says, "On that day [*yom*] the branch of the LORD shall be beautiful and glorious, and the fruit of the land shall be the pride and glory of the survivors of Israel" (Isa. 4:2). Some believe this verse refers to the millennium—a future one-thousand-year period of peace on earth. Others believe it refers to God's final establishment of his kingdom on earth. Either way, "day" clearly denotes a long period of time (cf. Zech. 14:1).

Second, interpreting the days of Genesis 1 as twenty-four-hour periods creates difficulties with the Genesis account. For one thing, in Genesis 1 the sun does not appear until the fourth day. This alone suggests that the "mornings" and "evenings" of the previous days were not marked off by the rising and setting of the sun. Even more importantly, at least two of the days include events that could not have fit into a twenty-four-hour period. On the third day God said, "Let the earth put forth vegetation." As a result, "the earth brought forth vegetation: plants yielding seed of every kind, and trees of every kind bearing fruit with the seed in it" (Gen. 1:11–12). This process of bringing forth vegetation is not something that could have occurred in a regular day.

Even more problematic, on the sixth "day" of creation God had Adam individually name all the animals (Gen. 2:18–20). This was not a capricious matter of slapping on titles, for ancient people believed that a name should reflect the character of a thing or person. The text itself suggests this, for it was through this process of naming that Adam discovered that none of the animals was an appropriate companion for him (Gen. 2:20). The process of naming the animals would have taken some consideration and thus some time on Adam's part.

Nonetheless, suppose Adam took a mere five minutes to name each pair of animals. That would mean he could name only 288 animals if he did nothing else for the entire twenty-four hours. Consider that there are roughly 12,000 species of mammals alone. According to a best-case scenario—allowing for no other activities, no sleep, and excluding all now-extinct species—it would have taken Adam more than forty days simply to name the mammals! Some young earth creationists insist that Adam named only the species in the Garden. However, to argue this they must reject the very "literal" hermeneutic on which they base their own case, for the text says, literally, "whatever the man called *every living creature*, that was its name" (Gen. 2:19, emphasis added). It seems much more natural to conclude that the "day" of human creation referred to in Genesis 1 is not a literal twenty-four-hour period.

Third, several passages of Scripture expressly teach that God's "days" are not measured like our "days." For example, the author of Psalm 90 says, "For a thousand years in your sight are like yesterday when it is past, or like a watch in the night" (v. 4). The theme is picked up by Peter when he writes, "But do not ignore this one fact, beloved, that with the Lord one day is like a thousand years, and a thousand years are like one day" (2 Pet. 3:8). Such teachings should caution us against a literal understanding of "day" in Genesis 1.

Along these same lines, Hebrews 4 teaches that we are still in the seventh day of creation on which God rests.

> For in one place [Scripture] speaks about the seventh day as follows, "And God rested on the seventh day from all his works." And again in this place it says, "They shall not enter my rest." So then, a sabbath rest still remains for the people of God; for those who enter God's rest also cease from their labors as God did from his. Let us therefore make every effort to enter that rest, so that no one may fall through such disobedience as theirs. (vv. 4–5, 9–11)

This passage suggests that God is still resting from his works on the previous six days. People can enter this rest if they do not resist God's will as the Israelites did in the Old Testament. What concerns us presently is the fact that the seventh day on which God rested apparently covers all of human history. We thus have good reason to conclude that the previous six days of creation were also long periods of time.

Finally, a number of passages teach that the earth is very old. For example, Habakkuk refers to "eternal mountains" and "everlasting hills" (Hab. 3:6). Micah refers to the "enduring foundations" of the earth (Mic. 6:2). The author of Proverbs says that "Wisdom" was created "long ago" and was established "ages ago . . . before the beginning of the earth" (Prov. 8:22–23). The author is presupposing that the earth is very old in order to exalt God's wisdom for being even older. The celebration of the antiquity of the earth found throughout Scripture is more consistent with the view that the earth is billions of years old than it is with the view that it is a mere ten thousand years old. At the very least, it demonstrates that there is nothing "ungodly" or "secular" about believing in a very old earth.

Supporting Arguments

1. *The truthfulness of God.* Scripture teaches us that God is completely truthful (Num. 23:19; John 14:6). It also teaches us that God's revelation comes to us through both Scripture and creation (Ps. 19:1–4; Rom. 1:19–20). This is important to remember when we consider that the cosmos appears very old. Consider one simple illustration. We know how fast light travels, and we know approximately how far away certain stars are from the earth. We thus naturally conclude that it has in some cases taken millions if not billions of years for the light from certain stars to reach us. Young earth creationists would have us believe that God created these stars in such a way that their starlight already reached the earth. God could of course do this if he wanted to, but it borders on deception. One could just as easily argue that we were all created five minutes ago with built-in memories.

2. *The credibility of the church.* We must learn from the past. The church lost a good deal of its credibility when it locked horns with science in the sixteenth century. Against Galileo and all who held to the heliocentric view of the solar system, the church insisted on a literal reading of certain passages of Scripture that subsequently were proven scientifically inaccurate. As Galileo himself warned, one must be hesitant to interpret the Bible in ways that openly conflict with the general findings of science, for creation too is "God's Word." Of course, if it is absolutely impossible to reconcile science with Scripture's teaching, we must side with Scripture. If there are ways of interpreting Scripture that do not conflict with science, however, these should be preferred. The day-age theory of Genesis 1 offers a way of reconciliation. Not only is there scriptural support for this view, but it does not harm the credibility of the church for the scientifically minded people we are called to reach with the gospel.

3. *The scientific evidence.* While it is true that science should not determine our exegesis, it is also true that we should not ignore science in our exegesis. Among other things, the credibility of our proclamation is at stake, as argued above. The fact of the matter is that the vast majority of scientists, from a wide variety of fields, agree that the earth is billions of years old. For example, almost all contemporary astronomers hold to the **big bang theory** of how the cosmos began. This view postulates that the universe began roughly fifteen billion years ago. Similarly, though young earth creationists try to explain this away with their **flood geology,** almost

all contemporary geologists find the evidence for a four- to five-billion-year-old earth to be compelling. Among other things, the stratification of the earth's layers cannot be accounted for adequately by the flood theory. Finally, the vast majority of biologists accept the view that life has been evolving on our planet for millions of years. Even most of the minority who reject macroevolution but accept microevolution argue that the changes we can discern from the fossil record require a time period far longer than ten thousand years. The day-age interpretation of Genesis 1 can accept this information without compromising fidelity to God's Word.

Responding to Objections

1. *Enumerated "days" were used in Genesis 1.* Some argue that the word *yom* can refer to an indefinite period of time only if it is not preceded by an ordinal (e.g., first, second). Since Genesis 1 numbers the days, this means the author intended for us to understand distinct twenty-four-hour periods. Three things may be said in response.

First, while it may be true that elsewhere in the Bible *yom* refers to a twenty-four-hour period when preceded by an ordinal, this is not a grammatical rule of the Hebrew language. In our view, Genesis 1 demonstrates that *yom* can refer to a period of time when preceded by an ordinal. Young earth creationists must presuppose their interpretation of Genesis 1 in order to make this argument, which, of course, constitutes circular reasoning.

Second, even if we grant that ordinarily *yom* refers to a twenty-four-hour period when preceded by an ordinal, we should not be surprised that Genesis 1 offers an exception to this. Most of the time when the Bible speaks of "days," it is referring to ordinary *human* days. The Bible simply does not have occasion to enumerate successive epochs—except in Genesis 1. This chapter deals with God's unique creation of the world, and humans are not even around until the end of the act. Therefore, if the epochal use of *yom* can be preceded by an ordinal, as we argue, this would be the only place where it would be appropriate to do so.

Third, having said all this, we should note that the claim that the epochal use of *yom* is never preceded by an ordinal may simply be mistaken. Hosea 6:2 proclaims that "after two days he will revive us; on the third day he will raise us up, that we may live before him." While Paul may allude to this as a type of Christ's resurrection (see **typology**) "on the third day" (1 Cor. 15:4), most commentators agree that Hosea was referring to epochs, not twenty-four-hour periods. If so, this is a clear instance of a Hebrew author enumerating epochs.

2. *The use of "evening" and "morning" suggests a twenty-four-hour period.* Young earth creationists often argue that the mention of "evening"

and "morning" after each creation day (e.g., Gen. 1:5, 8) signifies that each day was a twenty-four-hour period. The fact that the sun does not appear until the fourth day, however, proves that the terms "evening" and "morning" cannot be taken literally. Instead, they refer to the beginning and ending of epochs, much as we might refer to "the dawn of humankind" or "the twilight of the modern age."

3. *The word* 'olam *refers to an epoch*. Some argue that the author of Genesis 1 would have used the word 'olam instead of *yom* if he had wanted to refer to epochs. Two things may be said in response.

First, as we have already seen, there is a precedent in the Old Testament for interpreting *yom* as "age" or "epoch." This alone demonstrates that authors did not have to use 'olam when they wanted to refer to epochs.

Second, and even more to the point, it is not clear that 'olam could refer to "epoch" in biblical times. Post-biblical Hebrew used 'olam in this sense, but the term in the Old Testament has the connotation of something "everlasting" or "perpetual" (e.g., Gen. 9:16; Ps. 41:13). Since the author of Genesis is clearly referring to temporary periods of time, it seems natural for him to use *yom* instead of 'olam.

4. *Death entered the world with Adam*. It is sometimes argued that the old earth view of creation, which assumes that death was present millions of years before humans arrived on the scene, violates New Testament teaching that death entered the world through Adam's sin (Rom. 5:12).

First, as mentioned earlier, all the geological evidence suggests that animal death occurred before human death. Given this consensus, we should resist this conclusion only if Scripture absolutely demands that we do so. As we shall see, Scripture does not demand this.

Second, Paul is speaking specifically about humans in Romans 5. We are reading too much into the text if we apply this text to the entire animal kingdom. Indeed, if we are going to press the text this far, we could easily include all vegetation—forcing the awkward conclusion that God originally designed all animals and people to eat nothing.

Third, the "death" Paul refers to need not be physical death. It may refer to spiritual death. In fact, Genesis 2 may imply this, for God told Adam he would die on the day he ate from the tree (Gen. 2:17), yet Adam physically lived for a long while after his disobedience.

Finally, the problems that old earth advocates have with this text are less problematic than those young earth creationists must face. Young earth creationists must postulate not only that, for instance, the *Tyrannosaurus rex* was contemporary with Adam (in contradiction to modern science) but also that the *Tyrannosaurus rex* was originally a vegetarian. Most people consider this extremely implausible.

5. *The length of the Sabbath matches God's original Sabbath*. Finally, some argue that since the Sabbath day of rest commanded in Exodus

(Exod. 20:8; 31:12–17) is twenty-four hours, the original Sabbath of God's rest (and thus the other "days" in Genesis 1) must have been twenty-four hours as well. However, what is important in Exodus is not the *length* of the Sabbath but the *idea* of a Sabbath rest. For instance, there is a twenty-four-hour period of Sabbath rest every week but a yearlong period of Sabbath rest every seven years (Exod. 23:10–11; Lev. 25:1–7) and a Jubilee year of rest every fifty years (Lev. 25:8–17). What is consistent is a period of rest, not the length of the rest.

Restoring a Destroyed Creation (The Restoration View)

According to this view, the debate between young earth creationists and day-age theorists is unnecessary. While both sides make valid points, both sides start from a mistaken premise. They both assume that the first two chapters of Genesis are about the *original* creation of the earth. Advocates for the restoration interpretation of Genesis 1 argue that this is incorrect. After the first verse (Gen. 1:1), the first two chapters of the Bible are about the *restoration* of God's original creation, not the original creation itself.

The original creation expressed in Genesis 1:1 became corrupted through demonic forces and was judged. It became "a formless void" (Gen. 1:2). The author of Genesis 1 and 2 then describes how God restored the world and replenished it with beings (humankind) who would love God and administrate his lordship over the earth. Because adherents of this view suggest there is a "gap" between Genesis 1:1 and 1:2, this view has often been called the gap theory of creation. While this view may initially sound fanciful, it is supported by a careful reading of Scripture. It also offers a number of advantages over the young earth creation and day-age views.

The Biblical Argument

First, the description of the world in Genesis 1:2 as a "formless void" in which "darkness covered the face of the deep" is a pejorative description. In Scripture, "formless" (*tohu*) and "void" (*bohu*) almost always refer to something that has been corrupted, wasted, and/or judged (e.g., Deut. 32:10; Isa. 24:10; 49:4). Indeed, the only other verses in which the terms are used together refer explicitly to a desperate state of affairs *resulting from God's judgment* (Isa. 34:11; Jer. 4:23). It thus seems reasonable to assume that the state of affairs described in Genesis 1:2 refers to a state that was brought about by God's judgment. In contrast to the first verse, the second verse of the chapter does not describe God's original design.

This view is supported by the fact that Isaiah 45:18 says explicitly that the Lord "did not create [the world] a chaos [*tohu*]." Yet this is precisely how Genesis 1:2 describes the world. Some Old Testament scholars also argue that the verb "was" in Genesis 1:2 can be and perhaps should be translated "became." If so, Genesis 1:2 suggests that God did not originally create the world a chaos but that it eventually became one. The chaos is the result of God's judgment.

Second, a number of Old Testament scholars argue that "the deep" also has a negative connotation. In the ancient Mesopotamian world, "the deep" often signified something that opposed God, or in pagan literature, the gods. Perhaps this is why the author describes the Spirit of God as hovering over or guarding the deep (Gen. 1:2). Using imagery that ancient Hebrews could understand, the author reveals that God's Spirit was keeping demonic forces at bay. The sinister nature of the deep further suggests that the state of affairs referred to in Genesis 1:2 was not something God originally created.

Third, Genesis 1 and 2 are not the only passages of Scripture that refer to creation. Though evangelicals often overlook them, there are in fact a number of other creation passages in the Bible. Interestingly enough, many of these depict God doing battle with hostile forces (e.g., "waters," "the deep," "Leviathan") in order to bring the world into being (Ps. 74:12–17; 89:8–18; 104:1–9). Ancient Near Eastern people generally believed that a war of some sort preceded the creation of the world. These biblical passages appear to express this perspective but attribute the victory over hostile forces to Yahweh rather than to the pagan gods in whom other Near Eastern people believed.

The question that must be answered is this: How do these passages, which include conflict, fit into the creation story of Genesis 1 and 2? Along the same lines, one must also ask, Where does the rebellion and fall of Satan and his angels fit into the Genesis creation story (Jude 6; Rev. 12)? It is clear from Genesis 3 that Satan had already fallen by the time Adam and Eve were placed in the Garden. Yet we read nothing about him in the preceding chapters.

The restoration interpretation of Genesis 1:2 answers these questions. The conflict between God and hostile forces, expressed in the Old Testament, and the rebellion of Satan and the battle between him and God, expressed in the New Testament, are one and the same event. This rebellion and battle occurred sometime *after* the original creation (when all angels were created) but *before* the judgment and restoration of the creation. In other words, the battle occurred some time between Genesis 1:1 and 1:2.

As a result of the rebellion, ensuing battle, and ultimately God's judgment, God's original creation became a "formless void" characterized by "darkness" and covered by "the deep." Since this concept of a pre-creation battle was widely known among ancient Near Eastern people and among the Jews, as evidenced by the other creation passages that involve conflict, the Genesis author picked up his account where these other accounts left off. He began his narrative with the earth in its destroyed state. He then emphasized the ease with which God re-created his world, thus expressing the victory and sovereignty of the Creator over all forces that oppose him. No other reading of Genesis 1 and 2 can as easily harmonize itself with the biblical data about God's conflict with forces of evil prior to creation.

Fourth, it is significant that with the exception of animals and humans (Gen. 1:21, 26–27), Genesis 1 does not use the word "create" (*bara'*) but "make" (*'asah*). God fashions things out of preexisting material. This observation fits well with the view that Genesis 1 and 2 are talking about the restoration of the world, not its original creation from nothing.

Finally, certain otherwise puzzling features of the Genesis narrative become clear in light of the restoration interpretation. For example, God's command to humankind to "have dominion" seems to suggest that humankind would be met with resistance. The Hebrew term *kabash* ("dominion") usually suggests suppression, conquering, or enslaving hostile forces (e.g., Num. 32:22, 29; Josh. 18:1; Neh. 5:5; Jer. 34:16; Mic. 7:19; Zech. 9:15). Along the same lines, God's command to Adam to "keep" (*shamar*) the Garden (Gen. 2:15) conveys a sense of "guarding" it from something hostile. It is the same term used to describe the role of the cherubim in keeping Adam and Eve from reentering the Garden of Eden (Gen. 3:24).

But what were our primordial parents to subdue and guard against if in fact this was God's original creation and everything existed just as God intended it? There is no good answer. If the first two chapters of Genesis describe the restoration of a world from the ruins of an old one, however, these commands begin to make sense. One of the tasks God gave humanity, it seems, was the task of keeping the earth from falling back into the satanic bondage that led to its initial destruction.

Unfortunately, Adam and Eve failed to subdue the world and guard the Garden, for they succumbed to the temptations of the enemy (Gen. 3:1–7). In time sin ran its full course, and God once again had to cover the earth with the deep and start over (Gen. 6–9). As he did with the first destruction, he fashioned a new world from what could be salvaged from the old one. It is a process that Scripture tells us the world will undergo one final time when the Lord purges the world with fire in order to create "a new heaven and a new earth" (Rev. 21:1).

Supporting Arguments

1. *The flexibility of the restoration theory.* Most restoration theorists accept the young earth creation argument that the "days" of Genesis 1 are normal twenty-four-hour periods while also accepting the day-age argument that the earth is very old. According to the restoration view, the scientific evidence of an old earth applies to the first creation that was destroyed. The six twenty-four-hour periods of Genesis 1 apply to God's supernatural restoration of the creation after it had been destroyed. This interpretation can accept the strengths of both views while avoiding their weaknesses.

A restoration theorist need not hold to an old earth or a literal six-day creation, however. This too is one of the advantages of this perspective. It is theoretically consistent with either a young or old earth perspective, with either a literal or nonliteral understanding of the "days" of Genesis 1, and with either an evolutionary or non-evolutionary view of creation. Embracing this view allows one to follow both the scriptural and scientific evidence wherever it leads. As mentioned earlier, therefore, the debate between the young earth creationists and the day-age advocates is unnecessary, as is the debate between evolutionists and non-evolutionists.

2. *The problem of prehumanoid suffering.* One of the most difficult problems for both the young earth creationist and the day-age theorist is how to account for the presence of animal suffering prior to the arrival of human beings. All the fossil evidence suggests that nature was "red in tooth and claw" (Tennyson) millions of years before humans arrived on the scene. Most creationists argue against this on the grounds that Scripture teaches that creation was not corrupted and death did not enter the world until Adam sinned (Rom. 5:12). Only then did animals become carnivorous (cf. Gen. 1:30). As a result, they must reject the view held by almost all experts in the field that carnivorous animals roamed the earth millions of years before the advent of human beings. Day-age theorists accept this evidence but are faced with the difficulty of squaring their view with Scripture's teaching about the original vegetarian creation. They must also explain why an all-good and all-powerful God would use natural selection, a pain-filled, bloody, and barbaric means of bringing human beings on the scene, while pronouncing this state of affairs "very good" (Gen. 1:31).

The restoration view avoids both problems by affirming that both views contain an element of truth and an element of error. Young earth creationists are correct in affirming Scripture's teaching that animals *in this creation* were originally vegetarian, but they are wrong in thinking that this contradicts the evidence that animals have been carnivorous for millions of years. Day-age theorists are correct in affirming the evidence that animals have been carnivorous for millions of years, but they are mistaken in thinking that this characterized *this creation* from the start.

The most plausible view is that God's original creation became subject to demonic forces that corrupted it. The presence of vicious creatures such as meat-eating dinosaurs was the result of this alien corruption. God eventually destroyed this world and then restored it, placing humans over the earth as its authorities with the task of keeping it free from demonic influence. This they failed to do, and as a result, creation quickly lapsed back to the state it was in prior to God's judgment.

Responding to Objections

1. *This view is not traditional.* Opponents of the restoration view of creation often object that this view has few representatives in the church tradition. This is true, but two observations qualify its force as an objection.

First, evangelicals, and Protestants in general, look to Scripture as their sole authority in matters of doctrine. Therefore, while the absence of precedent for a view should make us cautious, it cannot itself constitute a decisive objection.

Second, no particular interpretation of the Bible's opening creation narrative can claim significant dominance in the church tradition. Indeed, one of the most popular interpretations of the creation story throughout church history, the allegorical interpretation, is now rejected by all evangelicals. The fact is that beyond the affirmation that God created all things from nothing, there has been no standard, let alone officially "orthodox," interpretation of Genesis 1 and 2.

2. *This view is based on circumstantial evidence.* One of the most frequently voiced criticisms of the restoration view is that it is based on inferences from circumstantial evidence. There is no single passage of Scripture that explicitly teaches this view. Indeed, many reject this view as fanciful speculation.

In response, all interpretations of Scripture are based on inferences from other Scripture passages. All evangelicals try to allow Scripture to interpret Scripture and to see each passage as a part of the whole. The restoration view is hardly unique in this regard and in fact is the best way of making sense of the whole of Scripture. It is the best way of harmonizing *everything* Scripture says about creation.

3. *This view is based on a distinction between "create" and "make."* Some have pointed out that Scripture uses "create" and "make" interchangeably. The restoration interpretation of Genesis 1 is thus mistaken in drawing conclusions based on this distinction.

It is true that "create" and "make" *can* be used interchangeably in Scripture. But when one author alters the terms throughout a single passage, it suggests that he is making a real distinction. In the case of Genesis 1, after the first verse in which God is said to have created everything, the author intentionally uses "create" only when referring to living beings—animals and humans. He is thereby contrasting what God "creates" with what God "makes," or "forms." This fact is important, for it demonstrates that Genesis 1 is mostly about God forming—or re-forming—the world rather than creating it *ex nihilo*.

4. *This view is inconsistent with the goodness of creation.* The restoration interpretation of Genesis 1 and 2 supposes that evil spirits existed before and after the creation (or re-formation) of this world. This belief is inconsistent with the fact that God pronounced his creation "good." How could he declare this if, in fact, there were myriad evil spirits menacing creation? In reply, we need only point out that God's declarations in Genesis have a specific focus. Each declaration refers to a new stage of God's restoration of the earth (Gen. 1:4, 10, 12, 18, 21, 25, 31). The declarations do not rule out the possibility that beings existed who were not part of his restoration process, and thus were not included in his pronouncements, and who were not good.

5. *This view is inconsistent with the fossil evidence.* If the original creation had been judged so severely that it could be described as a "formless void," contemporary scientists should not be able to find fossils of creatures (e.g., dinosaurs) who supposedly lived in this original creation. One would expect all evidence of the previous world to have been lost.

The argument does not work. Almost all geologists and paleontologists—including young earth creationists—agree that the earth has been through one or more global catastrophes in the past. Some believe the earth has undergone a global flood. Others believe it has experienced ice ages and revolutionary climate changes due to meteor showers. Yet all agree we can still find fossils of animals that existed prior to these alleged catastrophes. Why then should restoration theorists be accused of inconsistency on this account?

The fact of the matter is that we have no clear idea what the world looked like when the author described it as a "formless void" with "darkness" on the face of "the deep." There is no reason to assume that all evidence of previous life would have been destroyed.

Literary Theme over Literal Chronology (The Literary Framework View)

Young earth creationists try to force modern science into a literal reading of Genesis 1. Day-age theorists try to fit Genesis 1 into modern science. Proponents of the restoration view try to have their cake and eat it too by inserting a speculative gap between verses 1 and 2 of this chapter. All three views are fundamentally misguided and are rooted in contradictory opinions about the meaning and significance of various words and phrases in Genesis 1 (e.g., "day," "formless void"). None of them have seriously considered the more fundamental question concerning the kind of literature we are dealing with in Genesis 1.

More specifically, young earth creationists, day-age theorists, and restorationists all assume that the author of this passage was centrally concerned with providing his audience with a literal chronology of how creation came about—though they disagree over the length and nature of this chronology. The literary framework view is that the biblical author was interested in nothing of the sort. The discussion surrounding the seven days of creation was not meant to satisfy a quasi-scientific curiosity about the order of creation. Rather, it provided a literary framework within which the author could effectively express the Hebraic conviction that one God created the world by bringing order out of chaos. He was interested in thematic rather than chronological organization.

The Biblical Argument

We can appreciate the thematic organization of this chapter best if we step back from the various issues related to particular terms and look at the structure of the chapter as a whole.

The first verse (Gen. 1:1) functions as a general introductory statement. The second verse (v. 2) sets forth a problem that the rest of the chapter is going to solve. The problem is one with which ancient Near Eastern people would have been familiar: The world is engulfed in a primordial chaos. More specifically, the earth is enveloped in "darkness," covered by "the deep," and in a state that is "formless" and "void" (*tohu wabohu*). The author's goal was to show how Yahweh solved each of these problems and thus succeeded in bringing order out of chaos.

The creation week is divided into two groups of three days (days 1–3 and 4–6) with the seventh day acting as a capstone. Within each three-day grouping, four creative acts of God are identified by the phrase "Let there be . . ." Most significantly, the creative acts in the second group mirror the creative acts in the first group. That is, day four mirrors day one; day five mirrors day two; and day six mirrors day three.

The first set of three days addresses the problems of the darkness, the deep, and the formlessness of the earth as spelled out in v. 2. God addresses these problems by creating spaces within which things may exist. The second set of three days addresses the voidness problem of v. 2. God solves this problem by creating things to fill the spaces he created in the first three days.

More specifically, on day one God created light (which addressed the darkness problem) and separated it from the darkness (vv. 3–5). On day two God created the heavens (which addressed the watery abyss problem) and used it to separate the waters above from the waters below (vv. 6–8). On day three God created dry land and vegetation (addressing the formless earth problem) and separated the earth from the waters below (vv. 9–13). Thus, by the end of day three the first three problems had been addressed: darkness, water, formlessness.

The second set of three days addresses the final problem of voidness—the lack of things to fill the spaces God has created. This is how the second set mirrors the first set of days. Day four fills the space created on day one. Day five fills the space created on day two. And day six fills the space created on day three.

More specifically, on day four God creates the lights to fill the skies that he created on day one (vv. 14–19). On day five God creates fish and birds to fill the water and air that he created on day two (vv. 20–23). And on day six God creates animals and humans to fill the dry land that he created on day three (vv. 24–31). On day seven God rested from his labor, celebrating the goodness of creation (2:1–4).

The following chart summarizes the findings.

Problem	Solution: Stage 1	Solution: Stage 2
Formless void	Forming place (days 1–3)	Filling void (days 4–6)
Darkness	Day 1: light/separate darkness	Day 4: lights
The deep	Day 2: heavens/separate waters	Day 5: birds/fish
Formless earth	Day 3: earth/vegetation	Day 6: animals/humans

Genesis 1 is thematically and logically organized and expresses how the Creator solves the problems he needs to solve in order to bring creation out of chaos. Therefore, we have every reason to suppose that the succession of days was not meant to refer to a chronological succession but to a logical, thematic, and literary succession.

In this respect, Genesis 1 is not exceptional. Though it may strike modern historically minded people as odd, biblical authors frequently emphasized thematic unity over historical exactitude. For example, it is a well-known fact that some Gospel authors grouped Jesus' sayings and deeds by theme rather than by the order in which they occurred historically. As a result, the order of events in the Gospels differs considerably, just as the order of events in Genesis 1 and Genesis 2 differs significantly. This would be of concern only if the authors intended to provide an exact account of how things happened historically. If their concern was more thematic, as we suggest, then the contradictions are inconsequential.

Supporting Arguments

1. *The ancient Near Eastern background.* A number of considerations support the literary framework interpretation of Genesis 1. To begin with, an examination of ancient Near Eastern creation literature seems to confirm this view. Over the last century a number of ancient Near Eastern texts have been found that deal with creation and that to some degree parallel Genesis 1. There is often a "six plus one" literary structure to these texts, expressed as the seven "days" of creation. (This is found, for example, in the **Enuma Elish** as well as in several **Ugaritic** texts such as Keret, Aqhat, and Baal.) The general pattern of presenting creation in the form of a weeklong period has cultural precedent. It is difficult to avoid the conclusion that the Genesis author was following this cultural pattern to communicate his own view of creation.

2. *The theology of Genesis 1.* The theology of Genesis 1 takes on a more profound significance when read against the backdrop of ancient Near Eastern literature rather than against the backdrop of contemporary scientific concerns. Genesis 1 is a theological statement, not a scientific report, expressed in a rather typical ancient Near Eastern way. Its intended purpose is to tell us *who* the Creator is, not exactly *how* he created.

More specifically, when Genesis 1 is read against the ancient Near Eastern background, it becomes clear that the Genesis author is engaging in a polemic against his pagan neighbors. He utilizes their six-day structure but to a very different end. Unlike the pagan ancient Near Eastern view that many gods were involved in creation, the Genesis author affirms that the world was created by one God alone. Unlike their view that the cosmos was created as a result of a cosmic battle, the Genesis author affirms that God created the cosmos without opposition. Like a mighty king, the Lord simply said, "Let there be . . ."

What is more, unlike the pagan ancient Near Eastern view that the cosmos was formed out of preexistent material (often the body parts of defeated gods), the Genesis author affirms that God created the world simply by speaking it into existence (he created it *ex nihilo*). And unlike the common pagan view that the sun, moon, and stars were divine beings, the Genesis author emphasizes God's sole sovereignty over creation by depersonalizing them and depicting them as inanimate objects.

While modern people may be concerned with a scientific account of the origin of the cosmos, it seems the author of Genesis was not. His concern was simply to battle false theology with true theology. When we read his work against the backdrop of the theological concerns with which he was wrestling, it takes on a significance we miss if we are locked into modern issues. The "days" of Genesis 1 are part of a literary structure that serves to support the theological claim that Yahweh-God alone is Creator-King!

They are not meant to satisfy modern curiosity as to how long it took God to create the world.

3. *The weaknesses of alternative views.* Adherents of the literary framework view of Genesis 1 agree with young earth creationists that the word *day* (*yom*) as well as the "morning"/"evening" references probably indicate that the author was thinking of normal twenty-four-hour periods. The arguments against the epochal reading of *yom* in Genesis 1 are strong. At the same time, the arguments against the young earth creationists' position that the earth was created in six literal days and is only ten thousand years old are strong as well. Both views also have a difficult time explaining how plant life could survive for a day—or an entire age!—without a sun. The literary framework view not only avoids this problem but actually explains it. The order of the days is not meant to reflect the chronology of creation. It is rather meant to express thematically the problems of darkness, watery abyss, formlessness, and void expressed in Genesis 1:2.

4. *Genesis 1 and the scientific evidence.* The literary framework interpretation can easily be reconciled with any contemporary scientific theory of origin one chooses to embrace. Yet at the same time, reconciliation is not necessary. Genesis 1 has no bearing on science, for it is strictly interested in theology, not science.

Responding to Objections

1. *This view acquiesces to liberal theology.* Some conservative evangelicals object to the literary framework approach to Genesis 1 on the grounds that it acquiesces to liberal theology. A good deal of liberal theology is premised on the mistaken notion that people can embrace the symbolic meaning of an event while denying the event ever literally took place. So, for example, some liberal theologians have denied that the incarnation or resurrection literally took place, though they continue to insist that we can appreciate and benefit from their symbolic value. Evangelicals have always regarded this line of thinking implausible, if not incoherent. Unfortunately, some believe that the literary framework interpretation of Genesis 1 comes close to this sort of thinking. They argue that this view denies that creation literally took place as the passage says (namely, in six days) while it nevertheless insists that this does not affect the symbolic meaning of the passage.

The truth of the matter is that the literary framework interpretation of Genesis 1 has nothing in common with the agenda of liberal theology. The reason liberal theologians sometimes deny events such as the incarnation or resurrection is that they find Scripture impossible to believe. By contrast, literary framework theorists deny that Genesis 1 provides a literal chronology of how creation came about because they are convinced that the biblical author did not intend to provide a literal chronology. They are simply trying to remain true to the text. The literal reading of the passage is contrary to the authorial intent behind the text.

2. *This view overstates the parallels with other ancient Near Eastern texts.* Some Old Testament scholars have argued that literary framework theorists overstate the parallels between Genesis 1 and other ancient Near Eastern creation texts. More specifically, these scholars point out that the typical arrangement in other Near Eastern texts is three groups of two days, not two groups of three days, such as we find in Genesis 1.

In reply, this view does not deny that there are literary differences between Genesis and other ancient Near Eastern texts. This should not be surprising, for all the creation accounts differ in one way or another from all the others. Each author creatively arranged his material as he saw fit. The point is merely that the Genesis account parallels the other accounts by using "days" as thematic and literary benchmarks rather than literal quasi-scientific reports of how long it took for the world to come into being.

3. *"Day" is always used in a literal way in Hebraic literature.* Some object to the literary framework reading of Genesis 1 on the grounds that there are no other examples in Hebraic literature of "day" (*yom*) being used as a structural literary theme. This is true, but three considerations weaken it as an objection against this view.

First, most scholars agree that the concept of "day" *does* function as a structural literary device in other ancient Near Eastern texts, providing sufficient precedent for such an interpretation.

Second, the literary use of "day" in other ancient Near Eastern texts is always in creation passages. Too much should not be made, therefore, of the fact that this usage is found only in the Bible's fullest creation passage (Gen. 1).

Third, interpreting "day" in a literal fashion creates difficulties that the literary framework avoids. The literal interpretation forces us to accept that plant life arose before a sun existed. It also conflicts with modern science. Most importantly, if we approach the passage with the assumption that the author was concerned with chronology, we miss the profound thematic point the author is making throughout this passage, namely, that God brings order out of chaos.

4. *This view creates a false antithesis.* One could argue that the thematic structure that the literary framework highlights does not rule out the possibility that Genesis 1 *also* teaches the actual chronology of creation. That is, one could argue that God created the world in six twenty-four-hour periods or in six ages, and the reason the days occurred in the order they did is revealed by the literary framework theory. It is just as easy to credit God with being ingenious in the way he *actually brought about* creation as

it is to credit an ancient author with being ingenious in the way he chose *to structure a story* about creation.

One must admit that the scenario proposed by this objection is logically possible. But once we understand the literary purpose of the "days" in this passage, there is no need to interpret them as actual events, even if it remains logically possible to do so. In other words, the explanation of the text is not helped by this addition. What is more, if we accept this objection, we must once again wrestle with the biblical, logical, and scientific difficulties with which the other three theories of creation must deal. Why enter this arena if we do not have to?

5. *This view undermines the command to keep the seventh day holy.* Finally, some have argued that this theory undermines the motivation of the Sabbath commandment in Scripture. The command to rest on "the seventh day" presupposes the importance of the chronological, not simply logical, order of days in Genesis 1. Indeed, Exodus 20:8–11 sees the entire week of creation as a precedent for our workweek. As God worked six days and rested on the seventh, so we should work six days and rest on the seventh. This precedent makes no sense, it is argued, if chronology is not the point in Genesis 1.

This precedent makes perfect sense, however, even though chronology is not the point in Genesis 1. God rested when his work of bringing order out of chaos was complete. His work culminated in a rest that celebrated the goodness of creation (Gen. 2:2–3). *This* is the point of both the Genesis and the Exodus passages. It is not intrinsically connected to whether the "days" are twenty-four-hour periods or not, or whether the second day had to literally follow the first day. Indeed, Hebrews teaches us that God's seventh day is still in progress (Heb. 4:1–11), a point that decisively undermines the young earth creation objection.

Further Reading

Blocher, Henri. *In the Beginning: The Opening Chapters of Genesis.* Translated by David G. Preston. Downers Grove, IL: InterVarsity, 1984.

Custance, Arthur C. *Without Form and Void: A Study of the Meaning of Genesis 1:2.* Brockville, ON: Custance, 1970.

Hagopian, David G., ed. *The Genesis Debate: Three Views on the Days of Creation.* Mission Viejo, CA: Crux, 2001.

Moreland, J. P., and John Mark Reynolds, eds. *Three Views on Creation and Evolution.* Grand Rapids: Zondervan, 1999.

Morris, John D. *The Young Earth.* Green Forest, AR: Master, 1994.

Mortenson, Terry, and Thane H. Ury, eds. *Coming to Grips with Genesis: Biblical Authority and the Age of the Earth.* Green Forest, AR: Master, 2008.

Newman, Robert C., and Herman J. Eckelmann Jr. *Genesis One and the Origin of the Earth*. Downers Grove, IL: InterVarsity, 1989.

Ross, Hugh. *Creation and Time: A Biblical and Scientific Perspective on the Creation-Date Controversy*. Colorado Springs: NavPress, 1994.

Van Till, Howard D. *The Fourth Day: What the Bible and the Heavens Are Telling Us about the Creation*. Grand Rapids: Eerdmans, 1986.

Whitcomb, John C. *The Early Earth: An Introduction to Biblical Creationism*. Rev. ed. Grand Rapids: Baker Academic, 1986.

Wise, Kurt P. *Faith, Form, and Time: What the Bible Teaches and Science Confirms about Creation and the Age of the Universe*. Nashville: Broadman and Holman, 2002.

Young, Davis A. *Christianity and the Age of the Earth*. Grand Rapids: Academie/Zondervan, 1982.

Youngblood, Ronald F. *The Book of Genesis: An Introductory Commentary*. 2nd ed. Grand Rapids: Baker Academic, 1991.

——, ed. *The Genesis Debate: Persistent Questions about Creation and the Flood*. Grand Rapids: Baker Academic, 1990.

5

The Divine Image Debate

The Image of God Is the Soul (The Substantival View)
The Image of God Is Our God-Given Authority (The Functional View)
The Image of God Is Our Relationality (The Relational View)

Posing the Question

What makes a human being human? When does a human being become a person? When does a human being cease to be a person? What is the significance of being human? Is there an inherent value with inherent rights that go along with being human?

These are the kinds of questions that are addressed by the doctrine that humans are made in the *imago Dei* (Latin for "image of God"). They may seem theoretical, but they have many practical implications. For example, how you answer the question of what makes a human being human will significantly influence whether you believe mentally handicapped people should be able to reproduce at will or have the same access to limited medical resources. How you answer the question concerning the significance of being human will determine your views about what inherent rights people have, how people should be governed, and what authority, if any, they have to treat animals differently than they treat people.

Indeed, how you answer these questions will greatly affect your views on whether it is legal to allow severely deformed babies to die, whether people have the right or responsibility to take others off life support, whether and when people have the right to choose abortion, and whether human cloning should be pursued.

The Center and Its Contrasts

Christians throughout history have followed Scripture (esp. Gen. 1:26–28) and taught that humans are of inestimable value because they alone are created in God's own image. This belief sets Christians apart from non-Christians, who have taken a variety of perspectives on this issue.

Many people today believe that humans are essentially no different from "lower" animals from which we evolved. At the most fundamental level we are simply more complicated bundles of matter than other animals. This view of humans is sometimes called the naturalistic evolutionary view. Secular humanists hold to the naturalistic evolutionary understanding of humanity but stress that since we do not answer to a law or a being higher than ourselves, humans are the final measure of truth, morality, and value. Secular humanists tend to believe that humans possess an incredible potential to better ourselves and improve life on earth.

An increasing number of people in Western culture are being influenced by Eastern forms of thought. This influx of Eastern and ancient pagan forms of thought is often referred to as the New Age movement. In a variety of ways, members of this movement affirm that humans are intrinsically divine. Some go so far as to suggest that we are manifestations of God, or the One divine reality that encompasses all things (pantheism).

Many others today believe that no final answer can be given to questions such as, What makes a human being human? In their view, we can only express what various individuals or various cultures believe about humans. The "truth" of what makes a human being human is relative, depending on one's perspective. People who embrace this position are often labeled postmodernists and/or postmodern relativists. (See **postmodernism** and **relativism**.)

Finally, some agree with Christians that humans are created in the image of God, but by this they mean something very different from what Christians mean. For example, when Mormons affirm that humans are created in the image of God, they usually mean that God has a human form. Indeed, they believe that humans who follow God's will on earth will someday become gods themselves and beget children in their own image on their own planet. Few Christians throughout history have given any credence to the notion that the divine image refers to the body.

While Christians have always agreed that humans are made in the *imago Dei*, and while this sets them apart from naturalistic evolutionists, New Age theorists, and postmodern relativists, they have not always agreed on what this *imago Dei* refers to. Amid the variety of opinions expressed throughout history, three have at various times been popular.

The most popular answer has been that the *imago Dei* refers to the human soul. In other words, the spiritual substance of humans sets them apart from all other animals as beings who are uniquely created in the *imago Dei*. This view is often referred to as the **substantival view of the *imago Dei*.**

Theologians who espouse this view have often differed regarding what aspects of the human self manifest the soul. Many have emphasized that our ability to reason is the distinguishing mark of the soul. Others have argued that our ability to communicate sets us apart. Still others have stressed that our ability to love or to sense God or to make moral judgments manifests our *imago Dei*. Many theologians have concluded that all of these features manifest the soul. In each case, however, the divine image is located in the soul of humans. St. Augustine, Thomas Aquinas, and John Calvin are classic representatives of this perspective.

A different understanding of the *imago Dei* gained popularity in the twentieth century, though it had predecessors in earlier church history. This view locates the *imago Dei* in the commission of God for humans to "have **dominion**" over the earth. This view is sometimes referred to as the **functional view of the *imago Dei***, for it locates the essence of our divine image in what we as humans are called to do. As God is the loving Lord of the entire cosmos, humans are called to be the loving lords of the entire earth.

A third understanding of the *imago Dei* also gained popularity in the twentieth century, though it too had historical predecessors. In the early part of the twentieth century, Karl Barth argued that the central defining feature of the *imago Dei* is human relationality. Hence, this view is called the **relational view of the *imago Dei*.** Humans are created in the image of the Triune God and thus are meant to find their essence and destiny in community with one another and with God

The following three essays offer arguments in favor of each of these views.

The Image of God Is the Soul (The Substantival View)

What does the Bible mean when it says that humans are created "in the image of God"? In what ways is the human being a reflection of who God is? What sets humans apart from everything else in creation? According to the substantival view, the *imago Dei* means that in all of God's creation, humans alone have a soul. The *imago Dei* is not something we do; it is something we are. It is our essence. Five aspects of biblical revelation ground this perspective.

The Biblical Argument

First, the Bible repeatedly affirms that humans, in contrast to all animals, have an eternal soul (Matt. 22:37; 1 Thess. 5:23). Whereas the life of all animals ends with death, humans live on (Matt. 25:46; Rev. 6:9–11). Like God, humans are beings who shall never cease to exist spiritually.

Second, because we have a soul, we have the capacity to reason. Humans possess the unique ability as well as the innate need to pursue and discover truth. God invites people to reason with him (Isa. 1:18). Christians are encouraged to be ready to reason with unbelievers (2 Pet. 3:15). Indeed, throughout the Bible people are called on to make rational decisions (Deut. 30:19; Josh. 24:15). Like God, but unlike animals, humans have the capacity to think rationally.

Third, because we have a soul, we have the capacity for moral goodness. Whereas animals operate by instinct alone, humans can choose to do good. We can either obey or disobey God. Throughout the biblical narrative God, who is good by nature, calls on humans to pursue holiness and shun evil (2 Chron. 7:14; 2 Tim. 2:19–22). Like God, but unlike animals, humans possess a capacity for moral goodness.

Fourth, because we have a soul, we possess a "sense of the divine" (*sensus divinitatus*). Unlike animals, humans can and should sense the glory of God in all of creation (Ps. 19:1–4; Rom. 1:19–20). Humans can and should sense God's Spirit calling them into relationship with him (John 16:7–8).

Fifth, because we have a soul, we possess the capacity to love. Whereas animals are driven by instinct, humans possess the ability and therefore the responsibility to enter into self-sacrificial, loving relationships with God and other humans. Throughout the biblical narrative God calls people to enter into a loving, covenantal relationship with him and to love others as they love themselves (Lev. 19:18; Deut. 6:5; Matt. 22:36–40). Like God, humans possess the capacity to love.

In conclusion, the *imago Dei* is the soul of a person. Admittedly, the capacity of the soul to reason, aspire to moral goodness, sense God, and enter into loving relationships is diminished because of the fall. Indeed, in this fallen world the soul's capabilities may for a variety of reasons be altogether suppressed, as in the case of severely mentally handicapped people. But as long as the soul is present, the *imago Dei* is present.

Supporting Arguments

1. *Church tradition*. While there have been a number of views offered throughout history regarding the nature of the *imago Dei*, the view that

it refers to the soul is the most traditional. While this does not settle the issue for evangelical believers, it certainly counts in favor of this view.

2. *The essence of the human being.* We all have a sense that the value and dignity of human beings is associated with the sheer fact that they are human. Regardless of what they can and cannot do, they possess an inherent quality that sets them apart from the rest of creation. The biblical teaching regarding the *imago Dei* renders this intuition intelligible, but only if it is associated with who humans are, not with what they do.

If we associate the *imago Dei* with something humans do rather than with who they are, then individuals who cannot or do not perform these tasks cannot be regarded as truly human. This line of thinking could lead to the devaluation of unborn children, mentally incapacitated persons, or persons who have by their own choices made themselves into immoral, irrational, or loveless persons. According to the substantival view, all people are of infinite worth, regardless of their natural or acquired abilities or disabilities, simply because they possess a soul. It may be that certain persons cannot or do not exercise the capacities of their soul. Their intrinsic value, however, is rooted in the fact that they possess a soul, whether or not its capacities are exercised.

Responding to an Objection

This view is not rooted in Genesis 1:26–28. The most frequent objection to the traditional understanding of the *imago Dei* is that it is not adequately grounded in Scripture. Opponents of this view often point out that it is not rooted in an **exegesis** of Genesis 1:26–28, the central biblical text that discusses the *imago Dei.* Indeed, it is frequently argued that the view that the *imago Dei* refers to the soul is more influenced by Greek philosophy than by Scripture. More specifically, it is argued that the traditional emphasis on reason as one of the hallmarks of the *imago Dei* is a distinctly **Hellenistic,** not **Hebraic,** notion. Three things may be said in response to this objection.

First, it is true that the central text that declares the creation of humans in the image of God does not specify that this image is the human soul. Too much should not be made of this, however. This text tells us *that* we are made in the image but does not specify *what* this divine image is. We need to survey the rest of Scripture to discover what constitutes this image, and what we discover is that the image is the human soul.

Second, the argument that the traditional view of the *imago Dei* is more influenced by Hellenistic philosophy than by the Bible has never been proven. It is true that according to Hellenistic philosophy the most noble feature of humans was their possession of a divine soul. And it is true that

Hellenistic philosophers often affirmed that this soul lived on after physical death and gave people the capacity to reason and make decisions. But demonstrating parallels and proving a line of influence are two different things. One could just as easily argue, as traditionalists in fact have, that the parallels between Hellenistic philosophy and the traditional view of the *imago Dei* simply suggest that Hellenistic philosophers sometimes were correct.

Even if a line of influence could be proven, however, this would not invalidate the traditional view. Indeed, it has been plausibly argued that certain ideas in Scripture, especially in the New Testament, have their origin in Hellenistic culture. This simply demonstrates that God can use any means he chooses to reveal truth. The issue, then, is not whether the view that the *imago Dei* is the soul is influenced by Hellenistic philosophy. The issue is whether this view is true, and this must be decided primarily by a comprehensive study of Scripture. Where an idea originated historically is inconsequential.

This leads to a third response. The foundation for the view that the *imago Dei* is the soul is adequately rooted in Scripture. The fact that this view is not spelled out in any one text is of no consequence. Throughout the biblical narrative what sets humans apart from all animals is that humans alone possess a soul and therefore live eternally, reason, have moral capabilities, and can love. Unlike humans, nowhere are animals offered eternal life (John 3:15), commanded to think (Luke 10:27), held morally accountable (Ezek. 33:18–19), or commanded to love (John 15:17).

The Image of God Is Our God-Given Authority
(The Functional View)

We miss the full force of the *imago Dei* concept if we simply identify it with various ways humans are distinct from animals (e.g., reason, morality, love). The biblical concept instructs us as to how we are *like God*, not just how we are *different from animals*. To discover the meaning of the *imago Dei*, we must pay close attention to the way Scripture speaks about it.

The Biblical Argument

All Christians agree that the central text concerning the *imago Dei* is Genesis 1:26–28. Here the Lord says, "Let *us* make man in our image." Some argue that the "us" in this passage refers to the Trinity, but it is unlikely that the Old Testament author, traditionally identified as Moses, had the Trinity in mind. The revelation that God is Triune was not clearly revealed until the New Testament. It is therefore wrong to apply this New Testament understanding to an Old Testament text. (See **anachronistic**.) The most ancient and most probable interpretation is that the Lord was speaking to angels. This tells us that the *imago Dei* is something we share in common with the angels and gives us our first hint as to what the concept means.

Throughout Scripture we learn that angels are beings who are given authority to carry out certain tasks given to them by God. Some angels are charged with watching over nations (Dan. 10:13, 20–21; cf. Deut. 32:8–9), others with preserving justice (Ps. 82), still others with watching over people (Matt. 18:10; Heb. 1:14). Whereas God is the Lord of all creation, he delegates authority to angels to administrate his lordship. He is God over all creation, while angels are made to be "gods" over aspects of this creation. Hence, the Bible sometimes refers to angels (even fallen angels!) as "gods" (2 Cor. 4:4). This is the sense in which they bear the "image of God." Like God, they exercise authority over creation.

The same is true of human beings. We are made in the image of God because we are commissioned to have authority over creation. Our area of authority is the earth with all its inhabitants. Therefore, immediately after saying, "Let us make humankind in our image," the Lord says, "and let them have dominion over the fish of the sea, and over the birds of the air, and over the cattle, and over all the wild animals of the earth, and over every creeping thing that creeps upon the earth" (Gen. 1:26). The theme is reiterated for emphasis in the following verses: "So God created humankind in his image. . . . God blessed them, and God said to them, 'Be fruitful and multiply, and fill the earth and subdue it; and have dominion over the fish of the sea and over the birds of the air and over every living thing that moves upon the earth'" (Gen. 1:27–28).

The passage associates bearing God's image with exercising God's authority. Like angels, we bear the image of the Creator because we are commissioned to exercise lordship over an area of creation. Ultimately, it is God's authority that we exercise, for all creation belongs to him and the only authority we have comes from him. Yet it is our responsibility to exercise this authority in accordance with his will.

The teaching that the *imago Dei* is about exercising authority is disclosed elsewhere in Scripture. For example, in Psalm 8:4–6 we read:

> What are human beings that you are mindful of them,
>   mortals that you care for them?
> Yet you have made them a little lower than God,
>   and crowned them with glory and honor.
> You have given them dominion over the works of your hands;
>   you have put all things under their feet.

The supreme dignity of human beings is that they, like God, exercise authority over creation.

This teaching is applied in a more particular fashion when Scripture refers to certain individuals who are given authority over others as God's "sons." In a passage that most Old Testament scholars believe reflects the perspective of King David, the psalmist says:

> I will tell of the decree of the LORD:
>> He said to me, "You are my son;
>> today I have begotten you.
>> Ask of me, and I will make the nations your heritage,
>> and the ends of the earth your possession." (Ps. 2:7–8; cf.
>> 89:27–29)

The concept of "son" in this passage refers to a person's likeness to another. Whereas all humans are created in God's likeness in that they are given a domain of authority over the earth, the king is God's son in a unique sense because he exercises a greater scope of authority over the earth than most people.

Jesus Christ is the supreme example of this concept of sonship. His sonship is radically unique—he is "God's only Son" (John 3:16)—because he is fully God as well as fully human. And yet his sonship, like our sonship, is associated with the fact that he is given authority over creation. In the case of Jesus, however, he is given *all* authority in heaven and earth and will someday have *everything* in creation placed "under his feet" (1 Cor. 15:25, 27; Eph. 1:22). This is why he is the ultimate example of what it is to be in "the image of God" (2 Cor. 4:4; Col. 1:15; cf. 1 Cor. 15:45; Phil. 2:6–8; Heb. 1:3).

We humans lost much of our ability to exercise dominion over the earth when we surrendered our authority to Satan. He displaced humanity as "the god" of this world (2 Cor. 4:4; cf. 1 John 5:19). Since then the "whole creation has been groaning" as it waits "with eager longing for the revealing of the children of God" (Rom. 8:22, 19). Whereas humans should have had dominion over nature, nature now dominates us. When Satan is finally defeated and "the children of God" are revealed, when God's kingdom is established and humans once again exercise their authority as people who bear "the image of God," just as Jesus did, then God's will shall be done "on earth as it is in heaven" (Matt. 6:10) and creation shall be restored to what God originally intended it to be.

Supporting Arguments

1. *The biblical foundation.* Unlike alternative understandings of the *imago Dei,* the functional view relies on Scripture alone. The traditional view

that the *imago Dei* refers to certain features that distinguish humans from animals is unduly influenced by Hellenistic philosophy. And the contemporary view that it refers to our social nature is unduly influenced by modern existentialist (see **existentialism**) and psychosocial categories.

2. *The explanatory power of this view.* This understanding of the *imago Dei* sheds light on many other facets of biblical revelation and human experience. For example, this view explains how Satan was given lordship over creation. Our God-given authority was ours to use or misuse. Our first parents grossly misused it when they surrendered it to God's archenemy (Gen. 3:1–24; cf. Luke 4:6; 2 Cor. 4:4; Eph. 2:2; 1 John 5:19). This view further explains why nature has been corrupted (e.g., why we suffer from natural disasters, plagues, etc.). When authorities fall, everything for which they were responsible suffers accordingly.

This view also helps explain why God had to become a human being, for the authority over the earth had to be regained by those who gave it away. Unlike every other human being, Jesus never sinned and thus never came under Satan's authority (John 14:30; Heb. 4:15). As a result, he was the first person who could rightfully reclaim God's rule in the world. This is why he is called the "last Adam" (1 Cor. 15:45) and the head of a new humanity (2 Cor. 5:17; Eph. 2:13–15). Through him humanity is being restored to the role God originally intended for us, namely, co-rulers with him over all the earth (Rev. 5:10).

3. *Motivation for ecological missions.* Finally, this view provides a theological foundation for ecological concerns. The mandate to be good stewards of the earth is part of the essence of what it is to be human. The community of humans who are being restored to their God-given place of authority in Christ (the church) should therefore be at the forefront of the contemporary fight against the widespread abuse of nature and the unjust treatment of animals.

Responding to Objections

1. *This view is not traditional.* Admittedly, the view that the *imago Dei* refers to humanity's God-like authority over creation has not been frequently accepted in church history. Even worse, in the sixteenth century, this view was associated with **Socinianism,** which espoused it along with a number of heretical ideas, such as a denial of the Trinity and the atonement. This created an unfair prejudice against this view, which has to some extent prevented it from gaining a fair hearing.

If we acknowledge that Scripture, not tradition, is our final authority in matters of faith, and if we concede that groups such as the Socinians may be correct on some points even though they are grossly mistaken on others, we discover that there are many good reasons for accepting the view that the *imago Dei* refers to the God-like authority humans are commissioned to exercise on the earth.

2. *Dominion is not part of the* imago Dei. In Genesis 1:26–28, God first makes humans in his image and then gives the command to multiply and have dominion over the earth. Some argue that being created in the image of God is the **presupposition** of the command to have dominion over the earth, but it is not identical to it. While this is a possible interpretation of this passage, it seems to be strained. The proximity of the **stewardship mandate** to the declaration that we are made in God's image, together with other scriptural passages that associate "sonship" with "authority," warrants the conclusion that the divine image is essentially about exercising authority.

The Image of God Is Our Relationality (The Relational View)

The Biblical Argument

The heart of biblical revelation is the declaration that God is love (1 John 4:8, 16). Love is the essence of who God is. God's essence, therefore, is relationship, for love is intrinsically interpersonal. Hence, we find revealed throughout Scripture—dimly in the Old Testament but clearly in the New—that God's very being is constituted as the loving relationship between three Persons: Father, Son, and Holy Spirit (Matt. 28:19; John 17:21–23; cf. Gen. 1:26; Isa. 48:16).

This understanding of God provides the key to understanding what the Bible means when it declares that humans are made "in the image of God." The *imago Dei* means that humans, like God, are essentially beings who exist in relationship. We are created to exist in relationship with God and with each other. To the extent that we live in isolation from God and from each other, we are not fully human.

The central text that declares that humans bear the *imago Dei* reveals this truth. In Genesis 1:26, the Lord says, "Let us make humankind in our image." Such language is not employed when God creates anything else. Only with regard to humans, the pinnacle of God's creation, does God refer to himself as "us." This alludes to the Trinity and signifies that humans alone are made in the image of the Triune God.

Many contend that "us" refers to God and the angels. This interpretation, though ancient, seems unlikely on two accounts. First, if the author intended readers to understand that angels were included in the "us" of

Genesis 1:26, one would expect some previous allusion to angels in the creation account. Angels are never mentioned. Indeed, the suggestion that angels have a role in creation breaks the pattern of this chapter, which repeatedly emphasizes that God alone is the Creator of the world.

Second, and even more decisively, immediately after the Lord says, "Let us make humankind in our image," Scripture declares, "So God created humankind in *his* image, in the *image of God* he created them" (Gen. 1:27, emphasis added). The text explicitly states that humans are made in the image of God, not angels. This is supported by the rest of the Bible: It repeatedly says that humans are made in the image of God; nowhere does it say that they are also created in the image of angels (Gen. 9:6; cf. Ps. 8:4–6). These observations strongly support the understanding that "us" refers to God in his Triune nature, and therefore, that the *imago Dei* refers to our relationality. Like God, we are created to live life as an "us," not just as an "I."

But we have not yet addressed the strongest evidence for the relational understanding of the *imago Dei*. Immediately following the verse in which the Lord says, "Let us make humankind in our image," the author goes on to say, "So God created humankind in his image, in the image of God he created them; *male and female* he created them" (Gen. 1:27, emphasis added; cf. 5:1–2). To exist in the image of God is to exist in intimate loving relationship with others, epitomized here and throughout Scripture by the love between a husband and wife (cf. Gen. 2:23–24). Just as God's essence is a loving "us," humanity's essence is to be a loving "us." We are fully human only in community. When we enter into fully committed loving relationships with God and other people, we mirror the love that the Triune God is.

This is the central reason why God created the world. It is expressed beautifully in the prayer Jesus prayed just before his crucifixion:

> I ask not only on behalf of these, but also on behalf of those who will believe in me through their word, that they may all be one. As you, Father, are in me and I am in you, may they also be in us, so that the world may believe that you have sent me. The glory that you have given me I have given them, so that they may be one, as we are one, I in them and you in me, that they may become completely one, so that the world may know that you have sent me and have loved them even as you have loved me. (John 17:20–23)

Sin isolates people from God and from other people. It thereby destroys the essence of humanity, our *imago Dei*. Jesus came to restore this divine image by breaking down the walls that separate us from God and each other. Indeed, he is the paradigmatic "image of God" precisely because, unlike fallen humanity, he exemplifies a perfect love for God the Father and a perfect love for others. Through him humanity is being restored to become the "image of God" bearers that God always intended us to be. Jesus' prayer in John 17 is that this goal would be completed. The goal of creation is for humans to become one with God and one with one another just as Jesus and the Father are one. In fact, Jesus' prayer presupposes that we become one with each other only as we become one with him and his Father. As we mirror God's love in our relationship with God, we mirror God's love in our relationships with one another. And in this we discover our true humanity.

Supporting Arguments

1. *The Trinity*. This understanding of the *imago Dei* is the only view that weaves this concept into the central revelation of Scripture that God is Triune. How odd it would be if the defining feature of God in Scripture— namely, he eternally consists of Triune love—were altogether absent from the revelation that we are made in God's image. Yet this is what alternative understandings of the *imago Dei* must suppose. According to the relational view, the revelation that God is internally social and that humans are inherently social are inextricably bound together.

2. *Modern psychosocial theories*. While this view is rooted in Scripture, it is consistent with contemporary psychosocial perspectives on the human self. People always form their individual identities in relationship with others. The experience of an "I" presupposes an experience of a "you." A self can develop in a healthy manner only if it develops in community. This is confirmation of the accuracy of the exegesis of the biblical data.

Responding to Objections

1. *This view is not traditional*. It is true that until recently the view that the *imago Dei* refers to the inherent relationality of people was rarely taught in the church. This is due to the fact that early on the church accepted a Hellenistic view of the human self that focused too much on the rational and moral capacities of people.

Two considerations qualify this observation, however. First, the insight that the "us" of Genesis 1:26 alludes to the Trinity dates back to the early second century. Second, a number of theologians throughout church history have emphasized that relationality is a central aspect of human nature. Indeed, some have even made the connection between God's Triune relationality and our intrinsic relationality. What has been lacking until recently is the intrinsic connection between these observations and the teaching that we are made in God's image. In this light, the relationality view is not as novel as it might first appear, and for evangelicals who have always held that Scripture is a greater authority than church tradition, the new element in this view cannot be taken as grounds for rejecting it.

2. *This view is anachronistic.* The most frequent objection raised against this view of the *imago Dei* is that it is anachronistic. Since the Trinity was not clearly revealed until the New Testament, it is argued, we cannot suppose that the author was alluding to it in Genesis 1:26.

While it is anachronistic to read later ideas into earlier passages, all who acknowledge the inspiration of Scripture must allow for the possibility that inspired authors anticipated later revelations, perhaps even in ways they did not fully understand. To illustrate, Jesus rebukes his Jewish adversaries on the grounds that if they really believed Moses, as they claimed, they would believe in him, for Moses wrote about him (John 6:46). We do not need to suppose that Moses had a clear understanding of the Messiah to accept Jesus' teaching. So, too, we do not need to suppose that Moses had a clear understanding of the Trinity to accept that he, under inspiration, alluded to the Triune God in Genesis 1:26. Looking back on the passage in the light of subsequent revelation, we are able to discern that Moses was communicating more than he understood. There is nothing anachronistic about this supposition.

3. *This view accommodates contemporary thinking.* Finally, some argue that the view that the *imago Dei* refers to human relationality is the result of reading Scripture through the lenses of contemporary existentialist and/ or psychosocial paradigms. It is true that this view squares with contemporary insights into the social nature of the human self. This is one of its distinct advantages over alternative interpretations of the *imago Dei*. But this simply shows that certain insights into human nature are correct.

Some think it too coincidental that this understanding of the *imago Dei* just happened to coincide with the advent of modern theories that agree with it. But one could just as easily argue that mistaken ancient views of the self as essentially rational (the substantival view) or domineering (the functional view) prevented people from correctly understanding the *imago Dei*. The advent of truer views of the self allowed us to see what was always there but was hidden because of false presuppositions brought to the text.

Further Reading

Atkins, Anne. *Split Image: Male and Female after God's Likeness.* Grand Rapids: Eerdmans, 1987.

Barth, Karl. *Church Dogmatics.* Vol. 3, part 1. Translated by G. W. Bromiley. Edinburgh: T&T Clark, 1958.

Berkouwer, G. C. *Man: The Image of God*. Grand Rapids: Eerdmans, 1962.

Grenz, Stanley J. *The Social God and the Relational Self: A Trinitarian Theology of the* Imago Dei. Louisville: Westminster John Knox, 2001.

Hall, Douglas John. *Imaging God: Dominion as Stewardship*. Grand Rapids: Eerdmans, 1986.

Hughes, Philip Edgcumbe. *The True Image: The Origin and Destiny of Man in Christ*. Grand Rapids: Eerdmans, 1989.

Jonsson, Gunnlaugur A. *The Image of God: Genesis 1:26–28 in a Century of Old Testament Research*. Translated by Lorraine Svendsen. Revised by Michael S. Cheney. Stockholm: Almqvist & Wiksell, 1988.

McDonald, H. D. *The Christian View of Man*. Westchester, IL: Crossway, 1981.

Middleton, J. Richard. *The Liberating Image: The* Imago Dei *in Genesis 1*. Grand Rapids: Brazos, 2005.

Pyne, Robert A. *Humanity and Sin: The Creation, Fall, and Redemption of Humanity*. Nashville: Word, 1999.

Sherlock, Charles. *The Doctrine of Humanity*. Downers Grove, IL: InterVarsity, 1996.

Verduin, Leonard. *Somewhat Less Than God: The Biblical View of Man*. Grand Rapids: Eerdmans, 1970.

6

The Christology Debate

The Unavoidable Paradox of the God-man (The Classical View)
Christ Relinquished His Divine Prerogatives (The Kenotic View)

Posing the Question

"How can I follow the example of a guy who was God?" DeSean asked with an exasperated tone. Soel had been trying to help him through a spiritual crisis by posing the question, "What would Jesus do?" His encouragement was hitting a roadblock. "Come on, DeSean," Soel replied, "Jesus was a human being, just like we are. The Bible says we are to follow his example in all areas of our life." DeSean was not ready to accept something just because a Bible verse said he should. "I don't doubt he was a human being," he said, "but you Christians believe he was God. I don't get how a man can be God in the first place, and even if he were, I don't see how he can serve as an example of how we are to live. Being God kind of gives him an advantage over us, doesn't it?"

For a moment Soel was dumbfounded. Finally, several passages of Scripture came to mind, so he attempted a response. "No, it doesn't give him an advantage. The Bible says Jesus was tempted in every way that we are tempted." The response only intensified DeSean's questioning. "No advantage? Well, do you think Jesus could have sinned? And if so, since you say he was God, does that mean that God could have sinned?" Soel felt checkmated. On the one hand, he knew it wouldn't be correct to say that

God can sin. On the other hand, he didn't see how Jesus' temptations could be real if he couldn't sin. Soel worried that the months he had spent trying to bring DeSean to the Christian faith were going down the tube.

The Center and Its Contrasts

The theological issue at the root of Soel and DeSean's debate is this: How do we reconcile the fact that Jesus was fully God with the fact that Jesus was fully human? It is an issue that has been discussed in Christian circles throughout the church's history. All Christians believe that Jesus was both fully God and fully man. This doctrinal belief was formalized with the Council of Chalcedon in AD 451 and became one of the central beliefs of Christianity. It contrasts with the belief of a variety of heretical groups who hold that Jesus was the first and greatest creation of God. This view is called **Arianism** and is espoused today by the Jehovah's Witnesses as well as other unorthodox groups. The Christian view also contrasts strongly with that of Muslims and other groups who believe that Jesus was simply a prophet of God. It contrasts as well with various New Age views that see Jesus merely as a man who fully actualized his inner divinity. And it sharply contrasts with views of liberal scholars today (e.g., the **Jesus Seminar**) who try to argue that the **historical Jesus**—the Jesus "behind" the **mythologized** New Testament documents—was merely a Cynic philosopher or a religious and social revolutionary. The Bible, however, clearly teaches that Jesus was fully God as well as fully human (John 1:1; 20:28; Rom. 9:5; Col. 2:9; Titus 2:11–13).

But the question of how Jesus could be fully God and fully human has not been resolved to everyone's satisfaction. Within evangelical circles, the debate can be broken down into two broad camps. Many defend the more traditional view that Jesus exercised both his divine and human attributes at the same time. For example, this view maintains that Jesus could be omniscient as God and non-omniscient as human at the same time. Others, however, hold to what is called **kenotic Christology.** This group maintains that God had to "empty himself" (*kenosis* in Greek) to become a full human being. They argue that the Second Person of the Trinity laid aside his omniscience in order to become fully human, for a person cannot be fully human and omniscient at the same time. Clearly, how one answers this christological question would influence how that person would answer the questions DeSean posed to Soel.

The two essays that comprise this section offer a defense of the classical christological position and a defense of the kenotic christological position.

The Unavoidable Paradox of the God-man
(The Classical View)

Though it took nearly four centuries to iron out the details (at Chalcedon), the orthodox church has always interpreted Scripture as teaching that Jesus Christ was and is fully God as well as fully human. For most theologians and laypeople throughout history, this meant that Jesus exercised the full range of divine and human attributes. Though theologians have worked this out in many different ways, most have affirmed that Jesus was at one and the same time **omnipresent** (as God) yet spatially located (as human), omnipotent (as God) yet limited in power (as human), and omniscient (as God) yet limited in knowledge (as human). Jesus is one person, not two, but he has two natures, not one. The church has always admitted that this teaching constitutes a profound mystery, but it has always denied that it constitutes a contradiction.

Some evangelicals today are joining the ranks of those who insist that this teaching is not a paradox but a contradiction. While these evangelicals agree that Jesus was fully God and fully human, they insist that Jesus laid aside the use of his divine attributes in order to become a human. Though he retained his divine holiness and love, he temporarily relinquished his omnipresence, omniscience, and omnipotence. According to those who hold the classical view, these evangelicals are mistaken philosophically in thinking that the classical view constitutes a contradiction, and they are mistaken biblically in thinking that Jesus surrendered the use of certain divine attributes.

The Biblical Argument

If all that Scripture teaches about Christ is taken seriously, one cannot avoid the paradoxical conclusion that not only was Christ God and human, but he also *exercised* divine and human attributes.

To begin, while some in the early church denied that Jesus was a full human being (e.g., those who believed in **docetism**), few today question this truth. His humanity is revealed throughout the Gospels. For example, Jesus had to grow intellectually as well as physically (Luke 2:52). As a human, there were certain things Jesus did not know (Mark 13:32). As a human, his character had to mature through suffering (Heb. 2:10; 5:8–9). As a human, Jesus had to submit to the Father (Matt. 26:39; John 6:38), pray to the Father (Luke 6:12), and remain utterly dependent on the Father at all times. Though he was morally perfect, as a genuine human, Jesus experienced temptation (Luke 4:1–13; Heb. 4:15). And as a human,

Jesus experienced all the emotions that other humans experience: anger, sorrow, loneliness, and even fear (e.g., John 2:13–17; 11:35; Mark 15:34; Luke 22:41–44).

At the same time, Jesus' full divinity is revealed throughout the Gospels. While the authors clearly depict Jesus as at times limited in knowledge, they also depict him as exercising an omniscient mind. Upon meeting Nathanael for the first time, for example, Jesus declared, "Here is truly an Israelite in whom there is no deceit!" Nathanael saw this demonstration of supernatural knowledge as evidence of Jesus' divinity, for he exclaimed, "Rabbi, you are the Son of God! You are the King of Israel!" (John 1:47–50). John later makes it clear that this supernatural insight was not an occasional revelation: Jesus "knew all people and needed no one to testify about anyone; for he himself knew what was in everyone" (John 2:24–25).

In this light, we ought not be surprised when we find Jesus demonstrating an omniscient awareness of people's innermost thoughts and motives (Matt. 9:4; John 2:24–25). Nor should we be surprised when we find him expressing divine knowledge of Judas' deceitful heart and future betrayal (John 13:18–19, 21–27), of Peter's future denial (Luke 22:31–34) and exact mode of death (John 21:18–19), of a stranger who would open up his house to him and his disciples (Mark 14:12–16), or of a coin that would be found in a fish's mouth (Matt. 17:24–27). As a man, Jesus was indeed limited in what he knew. But it is also abundantly clear that as God, he was not limited. Somehow, Jesus was both simultaneously.

Scripture depicts Jesus as possessing other divine attributes as well. For example, the Gospels portray Jesus as the omnipotent Creator, even while also admitting that as a man he was limited in power. As God, Jesus was able to control the behavior of wind as well as the biting of fish (Luke 8:23–25; John 21:5–6). As a man, he could do nothing on his own (John 5:19). As God, his essence was and is unchangeable (Heb. 13:8; cf. Ps. 102:26–27; Mal. 3:6; James 1:17). As a man, he had to grow and be made perfect (Heb. 2:10). As God, he could not be tempted (James 1:13). As a real human being, however, he was tempted "in every respect" just as we are (Heb. 4:15). As God, he evoked and accepted worship (John 20:28). As a man, he prayed to and worshiped his heavenly Father (Luke 10:21). As God, he could confess that he was the great "I am" who spoke to Moses (John 8:58). The Jews understood that he was applying a divine title to himself, for they picked up stones to stone him (John 8:59). As a man, however, he acknowledged that the Father was greater than he was (John 14:28).

Scripture does not shy away from attributing both divine and human attributes, activities, and titles to Jesus Christ. The result may be paradoxical, but it is one we must accept, together with Christians throughout history, out of fidelity to Scripture. Not only was Jesus fully God and fully human, but he also acted out of capacities latent within each of these natures.

Supporting Arguments

1. *Rendering the two natures of Christ coherent.* The all-important question is this: Does this view constitute a contradiction? If it does, it must be abandoned. Professing contradictions is equivalent to professing nonsense. Though many argue otherwise, however, this view is not contradictory. A number of arguments and analogies have been offered that demonstrate this point. A recent one put forth by the Christian philosopher Thomas Morris of Notre Dame has two parts.[1]

First, there is a major difference between being "fully human" and "merely human," Morris argues. To be "fully human," one must possess all the attributes that constitute the essence of a human being. To be "merely human," however, one must possess these attributes *alone*. One cannot *also* possess other attributes that go beyond the human attributes. The Chalcedonian creed affirms that Jesus was "fully human" but not that he was "merely human." The latter contradicts certain divine attributes, but the former does not. Christ possessed all the attributes that constitute the essence of a human being, but in contrast to all "mere human beings," he also possessed all the attributes that constitute the essence of God.

Second, Morris argues, we may conceive of how Jesus was "fully human" as well as "fully God" by looking at his two distinct ranges of consciousness. (There is a long tradition among classical theorists of focusing on the two minds of Christ, to the point at which classical Christology is sometimes called **two minds Christology**.) If Jesus was "merely human," of course, he could have *only* a limited human consciousness. Since Jesus was not merely human, however, his limited human consciousness did not restrict (and thus rule out) his ability to possess an unlimited divine consciousness. Hence, Morris argues, the divine consciousness encompassed the human consciousness without thereby destroying it. We may further conceive that the divine mind always had access to the contents of the human mind, but not vice versa, for the divine mind is unlimited while the human mind is not. Thus, we may affirm that the human mind of Jesus genuinely had to grow, learn, confess ignorance at times, and so on, and that Jesus as a human had to go about acquiring information as all other humans do. At the same time, we may affirm, without contradiction, that Jesus was in a different sense omniscient.

2. *The glory of Jesus.* By explaining the biblical data in a noncontradictory way, classical Christology alone does full justice to the divinity of Jesus Christ. Conversely, by denying that Jesus could use certain divine attributes (e.g., his omniscience or omnipotence) while on earth, kenotic theorists subtly undermine Jesus' divinity and glory. After all, what is glorious about a divine nature that cannot be displayed? Kenotic theorists affirm that Jesus

was fully divine, but they divest this affirmation of any meaningful content by claiming Christ could not exercise his divine nature.

3. *The inconsistency of the kenotic view.* Classical Christology is consistent whereas kenotic Christology is not. The Bible suggests that Christ retained his human nature even after his ascension (e.g., Acts 17:3). The kenotic view seems to leave no possibility for a post-ascension humanity of Christ, however. If Jesus could become human only by emptying himself of certain divine attributes, then it follows that if Jesus ever reacquired the use of these divine attributes, he would no longer be human. To argue the point from the opposite direction, if the exercise of his divine attributes did not destroy Jesus' humanity *after* his earthly stay, on what basis can one insist that they would have destroyed his humanity *during* his earthly stay?

Responding to Objections

Beyond the objection that classical Christology is contradictory, which has already been addressed, several other objections have been brought against this view.

1. *How are two minds not two persons?* Some argue that two minds Christology cannot avoid the charge of **Nestorianism,** the ancient heresy that Christ was two persons in one body. (See **heretic.**) How can we conceive of a single person with two minds? Since a person's mind is the center of his personhood, to conceive of two minds is to conceive of two persons.

The objection does not work, however. *Ordinarily*, of course, there is a one-to-one correspondence between a person and a mind, but this is not a necessary truth. Thomas Morris provides an analogy of a person becoming aware that he is dreaming. There is in a real sense two "minds" involved in this awareness, yet no one would deny because of this that the person is one person. Morris offers another analogy of people with multiple personality disorder. Such people are psychologically ill because they lack a "mind" that encompasses and controls their other "minds"—something Jesus obviously possessed. But multiple personality disorder victims nevertheless illustrate the truth that one person can have distinct minds.[2]

2. *This view is not biblical.* Even if the classical view is philosophically possible, some argue that it is not biblical. The New Testament does not credit Jesus' miraculous powers to himself but to the Holy Spirit or the Father working through him (Luke 4:14, 17–21; John 5:19, 30). This, kenotic theorists argue, shows that Jesus had divested himself of his own authority.

It is true that some texts in the New Testament attribute Jesus' power to the Father and Spirit, but two points will suffice to show that this does not warrant the conclusion that Jesus did not possess his own power. First, certain Scripture passages attribute Jesus' miraculous powers to himself. For example, at one point Jesus told the Jews, "Destroy this temple [namely, his body] and in three days *I* will raise it up" (John 2:19, emphasis added). If Christ had relinquished all of his divine power, he certainly could not have raised himself up. Conversely, if he possessed the power to raise himself up, there obviously is no reason to deny him the power to do any of the other miracles he performed throughout his ministry.

Second, we must not draw too great a divide between the three Persons of the Trinity. In traditional teaching, the three Persons are so interwoven that what one does, they all do. (This is traditionally called the *perichoresis* of the three Persons.) For example, though Jesus says he will raise himself up, other passages say it is the Father and/or Spirit who raises Jesus up (John 2:18–21; 10:17–18; cf. Rom. 8:11; Gal. 1:1). One cannot legitimately use the fact that Scripture sometimes attributes Jesus' supernatural power to the Spirit or the Father to support the view that Jesus did not possess and exercise his own supernatural power.

3. *Jesus could not have been genuinely tempted.* A final objection is this: Some have argued that Jesus could not have been genuinely tempted, as Scripture says he was (Matt. 4:1), if his divine nature ensured that his human nature would never fall. Two things may be said in response.

First, though this problem is usually associated with two minds Christology, it actually is as much a problem for defenders of the kenotic view as it is for defenders of the classical view. Suppose Christ could have fallen by virtue of the fact that he had relinquished his divine prerogatives. What would have become of him had he done so? He obviously could not have continued to be fully God and fully human united in one person. Indeed, he would have become another sinner in need of salvation.

What would have happened had the all-holy, divine Son of God left the human Jesus? Humanity would have remained condemned in sin. God's plan for world history would have been thwarted. This suggestion also presupposes that Jesus was two persons rather than one person—for the divine person would have left the human person. Someone might suggest instead that the all-holy, divine Son of God would have ceased to exist. This is hardly an improvement, however. Such an event not only would have thwarted God's plan for world history but also would have destroyed God altogether! The Son of God, and therefore the Trinity, would have been annihilated! But God cannot be destroyed, any more than God can sin.

Second, anyone who suggests that Jesus could have fallen is thus walking on precarious ground. For good reason, most Christians throughout history have denied this possibility. But does this mean that Jesus could not have been tempted? Temptation is an experience someone undergoes when something evil pulls at him or her. The experience does not presuppose that the evil might actually win. It simply presupposes that the victory is not a forgone conclusion *in the mind of the person being tempted.* For example, a man who has developed a faithful character that will not allow him to enter into an adulterous relationship may nevertheless be tempted to cheat on his wife. Though it is (let us suppose) impossible for this man to fall, given his character, the temptation is real so long as the man does not know that it is impossible for him to fall. In the same way, we may suppose that Jesus' divine character made it impossible for him to fall. As God, he would of course have known that he could not fall, but as a man, he would not have known this. The experience of temptation would thus have been as real to Jesus as it is to any of us (Heb. 4:15).

Christ Relinquished His Divine Prerogatives (The Kenotic View)

A central tenet of the Christian faith is that God became a human being. This teaching is as beautiful as it is mysterious, but it does not create a *contradiction.* Believing that Jesus Christ was fully God and fully human does not require the belief that Jesus Christ was both omniscient and non-omniscient or omnipresent and non-omnipresent at the same time. According to the kenotic view, this belief *is* contradictory. Kenotic Christology holds that God the Son laid aside (*kenosis*) the use of certain divine attributes, such as his omniscience and omnipresence, precisely because these divine attributes would have precluded his ability to become a full human being. Everything inconsistent with being a true human was set aside in the incarnation. Jesus did not cease to be God, of course, and his divine attributes did not cease to exist. But the Second Person of the Trinity temporarily relinquished his ability to use these attributes.

The Biblical Argument

This is not simply an inference kenotic theorists make to avoid embracing a logical contradiction. Rather, it is the clear teaching of Scripture. For example, in Philippians the apostle Paul writes:

> Let the same mind be in you that was in Christ Jesus, who, though he was in the form of God, did not regard equality with God as something to be exploited, but emptied [*kenosis*] himself, taking the form of a slave, being born in human likeness. And being found in human form, he humbled

himself and became obedient to the point of death—even death on a cross.
(2:5–8)

This passage teaches that Jesus Christ became a real human because he
did not cling to his divinity. He was willing to "empty himself" in order to
take upon himself "the form of a slave" and be "born in human likeness."
If Jesus Christ continued to use his divine attributes, as classical Christology holds, what did Jesus empty himself of?

The teaching that Christ relinquished the use of certain divine attributes
is alluded to throughout the New Testament. Paul taught the Corinthians
that though Christ was originally "rich," he became "poor" in order to
make us "rich" (2 Cor. 8:9). He laid aside his treasure in order to open up
a way for us to share in his treasure. Jesus refers to this treasure that he laid
aside as his "glory" when he prays, "Father, glorify me . . . with the glory
that I had in your presence before the world existed" (John 17:5). Jesus
shared in the Father's glory prior to his becoming human. He was "rich,"
being in every way "equal with God." But he relinquished this glory to
become genuinely human. This is part of what is meant when John says that
Jesus *descended* into the world (e.g., John 3:13). Christ lowered himself to
become one of us. His prayer in John 17 is that he would soon regain his
glory through his death and resurrection (cf. Phil. 2:9–11). Without ceasing
to be God, Jesus divested himself of some of the riches, glory, rights, and
attributes of his divinity in order to invest himself fully in humanity.

Further evidence of Jesus' *kenosis* is found in the Gospels. While Scripture is clear that God knows all things (Ps. 139; 1 John 3:20), it is also clear
that Jesus did not know all things—even though he was fully God. Jesus
admitted that he did not know the "day or hour" of his return. Only the
Father knew this (Mark 13:32). He did not know who touched him to receive
a healing (Mark 5:30) or how long a young boy had been demonized (Mark
9:20–21). In the Garden of Gethsemane, he prayed that his Father would
find a way for him to avoid his crucifixion "if it [was] possible" (Matt.
26:39). Jesus could not have sincerely prayed this prayer if he as God knew
all along that it was not possible to avoid his crucifixion.

It seems clear, therefore, that as a full human being, Jesus was not
omniscient. He had a finite mind, for this is an essential part of what it
means to be human. Jesus had to learn and grow in wisdom just as all
other humans do (Luke 2:52). Indeed, Scripture says that God made Jesus
"perfect through sufferings" (Heb. 2:10). "He learned obedience through
what he suffered," and it was only after he had "been made perfect" that
he could become "the source of eternal salvation for all who obey him"
(Heb. 5:8–9). This does not imply that Jesus was *morally* imperfect, for
the Bible tells us he was sinless (Heb. 4:15). But it does imply that as with
all humans, Jesus had to grow spiritually as well as mentally and emotion-

ally. To do so, Jesus had to surrender temporarily the use of his infinite wisdom and power.

Only this *kenosis* explains how Jesus could have been tempted just as we are "in every respect," even though Scripture also states that God cannot be tempted (Heb. 4:15; James 1:13). Either we must accept the contradictory view that Jesus both could and could not be tempted, or we must conclude that Jesus relinquished the use of those aspects of his divinity (such as his omniscience) that prevented him as God from being susceptible to temptation.

Supporting Arguments

1. *The coherence of the kenotic view.* One of the strongest arguments in favor of kenotic Christology is that it avoids the logical contradiction created by traditional Christology. It allows believers to affirm that the infinite God became a finite human without contradicting themselves. Defenders of the classical view have made valiant but unsuccessful attempts to argue that their view is paradoxical, not contradictory. When all is said and done, the unity of Jesus' person hinges on the unity of his mind, will, and attributes. This is what personhood means. If Jesus had two minds, two wills, and two different sets of attributes (namely, omnipotent and not omnipotent), he simply was not one person.

2. *The humanity of Jesus.* Kenotic Christology empowers believers to take Jesus' humanity seriously. There simply is no way to affirm coherently that Jesus was a human in every respect while also affirming that he was omnipresent, omniscient, and omnipotent while here on earth. Classical Christology makes people conceive of Jesus either as two persons packed into one body (Nestorianism) or as God in a human body (**apollinarianism**).

3. *The example of Jesus.* Scripture encourages us to look to Jesus as the example of how we should live (1 Cor. 11:1; Phil. 2:5). But how can we follow the example of one who was omnipresent, omniscient, and omnipotent? Because it consistently affirms the full humanity of Jesus, kenotic Christology renders the mandate to make Jesus our example coherent.

Responding to Objections

1. *This view undermines the divinity of Jesus.* The most frequent objection raised against kenotic Christology is that it undermines Jesus' divine nature. While this objection applies to the views of certain liberal kenotic theologians who argued that Jesus actually *extinguished* his divine at-

tributes, it does not apply to the evangelical kenotic theory, which simply asserts that Jesus willingly gave up the *use* of those attributes that would have conflicted with his human nature.

2. *How did Jesus do miraculous deeds?* Many who hold to traditional two minds Christology argue that Jesus' miracles prove he did not relinquish his divine power, and his supernatural knowledge proves he did not relinquish his divine knowledge (e.g., Matt. 9:4; Mark 4:39). This conclusion is unwarranted, however. The New Testament almost always attributes Jesus' supernatural abilities to the Holy Spirit or to the Father, who was working through him (Matt. 12:28; Luke 4:1, 14, 17–21; John 5:19, 30).

This is why Jesus could tell his disciples that they would do "greater works" than the ones he performed (John 14:12). He could not have taught this if his miracles were a sign of his own divinity. The miracles Jesus performed evidenced his human submission to God and can thus, in principle, be performed by all humans. This also explains why Jesus' healing miracles were not always instantaneous and why his miracle-working power was contingent on other people's faith (Mark 6:5; 8:22–26). This would not have been the case if Jesus could have simply worked his power as Creator whenever he pleased.

3. *Paul's interest was not **metaphysical**.* Some have argued that kenotic theorists read too much into Philippians 2. In this passage, Paul celebrates Christ's humble attitude in becoming a human—an attitude all are to emulate (Phil. 2:5). True, he is not spelling out a theory of the incarnation, but two considerations dissipate the force of the objection.

First, kenotic christologists do not rely only on Philippians 2 for their view. It is based on a broad reading of Scripture. Second, the fact that Paul was not explicitly interested in metaphysics in this or any other "emptying" passage does not preclude the development of a theory of the incarnation partly on the basis of this passage. Paul's practical words often have metaphysical implications. As we wrestle with the question of how God could become a man, therefore, it is appropriate to ask, What is implied in Christ's emptying? The most plausible answer to this question is that he emptied himself of the use of attributes that would have been inconsistent with his ability to be fully human.

4. *Who ran the universe during the incarnation?* The Bible tells us that Christ holds all things together (Col. 1:17; Heb. 1:3). However, if Christ relinquished the exercise of his omnipresence and omniscience while on earth, there is no way he could have continued to perform this role.

In reply, the passages that celebrate Christ's role as Creator and Sustainer of the universe describe Christ's customary role. They do not rule out the possibility that Christ, for a season, set aside this function. The doctrine of the Trinity allows us to assert that God exists in three distinct ways at the same time. According to kenotic theorists, the second way God is God—the

Second Person of the Trinity—emptied himself and became a full human. But (thankfully) the universe was not thereby vacated. The Father and Spirit continued to exercise their omnipotent and omniscient capacities.

If it were exegetically necessary, we could argue that Christ still held all things together even while he was incarnate. Consider this example: The owner of a company who goes on vacation may nevertheless be credited with "holding the company together" if he has responsibly arranged for things to carry on a certain way while he is gone. So long as Christ's wisdom and power lie behind the sustaining of the universe, it can be said that he held all things together even after he temporarily surrendered the use of his infinite wisdom and power to become a man.

5. *What of Christ's post-ascension humanity?* Finally, some have objected to kenotic Christology on the grounds that it cannot explain how Jesus is both God and man now. Most scholars agree that the New Testament assumes that Jesus retained his humanity after his ascension (Acts 17:3). Yet everyone agrees that since his ascension, Jesus has exercised all of his divine attributes. That is, even evangelical kenotic theorists affirm that Christ is now omnipresent, omnipotent, and omniscient. But if the full exercise of divine attributes is consistent with Christ's humanity *after* his ascension, on what basis can kenotic theorists argue that they are inconsistent with his full humanity *before* his ascension?

Kenotic theorists respond to this objection in one of two ways. First, some concede that the *kenosis* of Christ was not necessary for him to become a human per se. It was necessary, however, for him to become the human who could save us from damnation, sin, and the devil. Some would argue that Christ had to experience and overcome temptation, for example, which means he had to empty himself of his omniscience. Others would argue that Jesus had to be vulnerable in order to lure Satan into orchestrating his crucifixion. This required that he surrender the use of his omnipotence. Some would further argue that as the sacrificial lamb of God, he had to experience genuine separation from the Father. Hence, he laid aside the use of his omnipresence. Most kenotic theorists would agree, however, that once his task of saving the world was complete, Christ reassumed the full exercise of divine attributes.

Second, some kenotic theorists would answer this objection by maintaining that it was indeed necessary for Christ to empty himself to become a human per se, but they would distinguish between humans in their present **probationary** state and humans in their glorified state in heaven. **Finitude** is intrinsic to humans in this probationary state, and its purpose is to allow humans to choose freely for or against God and thus determine their eternal destinies. All who choose for God will ultimately be transformed into a glorified state, through which they will enjoy perfect unbroken fellowship with God throughout eternity.

These kenotic theorists then argue that Christ had to become a sinless human *as humans are defined now* in this probationary period. It would have been logically impossible for Christ to do so without setting aside certain divine attributes. Once this stage of human existence is complete and the kingdom has been established, however, human nature will be transformed. No one except Christ will exercise omniscience, omnipresence, and omnipotence. But no one's nature will be such that these attributes are ruled out by definition, as they are now in this probationary period. Since Christ is in this glorified state now, he is able to exercise all of his divine attributes even though he is still, and shall always be, a full human being.

Further Reading

Erickson, Millard J. *The Word Became Flesh: A Contemporary Incarnational Theology.* Grand Rapids: Baker Academic, 1991.

Evans, C. Stephen. *Exploring Kenotic Christology: The Self-Emptying of God.* New York: Oxford University Press, 2006.

Hawthorne, Gerald F. *The Presence and the Power.* Dallas: Word, 1991.

Horton, Michael S. *Lord and Christ: A Covenant Christology.* Louisville: Westminster John Knox, 2005.

Koenig, Adrio. *The Eclipse of Christ in Eschatology: Toward a Christ-Centered Approach.* Grand Rapids: Eerdmans, 1989.

Macleod, Donald. *The Person of Christ.* Downers Grove, IL: InterVarsity, 1998.

Marshall, I. Howard. *Jesus the Savior: Studies in New Testament Christology.* Downers Grove, IL: InterVarsity, 1990.

Morris, Thomas V. *The Logic of God Incarnate.* Ithaca, NY: Cornell University Press, 1986.

Ramm, Bernard L. *An Evangelical Christology: Ecumenical and Historic.* Nashville: Thomas Nelson, 1985.

Sanders, Fred, and Klaus Issler, eds. *Jesus in Trinitarian Perspective: An Introductory Christology.* Nashville: Broadman and Holman, 2007.

Vinay, Samuel, and Chris Sugden, eds. *Sharing Jesus in the Two Thirds World: Evangelical Christologies from the Contexts of Poverty, Powerlessness, and Religious Pluralism.* Grand Rapids: Eerdmans, 1983.

Wells, David F. *The Person of Christ: A Biblical and Historical Analysis.* Westchester, IL: Crossway, 1984.

7

The Atonement Debate

Christ Died in Our Place (The Penal Substitution View)
Christ Destroyed Satan and His Works (The Christus Victor View)
Christ Displayed God's Wrath against Sin (The Moral Government View)

Posing the Question

You befriend a Muslim at the grocery store, and in time the two of you begin to discuss religion. At some point you tell him that you believe Jesus died for your sins. He immediately gets a puzzled look on his face. "What do you mean, 'died for your sins'?" he asks. You tell him that Jesus died in your place. His puzzled look intensifies. "How could an innocent man—indeed, one of God's prophets—be punished for what you deserve? Is that not unjust?" You have never thought of that question, and now you're the one with a puzzled look.

The Center and Its Contrasts

These are the kinds of questions we confront when we consider the doctrine of the atonement. Why did Jesus have to die? What did his death accomplish? How did it accomplish this? What relationship does Jesus' death have with his life, on the one hand, and his resurrection, on the other?

To non-Christians the death of Jesus is of no great consequence. Indeed, Muslims deny that Jesus ever died. The Qur'an teaches that God made someone look like Jesus (or, some teach, someone who already looked like Jesus) die on the cross. Most non-Christians do not have such an elaborate explanation, however. Some say that Jesus was a religious or a political martyr and so may grant that his death serves as an example of a person willing to die for his convictions. Others see his death simply as the inevitable and perhaps tragic fate of a religious zealot in the Roman Empire.

For Christians, however, Jesus' death and resurrection (which non-Christians usually deny) are nothing less than the centerpieces of world history. Here lies the key to all God's dealings with humanity. Through Jesus' death and resurrection, God freed us from the tyranny of evil and reconciled us to himself. Our relationship with God and our eternal destiny depend on what Jesus did when he died and rose again. On this all Christians have always agreed.

What exactly this reconciliation means and how exactly this reconciliation was achieved is a matter of dispute, however. The early church emphasized how Jesus' death and resurrection defeated Satan and thus set humankind free from his oppressive rule. This view is commonly referred to as the **Christus Victor** (Latin for "Christ is Victor") **view of the atonement.** While no Christian ever denied that Christ's death and resurrection defeated Satan, this understanding of the atonement became less prominent after the early Middle Ages. Recently, however, some Christians, including some evangelicals, have once again argued that this view portrays the primary significance of the atonement in the New Testament. Some recent defenders of this view are Gustaf Aulen, Thomas Finger, and Gregory Boyd.

In the eleventh century, Anselm offered the view that Jesus' death brought "satisfaction" between God and humanity by paying the penalty humanity's sin deserved. This view is usually referred to as the **satisfaction view of the atonement.** As the term was used in Anselm's day, "satisfaction" did not refer to a subjective emotion. Rather, it referred to the reparation that was due to someone after he had been wronged. In Anselm's view, humanity owed God infinite reparation because sin against God is an infinite crime. Hence, either humanity would have to pay for their wrongs by suffering eternal hell, or God himself would have to pay for this wrong. This is what God did by becoming a man and dying on the cross. Only those who reject God's sacrifice now need to suffer eternally. Though the influence of Anselm's satisfaction theory is apparent among some today, few contemporary evangelicals embrace it as an adequate way on its own to express the Bible's view of Jesus' death.

Abelard in the twelfth century brought a new dimension to the atonement when he argued that the primary significance of Jesus' life and death is that they serve as an example of how we are to live. The perfect love Jesus expressed, especially in his willingness to die for others, is a model for us to emulate. This view of the atonement is sometimes called the **subjective view of the atonement** because it emphasizes the subjective impact Jesus' death makes on us. While all concede that Jesus' life and death are models for us and that they should evoke obedient love toward God on our part, few contemporary evangelicals identify this as the primary significance of the atonement.

In the sixteenth century, John Calvin and Martin Luther advocated a view of the atonement that was somewhat different from all these. They believed that Jesus bore the punishment humanity deserved. Only in this way, they argued, could humanity be reconciled to an all-holy God. This view has similarities to Anselm's view, but it differs in stressing that Jesus actually bore the sin of humanity and actually took the punishment humanity deserved. This view is called the **penal substitution view of the atonement,** or the **substitutionary view of the atonement,** and is presently the view most often embraced by evangelicals. In recent years, it has been strongly defended by such theologians as Leon Morris and John Stott.

In the seventeenth century, a Reformer named Hugo Grotius found this view objectionable on a number of grounds. He argued that Jesus did not literally take on the sin of the world and suffer God's punishment on behalf of humanity. Jesus did indeed suffer the wrath of God, in Grotius's view, but as a demonstration of God's wrath against sin. This act was done to teach humanity the consquences of sin and to inspire us to holy living. The cross thus preserves God's moral government of the world. Hence, this view is called the **moral government view of the atonement.** It has found a number of noteworthy proponents throughout history and has in recent times been advocated by such evangelicals as Gordon Olson and George Otis Jr.

The three essays that follow provide examples of the kinds of arguments that evangelical theologians make on behalf of the penal substitution view, the Christus Victor view, and the moral government view of the atonement.

Christ Died in Our Place (The Penal Substitution View)

The Biblical Argument

We cannot understand or fully appreciate the significance of Jesus' death on the cross unless we understand and fully appreciate the dilemma God faced in wanting to save us and have eternal fellowship with us. The Bible says that we are individually and corporately at war with God. Every one of us willfully sins and falls "short of the glory of God" (Rom. 3:23). We have all "lived . . . in the passions of our flesh" and have thereby become "children of wrath" (Eph. 2:3). In our present fallen condition, we are now dead in sin (Eph. 2:1–3). Paul sums up our desperate condition when he writes:

> Jews and Greeks . . . are under the power of sin, as it is written:
>
>> There is no one who is righteous, not even one;
>>> there is no one who has understanding,
>>>> there is no one who seeks God.
>> All have turned aside, together they have become worthless;
>>> there is no one who shows kindness,
>>>> there is not even one. (Rom. 3:9–12)

This sinfulness poses a dilemma for God, for he perfectly loves us, on the one hand, but he is perfectly holy and cannot have anything to do with sin, on the other hand. Indeed, God cannot so much as look upon evil (Hab. 1:13). The only stance an all-holy God can have toward sin is one of holy rage (Rom. 1:18). The truth that "the wages of sin is death" (Rom. 6:2–3) flows out of God's very nature and can thus allow no exceptions. If God ever made light of sin, allowing it to go unpunished even once, he would be denying the perfection of his holy nature. This God cannot do.

God's utterly uncompromising stance toward sin may strike us as extreme and unwarranted, perhaps even prudish. But this is simply further evidence of how jaded our fallen reason has become and how little we understand either holiness or sin. To appreciate God's dilemma, and thus the reason Jesus had to die, we must in faith simply accept the truth as it is revealed in God's Word. Sin is antithetical (see **antithesis**) to God's holy nature. It is impossible for God simply to excuse it. And yet God loves sinners and wants us to enjoy perfect fellowship with him throughout eternity. How can this be achieved?

God's answer is as profound and mysterious as it is graciously beautiful. God himself decided to suffer "the wages of sin" that his own holiness demands. God the Son freely agreed with the Father to align himself with fallen humanity and to suffer God's wrath against sin by dying on the cross. This view of the atonement is called the penal substitution view, for Christ accepted the punishment for sin in our place.

The glorious truth that God would provide a substitute for humanity is foreshadowed in the Old Testament sacrificial practices. As a way of pointing forward to Christ's substitutionary sacrifice, people in the Old Testament were commanded to shed the blood "of goats and bulls" to atone for their sins (Heb. 9:13). The meaning of these sacrifices was explicitly substitutionary (e.g., Lev. 1:3–4). God was teaching the Israelites that "without the shedding of blood there is no forgiveness of sins" (Heb. 9:22). He was pointing to the time when God would shed his own blood as a substitute for sinful humanity (Acts 20:28; Rom. 3:25).

Isaiah expresses the Old Testament's anticipation of a Messiah who would be humanity's substitute: He would be "wounded for our transgressions, crushed for our iniquities" and would bear "the punishment that made us whole" (Isa. 53:5). God would "[lay] on him the iniquity of us all" (Isa. 53:6), for "his life [would be] an offering for sin" (Isa. 53:10). He would "[bear] the sin of many, and [make] intercession for the transgressors" (Isa. 53:12). These phrases clearly articulate the truth that Jesus would die in our place. Isaiah is clearly saying that the coming Messiah would play the role that sacrificed animals played in his day. He would die on behalf of others to make them acceptable to God.

The New Testament reinforces the connection between sacrifices and Christ's death. John the Baptist alludes to the sacrificed Passover lamb when he declares that Jesus is "the Lamb of God who takes away the sin of the world!" (John 1:29). Paul also declares that "our paschal lamb, Christ, has been sacrificed" (1 Cor. 5:7), and he draws a parallel with Old Testament sacrificial practices when he says that "Christ loved us and gave himself up for us, a fragrant offering and sacrifice to God" (Eph. 5:2).

However, the author of Hebrews makes the most extensive use of Old Testament sacrificial practices to express the meaning of Christ's death. He writes:

> [Christ] entered once for all into the Holy Place, not with the blood of goats and calves, but with his own blood, thus obtaining eternal redemption. For if the blood of goats and bulls . . . sanctifies those who have been defiled so that their flesh is purified, how much more will the blood of Christ, who through the eternal Spirit offered himself without blemish to God, purify our conscience from dead works to worship the living God! (9:12–14)

Later this author reiterates that whereas Old Testament priests had to offer sacrifices over and over, Christ "appeared once for all at the end of the age to remove sin by the sacrifice of himself" (Heb. 9:26). Christ did what Old Testament sacrifices could only foreshadow: He removed sin once and for all. This is why all who believe in him can enter into perfect fellowship with the all-holy God. Without this sacrifice, such fellowship would be utterly impossible.

The penal substitution understanding of Christ's death does not rest merely on the Old Testament sacrificial practices, however. In a variety of ways, it is declared throughout the New Testament.

Jesus made it clear that his death was to be a substitute for the death of others when he taught his disciples, "No one has greater love than this, to lay down one's life for one's friends" (John 15:13). He was, of course, alluding to his own love and his own forthcoming death. Paul makes essentially the same point when he teaches that "Christ redeemed us from the curse of the law by becoming a curse for us—for it is written, 'Cursed is everyone who hangs on a tree'" (Gal. 3:13). The sinless Son of God became a curse before his Father so that we who deserved to be cursed could be redeemed.

In fact, Paul goes so far as to say that Jesus, "who knew no sin," was "made . . . to be sin" so that "we might become the righteousness of God" (2 Cor. 5:21). This is how God "reconciled the world to himself" (2 Cor. 5:19). If we accept this teaching at face value, it is positively breathtaking. God placed our sin on Christ so that he might place his righteousness on us! Jesus became our sin! This is how the all-holy God resolved his dilemma of how to enter into eternal fellowship with sinners.

Another way the New Testament expresses the substitutionary significance of Christ's death is by saying that Christ was the **propitiation** for our sin. The term *propitiate* means "to appease." Hence, Christ's death appeased God's wrath toward sin because Christ received the punishment God's holiness demanded. Paul expresses this truth when he writes that even though "all have sinned and fall short of the glory of God" (Rom. 3:23), God makes us righteous "by his grace as a gift, through the redemption that is in Christ Jesus, whom [he] put forward as a sacrifice [literally, "propitiation"] of atonement by his blood, effective through faith" (Rom. 3:24–25).

John makes the same point when he declares, "In this is love, not that we loved God but that he loved us and sent his Son to be the atoning sacrifice for our sins" (1 John 4:10). Both Paul and John proclaim that by taking the punishment we deserved, Jesus satisfied God's holy requirement that no sin go unpunished. Every possible sin that could ever separate us from God— every wrong we did, every good we failed to do, every thought, word, or deed that "fell short of the glory of God"—has been "set aside" and "nailed to the cross" (Col. 2:14). God's wrath against sin has been appeased.

This is how God resolved his dilemma of how to share love with beings who by their own choice have made themselves antithetical to his holy nature. On Calvary, God's love bore the judgment of sin that his own holy nature required. Jesus died in our place.

Supporting Arguments

1. *How sinners are reconciled to God.* The penal substitution view of the atonement is the only view that takes at face value and with full seriousness

the Bible's teaching that Jesus died in our place. For this reason, it is the only view that makes clear how an all-holy God could reconcile sinners with himself. Neither the Christus Victor nor the moral government view of the atonement addresses this issue adequately. While they both contain truths—Christ defeats Satan (Christus Victor) and his death expresses God's wrath against sin (moral government)—neither clearly shows how sinners are objectively made pure before God. And unfortunately for these views, the acts of freeing us from Satan's power and showing God's wrath against sin do not do us any good unless we are really cleansed of past, present, and future sin.

2. *Jesus' life and death.* The penal substitution view of the atonement connects Jesus' death with his life in a way that the other two views do not. Jesus had to live a life of perfect obedience to God, for he could be our substitutionary sacrifice only if he was not himself in need of a sacrifice. He had to be the unblemished "lamb of God" (John 1:29, 36). Jesus' death is significant, therefore, only because his life was perfect.

Responding to Objections

1. *This view limits God.* Some argue that the penal substitution view of the atonement limits God, for it suggests that God has to punish all sin and thus that Jesus had to die for God to reconcile sinners to himself. God is not free, they argue, simply to forgive people. Some argue further that this view conflicts with biblical passages in which God forgives people simply on the basis of their repentance (cf. Luke 15:11–32). Two things may be said in response to this objection.

First, something can be said to "limit" God only if it is imposed upon God from outside himself. If a requirement *external to God* stipulated that God had to punish all sin, when God would just as soon let sin go unpunished, *this* would limit God. But the requirement that all sin be punished expresses God's own perfectly holy character. To say that God "can't" let sin go unpunished no more limits God than saying that God "can't" lie (Num. 23:19) or deny himself (2 Tim. 2:13).

Second, biblical passages that depict God forgiving sinners simply on the basis of their repentance do not contradict the penal substitution view of the atonement. God certainly forgives all who simply repent. The teaching that Jesus died in our place tells us *how* an all-holy God can do so without denying his own character. Whenever God forgives someone, he does so on the basis of the cross.

2. *This view encourages sinful living.* Some argue that the teaching that Jesus bore the punishment for our sins leads people to condone sinful living. Why not keep sinning if there are no longer any consequences for it?

First, we must note that Paul had to confront this very question several times in his ministry (e.g., Rom. 6:1–12). Therefore, if we are preaching what Paul preached, we should expect this kind of question from people. In other words, the objection indirectly confirms that our understanding of the significance of the cross is the same as that of Paul.

Second, Paul never answers believers who wonder if they can keep sinning by threatening them with God's judgment. He rather reminds believers that they are "a new creation" in Christ Jesus (2 Cor. 5:17). Believers have "died" with Christ and thus are now dead to sin. They have been raised from the dead with Christ and thus should now walk "in newness of life" (Rom. 6:3–5; Eph. 2:4–6). In other words, Paul motivates believers to holy living, not by threats but by reminding them of who they *already are* by faith in Christ. They have been made righteous and thus should reflect this in their living. This is the motivation the penal substitution view of the atonement provides to believers.

Third, if we followed the logic of this objection, it would rule out not only the penal substitution view of the atonement but also any doctrine of salvation by grace. In other words, the objection works only if salvation is a result of works (see **meritorious works**), not grace. The New Testament consistently teaches, however, that salvation is by grace alone.

3. *Guilt cannot be transferred.* Many object to this view, saying that the idea Jesus could be justly punished for our sins is incoherent, for guilt is an individual matter and cannot be transferred. Admittedly, there is an element of mystery to the penal substitution view of the atonement, but it is a mystery we must accept because it is rooted in Scripture.

However, we must also note that a large part of our difficulty in understanding this concept is due to the fact that we live in a highly individualistic culture that assumes moral responsibility is strictly an individual matter. The Bible, and most ancient and non-Western cultures, do not share this assumption. For example, the Bible teaches that all humanity is held accountable for Adam's fall (Rom. 5:12–14). Similarly, all of Israel was held accountable for David's sin (1 Chron. 21:1–17). And when Saul broke a four-hundred-year-old treaty that Joshua, the leader of Israel, had made with the Gibeonites, members of Saul's family had to pay (2 Sam. 21:1–9).

The same principle applies, but in an opposite direction, with Christ's death. As a member of the human race (this is why Jesus had to become a man), Jesus bore the sin of the world and the punishment it demanded. God treated this one individual as though he were the entire human race, and he treats all humans who accept Christ's death as though they were this one individual. We were all one "in Adam." Now we are all one "in Christ" (Rom. 5:12–21).

Perhaps we in modern Western culture have not completely lost this sense of corporate accountability, despite our rampant **individualism.** For example, most of us would understand how children of Nazi war criminals might continue to experience shame in the presence of Jewish children whose parents were murdered in concentration camps. We would understand if they felt they needed to make reparation. Why is this the case if moral responsibility is strictly an individual matter? Intuitions such as this serve as reminders that moral responsibility belongs to groups as well as to individuals.

4. *This view sets the Father against the Son.* Finally, some argue that the penal substitution view of the atonement destroys the unity of the Trinity, for it suggests that the Trinity experienced a rift between the Father and the Son when the Father judged the Son. On the contrary, though, this view posits a most profound unity between the Father and the Son, a unity that is revealed precisely at the moment when the Father judged the Son.

The crucifixion reveals the Father's willingness to sacrifice his Son (John 3:16) and the Son's willingness to be sacrificed on our behalf (Matt. 26:39). It declares that the Father and Son were both willing to experience a temporary severance in their eternal relationship for the sake of acquiring eternal unity with humanity. Their unified love for lost humanity and their unified will to save humanity led them to experience willingly a loss of unity in their own relationship. Hence, as paradoxical as it sounds, the perfect unity of heart and purpose between the Father and the Son was manifested precisely at the moment Jesus cried out, "My God, my God, why have you forsaken me?" (Matt. 27:46). This constitutes one of the most profound teachings of the entire Bible.

Christ Destroyed Satan and His Works (The Christus Victor View)

The Biblical Argument

The primary significance of Christ's death and resurrection is that they defeated God's archenemy, Satan. Scripture teaches that at some point in the distant past, probably before the creation of this cosmos, a great rebellion took place in heaven. According to the traditional understanding, the most powerful of all the angels (commonly named Lucifer) led multitudes of other angels in a war with God, a war that continues to this day (Rev. 12:13–17). Humans became enslaved to Satan and co-opted into his rebellion when Adam surrendered his authority to have dominion over the earth (Gen. 3:1–6; Luke 4:5–8; 1 John 5:19). Every individual does the same thing when he or she willfully sins (John 8:34).

As a result, the world is now "under the power of the evil one" (1 John 5:19), for Satan has become "the god of this world" (2 Cor. 4:4) and "the ruler of the power of the air" (Eph. 2:2). Indeed, Jesus refers to Satan as "the prince" of this present age (John 12:31; 14:30; 16:11 NIV). In the first century, "prince" (*archon*) was used to denote the highest official in a city or region. Jesus thus acknowledges that Satan is the highest power of this present fallen world, at least in terms of his present influence. This is why Jesus does not dispute Satan's claim that he has been given "authority" over "all the kingdoms of this world" (Luke 4:5–6).

Jesus came into the world primarily to overthrow Satan and his kingdom and to thereby free humans from his bondage. He came "to destroy the works of the devil" (1 John 3:8), to disarm "the rulers and authorities" (Col. 2:15), and to "destroy the one who has the power of death, that is, the devil" (Heb. 2:14). In fact, the first messianic prophecy in the Bible says that Jesus would "strike [the] head" of the serpent that deceived Adam and Eve (Gen. 3:15). And the Old Testament passage most frequently quoted in the New Testament (Ps. 110:1) says that Christ shall reign in the power of God "until [God] makes your enemies your footstool." The central significance of the Messiah is that he is victorious over everything and everyone who opposes God and all the evil forces that have enslaved humanity throughout the ages.

Jesus' ministry as well as his death and resurrection must be understood in this light. When Jesus exorcised demons, he demonstrated that through him the kingdom of God was advancing against the kingdom of darkness (Luke 11:20). Similarly, when Jesus healed people, he and his disciples understood that he was setting people free from Satan's oppression (e.g., Mark 9:25; Luke 11:14; 13:11–16). Hence, Peter later summarized Jesus' healing ministry by noting that he "went about doing good and healing all who were oppressed by the devil" (Acts 10:38). The New Testament as a whole regards sickness and disease as the direct or indirect results of satanic oppression. In healing people, therefore, Jesus was gaining ground against his cosmic archenemy.

The main way Jesus defeated Satan and his kingdom, however, was by his death and resurrection. This frequently missed theme runs throughout the New Testament. As alluded to above, the theme is first of all expressed in the way New Testament authors cite Psalm 110:1. For example, in the first sermon preached in church history, Peter depicts Christ's death and resurrection as fulfilling Psalm 110:1. By raising Christ from the dead, he says, the Father has made his Son "both Lord and Messiah" and has now set him at "his right hand" so he can reign over his enemies until they all are made his footstool (Acts 2:32–36). The author of Hebrews notes that by his sacrificial death Jesus has been enthroned over all his enemies (Heb. 1:13; cf. 10:12–13). And Paul applies this passage to the resurrection of Christ while noting that it means that "every ruler and every authority and power" will be "destroyed" (1 Cor. 15:22–25; cf. Eph. 1:20–22). The primary significance of Jesus' death and resurrection is that by means of these he triumphed over all human and spiritual forces that oppose God.

All of the passages that proclaim that Jesus is now exalted and seated at the right hand of God imply the same thing. For example, Peter and the other apostles proclaim that because Jesus was raised from the dead, "God exalted him at his right hand as Leader and Savior that he might give repentance to Israel and forgiveness of sins" (Acts 5:31). Through Jesus' death and resurrection, the former "ruler of the world" has been "driven out" (John 12:31) and a new "Leader" enthroned. Whereas the former illegitimate ruler held humanity in misery, sin, and bondage, this rightful Leader offers "repentance and forgiveness of sins."

Paul has something similar in mind when he writes that no one can condemn the believer because Jesus, who now justifies us, died, was raised to life, and is now seated "at the right hand of God" (Rom. 8:34). Because Christ now rules, Paul says, nothing can separate us from the love of Christ—neither angels nor rulers nor powers (Rom. 8:38). Along the same lines, Paul celebrates the power that is at work in believers because it is the same power that "raised [Christ] from the dead and seated him at his right hand in the heavenly places, far above all rule and . . . dominion" (Eph. 1:19–21). Similarly, Peter teaches that baptism is significant because we are saved "through the resurrection of Jesus Christ, who has gone into heaven and is at the right hand of God, with angels, authorities, and powers made subject to him" (1 Pet. 3:21–22).

The point is unmistakably clear. When Christ died and rose again, he "disarmed the rulers and authorities, and made a public example of them, triumphing over them in [the cross]" (Col. 2:15). He regained his rightful place and thus is in the position of power—at the right hand of God. As a result, Satan and all other powers of darkness have been subjected to him (cf. Phil. 2:9–11; Col. 1:15–20).

As already noted, this cosmic victory was revolutionary for humans. Because Christ defeated Satan by means of his death and resurrection, humans may now be set free from Satan's tyranny. All who say yes to Christ's lordship are "rescued . . . from the power of darkness and transferred . . . into the kingdom of [the] beloved Son" (Col. 1:13). We can now have our eyes opened and "may turn from darkness to light and from the power of Satan to God, so that [we] may receive forgiveness of sins" (Acts 26:18). This theme reoccurs throughout the New Testament.

For example, John writes that since Christ has overcome the devil, the one who is ultimately behind all sin (1 John 3:8, 12; 4:3; etc.), believers too can "overcome the evil one" (1 John 2:13–14) and live free from sin (1 John 3:6, 9; 5:18). We can now overcome "that ancient serpent, who is called the Devil and Satan, the deceiver of the whole world," for we war against him "by the blood of the Lamb and by the word of [our] testimony" (Rev. 12:9, 11). Similarly, the author of Hebrews proclaims that when Jesus destroyed "the one who has the power of death, that is, the devil," he set "free those who all their lives were held in slavery by the fear of death" (Heb. 2:14–15). The good news, Paul says, is that people may now "escape from the snare of the devil, having been held captive by him to do his will" (2 Tim. 2:26). When we receive this good news, we are "set free from this present evil age" (Gal. 1:4).

Finally, the Bible describes Jesus' death as a "ransom" (e.g., Matt. 20:28; Mark 10:45; cf. 1 Tim. 2:6; Heb. 9:15) and salvation as "redemption" (e.g., Rom. 3:24; 8:23; 1 Cor. 1:30; Eph. 1:7). Both terms refer to the price that had to be paid to release one from slavery, and both metaphors communicate the truth that Jesus did all that was necessary to release us from the bondage to Satan, sin, and condemnation.

Supporting Arguments

1. *Church tradition*. The Christus Victor view of the atonement was the dominant view of the atonement in the church until the eleventh century, when Anselm's satisfaction view became popular. The antiquity of this perspective counts in its favor.

2. *The unifying theme of Jesus' ministry*. The Christus Victor view of the atonement brings a thematic unity to Jesus' life, teachings, and ministry, while the other views do not. The unifying theme of Jesus' ministry was his warfare against the kingdom of darkness. His teaching, exorcisms, and healing ministry were all warfare activities. His death and resurrection simply culminated this activity. Hence, Jesus responds to Herod's threats by saying, "I am casting out demons and performing cures today and tomorrow, and on the third day I finish my work" (Luke 13:32). His resurrection "on the third day" completed the task for which he had been sent. While Jesus' death paid the price for human sin (substitutionary view) and/or demonstrated the severity of God's judgment against sin (moral government view), these views isolate Jesus' death and resurrection from the rest of his activity. They are combined with the Christus Victor understanding.

3. *The unity of Jesus' death and resurrection*. In the New Testament, Christ's death and resurrection are inextricably connected. Christ died *and rose again* to free us and reconcile us to God (2 Cor. 5:15; 1 Thess. 4:14). But the resurrection is not strictly necessary in either the penal substitution or moral government view of the atonement. If the body of Jesus had remained dead, our sins would still have been paid for and God's wrath against sin still demonstrated. Adherents of both these views find other reasons as to why Jesus had to rise again, but they are not inextricably connected to the atonement. This is not the case in the Christus Victor view. Jesus' victory over the grave and the lord of death was the point of his

death and resurrection. Had Jesus not risen, his death could not have saved us. In this respect, this view is more faithful to the New Testament.

4. *The cosmic dimension of evil.* People today often wonder how the gospel fits with contemporary knowledge of the vastness of the universe. Many also wonder how it is that this entire universe could be subject to "the bondage of decay" just because people on our small planet fell, and how it is that the entire cosmos can be set free from this bondage on the basis of what happened on our little planet (Rom. 8:19–23). The Christus Victor understanding of the atonement addresses these questions. The atonement is a cosmic issue before it is a **soteriological** issue because evil is a cosmic issue before it is a human issue. The primary battle that ravages creation is not the battle between God and rebellious humans but the battle between God and cosmic principalities and powers. Earth functioned in the cosmic war much like the beaches of Normandy functioned in the Second World War. It became the battleground where D-day took place. Christ entered our world as a man, conquered Satan, and then empowered the church to apply his victory to every area of life. As a result, not only is humanity freed from the power of the devil, but the entire creation is also restored.

Responding to Objections

1. *This view is imbalanced in its focus.* Some object to the Christus Victor understanding of the atonement on the grounds that the Bible is more interested in how the cross and resurrection reconcile us to God than in how they defeat Satan. Two things may be said in response.

First, while it is true that the New Testament places much emphasis on how the cross and resurrection reconcile us to God, it is not obvious that this emphasis is greater than the emphasis on Christ's defeat of Satan. As this essay demonstrates, the Christus Victor theme runs throughout the New Testament and is anticipated in the Old Testament.

Second, even if one insists that the reconciling theme of the atonement receives more emphasis, this does not affect the Christus Victor view of the atonement. The Bible is a practical book and is always centrally interested in humanity's relationship with God. It tells us only what we need to know. It would not be surprising, therefore, if the implications of Christ's death and resurrection for us receive much emphasis in the New Testament. But this does not alter the fundamental reason as to why the cross and resurrection can affect us as they do: By means of these activities God defeated Satan and his kingdom.

2. *This view is overly speculative.* Some object to the Christus Victor view of the atonement on the grounds that it is overly speculative. It is true that the Christus Victor motif was at times worked out in speculative

and fanciful ways in the early church. Theories were devised to explain exactly how God outwitted the devil by allowing Jesus to be crucified. Some supposed that God made a "deal" with Satan and then backed out of it. Others likened Jesus to a worm on a hook and Satan as a hungry fish. But one need not accept these fanciful ideas to accept the Christus Victor view of the atonement. The Bible simply does not spell out in any detail exactly how Jesus defeated Satan through the cross and resurrection.

We are told that demons recognized Jesus but did not know why he came to earth (Matt. 8:29), and we are taught that Satan and his minions were directly involved in orchestrating Christ's crucifixion (1 Cor. 2:7–8; cf. John 13:27). It seems, therefore, that God in some sense "baited" Satan by sending his Son into Satan's domain as a vulnerable human being, but we cannot with any degree of confidence go beyond this idea and spell out exactly *how* the cross and resurrection defeated Satan.

3. *This view gives Satan too much credit.* Finally, some object to the Christus Victor view of the atonement on the grounds that it gives too much power to Satan. They dislike the notion that the all-powerful, sovereign God of the universe would have to go to such extreme measures to defeat his archenemy.

This charge is unfounded. The Bible, not a human theory, says that the world is "under the power of the evil one" (1 John 5:19). The Bible teaches that Satan reigns as "the god of this world" (2 Cor. 4:4) and "the ruler of the power of the air" (Eph. 2:2). Of course, the Bible also clearly teaches that God is not threatened by Satan and that Satan cannot overthrow God's overall goals for world history. God has always been assured of winning the battle against his fallen chief angel. But this does not undermine the fact that Satan and his kingdom are genuine forces of evil with which God must reckon. The cross and resurrection are the central ways God reckons with them. This too the Bible explicitly teaches.

Perhaps some believe it would have been better if God had simply incinerated his foes when they fell. So much the worse for their theology. God is more exalted for having defeated them by his "manifold wisdom" (Eph. 3:10) than by relying merely on his sheer omnipotent power.

Christ Displayed God's Wrath against Sin
(The Moral Government View)

The Biblical Argument

All Christians agree that "God put [Jesus Christ] forward as a sacrifice of atonement by his blood," which is made "effective through faith" (Rom.

3:25). Most evangelicals assume that this means God punished Jesus for our sins. They believe we can be forgiven only because Jesus bore the punishment we deserved. And they believe that God considers them holy, despite sin in their life, because he sees them "under the blood" of his Son.

The moral government view of the atonement considers this view unbiblical and potentially harmful in that it can undermine God's call for believers to live holy lives. God does not have a quota of judgment that has to be poured out on someone (namely, his Son) in order for him to love and forgive sinners. As the Bible uniformly declares, God loves and forgives freely (Matt. 10:8; cf. Luke 15:11–32). Further, God does not consider people holy because of what Jesus did. He wants us actually to live holy lives. This is the central reason why Jesus died on the cross.

The meaning of Jesus' atonement is found in Romans 3:25b–26. Paul writes: "[God] did this [had Jesus crucified] to show righteousness, because in his divine forbearance he had passsed over the sins previously committed; it was to prove at the present time that he himself is righteous and that he justifies the one who has faith in Jesus." The point of Jesus' death was for God to "show righteousness." Because of his love, God demonstrated his wrath against sin to deter all humankind from sinning. The atonement, in other words, was the means by which God preserved his moral government of the world. A number of biblical motifs support this.

First, one of the central themes running throughout Scripture is that God is trying to raise up a people who walk in his ways (Exod. 19:5–6; 2 Chron. 7:14; Matt. 22:36–40). God is a holy God who desires to fellowship with a people who honor him and reflect his holiness (Exod. 19:6; Matt. 5:48; 1 Pet. 2:9). From the very beginning of the Old Testament, God sought to govern the world by teaching his moral principles to humans and motivating them to adhere to them. This is why he gave Adam the choice of obeying or disobeying him, with the warning of what would happen if Adam chose to disobey: "And the LORD God commanded the man, 'You may freely eat of every tree of the garden; but of the tree of the knowledge of good and evil you shall not eat, for in the day that you eat of it you shall die'" (Gen. 2:16–17).

The theme is repeated throughout the Old Testament. For example, the Lord says to the Israelites:

> See, I have set before you today life and prosperity, death and adversity. If you obey the commandments of the LORD your God . . . then you shall live . . . and the LORD your God will bless you. . . . But if your heart turns away and you do not hear . . . I declare to you today that you shall perish. . . . I have set before you life and death, blessings and curses. Choose life so that you and your descendants may live. (Deut. 30:15–19; cf. 11:26–28; Jer. 7:1–15; 17:19–27; 21:8; 22:1–5)

Similarly, in the New Testament, God's ultimate objective is to create people who are "holy and blameless before him in love" (Eph. 1:4). Paul declares that Christians "are what he has made us, created in Christ Jesus for good works, which God prepared beforehand to be our way of life" (Eph. 2:10). Though many believers mistakenly think holiness before God is merely a legal stance made possible because Christ took the punishment for sin, the Bible emphasizes that God's goal for his people is that they actually live holy lives (Lev. 11:44–45; 1 Pet. 1:15–16).

The moral government view of the atonement is consistent with this biblical teaching. Isaiah tells us that "the Lord was pleased, for the sake of his righteousness, to magnify his teaching and make it glorious" (Isa. 42:21). God magnified his teaching to the Israelites to inspire them to acknowledge God's righteousness by how they lived. He was willing to go to great lengths to give them vivid illustrations of the consequences of rebelling against his teaching. In the same way, it was "to show righteousness" that God "put [Jesus Christ] forward as a sacrifice of atonement by his blood" (Rom. 3:25). There can be no moral government with enforced consequences for sinful behavior. Therefore, God established his moral government by showing the severe consequences of disobedience, thus motivating people to walk according to God's law. One of the unfortunate consequences of the penal substitution view of the atonement is that it often has the opposite effect.

Second, throughout the Bible we learn that God is willing to forgive sinners simply on the basis of their faith and repentance. This idea is declared and demonstrated throughout the Old Testament (e.g., 2 Chron. 7:14), and it is even more clearly expressed in the New Testament (Mark 1:15; Acts 2:37–38; Rom. 2:4–8). Most importantly, the theme pervades the parables of Jesus.

One of Jesus' most famous parables is the parable of the prodigal son (Luke 15:11–32). A son shamelessly insists on his inheritance before his father's death—saying, in effect, "I wish you were dead." He leaves home and proceeds to squander all his money "in dissolute living" (v. 13). After a famine hits the land, he is reduced to feeding pigs (vv. 15–16), one of the most disgraceful forms of employment for a first-century Jew. On the verge of starvation, he comes to his senses and heads home, hoping to be a servant (vv. 16–17). Jesus continues:

> While [the son] was still far off, his father saw him and was filled with compassion; he ran and put his arms around him and kissed him. Then the son said to him, "Father, I have sinned against heaven and before you; I am no longer worthy to be called your son." But the father said to his slaves, "Quickly, bring out a robe—the best one—and put it on him; put a ring on his finger and sandals on his feet. And get the fatted calf and kill it, and let

us eat and celebrate; for this son of mine was dead and is alive again; he was lost and is found!" (vv. 20–24)

This powerful story beautifully displays the heart of God toward sinners. At the first sign of his son's return—"while he was still far off"—the father runs to him, embraces him, and restores him to his place in the family. There is no need for the son or anyone else to make reparation for the vast inheritance that was willfully squandered. The father does not need to punish someone—not even himself—before he can forgive his son. The father simply forgives—freely.

Another parable of Jesus makes the same point. In response to Peter's question concerning how often we should be willing to forgive one another, Jesus says, in effect, forgive without limit. Then he continues:

> The kingdom of heaven may be compared to a king who wished to settle accounts with his slaves. When he began the reckoning, one who owed him ten thousand talents was brought to him; and, as he could not pay, his lord ordered him to be sold, together with his wife and children and all his possessions, and payment to be made. So the slave fell on his knees before him, saying, "Have patience with me, and I will pay you everything." And out of pity for him, the lord of that slave released him and forgave him the debt. (Matt. 18:23–27)

The nature of forgiveness, we see, is that it erases debt, pure and simple. The king does not need someone else to pay the debt in order to forgive this slave. He simply does so "out of pity." So it is with God toward us. God takes "no pleasure in the death of the wicked" but rather wants "the wicked [to] turn from their ways and live" (Ezek. 33:11). When they simply do this, the Lord promises, "None of the sins that they have committed shall be remembered against them" (Ezek. 33:16). The only thing the Lord requires is that we turn from our sin and embrace him. Jesus displayed God's just wrath toward sin as a means of getting us to do just that.

A third aspect of Scripture supports the moral government view of the atonement. In Old Testament times, people were required to offer sacrifices to God because of their sin. Why was this required? It was not because these animals were substitutes for the punishment humans deserved. Indeed, if a person could not afford an animal, they were allowed to offer food (Lev. 5:11–13). There was clearly nothing substitutionary about the blood of animals. Indeed, the "scapegoat," which most closely symbolizes the sacrifice of Christ, was not killed at all. It was driven away (Lev. 16:10). Further, there were some sins for which no sacrifice could be made (Num. 15:30–31).

What then was the point of these sacrifices and offerings? They were to display to the Israelites the severity of God's judgment on sin. These bloody sacrifices or offerings served as constant reminders to the Israelites that "the wages of sin is death" (Rom. 6:23). In this sense, they foreshadowed the ultimate sacrifice, made by God himself, "for the sins of the whole world" (1 John 2:2). In a way that far transcended what the sacrifices of the Old Testament could accomplish, Christ "offered himself without blemish to God" to "purify our conscience from dead works to worship the living God!" (Heb. 9:14). In Christ's death, we see the full severity of sin, for we witness God's wrath against it borne by God's own Son.

Yet another aspect of biblical teaching that squares with the moral government view of the atonement is that guilt cannot be transferred. Ezekiel writes, for example: "The person who sins shall die. A child shall not suffer for the iniquity of a parent, nor a parent suffer for the iniquity of a child; the righteousness of the righteous shall be his own, and the wickedness of the wicked shall be his own" (18:20).

This view squares with what most people intuitively know. People cannot be justly punished for other people's crimes. Though they have made valiant efforts, exponents of the penal substitution view have never succeeded in clarifying how Jesus could literally bear the guilt of all people.

A final aspect of Scripture that squares with the moral government view is the New Testament teaching that there will be a **judgment seat** for believers. Paul writes, for example, that "all of us [believers!] must appear before the judgment seat of Christ, so that each may receive recompense for what has been done in the body, whether good or evil" (2 Cor. 5:10; cf. Rom. 14:10). There will be a fire that will test every believer's work (1 Cor. 3:12–15). And many of Jesus' teachings speak of punishments that are administered to servants who do not do what their master commands (Luke 12:45–48; 16:1–13; 19:11–27). How is this judgment possible if, in fact, all the sins of believers were already paid for on the cross of Calvary? Substitutionary theorists do not have a good answer.

Supporting Arguments

1. *The coherence and practicality of the moral government view.* The moral government view does not require people to believe the incoherent notion that Jesus literally bore the guilt of other people. Nor does it ask people to believe that God sees them as righteous even when their lives are sinful. The moral government view squares with what Scripture teaches and with what people ordinarily assume about the nature of justice. Relatedly, and perhaps most importantly, the moral government view of the atonement does not undermine but rather accentuates God's call for believers to live holy lives.

2. *The genuineness of God's forgiveness.* Suppose you owe me a financial debt you cannot pay. A friend of yours pays me instead. I then claim

to have "forgiven" your debt. Am I telling the truth? The answer is no. *A debt that is paid cannot be a debt that is forgiven.* So, too, if God demands that humanity's debt be paid, he never really forgives the debt. He has, in fact, been "paid in full." The moral government view, in contrast to the penal substitution view, shows that God forgives sinners, for he does not demand that their debt to him be paid—by anyone.

3. *The holiness and unity of the Trinity.* The penal substitution view of the atonement would have us believe that the Father literally made Jesus "to be sin" (2 Cor. 5:21) while he hung on the cross. But if God is so opposed to sin that he cannot have fellowship with sinners without punishing their sin, as this view argues, how are we to conceive of the all-holy Son of God *becoming* sin? Conversely, if God could literally *become* sin, the argument that God cannot have fellowship with sinners without punishing their sin does not stand up.

Paul is using the language of Old Testament sacrificial practices in this passage. He is not saying that Jesus literally became sin, only that Jesus played the role of a sin offering. The moral government view, therefore, avoids the problem of understanding how a God who can have nothing to do with sin could become sin.

Closely related to this, the penal substitution view requires us to believe that the Father literally rejected and judged the Son while he hung on the cross. But does this not destroy the unity of the Godhead? True, the Father and Son were united in their goal to save humanity, but this does not do away with the fact that a real separation occurred between the Father and the Son. This opinion runs counter to the biblical and traditional understanding that the three Persons of the Trinity are inseparable. The moral government view avoids this problem altogether. The Father expressed his wrath against sin *to us,* not to his Son, by having him die a cursed death on the cross. The Father was no more angry toward his Son on the cross than he was toward the animals that were sacrificed in the Old Testament.

Responding to Objections

1. *Jesus bore our sins.* Most evangelicals object to the moral government theory on the grounds that it conflicts with Scripture passages that speak of Jesus bearing our sins and appeasing God's wrath (e.g., Heb. 9:28; 1 Pet. 2:24; 1 John 2:2). The Old Testament also spoke this way about sacrificed animals (e.g., Lev. 1:4), yet no Christian thinks this implies that the animals literally were substitutes for people's punishment or appeased God's anger. They rather demonstrated God's anger and judgment. The same is true of Jesus' death. As with the sacrificed animals in the Old

Testament, Jesus bore our sin and was our propitiation in the sense that he made undeniably clear God's anger toward sin and the judgment it deserves.

2. *What becomes of God's justice?* Many argue that the moral government view undermines God's justice, for it means that the sins of forgiven people go unpunished. Indeed, one of the most frequent arguments made on behalf of the penal substitution view is that it makes sense of how an all-holy God can forgive sinners without compromising his just wrath toward sin. Two things may be said in response.

First, it is not at all clear how the penal substitution view makes sense of God's justice when it is premised on the incoherent notion that guilt can be transferred from a guilty party to an innocent party. To say that our sins were paid for when God smote Jesus does not clarify anything. It just adds another mystery to the discussion.

Second, there is nothing unholy about forgiving people. On the contrary, God's forgiveness is as much an expression of his holiness as is his just anger toward sin. This objection, like the penal substitution theory from which it arises, assumes there is a rule in the universe that says past sins *have* to be punished (though not necessarily the person who committed them!). But why assume this? We do not insist on this when we forgive people. Why must God? Indeed, as noted earlier, if God insists on payment, he does not truly forgive people. Furthermore, the Bible frequently teaches that God, out of his love and mercy, can and does simply forget the sins of the past when a person repents and turns to him (Ps. 103:8–14). He is a God who truly forgives, for he cancels their debt without payment.

Further Reading

Aulen, Gustaf. *Christus Victor.* Translated by A. G. Hebert. New York: Macmillan, 1969.

Beilby, James, and Paul R. Eddy, eds. *The Nature of the Atonement: Four Views.* Downers Grove, IL: InterVarsity, 2006.

Clark, Stephen B. *Redeemer: Understanding the Meaning of the Life, Death, and Resurrection of Jesus Christ.* Ann Arbor, MI: Servant, 1992.

Culpepper, Robert. *Interpreting the Atonement.* Grand Rapids: Eerdmans, 1966.

Driver, John. *Understanding the Atonement for the Mission of the Church.* Scottdale, PA: Herald, 1986.

Green, Joel B., and Mark D. Baker. *Recovering the Scandal of the Cross: Atonement in New Testament and Contemporary Contexts.* Downers Grove, IL: InterVarsity, 2000.

Hengel, Martin. *The Atonement: The Origins of the Doctrine in the New Testament.* Translated by John Bowden. Philadelphia: Fortress, 1981.

Hill, C. E., and F. A. James III, eds. *The Glory of the Atonement.* Downers Grove, IL: InterVarsity, 2004.

Jeffery, Steve, Michael Ovey, and Andrew Sach. *Pierced for Our Transgressions: Rediscovering the Glory of Penal Substitution.* Wheaton: Crossway, 2007.

Marshall, I. Howard. *The Work of Christ.* Grand Rapids: Zondervan, 1969.

Morris, Leon. *The Apostolic Preaching of the Cross.* Rev. ed. Grand Rapids: Eerdmans, 1994.

———. *The Cross of Jesus.* Grand Rapids: Eerdmans, 1988.

Murray, John. *Redemption Accomplished and Applied.* Grand Rapids: Eerdmans, 1955.

Shelton, R. Larry. "A Covenant Concept of the Atonement." *Wesleyan Theological Journal* 19 (1984): 91–108.

———. *Cross and Covenant: Interpreting the Atonement for Twenty-first Century Mission.* Tyrone, GA: Paternoster, 2006.

Wallace, Ronald S. *The Atoning Death of Christ.* Westchester, IL: Crossway, 1981.

8

The Salvation Debate

TULIP (The Calvinist View)
God Wants All to Be Saved (The Arminian View)

Posing the Question

From Nathan's perspective, the weekly Bible study had been going well for the several months of its existence. As the group made its way through Paul's Letter to the Romans, people seemed to be learning and growing together. The discussion time was always vigorous and challenging. It seemed that each evening ended with general agreement regarding what Paul had been trying to communicate and how his words could be applied, practically, in daily life.

Then came Romans 9. By the end of the evening, Nathan wasn't sure what to think. In fact, the only thing he was sure of was that the group discussion that night had produced far more "heat" than "light." Justin had argued strongly that this chapter clearly shows that God is sovereign over all things. More specifically, God has sovereignly chosen only some people—the elect—to receive salvation by grace. Alisha, on the other hand, strongly disagreed. She quoted 1 Timothy 2:4, which states that God desires all people to be saved. Nathan felt caught in between, because he believed both in God's sovereignty and his love. He left that evening with far more questions than he had arrived with.

The Center and Its Contrasts

Evangelical Christians agree on many things when it comes to the issue
of salvation. One of the central defining points of evangelicalism is the
conviction that a personal conversion experience is necessary for salvation. Evangelicals unanimously affirm that we are saved by grace through
faith and not of ourselves. "It is a gift of God—not the result of works, so
that no one may boast" (Eph. 2:8–9). Evangelicals of all varieties confess
that God is both our sovereign Creator and our loving Redeemer. There
is complete agreement that it is through the sacrificial death and victorious resurrection of Jesus alone that we find forgiveness of sins and peace
with God.

While there is much agreement on these central dogmas about salvation,
there is wide disagreement as to how these dogmas are to be understood in
terms of their doctrinal detail. For example, evangelicals concur that the
ideas of **predestination** and **election** are central to a biblical understanding
of salvation, for they are clearly and consistently taught in Scripture (e.g.,
Romans 8–9; Ephesians 1). However, when it comes to the questions of
how election works and on *what basis* God predestines people, evangelicals
exhibit a diversity of opinions.

This is not a new debate. The issue of the nature of salvation has been
debated throughout church history. Some of the more pressing questions
include: What is the proper balance between God's sovereignty and God's
love in the salvation process? What is the nature of God's grace, and how
does it work in a human life? To what degree has sin affected human freedom? And does human freedom play a central role in conversion?

With other orthodox Christians, all evangelicals agree at least in their opposition to one certain perspective on these matters: **Pelagianism.** Pelagius
was a fifth-century monk who gained a following in Rome and emphasized
the need for moral striving in the Christian life. Although his aspirations
were noble, the theology he developed to express them was problematic.
Among other things, he claimed that Adam's sin did not affect human nature. He thus maintained that human beings have the innate ability to live
sinless lives. God's grace helps us live holy lives before God, but he denied
that we are saved by grace alone. All evangelicals agree that Pelagius was
overly optimistic in his assessment of fallen human nature and thus did
not properly emphasize our need for grace in order to be saved. Although
evangelicals agree in this regard, they are divided on other matters related
to the nature of salvation.

The two essays that follow represent perspectives that have long and
distinguished histories. The Calvinist perspective, expressed in the first
essay, has roots that extend back to the famous fifth-century theologian
Augustine and his interpretation of Paul's Letter to the Romans. Other

well-known Christians who have held this view include the great Reformers Martin Luther and John Calvin, as well as the noted revivalists George Whitefield and Jonathan Edwards. Today, this view has been ably articulated and defended by evangelical scholars such as R. C. Sproul and John Piper. At the heart of this view is the conviction that in his wisdom and sovereignty and from before the foundation of the world, God mercifully chose to save a certain number of people—the elect—from among sinful humanity.

The second essay represents a perspective known as Arminianism, named after Jacob Arminius, an early seventeenth-century theologian. The roots of this view also wind their way back into the early church. In the fifth century, one of the people who challenged Augustine's interpretation of salvation and the workings of grace was a monk named John Cassian. He argued that while Augustine was right to challenge the errors of Pelagianism, he had gone too far in denying that human freedom had any real role in the salvation process. Cassian's basic conviction was reiterated during the Reformation age by the Catholic scholar Desiderius Erasmus and the Anabaptists. Others who have held to this perspective include the revivalists John Wesley and Charles Finney. In more recent years, this view has been espoused by Christian thinkers such as C. S. Lewis and Clark Pinnock. A fundamental conviction of the Arminian perspective is that while salvation comes to humans by God's sovereign grace alone, this grace allows human beings freely to accept or reject God's offer of eternal life. Put simply: God desires a love relationship with his human creatures, and love—real love—must be chosen.

TULIP (The Calvinist View)

The Biblical Argument

The Calvinist view of salvation is customarily organized around five points, signified by the acronym TULIP. The T in TULIP stands for **total depravity.** Scripture teaches that because of the fall all human beings are incapable of responding positively to God on their own. Had Adam not fallen, things would have been different. But as it now stands, we are "in Adam" (1 Cor. 15:22), a race of rebels incapacitated by our sin. Scripture goes so far as to say that humans are "dead in sin" (Eph. 2:1, 5). We are not merely wounded, as though the fall just made it more difficult to obey God, and therefore, God now has to assist us. We are corpses in relationship to the things of God. A corpse cannot respond to anything. Hence, if people are to enjoy a relationship with God, God must do nothing less than resurrect them. This, in fact, is precisely what Scripture declares God does to those he makes his children (Eph. 2:4–5). Apart from God's grace, all humans would be hopelessly doomed.

Scripture drives home our total depravity in a number of ways. Paul says unregenerate humans are "by nature children of wrath" (Eph. 2:3). We can no more change our nature on our own than we can change the color of our skin (Jer. 13:23). If we are to become objects of God's love, God is going to have to change our nature. God does this to those he makes his own (Eph. 2:1–7). Believers are literally made into new creations (2 Cor. 5:17) and form a new humanity (Eph. 2:15).

Scripture elsewhere declares that humans are "slaves to sin" (Rom. 6:16, 19–20) and slaves to Satan. Slaves cannot free themselves from their master. If slaves are to be set free, someone must help them. This is what God does for his elect. He frees them from the punishment and bondage to sin, frees them from the power of Satan, and frees them to do what they could never do on their own—namely, choose him, love him, and obey him.

Because of our self-chosen bondage, we cannot make a positive movement to God on our own. We cannot even choose to accept salvation unless God empowers us to do so (Rom. 9:14–23; Eph. 2:8). Paul powerfully summarizes our state when he writes:

> There is no one who is righteous, not even one;
>   there is no one who has understanding,
>   there is no one who seeks God.
> All have turned aside, together they have become worthless;
>   there is no one who shows kindness,
>   there is not even one. (Rom. 3:10–12)

No one on his or her own is righteous before God or even seeks after God. This is what total depravity means.

The U in TULIP stands for **unconditional election.** If we are indeed spiritual corpses, nothing in us merits God's choice to save us. If God nevertheless chooses to save us, the reason for doing so must lie in God, not in us.

Paul proclaims that "[God] chose us in Christ before the foundation of the world. . . . He destined us for adoption as his children through Jesus Christ, according to the good pleasure of his will" (Eph. 1:4–5). So, too, Paul says that God "saved us and called us with a holy calling, not according to our works but according to his own purpose and grace. This grace was given to us in Christ Jesus before the ages began" (2 Tim. 1:9). Before the foundation of the world, God chose some to be his children from among the mass of sinful humans, and he did this not in accordance with their works but in accordance with his own purpose. This is why Scripture refers to believers as God's elect (Matt. 24:22, 24, 31; Rom. 8:33), and this is why God's election is unconditional. Nothing in fallen human beings "conditions" God's choice.

The L of TULIP stands for **limited atonement.** Christ's death is sufficient for all the sins of the world, but it was intended to save only those whom the Father has predestined to be saved. Jesus does not work at cross-purposes with the Father, wasting his blood on people who are destined for destruction (Prov. 16:9).

We see something of Christ's particular focus on the elect in Jesus' high priestly prayer in John 17. Jesus prays to the Father, "I have made your name known to those whom you gave me from the world" (v. 6). Jesus did not intend to make the Father's name known to everyone, only to those the Father gave him. Shortly after this Jesus prays, "I am asking on their behalf; I am not asking on behalf of the world, but on behalf of those whom you gave me, because they are yours. All mine are yours, and yours are mine; and I have been glorified in them" (vv. 9–10).

The Son of God knows the Father's will perfectly. He thus knows from the start who belongs to the Father and who does not (John 10:14–16, 25–29). He knows who the Father is drawing to him and who the Father is not drawing (John 6:44, 65). He reveals the Father only to the elect, and he prays only for the elect. The same applies to the atonement. It would be odd indeed for Jesus to die with the goal of saving people the Father did not intend to save and people whom he knows will not be saved.

The I of TULIP stands for **irresistible grace.** Scripture makes it clear that people are saved by God's will, not their own wills. God's election "depends not on human will or exertion, but on God who shows mercy" (Rom. 9:16). Christians are born again "not of blood or of the will of the flesh or of the will of man, but of God" (John 1:13). Since humans are totally depraved, if matters were left up to them, they would willfully resist God forever. This, in fact, is precisely what those who are lost do. But God graciously changes the wills of his elect. God turns their hearts and places a love for him in their inner spirits (Jer. 31:31–34). God's grace is irresistible because God changes the wills of those who would otherwise resist it.

Finally, the P in TULIP stands for **perseverance of the saints.** (See **eternal security.**) When people have been elected by God and changed by God's irresistible grace, they cannot fall away. They will undoubtedly struggle and may even temporarily lapse into sin, but they will persevere in their faith until they receive their eternal reward. This marvelous teaching pervades the New Testament. For example, believers are said to have (not hope for) eternal life (John 3:36; 6:47). An eternal life that could possibly come to an end would not be eternal. Similarly, Jesus assures believers that they cannot be "snatched" out of the Father's hand (John 10:28–29). The New

Testament also consistently emphasizes that believers are "kept safe" by the power of God (1 Pet. 1:4–5; Jude 1).

The New Testament teaching on salvation begins with the grim but realistic teaching of the total depravity of humans and ends with the glorious proclamation of the eternal security of the elect. God's unconditional choice, Jesus' sufficient death, and the Spirit's irresistible work transform sinners into secure believers.

Supporting Arguments

1. *Logical coherence*. The five points of Calvinism are interconnected and thus form a logically coherent understanding of salvation that the Arminian view lacks. Because humans are totally depraved, God's choice to save some of them has to be unconditional. There clearly is nothing in humans that would merit God choosing some while leaving others in their sin. Because God's election is unconditional and restrictive (viz., not all are elect), Jesus' death could not have been intended to save all, for the Son cannot work at cross-purposes with the Father. Because the wills of the elect are as depraved as those of all sinners, the Spirit has to work irresistibly in their hearts so they will choose God rather than reject him. Finally, because individuals have nothing to do with being saved, they have nothing to do with their continuing salvation. They are called and kept by the power of the omnipotent God.

By contrast, the Arminian understanding of salvation is contradictory. It asserts that humans are depraved while also maintaining that God elects people on the basis of their faith. But how are humans capable of faith if they are truly depraved? And what is the force of saying that *God* elects people if the deciding factor as to whether a person is elect or not is what *they* do (namely, have faith)? Moreover, according to Arminianism, the intent of Jesus' death was to save all, but adherents also believe that not all are saved. This leads to the contradictory conclusion that Jesus' death was an atonement for many people whose sins are never atoned for. Either a person's sins are atoned for—in which case that person is forgiven and saved—or they are not. Hence, either Jesus' death is intended only for the people it actually atones for (the Calvinist view), or it is intended for all people and thus all are saved (universalism). Arminianism tries to find a middle ground between these two alternatives, which results in a contradiction.

Similarly, Arminianism is contradictory in maintaining that people can choose to yield to or resist the saving work of the Holy Spirit, though they also affirm that people are saved wholly by grace. If the difference between the saved and the unsaved is that the former yield to the Spirit while the latter do not, how can people avoid the conclusion that the saved are better than—or at least less sinful than—the unsaved? And how can people credit God alone with their salvation? Similarly, if people must keep themselves saved by continually producing faith, as Arminianism teaches, how can they avoid the conclusion that those who persevere are better than those who do not? Arminianism insists that it is God's grace that saves and keeps people, but it does so inconsistently.

2. *All the glory is God's.* Calvinism alone gives God all the glory for people's salvation. It does not credit the human with anything—not even with having enough goodness or spiritual insight to accept God's offer of salvation. God is the beginning, middle, and end of the salvation process. Calvinism thereby paints a picture of the sovereign, gracious Lord that is glorious and altogether consistent with the New Testament.

3. *The confidence of the believer.* Finally, because it identifies God as the sole originator and preserver of salvation, Calvinism offers believers a security and confidence that Arminianism cannot offer. Calvinists need not trust in their own ability to produce and sustain faith to become or stay saved. On their own, humans would not and could not produce or sustain anything of spiritual value. For adherents of Calvinism, their confidence rests in the power of the omnipotent God to rescue them from sin and to keep them from falling.

Responding to Objections

1. *God is not fair.* One of the most frequent objections people raise against the Calvinist understanding of salvation is that it isn't fair. It's not fair that God would choose to save some but not others when he could have saved all. Four points may be made in response.

First, suppose that God was in fact fair according to our human standards. Suppose God exerted the same effort toward all people to bring them into the kingdom. If this were the case, we would have to be consistent and conclude that ultimately people, not God, are responsible for their salvation, for God did to those who were saved exactly what he did to many other people who were not. But this undermines the clear New Testament teaching that salvation is the result of God's choice, not ours, and that we are saved by grace, not works.

Calvin makes this point when he writes:

> We shall never be clearly persuaded, as we ought to be, that our salvation flows from the wellspring of God's free mercy until we come to know his eternal election, which illumines God's grace by this contrast: that he does

not indiscriminately adopt all into the hope of salvation, but gives to some what he denies to others.[1]

In other words, either we must accept that God offers to some what he denies to others, or we must simply stop claiming that we are saved solely by grace.

Second, is it not obvious that salvation is not offered equally to all? Because of where and when people are born, some have an opportunity to believe that others lack. Yet apart from faith no one can be saved. This inequality presents a difficult problem for Arminianism, but it is perfectly consistent with Calvinism.

Third, we must understand that humanity as a whole has rebelled against God and deserves hell. It would be fair for God to leave all of us in our self-chosen sin and doomed fate. If we are considering things from a scriptural perspective, then, the mystery is not that God didn't save all—the mystery is rather that God saved any!

Finally, and most importantly, we must remember that God is God and we have no right to stand in judgment of him. When Paul considers the question of unfairness in God's election (note, Paul concedes that God's election may appear unfair to the natural mind!), he simply responds, "Who indeed are you, a human being, to argue with God?" (Rom. 9:20). The final scriptural answer to the objection that God is unfair is a rebuke! Before the sovereign God, humans must stand in silent reverence.

2. *What about our freedom?* Some people are troubled by the Calvinist teaching that humans in their present fallen state are unable to choose freely to accept or reject God's offer of salvation. This seems to undermine free will. They point out that Scripture repeatedly calls people to choose to believe in Jesus Christ, promising them that if they believe they will be saved (John 6:40; 20:31; Acts 16:31; Rom. 10:9).

First, Calvinists do not deny that God calls people to make a choice to believe in him. They deny that this choice is *the basis* of their salvation. It is one thing to say that people are saved *if* they believe. It is another thing to say that they are saved *because* they believe. People are saved because they are elected by God. If they are elect, they will believe. If they are not, they will not. Hence, Jesus tells unbelievers, "Whoever is from God hears the words of God. The reason you do not hear them is that you are not from God" (John 8:47). What comes first is that a person is either "from God" or "not from God." What comes second is that a person either accepts God's words or rejects them.

Second, Calvinists do not deny free will. Rather, they deny that fallen humans are able to choose God on their own. According to Scripture, all humans freely follow Adam and Eve in rebellion against God. The result of this rebellion is that humans are now totally depraved and unable to choose to respond positively to God. The freedom to do this is restored only when God opens their hearts (cf. Acts 16:14), changes their nature, and thus causes them to have a love for Christ they never otherwise would have had. "This is *the work of God*," Jesus says, "that you believe in him whom he has sent" (John 6:29, emphasis added).

3. *Does God want all to be saved?* Finally, many object to Calvinism on the grounds that certain passages of Scripture suggest that God loves the entire world, that he wants all to be saved (John 3:16; 1 Tim. 2:4; 2 Pet. 3:9), and that he takes no delight in "the death of the wicked" (Ezek. 33:11).

First, when the Bible says that God "loves the world" and that Jesus died "for the sins of the world" (John 3:16; 1 John 2:2), it means that God's love and Christ's death are for people (his elect) from every part of the world. In other words, his love is not for people in any particular geographical region. His kingdom shall be composed of people "from every nation" (Rev. 5:9; 7:9).

Second, God does not delight in the destruction of any person (Ezek. 18:32; 33:11), even though he has eternally decreed it. It is possible for God to will on one level what he takes no pleasure in on another level. Consider the crucifixion of Christ. This was an unjust event that was carried out by people with wicked intentions (Acts 4:27–28). On this level the crucifixion did not please God. Indeed, he despised the event and judged those who carried it out. It involved incomprehensible suffering for his one and only Son. Yet Scripture also tells us that "it was the will of the LORD to crush him with pain." Why? Because by doing so the Lord would "make his life an offering for sin" and "through him the will of the LORD [would] prosper" (Isa. 53:10; cf. Acts 2:23). The same can be said of the damnation of sinners. God does not delight in the destruction of any particular person, yet he chooses to incorporate it into his sovereign plan because of what it accomplishes. His glory is displayed in justly punishing sinners as well as in showing mercy toward his elect (Rom. 9:22–23).

God Wants All to Be Saved (The Arminian View)

The Biblical Argument

The Arminian understanding of salvation can be expressed and defended by discussing four motifs that run throughout Scripture. The first motif is that God loves all people. The second is that people are free to choose to accept or reject this love. The third is that God graciously influences people to accept his love, but he does not coerce them. The fourth is that believers must continue to maintain their relationship with God for their salvation to be secure.

First, all Christians agree that God is perfect love (1 John 4:8, 16). No greater and no purer love can be conceived of than the love that constitutes the eternal nature of the Triune God. This love entails that God loves all human beings with a perfect love and wants them to be saved. If God loves only some humans enough to save them, as Calvinism teaches, his love falls far short of perfection. Fortunately, Scripture's depiction of God's attitude toward all people is consistent with its teaching that God is perfect love.

Though the Israelites usually missed it, God repeatedly emphasized that his purpose was to use them, his elect people, to reach the entire world (Gen. 12:3; Exod. 19:6). Over and over again we read in Scripture that God is not a God who shows partiality to one group of people over another (Deut. 10:17–19; 2 Chron. 19:7; Job 34:19; Rom. 2:11). He is never unfair or arbitrary, Ezekiel tells us, but wants to have mercy on everyone (Ezek. 18:25). Jeremiah adds that God "does not willingly afflict, or grieve anyone" (Lam. 3:33), a teaching that contradicts the Calvinist teaching that God consigns some people to hell before he even creates them.

The first-century Jewish Christians also initially had difficulty accepting the truth of God's universal love. Though Jesus repeatedly stressed the universal scope of God's love and of his mission (Matt. 28:18–20; Acts 1:8), God had to take supernatural measures to prod the early believers to reach out to the world to fulfill the **Great Commission** (Matt. 28:18–20). He gave Peter a vision that motivated him to preach the gospel to the Gentile Cornelius (Acts 10:9–16). At the beginning of his sermon, Peter [finally!] declares, "I truly understand that God shows no partiality, but in every nation anyone who fears him and does what is right is acceptable to him" (Acts 10:34–35; cf. Eph. 6:9; 1 Pet. 1:17).

We must weigh Peter's words carefully: "*no* partiality." Though as fallen humans we are often selective in our love, God is not. This means that God does not create some people whom he loves and others whom he plans to send to hell. The God of perfect love creates people out of love for the purpose of sharing his love with all of them. He expressed this universal love in the person of Jesus Christ. "God so loved *the world* that he gave his only Son. . . . God did not send the Son into the world to condemn the world, but in order that *the world* might be saved through him" (John 3:16–17, emphasis added).

Because he loves all, he wants everyone to be saved. God takes no delight in the destruction of any wicked person but rather desires all to repent (Ezek. 18:23, 32; 33:11). In the words of the apostle Peter, God is "not wanting *any* to perish, but all to come to repentance" (2 Pet. 3:9, emphasis added). He "desires *everyone* to be saved and to come to the knowledge of the truth" (1 Tim. 2:4, emphasis added). Indeed, in explicit contradiction to the notion that Jesus died only for select individuals, Scripture tells us that God desires to be "the Savior of all people" (1 Tim. 4:10) and thus that Jesus died as "the atoning sacrifice . . . for the sins of the whole world" (1 John 2:2; cf. Heb. 2:9).

Second, God loves everyone, but love is a two-way street. While love is who God is, humans are contingent beings who thus must choose it. This is why throughout Scripture God calls people to make decisions. Beginning in the Garden of Eden and extending through the book of Revelation, God sets before us "life and death," all the while pleading with us to "choose life that you . . . may live" (Deut. 30:19; cf. Josh. 24:15; Acts 17:30–31). In the New Testament, this choice is the choice to place one's trust in Jesus Christ or to reject him. Over and over we read the call to "believe in the Lord Jesus Christ" with the promise that if you do so "you will be saved" (Acts 16:31; cf. John 3:16; Acts 2:21; Rom. 10:13). The invitation is offered to everyone with the hope that all will choose to accept it.

It does not make sense for God to command people to make decisions unless they are free to make these decisions. It does not make sense for God to offer people choices if he has already predestined the choices they will make. And it does not make sense for God to offer salvation to everyone and tell us he genuinely wants everyone to be saved if he has already determined that some of them (or, many would argue, *most* of them) will not believe and will thus be damned. If God gives us decisions and tells us he wants us to choose life, it can only be because we are capable of choosing life and because he genuinely wants us to do so.

Third, most Arminians agree with Calvinists that our present fallen condition is such that we cannot choose God *on our own*. Were it not for God's grace, all humans would be hopelessly lost. All of us have freely chosen to follow Adam in rebelling against God (Rom. 5:12). We have freely placed ourselves under Satan's power and have thus become his slaves (John 8:34; 1 John 5:19). We are so helpless that Scripture says we are "dead" in our sin (Eph. 2:1). Our hearts have become "devious above all else" and "perverse" beyond understanding (Jer. 17:9). Our very nature has become hostile to God (Eph. 2:3).

God is incomprehensibly gracious, however. He did not abandon us in our sin, and his grace leads him to work with us, by the power of his Spirit, to keep the evil in our hearts in check. (This is what some Arminians call **prevenient grace**.) There are times when God sees that people are hopeless, and so he withdraws his Spirit and hardens their hearts by "[giving] them up to their passions" (Rom. 1:26; cf. vv. 24, 28; Gen. 6:3). But otherwise God's Spirit is at work in people's hearts, trying to soften them to acknowledge his lordship and walk in his ways.

As people yield to this loving influence, their hearts and minds are opened to the truth (Acts 16:14; 2 Cor. 3:13–18). Believers must profess that they would not have had the ability to believe were it not for the working of the Holy Spirit (John 16:7–14; 1 Cor. 2:9–13; 12:3; 2 Cor. 3:18). In this sense, even faith is a gift from God (Eph. 2:8–9). At the same time, Scripture is clear that people retain the power to resist the Holy Spirit, if they so choose. Scripture explicitly says that people can and do "frustrate" the Holy Spirit (Isa. 63:10). People can be persistently "stiff necked" or stubborn in their sinful stance against God (e.g., Exod. 33:3, 5; 34:9; Deut. 9:6, 13; 10:16; 31:27; Judg. 2:19; 2 Kings 17:14; 2 Chron. 30:8; 36:13; Neh. 9:16; Isa. 46:12; 48:4; Jer. 7:26; Hosea 4:16). People can and do "reject God's purpose for themselves" (Luke 7:30). The God of perfect love "longs to be gracious" to these sinners (Isa. 30:18) and persistently pleads with them to yield to him (Isa. 65:2; Ezek. 18:30–32; 33:11; Hosea 11:7ff.; Rom. 10:21). Yet, he will not coerce them into believing.

This willful rebellion always grieves God to the heart, for he wishes it were not so. It is this grieving heart that Jesus expressed when he cried out to Jerusalem: "Jerusalem, Jerusalem, the city that kills the prophets and stones those who are sent to it! How often have I desired to gather your children together as a hen gathers her brood under her wings, and you were not willing!" (Matt. 23:37). Though the people of Jerusalem were persistently rebellious, rejecting God's invitations over and over again, God *still* wanted to forgive and shelter them. But *they* "were not willing." Passages such as this mean nothing if God always gets his way in terms of who is saved and who is not.

Finally, we have seen that God's Spirit works in hearts to bring people to the point of freely entering into a relationship with Christ. We must also say that God works in people's hearts to keep them in this relationship with Christ. He is forever at work not only to keep us in the faith but to help us grow in spiritual maturity (Eph. 4:11–24; 2 Pet. 3:18). Yet even here humans retain their free will. Hence, Paul says that we must "work out [our] own salvation with fear and trembling; for it is God who is at work in you, enabling you both to will and to work for his good pleasure" (Phil. 2:12–13). The text is clear: God is at work in us enabling us to do God's good pleasure, but we must cooperate with God's Spirit by working out our salvation. (See **conditional security.**)

This implies that it is possible for Christians to forsake their relationship with Christ and thus lose their salvation. This, in fact, is precisely what Scripture teaches. For example, Scripture warns that it is possible to have your name blotted out of the Book of Life by rejecting the Lord who first wrote it there (Ps. 69:28; Rev. 3:5). Paul worries that this is the case with certain Christians at Galatia: He suspects they have "fallen from grace" (Gal. 5:4). So, too, Paul warns Timothy about "Hymenaeus and Philetus . . . who have swerved from the truth" (2 Tim. 2:17–18), while Peter speaks of certain "false teachers" who "will even deny the Master who bought them—bringing swift destruction on themselves" (2 Pet. 2:1). These passages argue against the Calvinist teaching that anyone who falls from the faith was never really saved in the first place. The names of the people spoken of in these passages were written in the Book of Life, and these people were in grace and bought by the Master.

The possibility of believers losing their salvation is also clear in Scripture's many warnings to believers not to fall away. For example, Peter writes:

> For if, after [people] have escaped the defilements of the world through the knowledge of our Lord and Savior Jesus Christ, they are again entangled in them and overpowered, the last state has become worse for them than the first. For it would have been better for them never to have known the way of righteousness than, after knowing it, to turn back from the holy commandment that was passed on to them. (2 Pet. 2:20–21)

Clearly, it is possible for people who have been made righteous "through the knowledge of our Lord and Savior Jesus Christ" to reject this salvation and end up in a state worse than the one from which they were saved. This is why Jesus taught that "[anyone] who endures to the end will be saved" (Matt. 24:13). Those who fall away from the faith are no longer saved.

Supporting Arguments

1. *Affirmation of God's perfect love.* One of the greatest advantages of the Arminian understanding of salvation is that it alone can affirm with logical consistency the perfection of God's love. There simply is no way to do so if one believes that God chooses not to save some (or most) of the people he could save. While not denying that God would be just in sending all humans to hell, Arminians simply deny that God is perfectly loving if he does not save all whom he could save. A person who threw out only one lifeline to ten drowning people when he had ten lifelines available would not be considered perfectly loving—even if the people themselves were responsible for going overboard. God throws out lifelines to everyone. That some choose to drown is not his fault nor his desire.

2. *Confidence in evangelism.* Arminians can be confident that God loves all people, that Jesus died for their sins, and that the Holy Spirit is at work in their hearts. These facts provide a confidence and motivation to preach the gospel "to the whole creation" (Mark 16:15; Col. 1:23). While Calvinists sometimes make great evangelists, their theology cannot supply this confidence or motivation. If they are consistent with their theology, they cannot say to every person they meet, "God loves you" or "Jesus died for you," because the person they are talking to may not be one of God's elect.

Conversely, since Calvinists believe there is no chance that the elect will *not* be saved, Calvinism undermines the urgency of evangelism. In the Arminian view, since people are saved only when they believe, and since they cannot believe unless they hear the gospel preached to them (Rom. 10:13–17), it is urgent that Christians take upon themselves the responsibility to evangelize.

Responding to Objections

1. *This view is not consistent with election.* Many argue that Paul's theology of election is not consistent with Arminianism. Paul says that "[God] chose us in Christ before the foundation of the world" (Eph. 1:4) and that God "saved us" and gave us grace "in Christ Jesus before the ages began" (2 Tim. 1:9).

The classic Arminian interpretation is that God elected people on the basis of his foreknowledge of their faith. Before the foundation of the world God foreknew who would and would not believe. He chose (elected) those who would believe to be his children and predestined them "to be holy and blameless before him in love" (Eph. 1:4). These individuals are in this sense saved and given grace "in Christ Jesus before the ages began."

An alternative Arminian interpretation maintains that Paul's concept of election in these passages is corporate, not individual. The church is God's elect people in the same sense that Israel was God's elect nation. According to this interpretation, before the foundation of the world God chose to have a people (the church) who would believe in him and would be predestined "to be holy and blameless before him in love." When a person chooses to be incorporated into this group by believing in Jesus, all that is predestined *for the group* now applies to that person. Hence, Paul can say to all who have chosen to become part of the church, "He chose us [as a group] in Christ before the foundation of the world to be holy and blameless before him in love. He destined us for adoption as his children" (Eph. 1:4–5).

Either of these interpretations is more plausible than the Calvinist interpretation, which depicts God as deciding who would (and thus who would not) believe in him before the foundation of the world.

2. *This view suggests that we get credit for our salvation.* It is often argued that Arminianism logically undermines the scriptural teaching that we are saved by grace alone. If the ultimate reason a person is saved or not lies in that person, not in God, then the credit for salvation must go to the person, not to God. Three things may be said in response to this argument.

First, salvation is a gracious gift by God, but a gift is not less of a gift because it is accepted. For example, a man recently donated several million dollars to a trust fund for disadvantaged teenagers. Would it not be absurd for someone to claim that his gift was not really a gift because the trustees of the trust fund accepted the gift? Would anyone claim that the trustees must take credit for the donation because they could have rejected the gift? So it is with God's offer of salvation. The gracious gift is offered to all and is no less a gift because we must choose to accept it.

Second, Scripture never portrays the choice to have faith as a work. When New Testament authors stress that salvation is not arrived at by works, as first-century Jews, these authors are referring to works *of the law*. They are saying that God's righteousness does not come by external obedience to the law, as some Jews of their day supposed. God's righteousness cannot be earned. It can come only as a gift (Rom. 4:4–16). But the New Testament nevertheless also teaches that the gift must be accepted by faith.

Finally, most Arminians agree that even the ability to accept the gift of salvation is given by God, as said above. Arminians differ from Calvinists on this matter only in that they deny that the Spirit works *irresistibly*. God graciously makes it *possible* for people to believe, but he does not make it *necessary* for them to believe. It is one thing to claim that without the Holy Spirit we *cannot* believe and quite another to say that with the work of the Holy Spirit we *must* believe. Scripture affirms the former but not the latter. In any event, this demonstrates that Arminianism does not undermine the truth that God is to receive all the glory for salvation.

Further Reading

Basinger, David, and Randall Basinger, eds. *Predestination and Free Will: Four Views of Divine Sovereignty and Human Freedom*. Downers Grove, IL: InterVarsity, 1986.

Cottrell, Jack W., et al. *Perspectives on Election: Five Views*. Nashville: Broadman and Holman, 2006.

Forster, Roger T., and V. Paul Marston. *God's Strategy in Human History*. Minneapolis: Bethany, 1973; Eugene, OR: Wipf and Stock, 2000.

Jewett, Paul K. *Election and Predestination*. Grand Rapids: Eerdmans, 1985.

Klein, William W. *The New Chosen People: A Corporate View of Election*. Grand Rapids: Academie/Zondervan, 1990.

Olson, Roger E. *Arminian Theology: Myths and Realities*. Downers Grove, IL: InterVarsity, 2006.

Peterson, Robert A., and Michael D. Williams. *Why I Am Not an Arminian*. Downers Grove, IL: InterVarsity, 2004.

Pinnock, Clark, ed. *The Grace of God and the Will of Man*. Minneapolis: Bethany, 1989.

———, ed. *Grace Unlimited*. Minneapolis: Bethany, 1976.

Piper, John. *The Justification of God*. 2nd ed. Grand Rapids: Baker Academic, 1993.

Schreiner, Thomas R., and Bruce A. Ware, eds. *The Grace of God, the Bondage of the Will*. 2 vols. Grand Rapids: Baker Academic, 1995.

Shank, Robert. *Elect in the Son*. Minneapolis: Bethany, 1989.

Sproul, R. C. *Chosen by God*. Wheaton: Tyndale, 1986.

Storms, Sam. *Chosen for Life: The Case for Divine Election*. Wheaton: Crossway, 2007.

Walls, Jerry L., and Joseph Dongell. *Why I Am Not a Calvinist*. Downers Grove, IL: InterVarsity, 2004.

9

The Sanctification Debate

Sanctification as a Declaration by God (The Lutheran View)
Sanctification as Holiness in Christ and in Personal Conduct
(The Reformed [Calvinist] View)
Sanctification as Resting-Faith in the Sufficiency of Christ
(The Keswick "Deeper Life" View)
Entire Sanctification as Perfect Love (The Wesleyan View)

Posing the Question

Ernie struggles with a habitual problem of lustful thoughts. He has prayed frequently that God would deliver him, but no release has come. Ernie believes that because God cannot look upon sin, God can no longer accept him in the same way he did before the sin occurred. Ernie sincerely desires to live a life pleasing to God but up to now has failed to realize his goal.

What should Ernie do? Should he (1) reaffirm the belief that persons stand before God by faith alone, rest in this biblical fact, and simply seek professional help for his personal problem; (2) recall that he is united with Christ and simply trust that Christ's life will be increasingly manifested in him; (3) recall that the Holy Spirit has already given him the power to say no to sin and develop this power through obedient discipleship; or (4) seek a special empowerment of the Holy Spirit that cleanses the heart from impurity and fills it with power for spiritual and moral victory? How you advise Ernie reflects your understanding of sanctification.

The Center and Its Contrasts

Orthodox Christians have always understood that God calls his people not only to *believe* the truth he has revealed but to *live* according to that truth. When people place their trust in Jesus Christ, they are given a new nature and are indwelt by the Holy Spirit, who empowers them to live lives that honor God. God's holy character, revealed in Scripture, is the standard against which all behavior is judged. The process by which believers come to live a God-honoring life is called **sanctification.**

Of course, many non-Christians believe it is important to live a moral life. What distinguishes the Christian perspective, however, is the understanding that humans cannot live up to God's standards on their own power. It is only because God graciously works in and through believers' lives in the power of the Holy Spirit that they can ever hope to live lives that honor God.

Beyond the common understanding that believers are called to live holy lives, there is much disagreement among Christians. The disagreements among evangelicals arise primarily over the relationship between **justification** and sanctification. All agree that believers are justified by grace through faith. But what then does sanctification accomplish? Does it in any sense make one more holy? Is it a necessary part of salvation? And how are Christians to grow in it?

The evangelical options considered in this section offer various answers to these questions. Each view proposes a theological interpretation of the promise, "For sin will have no dominion over you, since you are not under law but under grace" (Rom. 6:14). The first essay expresses the Lutheran perspective, which defines sanctification as living in the faith that one has already been justified. The Reformed view defines sanctification as an outgrowth of participation in Christ. According to the Keswick view, sanctification is achieved only as believers enter into the resting-faith that is the promised gift to all believers through a crisis experience with the Holy Spirit. The final essay articulates the Wesleyan understanding that entire sanctification is not only possible here on earth but is the calling of God for all believers.

Sanctification as a Declaration by God (The Lutheran View)

According to this view, justification and sanctification should never be considered apart from one another. In truth, they are two sides of the same coin. Sanctification is nothing other than learning to live by faith that one is justified because of God's free gift in Jesus Christ. The motivation for living a sanctified life is the belief that God alone saves sinners, independent of anything the believer can do. "For by grace you have been saved through faith, and this is not your own doing; it is the gift of God—not the result of works, so that no one may boast" (Eph. 2:8–9). Sanctification is nothing over and above living out the faith that one has already been declared perfectly holy and righteous for Jesus' sake.

If we as sinners are justified and sanctified by faith alone, there is clearly nothing for us to do—except trust God. This faith foundation creates a dilemma, however. If people cannot contribute to their righteous standing before God, won't they cease living holy lives? In order to resolve this dilemma, many Christians see sanctification as a way of life they must live distinct from and subsequent to justification. They create religious schemes—good and virtuous responsibilities—to present before God in an attempt to secure the divine promise beyond simply accepting it in faith. Justification is thereby transformed into a kind of necessary religious activity that initiates people into the more *serious* business of becoming sanctified. The glory and power of God's declared righteousness (justification) is thereby lost, replaced by human striving to improve on what God has already done. This understanding of sanctification is unbiblical and spiritually disastrous. The proper biblical understanding is that sanctification is nothing over and above the confident trust that God has done what he said he would do in believers when they trust in Christ. He declares them to be holy.

The Biblical Argument

First, fundamental to biblical teaching is the claim that all people are sinners. Scripture is unequivocal on this point: "All have sinned and fall short of the glory of God" (Rom. 3:23). "There is no one who is righteous, not even one" (Rom. 3:10). This biblical assertion is basic to the Lutheran perspective on the Christian life. Sinners are void of the rational and moral capacity to find God apart from divine assistance. Humanity is utterly lost. Sin is not simply a misdeed that needs to be forgiven. It is a state of total rejection of God's right to be God (Rom. 1:21–23), prompted by a lack of faith over against the incredible goodness of God (Rom. 1:21, 25).

The law of God was given to humans because of sin. Its primary purpose was and is to imprison humans in their sinful state. The law bars the door to salvation through all avenues except faith in the redemptive promise of God in Jesus Christ. As the apostle Paul teaches, "But law came in, with the result that the trespass multiplied" (Rom. 5:20), for "no human being will be justified in [God's] sight by deeds prescribed by the law, for through the law comes the knowledge of sin" (Rom. 3:20). The law, therefore, does not exist as a guide for the promotion of holiness; it simply functions to intensify sinfulness. "For sin, seizing an opportunity in the commandment, deceived me and through it killed me" (Rom. 7:11). All attempts to fulfill a set of commands in order to be righteous before God come under the category of the law. As such, all such attempts can succeed only in exposing and increasing sin. The only hope for redemption is to trust that God justifies sinners simply because they trust in the sufficiency of Christ's atoning sacrifice.

While justified sinners remain sinners throughout their earthly lives, they are, nevertheless, at the same time declared righteous and holy by faith on the basis of what Christ has done. This is the unconditional promise of God. An unconditional promise grants something to be true on the basis of the one who promises it. Hence, sinners are declared righteous and holy before God through faith alone in the atoning work of Christ. Scripture permits no other basis. Paul states, "Now to one who works, wages are not reckoned as a gift but as something due. But to one who without works trusts him who justifies the ungodly, such faith is reckoned as righteousness" (Rom. 4:4–5).

True sanctification, then, is simply trusting that God has taken charge of the matter. Sinners realize that their ways are at an end. Nothing can be added to justifying faith. It is a matter of being grasped by the unconditional promise of God and living on the basis of that promise. Here works and religious schemes are nullified. Human efforts—no matter how moral or well intentioned—are excluded. What matters is that God has unconditionally promised righteousness and holiness to sinners through faith in Christ. As Paul proclaims, sinners find not only "wisdom," "righteousness," and "redemption" but also "sanctification," in Christ alone (1 Cor. 1:2, 28–31).

Second, as sinners declared just and holy (sanctified) by faith alone in what Jesus has done, we still struggle. The struggle, however, is not a Dr. Jekyll/Mr. Hyde conflict between two opposing dispositions (old nature versus new nature or flesh versus the Spirit). Rather, the old self denotes the unwillingness to rely completely on the unconditional promise of justification by faith alone (Eph. 2:8–9). As old beings, we add requirements to sanctification, separating it from justification, believing that our good, virtuous deeds matter before the bar of divine accountability, for if justification by faith alone is true, all works are eliminated and the old being must die—die to the possibility of contributing to righteousness by deeds. But old beings do not want to die, to be shorn of all defenses and claims. Justification by faith alone means we must be reborn, not by our efforts, even our sanctifying ones, but by God (John 3:1–8). Thus, the question is, Can we live as though justification by faith alone is true?

Finally, the Christian life is not a matter of moving toward a goal but rather having a new life supernaturally arise in us. As Paul emphatically states, "If anyone is in Christ, there is a new creation: everything old has passed away; see, everything has become new!" (2 Cor. 5:17). God alone brings forth a new creation through the Holy Spirit independent of our good deeds (Gal. 6:15). Progress or growth in the Christian life lies in beginning again, and beginning again means being continually captivated by the unconditionality of the grace of God. It is a matter of accepting the fact that if we are to be saved, it will have to be by grace alone. We are sanctified when we come to trust that God will in the end have his way with us—independent of our supposed spiritual achievements.

Supporting Arguments

1. *Christian realism*. The Lutheran understanding of sanctification best squares with common Christian experience. Regardless of how earnestly Christians strive to live holy lives, every Christian knows deep in his or her heart that he or she remains a sinner saved by grace. As Scripture teaches, "If we say that we have no sin, we deceive ourselves, and the truth is not in us" (1 John 1:8). The Lutheran view of sanctification simply accepts this as fact. While growth in the life of faith is expected, believers know they will never outgrow their radical dependence on God's grace to be reconciled to him.

2. *Faith and pride*. If people think that sanctification adds anything to their justification, there is room for them to become spiritually prideful. At the very least, they can begin to congratulate themselves that they are less in need of God's sheer grace than they once were and no doubt less in need than other believers now are. They may think this is the result of their persistent obedience (the Reformed view), their increased faith in their identity in Christ (the Keswick view), or their becoming open to the infilling of the Holy Spirit (the Wesleyan view). By contrast, when believers emphasize that they are always saved sinners, whatever level of maturity they have attained, they remain aware that they are totally dependent on God's grace. Thus, this view preserves humility in the hearts of Christians.

Responding to Objections

1. *Faith requires expression through good works*. While all evangelicals agree that sinners are justified by faith alone, some object to the Lutheran view on the grounds that faith has to be expressed through works. James writes, "What good is it, my brothers and sisters, if you say you have faith

but do not have works? Can faith save you? . . . Faith by itself, if it has no works, is dead" (James 2:14, 17). Thus, some claim that the Lutheran perspective can easily lead one to adopt a view of **cheap grace.**

Admittedly, Scripture presents commands to believers, summoning them to walk in obedience to these commands. They are, for example, commanded to "live in love" (Eph. 5:2), "please" God (2 Tim. 2:4), "pursue . . . holiness without which no one will see the Lord" (Heb. 12:14), and not let sin reign in their mortal bodies (Rom. 6:12). But these commands do not mean that humans are to add good behavior to their righteousness in Christ. Rather, they are the means by which believers open their lives to the transforming grace of God through the work of the Holy Spirit. Believers are called to express their exclusive relationship with Christ by the way they live. Believers are not to remain stagnant but are summoned to grow in Christlikeness and to progress in victory over sin. While believers must constantly return to their foundation in the grace of God, they are nevertheless to progress toward the goal of spiritual maturity (Heb. 6:1). Paul writes, "Now to one who works, wages are not reckoned as a gift but as something due. But to one who without works trusts him who justifies the ungodly, such faith is reckoned as righteousness" (Rom. 4:4–5). If faith includes works in any form, then faith is no longer faith but obligation.

The importance of living a life pleasing to God is not neglected or abandoned by Lutherans. Good works simply constitute an expression of a believer's faith. Lutheran believers walk in righteousness, holiness, and love because they believe (trust) that God's directives constitute the right way to live, not because such good deeds form a new basis by which believers stand before the grace and love of God.

2. *This view turns imputed righteousness into a legal fiction.* Critics of this view often argue that its understanding of justifying grace is defective. According to the Lutheran view, justification is that work of Christ that transforms believers positionally; in the act of justification, God declares believers to be, legally speaking, righteous before him. This declaration, however, has absolutely nothing to do with actual behavior, since if it did, believers would be right back in the quagmire of works-righteousness. However, critics suggest that this view reduces sanctification to nothing more than a legal fiction—God declares believers to be something that they, in fact, are not. Ultimately, believers cannot truly expect to be anything more than relationship-breaking sinners until they reach heaven. The supposed example that Christ left is something believers can never really expect to follow. But the simple fact that Paul himself imitated Christ in his walk and calls Christians to do the same (1 Cor. 11:1; Eph. 5:1–2; Phil. 2:5–11; cf. 1 John 2:3–6) reveals the inherent problem of the Lutheran view's pessimistic attitude regarding a believer's ability to attain to true holiness on earth.

In response to this objection, we note that a criticism similar to this was entertained by Paul when he set out his understanding of justifying grace. Upon explaining the notion of justification by grace through faith alone, Paul anticipated the critic's question: "What then are we to say? Should we continue in sin in order that grace may abound?" (Rom. 6:1). This criticism is precisely the sort of question one would raise if he or she truly understood the gift of free grace in Jesus Christ! The justifying grace of God is radical, total, and uncompromising. It cannot be gained or supplemented—either before or after conversion—in any way, shape, or form. Some may complain that this reduces holiness to a mere legal fiction, but this is to cast the glorious gift of pure and free grace in an unnecessarily negative light. Justification is not a legal fiction; it is rather a legal fact! The Greek term used in the New Testament for "righteousness" is derived from the Roman court system and literally means "to declare righteous." Justification means that apart from human works God declares sinners to be righteous before him. Declared, imputed righteousness is a scandal to be sure, but it is not a scandal of legal fiction. Rather, it is a scandal of the infinite and uncompromising love of God toward sinners, such that he utterly and completely saves them apart from even the slightest effort on their part. It is the scandal of grace without works, of love without strings, of right-standing before God without human effort or boasting of any kind.

Sanctification as Holiness in Christ and in Personal Conduct (The Reformed [Calvinist] View)

The Reformed view of sanctification arises from the biblical exposition advanced primarily at the time of the Reformation. It is particularly associated, however, with the writings of John Calvin. The Reformed view anchors its interpretation in the biblical teaching that believers are united with Christ in his death and resurrection through faith and that from participation *in Christ,* holiness of life can emerge.

The Biblical Argument

The New Testament unequivocally declares Christ to be the author and guarantor of sanctification (Heb. 12:2). Christ is the first and only fully sanctified person. "He has climbed God's holy hill," writes Reformed theologian Sinclair Ferguson, "with clean hands and a pure heart (Ps. 24:3–6). It is as the *Lead Climber* that he gives the sanctification he has won to others (Acts 5:31)."[1] "For their sakes I sanctify myself," declared Jesus, "so that they also may be sanctified in truth" (John 17:19). "The one who sanctifies and those who are sanctified all have one Father" (Heb. 2:11). Jesus has sanctified human nature in himself so that those who believe in him may share in that sanctification through union with him by faith. Paul, therefore, writes, "He is the source of your life in Christ Jesus, who became for us wisdom from God, and righteousness and sanctification and redemption" (1 Cor. 1:30). The sanctification Christ imparts to believers through the Holy Spirit is, on the one hand, *definitive,* and on the other, *progressive.*

Definitive sanctification means that believers are sanctified in Christ and that no further sacrifices or rituals are required to keep them in that sanctified condition. While Reformed teachers recognize that sanctification is a lifelong process, they note that the more characteristic teaching in the New Testament refers not to a process but to a once-and-for-all—never needing to be repeated—definitive act. The author of the Epistle to the Hebrews explains this once-and-for-all definitive act of sanctification by which God consecrates people through Jesus' sacrifice for sin with the words "we have been sanctified" (Heb. 10:10). By the once-and-for-all offering of himself in death, Christ "has perfected for all time those who are sanctified" (Heb. 10:14). Paul, therefore, can refer to believers as "those who are sanctified in Christ Jesus" (1 Cor. 1:2) or as "saints" (Rom. 1:7; Eph. 1:1). Definitive sanctification, therefore, means that believers are sanctified through their union with Christ and that this sanctified state constitutes their permanent status before God.

While believers are definitively sanctified through union with Christ, they are also called to express this distinctive and exclusive relationship by the way they live. Reformed teaching asserts that upon union with Christ, believers are transferred from the household of Adam—from the reign of sin—into the family of Christ and into the provisions of God's grace (Rom. 6:3–4). Paul refers to this transfer when he writes that believers are both "baptized into [Christ's] death" (Rom. 6:3) and "baptized into one body" (1 Cor. 12:13). Upon repentance and faith, believing sinners are united with Christ through the baptizing work of the Holy Spirit. The Holy Spirit indwells believers and changes them motivationally and dispositionally in the core of their being. This is what is meant by regeneration or being born again. Because the Spirit indwells believers at conversion, the Spirit is the source by which this new life grows from infancy to spiritual maturity. Paul, therefore, admonishes, "Live by [walk in] the Spirit . . . and do not gratify the desires of the flesh" (Gal. 5:16).

Union with Christ emits further benefits for progressing in godliness. Paul states that believers have died to sin (Rom. 6:2; Col. 3:3). "Death to sin" does not mean that believers have died to the enticements and allurements of sin, nor does it mean that they cannot sin (Rom. 6:12; 1 John 2:1). Rather, it means that the reign or dictatorial control of sin has been broken for those who are united with Christ. It teaches that a once-and-for-all definitive and irreversible break with the realm in which sin reigns has occurred. Having been transferred from the realm of sin and incorporated (baptized) into Christ's death, believers now reside in a household in which sin no longer has the right to dictate (Rom. 6:14) and where condemnation no longer exists (Rom. 8:1).

As new persons, however, believers must avoid the conclusion that being a new self implies a life of sinlessness. Believers are *genuinely new*, though not yet *totally new*.[2] John Murray expresses the Reformed view clearly:

> The newness of the new self is not static but dynamic, needing continual renewal, growth, and transformation. A believer deeply conscious of his or her shortcoming does not need to say, because I am still a sinner, I cannot consider myself a new person. Rather, he or she should say, I am a new person, but I still have a lot of growing to do.[3]

Believers are new persons who are being progressively renewed. They still battle sin and will sometimes fall into sin, but they are no longer slaves to sin. Through union with Christ and the power of the Holy Spirit, they are now able to resist sin, because for every temptation God will provide a way of escape (1 Cor. 10:13).

The primary agent of change in the lives of believers is the Holy Spirit. The Spirit transforms believers at the center of their being so that the desires and attitude of Christ are reproduced in them. The Spirit is the power that induces and energizes the newly implanted desire to love, trust, obey, and praise God. The Spirit's ministry, however, is complemented by obedience to God's law and the practice of Christian discipleship.

Obedience entails more than conformity to a preestablished set of behavioral standards. It involves an unconditional commitment of faith in Christ and centers on the lordship of Christ. Because no other source for the realization of the freedom purchased by Christ exists, believers are exhorted to obey their new Master with a slave-like commitment that leads to holiness (Rom. 6:15–22). "But now that you have been freed from sin and enslaved to God, the advantage you get is sanctification. The end is eternal life" (Rom. 6:22). Obedience, therefore, is essentially an issue of faith and love. Faith shows in obedience to Christ, because believers cannot confess Jesus as Lord of their lives and at the same time ignore his gracious guiding of their lives. Further, God loved humans so much that the only appropriate response is to love God in return (1 John 4:10–11). Love for God is shown in obedience to him—a heartfelt willingness to do all for God who has done all for us.

Supporting Argument

Balancing realism and optimism. The Reformed understanding of sanctification balances the New Testament's optimism in believers' ability to conquer sin with the undeniable reality that they remain sinners in need of God's grace throughout life. This cannot be said of the other three views of sanctification.

The Lutheran perspective is certainly realistic in acknowledging the Christian's ongoing struggle with sin, but it is not adequate in affirming the *real change* that occurs when a person is united with Christ. While believers are not all they should be, can be, and shall be, they are also not what they once were. "In Christ" they are new creations!

The Wesleyan and Keswick views affirm that a believer is a new being in Christ and has therefore been empowered to live a holy life. But they do not adequately account for the undeniable reality that, despite their most earnest efforts, believers remain sinners saved by grace. Despite the truth that they have been changed in Christ, Christians must perpetually strive against the flesh to set aside the old self that continually plagues them. The Reformed view best explains and balances these two realities. It thus encourages believers to be humble before God while being confident in their ability to make progress in sanctification.

Responding to Objections

1. *This view risks the danger of human pride.* We must take great care in talking about progress in sanctification as though we can bring it about. In this light, some fault the Reformed view for failing to accept fully the fact that, *even as Christians*, we are still sinners and that our justification and sanctification reside fully in God's declaration. Sanctification is not something sinners can achieve. It is the exclusive work of God through the agency of the Holy Spirit. Changes in attitude and actions lie entirely in the work of God. To claim that we are in any sense responsible for the production of spiritual change not only expresses human pride—the essence of all sin—but also nullifies the central biblical teaching that sinners are justified by faith alone.

In response to this objection, we reiterate the Reformed conviction that sanctification is grounded exclusively in Christ. The Reformed view emphasizes that sanctification is never the consequence of human effort; it lies exclusively in the life, death, and resurrection of Christ. Christ alone is the source and guarantor of sanctification. John Calvin put the point unequivocally.

> We see that our whole salvation and all its parts are comprehended in Christ (Acts 4:12). We should therefore take care not to derive the least portion of

it from anywhere else. If we seek salvation, we are taught by the very name of Jesus that it is "of him" (1 Cor. 1:30). If we seek any other gifts of the Spirit, they will be found in his anointing . . . if purity, in his conception; if gentleness, it appears in his birth; . . . if newness of life, in his resurrection. . . . In short, since rich store of every kind of good abounds in him, let us drink our fill from this fountain, and from no other.[4]

2. *Sanctification is more than moral imperatives.* Some argue that the Reformed view interprets sanctification within a performance context, that is, a life of obedience, while Scripture presents sanctification within a relational context, that is, the living of a life of love toward God and one's neighbor. Paul admonishes, "Owe no one anything, except to love one another; for the one who loves another has fulfilled the law" (Rom. 13:8). Jesus likewise summarized the law as "love the Lord your God with all your heart, and with all your soul, and with all your strength, and with all your mind; and your neighbor as yourself" (Luke 10:27). The heart of sanctification is not first doing but first being—being a person whose life is dominated and guided by the love of God.

As previously stated, according to the Reformed view, obedience constitutes a response of gratitude and love and does not create a second basis beyond justification for remaining in the grace and love of God. The Heidelberg Catechism expresses the Reformed view.

Since we are redeemed from our sin and its wretched consequences by faith through Christ without any merit of our own, why must we do good works? Answer: Because just as Christ has redeemed us with his blood, he also renews us through his Holy Spirit according to his own image, so that with our whole life we may show ourselves grateful to God for his goodness and that he may be glorified through us; and further, so that we ourselves may be assured of our faith by its fruits and by our reverent behavior may win our neighbors to Christ.[5]

In the Reformed view, moral imperatives (commands) are always derived from the indicatives (our being in Christ). The indicatives of the Christian life refer to the life, death, and resurrection of Christ—i.e., to the fruit of Christ's redemptive work on behalf of sinners. They constitute the basis for God's granting forgiveness and holiness to sinful persons. The call to obedience always flows from or follows the indicatives by way of a conclusion. The biblical teaching is "because . . . therefore." *Because* Christ has triumphed over sin, we are *therefore* summoned to walk in newness of life. To draw an analogy: *Because* I place ten million dollars in your bank account (the indicative), I can *therefore* admonish you to pay your bills. The admonition to obey (the imperative) is extended *because* the provision has already been made that makes possible the response of obedience. The imperatives (commands) of the Christian life, therefore, never form new indicatives but emerge as a *consequence* of the indicative.

Sanctification as Resting-Faith in the Sufficiency of Christ (The Keswick "Deeper Life" View)

The higher or deeper life view of holiness is associated, though not exclusively, with the Keswick message. Keswick locates its historical origin in England (1873–1875) and later adopted the name of an English town, Keswick, located in the North Lakes district of the United Kingdom, where its annual convention was held for many years. (Keswick conferences were also held in the United States, Canada, Asia, etc.) Keswick is a nondenominational movement that interprets the life of holiness principally through the lens of Paul's teaching encapsulated in Romans 6–8.

The Keswick message was pointedly expressed in its first publication:

> We believe that the Word of God teaches that the *normal* Christian life is one of uniform sustained victory over known sin . . . that a life of faith and victory, of peace and rest, are the rightful heritage of every child of God, and that he [she] may step into it . . . not by long prayers and laborious effort, but by a deliberate and decisive act of faith. The normal experience of the child of God should be one of victory instead of constant defeat, one of liberty instead of grinding bondage, one of "perfect peace" instead of restless worry . . . that in Christ there is provided for every believer victory, liberty, and rest, and that this may be obtained not by a lifelong struggle after an impossible ideal but by a surrender of the individual to God, and the indwelling of the Holy Spirit.[6]

The Biblical Argument

The death and resurrection of Christ have provided for every believer a life of victory over sin. Christ has conquered sin and only through union with him through the Holy Spirit is his accomplished victory available to believers. They have no life or holiness except as they abide in Christ and Christ in them (John 15:4–5). By believers' consent, Christ gains and keeps the heart, transferring his victory and his life to their spiritual needs. Christ meets the force of sin through the Holy Spirit to the extent that believers are no longer hindered in their spiritual progress or robbed of their peace. Paul writes, "How can we who died to sin go on living in it? Do you not know that all of us who have been baptized into Christ Jesus were baptized into his death? Therefore we have been buried with him by baptism into death, so that, just as Christ was raised from the dead by the glory of the Father, so we too might walk in newness of life" (Rom. 6:2–4). This blessing of victory, liberty, and rest actualized through Christ's death and resurrection is the rightful heritage of every believer.

Still, the sinful nature remains in the believer following conversion, contending with the new (Spirit-given) nature for control of the believer's attitudes and conduct. Scripture affirms that there is a constant struggle within every believer between the old nature and the new nature or between the flesh and the Spirit. These two natures stand armed and militant against each other, battling for control of the believer's life. The consequence is that spiritual conflict—often of desperate proportions—erupts in the life of the believer, distinctly illustrated in Romans 7:15, 22–24: "I do not understand my own actions. For I do not do what I want, but I do the very thing I hate. . . . For I delight in the law of God in my inmost self, but I see in my members another law at war with the law of my mind, making me captive to the law of sin that dwells in my members. Wretched man that I am! Who will rescue me from this body of death?" Writing to the Galatian believers, Paul again describes this unremitting struggle between the two opposing impulses in the heart of the believer: "For what the flesh desires is opposed to the Spirit, and what the Spirit desires is opposed to the flesh; for these are opposed to each other, to prevent you from doing what you want" (Gal. 5:17). The reason for the failure lies in the flesh that prevents the Spirit-initiated desires from coming to fruition. No matter how disciplined or determined the believer is in his or her natural self, the believer is powerless in the struggle against sin and the flesh.

Victory over sin and, consequently, a life of holiness require total surrender to God. Paul admonishes, "Present [yield, surrender, offer] yourselves to God as those who have been brought from death to life" (Rom. 6:13). Upon unconditional surrender to God, the Holy Spirit takes control of the life of the believer. Deliverance from the dictatorial reign of sin is the result of a higher and mightier power—the power of the Spirit of life in Christ Jesus. Victory over sin, therefore, is not a matter of suppression, eradication, or the ability to perform virtuous deeds; rather, it lies in the counteraction of the Spirit, who controls the surrendered believer.

Total surrender, however, normally involves a crisis experience in which the believer comes to the realization of his or her total impotence in the presence of sin's overwhelming power. The crisis is further deepened by the awareness that even the believer's striving to be holy is often done in the flesh, creating the cry, "Wretched man that I am! Who will rescue me from this body of death?" (Rom. 7:24). The experience of spiritual victory emerges as the direct consequence of (1) a total surrender to God, acknowledging that the natural self cannot overcome sin, and (2) resting-faith in Christ, who has conquered sin. This act of complete surrender to God and the indwelling Holy Spirit is analogous to the surrender of a believer's life in faith to the justifying Christ.

Resting-faith in the provisions of Christ's death and resurrection is the key to victory over sin and a life of godliness. The believer ceases striving to be holy in his or her natural self, confesses his or her spiritual bankruptcy, and reckons himself or herself dead to sin but alive to God (Rom. 6:11–12). Faith alone resting in Christ's accomplishments constitutes the path to holiness, characterized by freedom over sin and a life of joy and peace through the indwelling Holy Spirit (Rom. 6:8–11). "A sabbath rest still remains," writes the author of the Epistle to the Hebrews, "for the people of God; for those who enter God's rest also cease from their labors as God did from his" (Heb. 4:9–10).

Upon the act of surrender, the Holy Spirit fills (takes control of) the believer, empowering him or her to resist sin and to live a life pleasing to God. The Holy Spirit is the counter-effecting power to sin and the sinful nature. Paul writes, "For the law of the Spirit of life in Christ Jesus has set you free from the law of sin and of death" (Rom. 8:2). This disposition of resting-faith constitutes a definite act separate from regeneration. It is the response of the believer to the biblical command to surrender his or her life to the indwelling Holy Spirit (Eph. 5:18) and to rest by faith in the victory accomplished by Christ's death and resurrection (Rom. 6:11–13; 8:13–14; 12:2; Col. 3:9–10; 1 Thess. 4:1–2).

Supporting Argument

Experiencing freedom here and now. Of all the views, the Keswick view offers believers the most practical way to gain victory over sin. Often believers despair of living a victorious life, for they assume that because their struggle with sin is severe, this is a far-off if not unattainable goal. They may simply accept that they are sinners (the Lutheran view). They may conclude that, though they are united with Christ, they can make only slow and gradual progress over years of obedient living (the Reformed view). Or they may conclude that they must wait for a supernatural experience (the infilling of the Holy Spirit) that will free them from sin once and for all (the Wesleyan view). These views fall short of empowering believers *here and now* because none of these views frees believers from the mistaken belief that sin still has power over them.

Things immediately change for people, however, when they are encouraged to have faith, on the authority of God's Word, that sin has no power over them. It is only their lack of faith that prevents them from experiencing this truth. When believers exercise faith and cease from their own striving, they can experience here and now the truth that they are "dead to sin and alive to God in Christ Jesus" (Rom. 6:11).

Responding to Objections

1. *This view focuses exclusively on the act of surrender.* Some critics of the Keswick view argue that its danger lies in the presumption that one does not really possess the Spirit—i.e., the Spirit's power—until the act of total surrender is made. Such an inference, they say, tends to focus the believer's concern exclusively on this one supreme act of surrender to the Spirit, indirectly divorcing the Spirit's task from its connection with the atoning work of Christ. These critics see this as a deviation from New Testament teaching. John writes, "When the Spirit of truth comes, he will guide you into all the truth; for he will not speak on his own. . . . He will glorify me, because he will take what is mine and declare it to you" (John 16:13–15). So inseparably connected is the Spirit with the work and person of Christ, critics argue, that the New Testament knows no work of the Spirit except in and through the context of the work of Christ. Moreover, they ask, what happens if a believer unfortunately is never taught the necessity of this one supreme act of surrender? Will his or her Christian life always remain in some sense deficient? To be a Christian in the New Testament sense means to possess the Spirit (Rom. 8:9–11), whose indwelling presence is constantly striving to reproduce in believers spiritual fruit as a consequence of Christ's atoning work.

In responding to this objection, it must be reiterated that the ground of this act of surrender is nothing more nor less than the powerful saving work of Jesus Christ! The surrender is surrender to God through Jesus Christ. The result is the empowerment of the Holy Spirit. Surrendering to God is not an act of resignation; rather, it entails placing one's life completely in the hands of God. It is not surrender *from* but surrender *to*—a relinquishing of oneself to a new master who alone possesses the spiritual resources for victory over sin. It is an act of complete faith in God's promise that Christ's victory over sin has been secured. The surrender constitutes an abandonment of self-effort and a reliance by faith on the indwelling Holy Spirit. There is no rivalry between an original conversion to Christ and a subsequent act of surrender to that same Christ.

2. *Resting-faith is itself a crisis.* Some critics of the Keswick view pose a more practical problem: What happens if the victory over sin does not occur? If victory lies in resting-faith and the victory does not happen, the failure, then, must lie in the resting-faith, since Christ's victory is not deficient. But how does a person acquire more resting-faith? This dilemma, they say, causes the experiential basis of victory to reside in the believer's capacity to actualize the resting-faith. Thus, the life of holiness and victory is now transferred from Christ to the believer's ability to offer a sufficient

amount of consecrating-faith to actualize the victory, making the acquisition of more resting-faith itself a serious issue.

In response to this objection, we stress that resting-faith centers in Christ alone, not in the believer's ability to create the resting-faith. As Scripture clearly states, "Those who enter God's rest also cease from their labors as God did from his" (Heb. 4:10). Resting-faith lies wholly in the One who has promised the victory. It constitutes a personal commitment to God, who has offered victory over sin and newness of life in Christ. It is the object of the resting-faith—not the disposition of faith—that constitutes the sum and substance of the act of faith.

3. *Not all spiritual striving is of the flesh.* Critics object to the Keswick inference that all human initiative to walk in holiness is tainted by the energy of the flesh. The admonition to yield or surrender to God, however, is not a summons to inactivity but a call to report for duty. Believers should build spiritual disciplines in their lives that assist them in saying no to sin and yes to those biblical principles that promote Christian character and conduct. J. I. Packer rightly counsels, "If you are fighting a bad habit, work out before God a strategy for ensuring that you will not fall victim to it again, ask [God] to bless your [strategy], and go out in [God's] strength, ready to say *no* the next time temptation comes."[7] Surrender means presenting oneself to God and then serving God and believing that in every temptation God has provided a way of escape (1 Cor. 10:13).

Entire Sanctification as Perfect Love (The Wesleyan View)

The Wesleyan view of sanctification begins with the insight that in the Bible the concept of holiness centers on relationship with God. It denotes not what believers are separated from but to whom they are consecrated. The temple, the priests, the temple objects, and so on were holy because they belonged exclusively to God. Holiness or sanctification, therefore, refers first and foremost to an exclusive relationship with Christ, the holy One. It is a matter of the heart, of right relationship, and is not to be judged in terms of a predetermined set of objective religious standards.

The Biblical Argument

A right relationship with God entails cleansing from sin. The notion of cleansing permeates Scripture. Words such as *wash*, *purge*, *prune*, and so on, writes Charles Carter, "transcend their material sense and refer to a work of God that relieves the human heart of its impurity as earthly detergents remove material contamination. The emphasis is on the thoroughness of the cleansing rather than on the choice of the figure under which it is presented."[8] The focus of cleansing is the removal of the cause of the defilement, namely, inbred sin. "Purge me with hyssop," requests David, "and I shall be clean; wash me, and I shall be whiter than snow. . . . Wash me thoroughly from my iniquity, and cleanse me from my sin" (Ps. 51:7, 2). The thorough cleansing from the pollution of inbred sin makes possible a relationship of unbroken fellowship with Christ.

The promise of unbroken fellowship is reenforced by the biblical view of sin. Sin is not a thing, like a decayed tooth, but an attitude of the heart—a disposition of pride that God promises to cleanse from the life of the consecrated believer. This cleansing explains John's perplexing words: "Those who have been born of God do not sin, because God's seed abides in them; they cannot sin, because they have been born of God" (1 John 3:9). If sin is understood in a legal sense—i.e., any breaking of God's law, accidental or deliberate—then John's words are difficult to explain, since no one is perfect in external conduct. But if sin is a matter of the heart, and if the heart is cleansed from inbred sin, a believer can be perfect in attitude or heart even though his or her external actions may, at some point, be defective. This gift of God's grace, through the Holy Spirit, that cleanses the heart from inbred sin and fills it with the love of God is available to every believer following conversion. Wesleyans call this gift entire sanctification. Paul, himself, refers to this idea when he prays, "May the God of peace himself sanctify you entirely; and may your spirit and soul and body be kept sound and blameless" (1 Thess. 5:23).

According to the Wesleyan view, the first gift of grace is forgiveness of sin through the Son. Entire sanctification is the second gift of grace. Wesleyans take seriously the scriptural texts that call believers to a higher life of Christian devotion, to having their hearts *entirely* cleansed from sin (1 Thess. 5:23; Heb. 9:14; 10:22). The word *entire* should not be taken in a static, rationalistic way. It denotes "a quality of being, not a quantitative measurement." In other words, it refers to the quality and purity of love, not to the degree of love.[9]

The fact that a second gift of God's grace is available to all believers finds its confirmation in Scripture (cf. Acts 1:8). Acts 8:14–17 and 19:1–7, for example, record the experience of the Samaritan and Ephesian believers and illustrate the truth that one may have faith in Christ and yet not have received the empowering fullness (cleansing) of the Holy Spirit. The New Testament, therefore, makes a distinction in Christian experience between the reception of the Son and the reception of the Holy Spirit (Acts 10:1–46; 18:24–26). Thus, a believer may experience the forgiveness of sin through the Son and then subsequently enter into the empowerment of the Spirit, who cleanses the heart from inbred sin and fills it with the love of God.

Entire sanctification is nothing more or less than having the heart filled with the love of God. John wrote:

> God is love, and those who abide in love abide in God, and God abides in them. Love has been perfected among us in this: that we may have boldness on the day of judgment, because as he is, so are we in this world. There is no fear in love, but perfect love casts out fear; for fear has to do with punishment, and whoever fears has not reached perfection in love. (1 John 4:16–18)

Wesley described the experience of entire sanctification as having "the mind of Christ," as "walking as Christ walked"; it is "to have a heart so all-flaming with the love of God . . . as continually to offer up every thought, word and work, as a spiritual sacrifice, acceptable to God through Christ."[10] It is love expelling sin and governing both the heart and life. Wesley further described it as a "circumcision of the heart" (Rom. 2:28–29)—"that habitual disposition of soul which, in the sacred writings, is termed holiness." It refers to a "cleansing from all filthiness of both flesh and spirit and, by consequence, [to a person] endued with those virtues which were also in Christ Jesus."[11] Entire sanctification is a gift available to every believer through the Holy Spirit and is entered into by faith and surrender to God following conversion.

Supporting Arguments

1. *The root of the problem*. Of the four views evangelicals hold on sanctification, the Wesleyan view alone focuses the process of sanctification on its proper object—the love of God. The problem of ongoing sin in the lives of believers is nothing other than a deficiency of heartfelt love for their Creator and Savior. This is the fundamental issue involved in the process of sanctification.

The other three views fail to articulate the power available to believers for holy living because they mistake *symptoms* of a problem for the *source* of the problem. By focusing on sinfulness, the Lutheran and Reformed views underemphasize the power that perfect love for God has to transform believers in this life. People can believe they are holy in Christ and can strive to live out this holiness, but unless they are filled with perfect love for God, their motivation will fall short of attaining their objective.

Similarly, by focusing exclusively on the faith of believers, the Keswick view underemphasizes the role the heart plays in motivating people to live out what they know to be true. People can seek to rest in the faith that they are free from sin in Christ all they want, but unless their hearts are filled with a passionate love for God, resting in this faith will not result in sin-free living. Only a perfect love for God can cause what one *believes* to make a profound impact on how that person *lives*.

2. *Optimism and dependency*. With the Keswick view, and against the Lutheran and Reformed views, the Wesleyan view of sanctification emphasizes the power of God to transform believers in the present. God's promise to believers that they can live victoriously is not a legal fiction or merely an eschatological promise.

At the same time, the Wesleyan view does not accept that this victorious living can come about merely by exercising a stronger faith, as the Keswick view teaches. This almost reduces sanctification to a version of "the power of positive thinking" theme that is popular in our culture. Rather, faith is only as powerful as the love that motivates it. As Scripture uniformly teaches, this love is not something believers can *will* or *think* themselves into. It can come only as a gift from God, through the power of the Holy Spirit filling a heart. In this way, the Wesleyan view captures the optimism of the Keswick view while preserving the necessity of dependence on God advocated by the Lutheran and Reformed views.

Responding to Objections

1. *This view minimizes the work of justification and misunderstands the work of the Holy Spirit*. Some critics of the Wesleyan view claim that the two-stage process minimizes the reception of justifying grace in Christ at conversion. It implies, they say, that the first experience of grace is somehow less important than the subsequent one. In other words, the first step in the process appears more or less a platform for the subsequent second bigger and better step. This two-stage scheme unfortunately minimizes the unconditional justifying grace of God, reducing it to an initiatory role. Beyond this, critics often argue that if regeneration is an indispensable component of conversion, and if regeneration is the work of the Holy Spirit, and if the Holy Spirit is a person and therefore cannot be segmentally divided, then believers receive the complete personhood of the Holy Spirit at conversion. To experience a heart captivated by the love of God, or to have one's soul abound with kindness, meekness, gentleness, and so on does not require a separate or second reception of grace. It simply entails the ongoing work of the indwelling Spirit, who produces spiritual fruit in the life of the believer. While the experience is right, the requirement of a second step of cleansing faith beyond justification is theologically inaccurate.

In response to these criticisms, we begin, first, with a clear proclamation that justification in Christ is the grounding, root, and source of all spiritual blessings a believer will ever inherit. The Wesleyan view does not minimize justifying grace. On the contrary, the Wesleyan perspective emphasizes the power of justifying grace by boldly proclaiming that this first work of grace was designed to eventuate in something more than a mere forensic declaration of righteousness. According to the Lutheran view, for example, believers are understood as receiving an "imputed" righteousness that may or may not actually result in a holy life. But this kind of righteousness is mere legal fiction. Believers are declared righteous without necessarily living out this righteousness in their thoughts, words, and deeds. This is a defective and weak view of justifying grace. According to the Wesleyan view, however, when God makes believers righteous, he does not merely impute it in a legal fashion. Rather, at the same time he truly *imparts* righteousness to the believer, as evidenced by the living of a sanctified life.

Regarding the argument against a two-stage scheme, we simply note that Scripture itself makes a clear distinction between baptism/conversion and the reception of the Holy Spirit at Pentecost. Representative texts are found in the experience of the Samaritan believers (Acts 8:4–25), the experience of the Ephesian believers (Acts 19:1–7), and the experience of the disciples (John 20:22; Acts 2:1–21). In John 20:22, for example, Jesus breathed on the disciples and said, "Receive the Holy Spirit." Then in Acts 2:1–4 these same disciples received the Spirit a second time on the day of Pentecost. The New Testament, therefore, distinguishes between the dispensation of the sending of the Son and the sending of the Spirit as it does between the ministry of the cross and that of the Pentecostal Spirit (or between the Exodus deliverance and the promised rest in the land of Canaan). These two dispensations represent two gifts, two ministries of God's grace: forgiveness of sin and the empowering presence of the Spirit. Holiness of life will remain only a quest and never an experience apart from the cleansing and filling gift of the Holy Spirit.

2. *Perfection is a heavy burden.* Many critics of the Wesleyan view point out that the admonition to live a life of perfection is a heavy burden to carry, even if it is a perfection of the heart and not a perfection of deeds. The burden, they say, is intensified by the fact that the status of perfection is bound up with the believer's ability to consciously resist sin in his or her heart. The New Testament, however, does not speak of the Christian life in terms of human perfection but in terms of developmental growth toward spiritual maturity. Hence, the New Testament word for "perfect" is best translated in a developmental context as (personal) maturity. The admonition, "Be perfect . . . as your heavenly Father is perfect" (Matt. 5:48), for example, is not a summons to moral perfection of the heart but a call to believers to respond in acts of mercy and kindness, especially toward their enemies, in the same manner as God responds. This insight, critics

argue, even calls into question the Wesleyan distinction between deliberate sin and sin as attitude or intent. The New Testament's declarations of sin as propensity and sin as act are related to each other as cause and effect. There are not two kinds of wrong deeds, those of the heart and those of conduct. Sinful acts are produced by a sinful disposition. Sin is sin, whether done accidentally or deliberately. John writes, "Everyone who commits sin is guilty of lawlessness; sin is lawlessness [law breaking]" (1 John 3:4).

In response, we can only emphasize once again that—like it or not— perfection is a biblical admonition. The summons to a life of perfection or blamelessness is not a Wesleyan creation but is decreed by Scripture. Scripture demands that righteousness exceed the perfection of deeds displayed by the Scribes and Pharisees (Matt. 15:20) and that believers are to be perfect as the heavenly Father is perfect (Matt. 5:45). Believers are summoned to a perfection in love that casts out all fear (1 John 4:12, 18). This promised perfection is the work of the Holy Spirit, who cleanses the heart from inbred sin and fills it with divine love, which expresses itself in perfect devotion to God and love for one's neighbor (1 John 4:12).

In answering the claim that the Bible makes no distinction between deliberate sin and sin as attitude or intent, Wesleyans point to Scripture. In the Bible, sin is an ethical concept. If sin is interpreted in a legal context, that is, in terms of the deeds we perform, the words of John, namely, "Those who have been born of God do not sin, because God's seed abides in them; they cannot sin, because they have been born of God" (1 John 3:9), become impossible to understand. But if sin is interpreted as a matter of the intent of the heart, as an ethical concept, the text becomes comprehensible. Freedom from sin has to do with the heart. If the heart is thoroughly purged, right deeds naturally will follow. Believers, therefore, are promised freedom from willful or deliberate sin in their hearts, though they may be defective in some unknown requirement of external conduct. But even though believers may be made perfect in love, they are still in need of the atoning work of Christ.

Further Reading

Alexander, Donald L., ed. *Christian Spirituality: Five Views on Sanctification*. Downers Grove, IL: InterVarsity, 1988.

Barabas, Steven. *So Great Salvation: The History and Message of the Keswick Convention*. Eugene, OR: Wipf and Stock, 2005.

Bayer, Oswald. *Living by Faith: Justification and Sanctification*. Translated by Geoffrey Bromiley. Lutheran Quarterly Books. Grand Rapids: Eerdmans, 2003.

Beeke, Joel R. *Holiness: God's Call to Sanctification*. Edinburgh: Banner of Truth Trust, 1994.

Brower, Kent E., and Andy Johnson, eds. *Holiness and Ecclesiology in the New Testament*. Grand Rapids: Eerdmans, 2007.

Burgess, Stanley M., ed. *Reaching Beyond: Chapters in the History of Perfectionism*. Peabody, MA: Hendrickson, 1986.

DeMoss, Nancy Leigh. *Holiness: The Heart God Purifies*. Chicago: Moody, 2005.

Dieter, Melvin E., et al. *Five Views on Sanctification*. Grand Rapids: Zondervan, 1987.

Drury, Keith W. *Holiness for Ordinary People*. Indianapolis: Wesleyan Publishing, 2004.

Earle, Ralph. *Sanctification in the New Testament*. Kansas City, MO: Beacon Hill, 1988.

Kärkkäinen, Veli-Matti. *One with God: Salvation as Deification and Justification*. Collegeville, MN: Liturgical Press, 2005.

Peterson, David. *Possessed by God: A New Testament Theology of Sanctification and Holiness*. Downers Grove, IL: InterVarsity, 2001.

Ryle, J. C. *Holiness*. 2nd ed. Grand Rapids: Baker Books, 1979.

Toon, Peter. *Justification and Sanctification*. Westchester, IL: Crossway, 1983.

Warfield, B. B. *Perfectionism*. Grand Rapids: Baker Academic, 1991.

10

The Eternal Security Debate

Secure in the Power of God (The Eternal Security View)
The Need to Persist in Faith (The Conditional Security View)

Posing the Question

Marty has been a Christian for many years. Nonetheless, he continues to struggle with a certain pattern of habitual sin in his life. Time after time, year after year, he repents, but inevitably he falls back into the same pattern of sinful behavior. He finally asks two mature Christian leaders in his church what he can do about this bondage in his life—and whether he is even a true Christian.

The first leader, Sage, assures him that God's grace and the gift of salvation are absolutely free. As Ephesians 2:8–9 proclaims, there is nothing Christians can do to add to God's grace in their lives. Because Marty trusted Jesus for salvation, nothing—including ongoing, habitual sin—can separate him from God. "In other words," Sage says enthusiastically, "absolutely *nothing* can separate you from God once you have trusted Christ. Christian growth is important, and God will use these sorts of things in your life to help you mature. But always remember, Marty, you are eternally secure in your salvation!"

The second leader, Rylie, also assures Marty that God loves him wholeheartedly, but she also strongly urges Marty to earnestly seek God's power and, with the help of the Holy Spirit, to pursue freedom from the sin in his life. She gently but firmly warns Marty that—as Hebrews 10:26–31 reminds us—a lifestyle of ongoing, willful sin may lead to the loss of salvation. Marty is left wondering how to balance the Scripture passages and what implications they have for his relationship with God.

The Center and Its Contrasts

Evangelical Christians agree that God is the initiator of salvation (Titus 2:11). By his love he has called us, redeemed us, and justified us (Rom. 8:30). His intention for believers is that they would continue to grow in grace (2 Pet. 3:18) until they are sanctified in all aspects of their being (1 Thess. 5:23). The vast majority of evangelicals agree that this process of sanctification will never be completed this side of death. However, there is significant disagreement as to whether Christians can lose their salvation due to ongoing, willful, and unrepentant sin in their lives. (See **apostasy**.)

Since the time of Augustine, the question of Christian perseverance—whether God ensures that Christians will persevere in their saving faith until the end—has been an issue of debate. Especially in his later writings, Augustine emphasized that the gift of perseverance was something given by God to all whom God graciously chooses to receive salvation. For Augustine, the gift of perseverance was in no way a reward for a life well lived. Rather, it was a gift of pure grace given to some, in order that it might be according to mercy and not according to merit. The Pelagians were not the only ones to take issue with Augustine's understanding of grace; the moderate monks of Gaul, such as John Cassian, did so as well.

During the Reformation period, John Calvin took up Augustine's position and developed it. He understood the gift of perseverance to be a confirmation, for the elect, of their status before God. It offered assurance to believers of their eternal security in Christ. Others, such as the Anabaptists and the Roman Catholic Church (at the Council of Trent) rejected a strong Augustinian understanding of perseverance. The perspective of conditional security—that it is possible for believers to lose their salvation—was espoused by the Arminian Remonstrant Articles in 1610. The Calvinist perspective—rooted in the idea of irresistible grace—was championed at the Synod of Dort and was codified as the letter P (for "perseverance of the saints") in the five-point acronym TULIP.

Today, evangelicals continue to debate this issue. Many who adhere to the unconditional security position are within the Augustinian-Calvinist tradition, but this is not always the case. The historic Arminian view has been one of conditional security, yet today some Arminians claim that once a person has freely made a commitment to Christ, that person becomes unconditionally secure in his or her salvation. The following two essays present each of these perspectives in turn.

Secure in the Power of God (The Eternal Security View)

The Biblical Argument

The Bible emphasizes that believers continually need to trust in Jesus Christ and walk with God to be saved. The Bible also teaches that believers do not do this on their own: They are empowered by God to persevere in the faith. The assurance that they will persevere to the end is fortunately not rooted in their own feeble strength and carnal character. Rather, their confidence is rooted in God's omnipotent power and unwavering faithfulness. Because the foundation of salvation is God, the salvation of believers is eternally secure. Once acquired, salvation cannot be lost.

Believers may occasionally stumble in their walk, of course. But they will, by God's grace, eventually return to a relationship with the Lord. If a "Christian" completely and permanently abandons the faith, Scripture suggests that this person was never genuinely saved in the first place. "They went out from us," John says, "but they did not belong to us; for if they had belonged to us, they would have remained with us. But by going out they made it plain that none of them belongs to us" (1 John 2:19). For John, believers by definition persevere in their relationship with the Lord. When they utterly abandon the faith, they make it plain that they never really had a saving relationship and thus never really belonged to the community of God's people.

The passages that address the security of the believer focus on three themes: God's will, God's power, and God's life.

The first theme roots the security of the believer in the fact that God's unfailing will is that no believer should ever perish. Jesus is explicit on this point. "This is the will of him who sent me," he says, "that I should lose nothing of all that he has given me, but raise it up on the last day" (John 6:39). None of those who are drawn by the Father and given to Christ (John 6:35–44) can fail to be raised up on the last day.

Paul puts the matter even more forcefully when he writes: "For those whom he foreknew he also predestined to be conformed to the image of his Son. . . . And those whom he predestined he also called; and those whom he called he also justified; and those whom he justified he also glorified" (Rom. 8:29–30).

It should be noted that most defenders of eternal security are Calvinists who believe that God foreknows who will be saved because he predestines them to be saved. Some, however, are Arminians who believe that God simply foreknows who will believe and then on this basis predestines them to go through the process of salvation. Nevertheless, all who believe in eternal security agree that at least *at the point of their faith*, God predestines believers to be conformed to the image of his Son. Hence, one cannot be truly saved and fail to be conformed to Christ's image.

In the above passage, Paul says that all who are foreknown shall be called, justified, and eventually glorified. The passage assumes that it is impossible to be present at the beginning of this process (foreknown by God) and not present at the end (glorified by God). If one is a believer, in other words, that person's future conformity to Christ's image and future glorification is absolutely secure. No wonder Paul can later proclaim without qualification that nothing "in all creation [is] able to separate us from the love of God in Christ Jesus our Lord" (Rom. 8:39; cf. vv. 33–38). The love that saves believers is the same love that preserves them until the end.

Paul's assurance also explains how he could in this same context share with his audience the remarkable claim that "all things work together for good for those who love God, who are called according to his purpose" (Rom. 8:28). If believers could conceivably fall away, Paul could not have said this confidently. Something could potentially cause believers to lose their salvation and thus could not possibly work together for their good. Since the destiny of believers is secure, however, Paul could be certain that *everything* that happens to them will be designed by God to somehow contribute to their good.

A second set of passages that concern the eternal security of believers centers on God's power. While humans are limited in strength and waver in character, God possesses unlimited strength and an unwavering character. Part of the Good News is that their continual salvation is rooted in who *he* is, not in who *they* are!

Even in the Old Testament, when the nature of salvation was not yet fully revealed, David proclaimed, "Our steps are made firm by the LORD." Because of this, he continued, "though we stumble, we shall not fall headlong, for the LORD holds us by the hand" (Ps. 37:23–24). The firmness of believers' steps and the confidence that they shall not fall headlong is located in God's strength and faithfulness, not their own. David elsewhere celebrated how God "will not forsake his faithful ones," with the implication that "the righteous shall be kept safe forever" (Ps. 37:28). Believers are kept safe; they do not keep themselves safe.

The teaching that God's children are kept by God's power is more clearly revealed in the New Testament. Paul expresses it when he confesses to the Philippians, "I am confident of this, that the one who began a good work among you will bring it to completion by the day of Jesus Christ" (Phil. 1:6). Similarly, Paul prays that the Thessalonians will be entirely sanctified, adding that "the one who calls you is faithful, and he will do this" (1 Thess. 5:24). The continual growth of believers is as much dependent on God's power as was their original salvation. For this reason, it is just as secure.

Peter teaches the same truth when he proclaims that God has given believers "an inheritance that is imperishable, undefiled, and unfading, kept in heaven for [us], who are being protected by the power of God through faith for a salvation ready to be revealed in the last time" (1 Pet. 1:4–5). Jude speaks in similar terms when he refers to believers as "those who are called, who are beloved in God the Father and kept safe for Jesus Christ" (Jude 1). Later Jude prays, "Now to him who is able to keep you from falling, and to make you stand without blemish in the presence of his glory with rejoicing" (Jude 24). This is a marvelous teaching! The inheritance of believers is "imperishable": It *cannot* perish or fade because its preservation does not depend on human power but on God's power. It is kept in heaven as believers are protected by the power of God and kept safe for Jesus Christ. If their safety, protection, and perseverance are up to God, believers can rest assured that their destiny is absolutely secure. Their salvation is indeed imperishable.

Finally, the security of believers is rooted in the fact that when they believe, they are given God's own eternal life. A life that is eternal by definition cannot come to an end. The background for this teaching is found in the Old Testament. Even before the full glory of God's salvation was revealed in the New Testament, salvation was described as an everlasting gift. For example, Isaiah proclaims that Israel "is saved by the LORD with everlasting salvation." For this reason he assures Israel that they "shall not be put to shame or confounded to all eternity" (Isa. 45:17). Similarly, through Jeremiah the Lord says, "I will make an everlasting covenant with [my people], never to draw back from doing good to them; and I will put the fear of me in their hearts, so that they may not turn from me" (Jer. 32:40). This passage is significant not only because the Lord states that his **covenant** with his people is to be everlasting but also because he acknowledges that *he* is the one who places reverent fear in the hearts of believers "so that they may not turn from me." He keeps believers; they do not keep him.

The eternal nature of salvation is made even clearer in the New Testament. Jesus teaches that "anyone who hears my word and believes him who sent me has eternal life, and does not come under judgment, but has passed from death to life" (John 5:24; cf. 3:36). Note that Jesus says believers have *already been given* eternal life. In the words of Peter, they have "been born anew, not of perishable but of imperishable seed, through the living and enduring word of God" (1 Pet. 1:23). Eternal and imperishable life is not a future hope for believers: It is a present reality! This is why Jesus can say that believers have already "passed from death to life" and do not have to worry about coming under judgment. If believers were yet on probation before God, Jesus could say only that believers *might* receive eternal life, *might* pass from death to life, and *might* not come under judgment. But this is not at all how Jesus talks. Believers receive God's eternal life the moment they believe, and God's life cannot be extinguished.

Jesus develops the theme still further when he says: "My sheep hear my voice. I know them, and they follow me. I give them eternal life, and they will never perish. No one will snatch them out of my hand. What my Father has given me is greater than all else, and no one can snatch it out of the Father's hand" (John 10:27–29). The sheep receive the uncreated and unending life of God. For this reason, Jesus promises them they will never perish and no one will snatch them away. The gift of salvation and the call of God are irrevocable (Rom. 11:29). Through the blood of Jesus, believers are reconciled to God once and for all. In the words of the author of Hebrews, Jesus' sacrifice has "perfected for all time those who are sanctified" (Heb. 10:14).

Supporting Arguments

1. *Perseverance by grace.* The eternal security position emphasizes that believers' perseverance is as much a matter of grace as is their original salvation. If perseverance is contingent on continual willing and working, then victory in the end is to believers' credit, not God's.

2. *Forever a child of God.* The Bible teaches that when people place their trust in Jesus Christ, they become God's children (John 1:12–13; Rom. 8:14–17). What kind of parent would disown his own child (cf. Isa. 49:15–16)? Indeed, when Scripture metaphorically describes salvation as being conceived with an imperishable seed, it suggests that God gives believers his own "gene pool," as it were (1 Pet. 1:23). He can no more reject his children than a father or mother can reverse the biological fact that he or she has a child.

3. *Courtship and marriage.* If believers are not eternally secure, then their relationship with God is always on probation. Prior to death, believers cannot enter into an unconditional love relationship with God the way a husband and wife are meant to love one another. Rather, in this life they are always "courting." Yet the Bible says believers *are* the bride of Christ (Eph. 5:25–32; cf. 2 Cor. 11:2; Rev. 19:7–9).

4. *The security of the believer.* If their relationship with God is always on probation, believers cannot be sure they are saved. They cannot celebrate *with absolute assurance* their future life with God. To some extent, an element of anxiety is always in order, for they are, every minute of their

lives, on trial. This undermines the joy of the Christian life and encourages believers to relate to God more as an employer than a lover.

Responding to Objections

1. *Several Scripture passages contradict this view.* Objectors to the eternal security position cite a number of passages they believe contradict this view. For example, Paul worries that the Galatians have "fallen from grace" (Gal. 5:4). The author of the book of Hebrews warns his audience that if they "willfully persist in sin after having received the knowledge of the truth, there no longer remains a sacrifice for sins" (Heb. 10:26). And Peter warns that if those who have "escaped the defilements of the world through the knowledge of our Lord and Savior Jesus Christ" become "again entangled in them," their "last state [is] . . . worse for them than the first" (2 Pet. 2:20). Critics of the eternal security position argue that these passages imply it is possible for believers to lose their salvation. Three things may be said in response.

First, since a host of other Scripture passages teach that believers cannot lose their salvation, we must conclude that whatever these passages mean, they cannot mean that believers *can* lose their salvation. If this were so, Scripture would contradict itself.

Second, neither these nor any other passages of Scripture explicitly say that a saved person became unsaved. Paul speaks of people who have been freed from the yoke of the law and who now want to go back to it. In this sense, they have "fallen from grace." But this does not mean they were saved and now are unsaved. So, too, when Peter refers to people who have "escaped the defilements of the world through the knowledge of our Lord," he is not necessarily referring to people who were genuinely saved believers. According to 1 John 2:19, when a person abandons Christ, it is proof that that person never really belonged to Christ.

Third, while many passages of Scripture warn believers to persevere in the faith and not fall away, they do not imply that true believers *can* fall away. Rather, it is in part by means of passages such as these that genuine believers *do not* fall. Believers need to persevere in their faith, but by the sovereign grace of God it is certain they will do so. Warning passages are one of the means by which God ensures this.

2. *Eternal security undermines free will.* Some object to the eternal security position on the grounds that it eliminates free will. A Calvinist would respond that fallen humans are never free in the sense that they possess the power to choose for or against God on their own. On their own, fallen humans would always choose against God. By God's grace, elect individuals inevitably want to choose God. This does not undermine

freedom, for freedom is simply the ability to choose what a person wants. What a person wants, however, is decided either by fallen nature or by God's gracious will (if that person is elect). In this sense, the fact that God keeps believers secure no more undermines free will than does the fact that God had to unconditionally save them in the first place.

Along different lines, an Arminian would respond that while humans can choose to accept salvation or not, once they have chosen to accept it they cannot permanently choose to reject it. God keeps them from falling permanently. Their initial choice lets God in the door, as it were, and once in, God refuses to move out. The reality is that some choices have eternal ramifications; they cannot be reversed. Once pregnant, for example, a woman cannot ever choose *not* to have been a mother (at least in a biological sense). So, too, the choice to make Christ Lord is irrevocable. This restriction of freedom on this one point does not undermine freedom regarding other decisions, and it does not undermine the freedom with which people initially make the decision to accept Christ.

The Need to Persist in Faith
(The Conditional Security View)

The Biblical Argument

Personal relationships require people to choose freely to enter into a relationship and to choose freely to sustain the relationship. According to Scripture, God wants to have a personal relationship with humans. Indeed, God desires a relationship with humans that is like the intimacy and commitment a husband and wife should share (Eph. 5:22–32). This means that a relationship with God is one a person must choose to enter into and choose to sustain. If a person decides to terminate the relationship—if he or she "divorces" God—the relationship ends. Since there is no salvation outside of a personal relationship with God, this means it is possible for a person to lose salvation. Christians can and sometimes do revoke their vows to walk faithfully with God.

This is not simply an inference made on the basis of the nature of interpersonal relationships; it is explicitly taught in Scripture. (1) The Bible describes salvation in conditional terms. (2) It warns believers not to fall away. (3) It identifies certain people who in fact lost their salvation. The following argument explores these three motifs.

First, though Scripture declares that salvation is eternally secure *from God's side,* it stresses that it is conditional *from the human side.* That is, believers never need to concern themselves with whether God is doing his part in saving them, but they do need to be concerned with whether they are doing their part in the salvation process. God's part is to love believers, pay the price for their sin, and continually work not only to keep them from falling but also to help them grow in their faith. This much is eternally secure. The part of believers is simply to yield to God's love and God's Spirit working in their lives. This much is not eternally secure, for it is up to humans to choose it. God *wants* everyone to be saved, but he is not willing to override their freedom (2 Pet. 3:9). He wants a personal relationship with humans, and this involves choice. People must respond to God's grace by consistently choosing to trust in Christ and thus walk with God.

The conditional nature of salvation is revealed throughout Scripture. For example, the Lord frequently "tests" his covenant partners "to know" whether they will remain faithful to him (e.g., Gen. 22:12; Deut. 8:2; 13:1–3; Judg. 2:22; 3:4; 2 Chron. 32:31). Those who do not pass God's tests are no longer considered covenant partners with him (e.g., Ps. 95:10–11; Heb. 3:7–10; cf. Isa. 63:10; Acts 7:51; Eph. 4:30; Heb. 4:7). They may repent and return to the Lord, of course, but in their state of rebellion, they are "cut off" from God's covenantal promises—including the promise of salvation (Rom. 11:17–24). God would have no reason to test believers and could not possibly cut off certain covenant partners if salvation were eternally secure.

The conditional nature of salvation is taught in other ways as well. For example, Jesus taught that "the one who endures to the end will be saved" (Matt. 10:22; cf. 24:13). Salvation clearly is conditioned on whether one endures. Paul emphasizes this truth even more strongly when he tells Timothy's congregation, "If we endure, we will also reign with him," but "if we deny him, he will also deny us" (2 Tim. 2:12). Similarly, Paul assures the Christians at Colossae that they will be "holy and blameless and irreproachable" before the Lord "provided [they] continue securely established and steadfast in the faith" (Col. 1:22–23). We must consider that Paul is speaking to people he assumes are at the present time saved. The conditional nature of his promises and warnings suggests that it was possible for saved people to fail to endure, to deny Christ, to fail to be steadfast, and thus to lose their salvation.

Second, the possibility of falling away from God's grace is implied in the many warnings in Scripture *not* to fall away. The author of Hebrews warns his readers not to be like Esau and sell their birthright, for later Esau "wanted to inherit the blessings [but] was rejected, for he found no chance to repent" (Heb. 12:17). The passage clearly implies that it is possible to sell one's birthright and that if one does so, he or she will not inherit the blessing that came with the birthright.

Along similar lines, Peter warns of false teachers who "deny the Master who bought them" and thus bring "swift destruction on themselves"

(2 Pet. 2:1). Some try to maintain the doctrine of eternal security while acknowledging the obvious fact that people sometimes abandon their faith by claiming that such people were never "truly saved" in the first place. In this passage, however, Peter explicitly claims that these teachers denied the Master who bought them. Apparently, they were once bought with Christ's blood, though it now did them no good.

Peter provides an even more forceful teaching—and warning—on the conditional nature of salvation when he writes:

> If, after [people] have escaped the defilements of the world through the knowledge of our Lord and Savior Jesus Christ, they are again entangled in them and overpowered, the last state has become worse for them than the first. For it would have been better for them never to have known the way of righteousness than, after knowing it, to turn back from the holy commandment that was passed on to them. (2 Pet. 2:20–21)

Peter suggests it is possible for people who have been made righteous "through the knowledge of our Lord and Savior Jesus Christ" to later reject this salvation and end up in a state worse than the one from which they were initially saved. If it is not possible for Christians to lose their salvation, it is not clear what Peter is trying to teach in this passage. Nor is it clear what Peter intends to teach when he later warns, "Beware that you are not carried away with the error of the lawless . . . but grow in the grace and knowledge of our Lord and Savior Jesus Christ" (2 Pet. 3:17–18). If people who are under grace and who know the Lord cannot be carried away, what is the point of warning them about this?

Finally, consider the Lord's warnings to the church of Laodicea in Revelation 3. Though these Christians were once on fire for the Lord, they had grown lukewarm. Consequently, the Lord was ready to "spit [them] out of [his] mouth" (v. 16). He "[stood] at the door, knocking," for he wanted to renew his fellowship with these former disciples (v. 20). The Lord promised them that "to the one who conquers I will give a place with me on my throne" (v. 21). But this promise was clearly conditioned on whether people responded. Those who abandoned their walk would be rejected and would have their names blotted out of the Book of Life (v. 5). Throughout Scripture the Book of Life referred to a register of all citizens in the kingdom community. Names could be added or deleted from this register, depending on the state of a person's heart (e.g., Exod. 32:32–33; Ps. 69:28; cf. Rev. 22:19). The warning about having one's name blotted out of the Book of Life as well as the warnings about being spit out of the Lord's mouth are meaningless if in fact believers are eternally secure.

Third, Scripture teaches that salvation is conditioned on continual faith and obedience by providing examples of people who fell away from God's grace. For example, Saul was once a person who knew God and walked with God. God was with Saul, and Saul even prophesied the Word of God (1 Sam. 10:6–7). Indeed, God promised Saul that he would bless him and his descendants, *if* Saul would remain faithful to him (1 Sam. 13:13). Unfortunately, Saul rebelled against God and became so wicked that God regretted making him king (1 Sam. 15:11; cf. v. 35). Saul became an example of someone who once enjoyed God's favor but eventually was rejected by God because of his own evil choices.

The history of Israel also illustrates the conditional nature of salvation. Paul teaches that Israel as a nation was "broken off" the vine while Gentiles who believed were "grafted in their place" (Rom. 11:17). If Israel was broken off, their relationship with the Lord was clearly not eternally secure. Neither is the relationship between the Lord and the newly grafted in Gentiles, however. Paul warns, "If God did not spare the natural branches [the nation of Israel], perhaps he will not spare you" (Rom. 11:21). In both cases, God's promises are conditioned on the response of the people. When believers grow hard in their hearts and become unbelievers, they are rejected.

Along similar lines, Paul says to those who "want to be justified by the law" that they have "cut [themselves] off from Christ; [they] have fallen away from grace" (Gal. 5:4). At one time they had been "running well," and Paul had assumed they were true believers. Now, however, they are not "obeying the truth" (Gal. 5:7). In this respect, they are like Hymenaeus and Philetus, who "swerved from the truth" by denying the future resurrection from the dead (2 Tim. 2:17–18). Such warnings imply that it is possible to fall from grace and thereby forfeit one's place in the eternal kingdom (cf. Rev. 22:19).

Undoubtedly, the strongest and most frequently misunderstood warning not to fall away comes from the author of Hebrews. The author writes:

> It is impossible to restore again to repentance those who have once been enlightened, and have tasted the heavenly gift, and have shared in the Holy Spirit, and have tasted the goodness of the word of God and the powers of the age to come, and then have fallen away, since on their own they are crucifying again the Son of God and holding him up to contempt. (6:4–6)

This passage clearly implies that a person can lose his or her salvation. The author also seems to suggest that a person cannot be saved again if this happens. Perhaps his meaning is made clearer when he writes, "If we willfully persist in sin after having received the knowledge of the truth, there no longer remains a sacrifice for sins, but a fearful prospect of judgment" (Heb. 10:26–27). If believers *willfully persist* in the sin that the Hebrew Christians were being warned about—the sin of holding Christ up to contempt through unbelief and disobedience—then there no longer remains a sacrifice but only judgment. *Persistence* is the crucial element here. Since Christ is always ready and willing to forgive all sin, the author must be warning Christians that if they do not repent, they may in time find themselves unable to repent. They will have hardened themselves to the Holy Spirit and thus committed the sin that is mortal (1 John 5:16).

Supporting Argument

Cheap grace. Most defenders of eternal security stress the importance of believers living a holy life. At the same time, the doctrine of eternal security easily leads to a cheapened view of God's grace. Some conclude that if they are eternally secure by virtue of their faith in Christ, they can live however they please without fear of eternal consequences. Scripture often warns believers not to live unholy lives precisely because they could lose their salvation. This warning means little if the doctrine of eternal security is accepted.

Responding to Objections

1. *This view contradicts the security passages in Scripture.* The main objection to the conditional security position involves Scripture passages that suggest the security of salvation. This objection is invalid, however, because there are other ways of interpreting these passages that are consistent with scriptural evidence for conditional salvation.

For example, Paul writes, "I am confident . . . that the one who began a good work among you will bring it to completion by the day of Jesus Christ" (Phil. 1:6). Defenders of eternal security often cite this passage in support of their doctrine. But are we really to believe that Paul was confident no Philippian Christian would ever fall away? This seems unlikely, since Paul later considers the possibility that the Philippians *would not* hold firmly to their salvation, in which case Paul says he would have carried out his missionary endeavors among them in vain (Phil. 2:16). A preferable interpretation is that Paul was simply expressing confidence in *God's* willingness and ability to do all he could do to keep the Philippians strong in the faith. Many of Paul's statements regarding the security of believers can be understood in this way (e.g., 1 Thess. 5:24).

Another example is found in 1 Peter, where the apostle says that God has given believers "an inheritance that is imperishable" and that believers are "protected by the power of God through faith for a salvation ready to be revealed in the last time" (1 Pet. 1:4–5). Defenders of eternal security interpret this as an assurance that believers cannot lose their salvation. But this seems unlikely, for Peter elsewhere warns his audience in strong terms of the dire consequences for those who abandon the faith (2 Pet. 2:20–21; 3:17–18). Notice that Peter says believers' *inheritance* is imperishable. He does not say that access to this imperishable inheritance is unconditional. If believers meet the condition of persistent faith, they inherit the imperishable inheritance.

Regarding Peter's claim that believers are "protected by the power of God," notice that he immediately adds, "through faith." God will certainly protect believers, keep them, strengthen them, and so on to the very end, as long as they do not revoke their commitment to Jesus Christ as Lord and Savior of their lives. If they revoke this, all the desire and power of the Creator profits them nothing. Many of the passages that advocates of eternal security appeal to can be explained in a similar fashion (e.g., Jude 1, 24).

2. *This view promotes insecurity.* Some object to the doctrine of conditional security on the grounds that it leaves believers perpetually insecure about their salvation. If people can lose their salvation, it is argued, then they can never in this life confidently celebrate their future reward in heaven. But this objection is misguided.

Consider an analogy. When people get married, they know they may divorce their spouse in the future if they choose to. At the same time, they do not enter into the marriage with a fear that the marriage will dissolve. They know that it is *up to them* to enter into the marriage and, if they so choose, to dissolve the marriage. But *for just this reason* the conditional nature of marriage does not make them insecure. Of course, if the stability of a marriage were rooted in *factors outside their control*, they would indeed have cause to worry. As it stands, however, it is conditioned on their own will. Hence, there are no grounds for insecurity. The same thing is true of salvation. It is conditioned on nothing other than the will of the person.

Finally, it is worth noting that most who affirm eternal security agree that if a person who once believed chooses to abandon the faith, that person cannot claim to have assurance of salvation. People who affirm eternal security assert that this falling away proves only that the person was never really saved in the first place. People who affirm conditional security accept that the person was once saved but is so no longer. What this shows is that when it comes to believers being confident of their salvation, defenders and detractors of conditional security are in the same boat! Both schools of thought affirm that a person who walks with God in faith should feel secure, and both schools of thought affirm that a person who has rejected God, even if that person once walked with God, cannot feel secure and must be warned that his present lack of faith may lead to everlasting destruction. In short, the affirmation of conditional security should never produce anxiety in believers who continue to choose to believe in Christ.

Further Reading

Arrington, French L. *Unconditional Eternal Security: Myth or Truth?* Cleveland, TN: Pathway, 2005.

Bateman, Herbert W., IV. *Four Views on the Warning Passages in Hebrews*. Grand Rapids: Kregel, 2007.

Berkouwer, C. G. *Faith and Perseverance*. Grand Rapids: Eerdmans, 1958.

Corner, Daniel D. *The Believer's Conditional Security: Eternal Security Refuted*. 3rd ed. Washington, PA: Evangelical Outreach, 2001.

Gundry Volf, Judith M. *Paul and Perseverance: Staying in and Falling Away*. Tübingen: Mohr Siebeck, 1990.

Horton, Michael S., et al. *Four Views on Eternal Security*. Grand Rapids: Zondervan, 2002.

Marshall, I. Howard. *Kept by the Power of God: A Study of Perseverance and Falling Away*. London: Epworth, 1969.

Oropeza, B. J. *Paul and Apostasy*. Tübingen: Mohr Siebeck, 2001.

Schreiner, Thomas R., and Ardel B. Caneday. *The Race Set before Us: A Biblical Theology of Perseverance and Assurance*. Downers Grove, IL: InterVarsity, 2001.

Shank, Robert. *Life in the Son: A Study of the Doctrine of Perseverance*. Springfield, MO: Westcott, 1960.

Stanley, Charles F. *Eternal Security: Can You Be Sure?* Nashville: Oliver-Nelson, 1990.

Waterhouse, Steven W. *Blessed Assurance: A Defense of the Doctrine of Eternal Security*. Amarillo, TX: Westcliff, 2003.

11

The Destiny
of the Unevangelized Debate

No Other Name (The Restrictivist View)
God Does All He Can Do (The Universal Opportunity View)
Hope beyond the Grave (The Postmortem Evangelism View)
He Has Not Left Himself without a Witness
(The Inclusivist View)

Posing the Question

Imagine that you are called by God to bring the gospel to an unreached people group on the far side of the globe. After months of language instruction, preparation, and prayer, you head to the mission field. Within a year, after much relationship building, you see God at work among the hearts of the people. The first conversions begin to take place. Eventually a small church is born where once there was no sign of the gospel.

One day, Jamil, one of the first converts, asks to talk with you in private. He tells you how thankful he is that God sent you to share the news of his Son, Jesus Christ. Then he asks a question that has been plaguing him for some time. He recounts the fact that six months before you came to his land, his father died. His father was a good man, respected and loved by everyone in the village. However, he died without ever hearing the gospel of

Jesus Christ. With tears in his eyes, Jamil asks you, "Is there any chance I might see my father again in heaven? Or does the fact that he died without hearing the gospel seal his fate in hell for eternity? Is there a chance that my father will somehow come to know the God that has finally been revealed to the village? Or will he be eternally condemned simply because he was born at the wrong time and place?" What would you say to Jamil?

The Center and Its Contrasts

The issue of the destiny of the unevangelized forces Christians to wrestle with the seeming tension between two clear truths of Scripture: the *universality* of God's love and the *particularity* of the path to salvation, a personal relationship with Jesus Christ. Evangelicals together affirm that God loves humanity and desires to save sinners (John 3:16; 1 Tim. 2:4; 2 Pet. 3:9). Nonetheless, they also hold firm to the conviction that Jesus Christ is the only means of salvation for all humanity (John 3:18; 14:6). As the author of the book of Acts records, "There is salvation in no one else, for there is no other name under heaven given among mortals by which we must be saved" (Acts 4:12). How are we to understand the relationship between these two fundamental convictions? What happens to those who never hear about Jesus Christ?

Many theologians today categorize the three common ways of approaching this issue as follows:

1. **exclusivism.** This view holds that Jesus is the only Savior for all humanity and that it is *not possible* to attain salvation apart from explicit knowledge of him. Thus, Jesus is both ontologically (see **ontology**) and epistemologically necessary for salvation (people must know him and know that they know him).
2. **inclusivism.** This view maintains that Jesus is the only Savior for all humanity but that it *is possible* to attain salvation apart from explicit knowledge of him. One can be saved by expressing faith in God based on the general knowledge of him that is available to everyone. Thus, Jesus is ontologically but not epistemologically necessary for salvation (people must know him but not necessarily know that they know him).
3. **pluralism.** This view holds that Jesus is only one of many saviors available in the world's religions. Thus, Jesus is neither ontologically nor epistemologically necessary for salvation.

The last solution to this question—pluralism—has been universally rejected by evangelical Christians. While there are a number of distinct models of pluralism, all of its forms hold that Jesus is only one of many possible saviors. Thus, pluralists claim that all the great world religions offer viable paths to salvation in their own right. This perspective must disregard or explain away the clear proclamation in the New Testament that Jesus is the single and indispensable Savior of humanity. Pluralism also leads to the denial of such basic Christian dogmas as the deity of Christ, the Trinity of God, and atonement by the death and resurrection of Jesus. For these and other reasons, evangelicals have never regarded pluralism as a viable option.

When it comes to answering the question of the destiny of the unevangelized, evangelicals find various forms of exclusivism and inclusivism to be the most plausible and biblically faithful solution. In fact, at least four views on this matter have emerged among evangelicals. The first three are types of exclusivism, since they each in various ways affirm that a person must know and believe in the name of Jesus to be saved. These three views are known as **restrictivism, universal opportunity,** and **postmortem evangelism.** The final perspective is a form of inclusivism, for it maintains that although Jesus is the necessary means of salvation, someone does not need to know this fact to be saved by Christ.

The following four essays argue for each of these four evangelical perspectives.

No Other Name (The Restrictivist View)

The first view has been labeled the restrictivist view, for it advocates that salvation is restricted to those who have heard the gospel and have made a conscious decision to accept it. Those who never hear the gospel are judged on the basis of what they know or should have known. What they should have known is sufficient to condemn them, for God's general revelation of himself in creation leaves all without excuse (Rom. 1:18–22).

The Biblical Argument

Several themes in the Bible make it clear that salvation is restricted to believers. First, the New Testament explicitly teaches that salvation is found only in Jesus Christ. In the words of Peter, "There is salvation in no one else, for there is no other name under heaven given among mortals by which we must be saved" (Acts 4:12). The only mediator between God and humans, Paul teaches, is Jesus Christ (1 Tim. 2:5). Jesus himself taught that he was "the way, and the truth, and the life. No one comes to the Father except through [him]" (John 14:6).

The way to reach the Father through Jesus is by believing in him. Those who do not believe cannot be saved. In the words of John, "Those who believe in him are not condemned; but those who do not believe are condemned already, because they have not believed in the name of the only Son of God" (John 3:18). In his first epistle, John writes, "This is the testimony: God gave us eternal life, and this life is in his Son. Whoever has the Son has life; whoever does not have the Son of God does not have life" (1 John 5:11–12). This is why in his high priestly prayer, Jesus prayed for all throughout history who would believe in him through the testimony of his disciples (John 17:20–21).

The condition for salvation given throughout the New Testament is that a person place his or her trust (faith) in the Savior God has provided for the world. Only if a person is willing to "confess with [his] lips that Jesus is Lord and believe in [his] heart that God raised him from the dead" can that person inherit the promise that he or she will be saved (Rom. 10:9).

Doesn't this make evangelism a matter of utmost urgency? It certainly does, as Paul himself teaches.

> "Everyone who calls on the name of the Lord shall be saved." But how are they to call on one in whom they have not believed? And how are they to believe in one of whom they have never heard? And how are they to hear without someone to proclaim him? And how are they to proclaim him unless they are sent? As it is written, "How beautiful are the feet of those who bring good news!" (Rom. 10:13–15)

Unless someone preaches the gospel to the lost, the lost cannot believe and cannot be saved. Some hold out hope that people may be given a chance to believe after death if they are not afforded the opportunity in this lifetime. The Bible offers no such hope, however. On the contrary, it teaches that "it is appointed for mortals to die once, and after that the judgment" (Heb. 9:27).

Others hold out hope that at least sincere people of other religions will be saved. But again, the Bible offers no such hope. Indeed, the biblical perspective on pagan religions is that they are deceptive and are under God's judgment (Exod. 20:3–6; 2 Chron. 13:8–9; Isa. 37:18–19; Acts 26:17–18; Col. 1:13). This is why we find a number of examples in Scripture of people who were sincerely religious but who had to receive the knowledge of Jesus Christ in order to be saved (e.g., Acts 9:2; 10:30–33).

Doesn't this mean that the majority of people who have existed throughout history will be lost? This is not only an implication of restrictivist theology but also the explicit teaching of Jesus himself. "Enter through the narrow gate; for the gate is wide and the road is easy that leads to destruction, and there are many who take it. For the gate is narrow and the road is hard that leads to life, and there are few who find it" (Matt. 7:13–14).

There is undeniable pressure to compromise the narrowness of this teaching in our pluralistic age, which celebrates the diversity of religions and philosophies as different paths to God, or at least to self-actualization. But in fidelity to the Word of God and the teachings of Jesus in particular, believers must resist this pressure. There is in fact "no other name under heaven given among mortals by which we must be saved" (Acts 4:12).

Supporting Argument

Church history. While there has been no single perspective on this issue in church history, the restrictivist position has had a large number of weighty defenders, including Augustine, John Calvin, and Jonathan Edwards. Today the view is defended by such noted evangelical theologians as Carl Henry, R. C. Sproul, and Ronald Nash.

Responding to Objections

1. *This view is unfair.* One of the primary objections to this view is that it is unfair. It is not a person's fault for being born in a time and place when and where he or she cannot hear the gospel.

Four things may be said in response to this objection. First, people are judged on the basis of what they did know, or should have known, not on the basis of what they did not know. They are left without excuse because the glory of God is revealed throughout nature and is available to all (Rom. 1:20).

Second, we must be careful about concluding that God is unfair, regardless of how matters look to us. Consider that we must come to this conclusion using the brain and moral sensitivity that God himself gave us. It is presumptuous for the clay to criticize the potter. To what standard of justice are we going to hold God accountable? His own character *is* the standard of justice and holiness against which everything else is measured.

Third, many of those who embrace the restrictivist position are Calvinists who believe in particular election—the belief that God selects from all eternity who will be saved. From this perspective, if a person is not reached by the gospel, this is only because that person was not among God's elect. In other words, the "good fortune" of being given the opportunity to believe is another aspect of the electing grace that destined a person to heaven from all eternity.

Finally, one might argue that the apparent unfairness of this view actually gives the restrictivist perspective a ring of truth that other views lack, for if there is anything that is clear, it is the fact that life is not fair. Indeed, whatever criticisms could be leveled against the restrictivist doctrine of salvation could be raised against just about everything in life! For example, some people are born into great wealth while others are born into terrible poverty. Some are born with perfect health, others with sickness, deformities, and/or a destiny to die at a young age. Some are born intellectually gifted, others intellectually challenged. And so on. The fact that some are given the opportunity to enter into the narrow gate while others are not may not sit well with us, but it certainly squares with everything else we know about life.

2. *According to this view, babies and the mentally disabled cannot be saved.* Some object that if a person must believe in order to be saved, then all people incapable of choice—including infants and mentally disabled people—must be doomed, and this seems grotesquely unfair.

First, as was said in regard to the first question, we must be careful about charging God with unfairness, for the reasons given above.

Second, whereas with most people we can appeal to what they should have known on the basis of general revelation, we obviously cannot do this in regard to infants or mentally disabled people. What is more, if people cannot make responsible decisions, they cannot sin. Hence, most restrictivists today would hold that infants and mentally disabled people are saved, for they did not ratify Adam's fall in their life.

Nevertheless, some restrictivists of the Calvinist persuasion argue that we must resist making ourselves judges for God. Perhaps the question of the salvation of infants and mentally disabled people is one of the "secret things" of God we simply cannot know (Deut. 29:29). For all we know, God may elect some infants and mentally disabled people while passing others by. If so, this is his holy prerogative, and we must trust that it is wise and good.

God Does All He Can Do
(The Universal Opportunity View)

Two truths condition the universal opportunity view. First, the Bible teaches that God is all-powerful. He can do whatever he wants. He uses humans when it pleases him. But he does not need them to get the job done. Second, the Bible teaches that God wants everyone to be saved. He takes no delight in the destruction of any soul, however wicked (Ezek. 18:32; 33:11).

From these two truths it would seem to follow that if a person is willing to accept Christ as Lord, the all-powerful God will find a way to give that person the opportunity to do so. He will send a missionary, an angel, or perhaps come to a person in a dream or deathbed vision. One way or another, all who have a heart to believe will be given the chance to do so. On the judgment day no one will complain, "I would have believed, if only I had been given the opportunity." No other view is consistent with the scriptural data.

The Biblical Argument

Adherents of this view agree with restrictivists in that one must believe in Jesus Christ to be saved (Acts 16:31; Rom. 10:13–17). There is no basis for holding out hope that nonbelievers will be saved or that people will get a chance to accept Christ after death. Nevertheless, they deny that people end up going to hell because they were born in the wrong place at the wrong time. Such a notion is unscriptural on at least two accounts.

First, as noted above, the Bible depicts God as one who loves all people, wants all people to be saved (1 Tim. 2:4; 2 Pet. 3:9), and thus does whatever he can to save people. For example, depicting himself as a farmer and his people as a vineyard, the Lord says, "What more was there to do for my vineyard that I have not done in it?" (Isa. 5:4). Clearly, God does all he can to bring people into a relationship with him. He holds out his welcoming arms "all day long" to people, despite their rebellion (Rom. 10:21). Jesus manifested this grieving heart of God's when he expressed his desire to protect "as a hen gathers her brood under her wings." Unfortunately, Jesus adds, the inhabitants of Jerusalem "were unwilling" (Matt. 23:37–39). The only thing that can thwart the desire of the omnipotent Creator to save all people is their own unwillingness to be saved. If a person has a will to be saved, God will find a way to save that person. He is a God who "rewards those who seek him" (Matt. 7:7–8; Heb. 11:6).

Second, Scripture contains examples of God reaching people through extraordinary means. For example, in the case of the Ethiopian eunuch who was seeking truth, God supernaturally arranged for him to come in contact with the missionary Philip (Acts 8:26–40). In the case of the Gentile Cornelius, who had a heart to believe, God employed special messengers and visions (to Peter) to ensure that he and his household heard the Word of the Lord (Acts 10:1–48). Elsewhere in Scripture God spoke to pagans through dreams, visions, and/or angels (e.g., Gen. 20; Dan. 2).

This is sufficient to show that people will not be damned who would have believed had they been placed in different circumstances. If they are salvageable, God will find a way to salvage them. One way or another, God will give them a chance to come to a saving faith.

Supporting Arguments

1. *Church tradition.* While the church has had a diversity of opinions on the matter of the salvation of the heathen, it is worth noting that the universal opportunity position has had some weighty defenders in the church tradition. Thomas Aquinas, Jacob Arminius, and John Henry Newman advocated this perspective. Two noteworthy modern-day advocates are Norman Geisler and Robert Lightner.

2. *Reason.* The notion of a person going to hell because he or she was never given the chance to hear the gospel violates reason. What kind of loving God would wager eternal happiness or eternal misery on where and when a person was born? People obviously cannot be responsible for where or when they were born, so it is unjust to punish them on the basis of these matters.

Some may respond that we have no right to question God's justice. But surely if there are two available theological perspectives, one that attributes to God a justice that looks just to us, while the other attributes to God a justice that offends our moral sensibility, we should prefer the first, all other things being equal. The universal opportunity position is the only position that is able to affirm with logical consistency God's loving character while also holding to the necessity of belief in Jesus.

Others might respond to the objection of unfairness by claiming that people who do not hear the gospel are judged on the basis of what they know, not on the basis of what they do not know. This is hardly an adequate response to this objection, however. It cannot be coincidental that only those who get an opportunity to believe end up being saved. Nor is it coincidental that all who are not given this opportunity end up not being saved. There is every reason to conclude that the final explanation as to why some (at least) are not saved is because they were born in the "wrong" place and at the "wrong" time—matters that were outside their control. This is an irrational thing to believe.

Responding to Objections

1. *There is inadequate evidence for this view.* Some object to the universal opportunity position on the grounds that it lacks adequate grounding in the New Testament. True, God uses angels and visions to bring the gospel to people, but this never happens apart from people eventually coming in contact with an actual human missionary. This cannot be denied, but three points will show that this objection is not decisive.

First, John states that not everything that happened in the early church is recorded in Scripture (John 21:25). Because we have no explicit example of someone arriving at a saving faith through dreams, visions, or private revelations does not mean that it did not or could not happen. Second, the fact that we do have clear precedent for God sending messages to people through dreams, visions, and revelations suggests that God could easily use these means to send the most important message of all to those who truly desire spiritual truth. Indeed, given this pattern, wouldn't we expect God to use these means if he needed to? Third, there are several cases reported in recent history of certain people groups who came to a knowledge of the incarnation on their own, testifying to the fact that God can and does use any method he chooses to bring people to a saving faith in him.

2. *This view compromises the urgency of missions.* Some worry that if we open up the possibility that people can be saved through dreams, visions, or supernatural revelations, the urgency of evangelism and missions will be compromised. The confidence that God will somehow reach all who want to believe should not undermine this urgency, however. God has clearly ordained that the ordinary means by which people become his children is through human witnesses. If God wants to work through other means, that is his prerogative (cf. Deut. 29:29). Christians are to obey God, not speculate about how he might save people even if his followers do not obey him. Christians must therefore proceed on the assumption that the eternal destiny of people depends on their willingness to preach the gospel.

Hope beyond the Grave
(The Postmortem Evangelism View)

Do people who die without knowing Jesus Christ necessarily go to hell? According to the postmortem evangelism view, the answer is no. People are given a chance to accept or reject Christ after death.

The Biblical Argument

The postmortem evangelism position can be defended on two accounts: The first relates to the general portrait of God in Scripture; the second relates to specific passages that support it.

The great overarching theme of the Bible is that the Creator lovingly and persistently pursues humans to bring them into a loving relationship with himself. He has a passionate love for all those he has created (John 3:16; 1 Tim. 2:4) and does not want any to perish (Deut. 30:15–20; 2 Pet. 3:9). Though many choose to resist him to the bitter end and thereby condemn themselves, this is not God's desire. He explicitly says that he takes no delight in this (Ezek. 18:32; 33:11). God does not willingly afflict or grieve anyone (Lam. 3:33). When God's justice demands that he afflict and grieve people, we must be assured that such an act was not God's first choice. God's first choice is always for people to receive his love, to enter into his salvation, and to enjoy him and reign with him throughout eternity. As long as there is hope for people, God will not give up on them.

Most evangelicals assume that death terminates all hope. People can choose for or against God as long as they are alive, but at the moment of death, their fate is eternally sealed. If, for whatever reasons, a person has not accepted Christ, then that person is destined to hell.

The assumption that death necessarily terminates hope—even for God—is unfounded. Why should we assume that death is an insurmountable obstacle for the Lord when his most definitive act involved defeating the one who had the power of death and overcoming the grave (Heb. 2:14)? Because of his resurrection, Jesus now holds "the keys of Death and of Hades" (Rev. 1:18). If someone died whose heart was not irreversibly set against Christ, it seems natural to assume that Christ would be willing and able to continue trying to win that person over.

This view is not based on merely a logical inference from God's love and Christ's victory over the grave, however. A number of Scripture passages explicitly teach it. Perhaps the most important of these is 1 Peter 3:18–20:

> For Christ also suffered for sins once for all, the righteous for the unrighteous, in order to bring you to God. He was put to death in the flesh, but made alive in the spirit, in which also he went and made a proclamation to the spirits in prison, who in former times did not obey, when God waited patiently in the days of Noah, during the building of the ark, in which a few, that is, eight persons, were saved through water.

Peter reiterates his point in the next chapter when he writes, "For this is the reason the gospel was proclaimed even to the dead, so that, though they had been judged in the flesh as everyone is judged, they might live in the spirit as God does" (1 Pet. 4:6). Paul also mentions the fact that Christ "descended into the lower parts of the earth" before he "made captivity itself a captive" (Eph. 4:8–9; cf. Rom. 10:7).

Admittedly, both of these passages are controversial. Space does not permit a detailed discussion of the issues that have been raised regarding these texts. But it is interesting to consider how much of this controversy is due to the ambiguity of these texts, and how much is due to the *clarity* of the texts. While there is some exegetical ambiguity, to be sure, one thing that is rather clear about these passages is that they seem to teach that at least some people get a chance to accept Christ and be delivered by Christ after death.

Other passages seem to refer to postmortem evangelism as well. For example, Jesus taught that "the hour is coming, and is now here, when the dead will hear the voice of the Son of God, and those who hear will live" (John 5:25). Most evangelicals assume that "those who hear" are those who believed while they were alive. When they hear the Son's voice, they come alive again. This is a possible interpretation, though one wonders how corpses can hear *before* they come alive. It is possible that the Lord is saying that those who are physically dead but who as spirits receive (hear) the Word of the Son of God will receive eternal life.

Jesus also taught his contemporary audiences that he had many tribes who were not of the house of Israel (John 10:16). Since one must believe in Christ to be saved, and since only the small audience Christ was speaking to at the time were being presented with the opportunity to believe in him, one must wonder how these other tribes came to belong to Jesus. The most plausible answer is postmortem evangelism.

Further, Jesus spoke of a sin that would not be forgiven "either in this age or in the age to come" (Matt. 12:32). Does this not presuppose that there are other sins that may be forgiven "in the age to come"? Several other passages suggest that some people who did not praise God in life will praise him after death (e.g., Phil. 2:10; Rev. 5:13). Paul taught that if "for this life only we have hoped in Christ, we are of all people most to be pitied" (1 Cor. 15:19). The passage suggests that there is also hope in Christ in the next life. And perhaps most intriguingly, it is significant that the gates of the new Jerusalem will never be shut (Rev. 21:25). Nothing unclean can enter the holy city, but the door is open, it seems, for people to change and come in.

Supporting Arguments

1. *Church history.* The church has always had a diversity of opinions on the salvation of non-Christians. Still, several versions of the postmortem evangelism position were popular in the early church and were advocated by such noteworthy theologians as Hippolytus, Clement of Alexandria, Origen, Athanasius, Gregory of Nazianzus, and Ambrose. It is also significant to note that the idea of Christ descending into hell is found in the two earliest ecumenical creeds of the church, the Nicene and the Apostles' Creed. While such information does not settle the issue for Protestants, it does lend exceptional credibility to this position. Finally, this view is defended by noteworthy contemporary evangelicals such as George McDonald, Donald Bloesch, Gabriel Fackre, and Stephen Davis.

2. *The freewill defense.* Among evangelicals, the most common explanation for the problem of evil is the freewill defense. In essence, this argument states that evil exists in the world because creatures must have the freedom to choose evil if they are to have the freedom to choose love. If this view is accepted, then it follows that no one can enter into God's love without choosing for it, and no one can be excluded from God's love without choosing against it. If even one person could automatically go to heaven without choosing it, the entire freewill defense falls to the ground. Yet many people obviously die without having made a resolved choice for or against God. The postmortem evangelism position is the most natural way of reconciling the need for choice with the fact that in this life choice is often unavailable to people.

Responding to Objections

1. *Scripture rules out the possibility of an offer of salvation after death.* The verse most frequently cited against the postmortem evangelism position is Hebrews 9:27: "And just as it is appointed for mortals to die once, and after that the judgment." According to some, this verse means that immediately after death humans experience judgment. This, they argue, rules out the possibility of an offer of salvation after death.

This interpretation, however, reads too much into the text. The author is simply drawing a parallel between Christ's death "once and for all" and our death (Heb. 9:23–28). While this verse certainly rules out **reincarnation,** it does not rule out the possibility of intermediate events between death and judgment. Indeed, most evangelicals agree that a multitude of events will take place between death and the final judgment—e.g., Jesus' return, the defeat of evil, the bodily resurrection, and so on. The postmortem view simply adds one more event (or process) to this eschatology between death and judgment: the evangelization of the previously unevangelized.

2. *This view undermines missions.* Some people allege that if people are given a chance to accept or reject Christ after death, the urgency of evangelizing them in this life is undermined. In response, if this objection carries any weight, it does so against all evangelical views about the destiny of the unevangelized except the restrictivist view. All other views hold out hope for some people who die without Christ. Indeed, it has been argued that even the Calvinist form of restrictivism undermines the urgency of evangelism, for Calvinists believe that the elect are predestined to be saved.

There is no reason, however, to give this objection much weight. Motivation for evangelizing the world is rooted in a desire to obey the Lord who commands it, to share the joyful Good News of redemption with people who lack it, and to glorify God by having as many people as possible acknowledge him in this lifetime as the rightful Lord of all creation. Believers do not need to be convinced that the eternal destiny of people hinges on their evangelism efforts to feel compelled to share the gospel with them.

He Has Not Left Himself without a Witness (The Inclusivist View)

Adherents of this view, along with those who adhere to the other three evangelical options, believe that Jesus is the only Savior, the one mediator between God and humans (1 Tim. 2:5–6). They believe there is no other name given to humans whereby we must be saved (Acts 4:12). They agree that no one can go to the Father except through Jesus Christ (John 14:6). And they agree that the pluralist position, which holds that all religious roads lead to God, is both unbiblical and incoherent.

Where adherents of this view part company with other evangelical brothers and sisters is over the assumption that a person must explicitly *know about* and *believe in* Jesus to be saved by Jesus. All must be saved *through* Jesus—whether they know him or not! In other words, people cannot be saved apart from Jesus, but they can be saved apart from *knowing* they are saved by Jesus. At no time in history has God left himself without a witness (Acts 14:17), and people are judged based on how they respond in their innermost heart to this witness. This view is often called the inclusivist view, for it holds that salvation is inclusive for all who have a heart that is open to Christ, whether they know him by name or not.

The Biblical Argument

The Bible teaches that God is Lord of the entire world; he is in love with the entire world; and he wants to save the entire world. Therefore, he has not left himself without a witness throughout the entire world (Ps. 19:1–4; Acts 14:17; Rom. 10:18; 1 Tim. 2:4; 2 Pet. 3:9). God's "eternal power and divine nature" can be "understood and seen through the things he has made" (Rom. 1:20). When people do not have the written revelation of God, God works with them and judges them on the basis of the internal witness they do have. In the words of the apostle Paul:

> When Gentiles, who do not possess the law, do instinctively what the law requires, these, though not having the law, are a law to themselves. They show that what the law requires is written on their hearts, to which their own conscience also bears witness; and their conflicting thoughts will accuse or

perhaps excuse them on the day when, according to my gospel, God, through Jesus Christ, will judge the secret thoughts of all. (Rom. 2:14–16)

All people have some degree of light available to them, and this light is Jesus Christ (John 1:9; 8:12). How they respond to this light determines their eternal nature and destiny. People are judged on the basis of what they know. This is the point of several of Jesus' parables. In Luke 12, for example, Jesus provides this teaching:

That slave who knew what his master wanted, but did not prepare himself or do what was wanted, will receive a severe beating. But the one who did not know and did what deserved a beating will receive a light beating. From everyone to whom much has been given, much will be required; and from the one to whom much has been entrusted, even more will be demanded. (vv. 47–48)

Restrictivists hold that God condemns people even when the reason they did not believe was no fault of their own. Either they were not one of God's elect, as Calvinist restrictivists believe, or they were simply born in a place where the gospel unfortunately was not preached, as Arminian restrictivists hold. Either way, a fundamental sense of morality is undermined. If God wagers a person's eternal destiny either on his own arbitrary election or on the contingent vicissitudes of where and when that person happens to be born, it is difficult to confess with integrity that God is all-loving and all-good. What Jesus teaches in the above parable, however, is that our basic sense of fairness, justice, and morality is not eschewed. God does not consign people to hell who never had a genuine chance of going to heaven. Rather, salvation is available to all, and God genuinely wants all to receive it.

Though he was stubbornly locked in a myopic first-century Jewish mindset, Peter finally woke up to the universality of God's love after receiving several bizarre visions. "God shows no partiality," he later told his Gentile audience. Rather, "in every nation anyone who fears him and does what is right is acceptable to him" (Acts 10:34–35). God rewards all who seek him by faith, however enculturated their faith may be (Heb. 11:6). Indeed, according to Paul, God was providentially involved in determining "the times of their existence and the boundaries of the places where [each nation] would live *so that they would search for God* and *perhaps grope for him* and find him—though indeed he is not far from each one of us" (Acts 17:26–27, emphasis added).

The center of God's global providential activity is getting people to seek him and in some form or other have faith in him. This is why the Bible repeatedly praises the saving faith of many people who not only did not know Jesus but also were not part of Israel and therefore could not be expected to know even Yahweh. One thinks of such faith-filled people as Melchizedek, Jethro, Job, and Rahab (Gen. 14:17–20; Exod. 18:1–12; Job 1:1; Heb. 11:31). These people were sinners and thus in need of the Savior as much as anyone. But through no fault of their own, they were unable to have an explicit faith in Jesus. Yet there is no doubt they were saved. How is this possible? God includes people under the work of Christ on the basis of their heart, not their head (which is prevented from faith for chronological or geographical reasons).

The Bible offers a number of other suggestions that God accepts all who have faith, whatever their level of understanding (or misunderstanding). Paul says all should "have [their] hope set on the living God, who is the Savior of all people, especially of those who believe" (1 Tim. 4:10). This passage reveals that the scope of God's saving activity encompasses more than just "those who believe."

Similarly, Jesus spoke of "sheep" who "do not belong to this fold" (John 10:16). These sheep could not have known they were sheep, of course, for they had not yet had contact with the shepherd. But their hearts were toward him nonetheless. Perhaps Jesus was referring to these same anonymous sheep in Matthew 25, when he gave his dire eschatological warning about the judgment day. In this passage, Jesus welcomes many who did not know him explicitly but who lived out an implicit faith by clothing him, feeding him, visiting him in prison, and so on (vv. 36–40). Conversely, many who thought they knew Jesus will be excluded by Jesus because their faith was disingenuous, as evidenced by the fact that they did not demonstrate any Christlike works (vv. 41–46). The judgment day, Jesus is saying, is going to have some surprising twists and turns.

Supporting Arguments

1. *Church history*. While never the dominant view, the inclusivist view is well represented in church history. It was embraced by such authorities as Justin Martyr, Ulrich Zwingli, John Wesley, and C. S. Lewis. Among evangelicals today, the view is defended by Sir Norman Anderson, Clark Pinnock, and John Sanders.

2. *God's love and justice*. The inclusivist view allows us to embrace the exclusivity of Jesus Christ without sacrificing either the universality of God's love or the just nature of God's character. This view creates no sense in which people can be condemned because God did not select them or because they were born in the wrong time and wrong place. But neither do we have to wager everything on an obscure hope that people will have a special divine visitation before they die (the universal opportunity view)

or that they will be evangelized after death (the postmortem evangelism view). This view simply says that God sees the hearts of people perfectly and applies the reconciling work of Christ to all who have a heart to receive it—whether they know it or not.

Responding to Objections

1. *This view constitutes a drift toward religious pluralism.* One of the most frequent objections to the inclusivist view is that it constitutes the beginning of a slippery slope toward the heresy of religious pluralism. This common objection is based on a significant misunderstanding of the position, however.

There is a great difference between the claim that Jesus is not *epistemologically* necessary for salvation (the inclusivist view) and the claim that Jesus is not *ontologically* necessary for salvation (the pluralist view). This line is so fundamental and decisive that there is no fear of a slippery slope from one to the other. Inclusivists hold passionately—as do all evangelicals—that Jesus is the divine Son of God and that no one can be saved apart from his redemptive work on the cross. Inclusivists simply maintain that God can recognize faith even in a person who has been chronologically or geographically cut off from the explicit message of Jesus Christ.

2. *This view undermines missions.* Another common objection to the inclusivist perspective is that it compromises the urgency of missions and evangelization. In fact, some have argued, if the severity of people's judgment is based on how much light they receive, perhaps Christians are doing them a disservice by bringing them more light!

The first thing to note in response to this objection is that the only people not affected by it are Arminian restrictivists, for they are the only ones who consistently hold that the eternal fate of people literally hangs on whether Christians evangelize them. This view is so problematic, however, that few embrace it.

Second, there are many reasons one can and should be passionate about evangelism, apart from the frightful conviction that the eternal salvation of people hangs on whether Christians effectively present the gospel to them. For starters, the Lord commanded his followers to evangelize the world (Matt. 28:18–20), and all true believers want to please their Lord. Second, it is natural for every passionately committed Christian to want to share with others the glorious Good News of eternal life. Third, Christians should evangelize for the glory of God and the joy of people, for life is lived more fully and God is more glorified when individuals are disciples of Jesus. Finally, the New Testament presupposes that only people who explicitly confess Jesus as Lord and Savior can have assurance of salvation. Because we *hope* godly non-Christians are saved does not mean we are *confident* they are saved. We can only be confident of a person who confesses Christ as Lord and Savior. Hence, it is urgent that we rescue these souls from the danger they are in.

Further Reading

Clendenin, Daniel B. *Many Gods, Many Lords: Christianity Encounters World Religions.* Grand Rapids: Baker Academic, 1996.

Crockett, William V., and James G. Sigountos, eds. *Through No Fault of Their Own? The Fate of Those Who Have Never Heard.* Grand Rapids: Baker Academic, 1991.

Erickson, Millard J. *How Shall They Be Saved? The Destiny of Those Who Do Not Hear of Jesus.* Grand Rapids: Baker Academic, 1996.

Kärkkäinen, Veli-Matti. *An Introduction to the Theology of Religions: Biblical, Historical, and Contemporary Perspectives.* Downers Grove, IL: InterVarsity, 2003.

Morgan, Christopher W., and Robert A. Peterson, eds. *Faith Comes by Hearing: A Response to Inclusivism.* Downers Grove, IL: IVP Academic, 2008.

Nash, Ronald H. *Is Jesus the Only Savior?* Grand Rapids: Zondervan, 1994.

Netland, Harold A. *Encountering Religious Pluralism: The Challenge to Christian Faith and Mission.* Downers Grove, IL: InterVarsity, 2001.

Okholm, Dennis L., and Timothy R. Phillips, eds. *Four Views on Salvation in a Pluralistic World.* Grand Rapids: Zondervan, 1995.

Pinnock, Clark H. *A Wideness in God's Mercy: The Finality of Jesus Christ in a World of Religions.* Grand Rapids: Zondervan, 1992.

Sanders, John. *No Other Name: An Investigation into the Destiny of the Unevangelized.* Grand Rapids: Eerdmans, 1992.

———, ed. *What about Those Who Have Never Heard? Three Views on the Destiny of the Unevangelized.* Downers Grove, IL: InterVarsity, 1995.

Tiessen, Terrance L. *Who Can Be Saved? Reassessing Salvation in Christ and World Religions.* Downers Grove, IL: InterVarsity, 2004.

Yong, Amos. *Beyond the Impasse: Toward a Pneumatological Theology of Religions.* Grand Rapids: Baker Academic, 2003.

12

The Baptism Debate

Baptism and Christian Discipleship (The Believer's Baptism View)
Covenanting with the Community of God (The Infant Baptism View)

Posing the Question

"You have made arrangements with your pastor to have your baby baptized, haven't you?" Denay didn't know quite how to answer her mother-in-law, especially since Linda had a rather intense look on her face and a sense of urgency in her voice. Linda didn't mind that her son and his wife, Denay, had decided to attend the church in which Denay had been raised. With some effort, she had even remained gracious when her son announced that he was going to be baptized by immersion—though she did not understand why her son thought his infant baptism was no longer adequate. But now there was a child involved, and in her opinion, children of Christian parents needed to be baptized.

"We believe that baptism should take place when a person is old enough to make a responsible, personal decision to be a disciple of Jesus," Denay sheepishly responded. A long moment of awkward silence followed as Linda gathered her thoughts.

"This is not right, Denay! Doesn't your church believe the Bible? Children have always been part of God's covenant, and the church has always baptized children. Now you're denying your child and my grandchild this privilege. You're excluding him from God's covenant, hoping he'll accept it for himself later on. God forbid, but what if he were to die before he is old enough to do this?"

The Center and Its Contrasts

All Christians throughout history have agreed, on the basis of Scripture, that baptism is important. Historically, baptism has not been understood to be an optional practice. It is commanded by God. But there has often been disagreement about whom baptism is for, how it should be done, and why it is significant.

The dominant practice throughout church history has been to baptize infants by sprinkling or pouring water on them. In Catholic theology, this is done primarily to wash away original sin. In the Eastern Orthodox Church, however, baptism is understood primarily as the rite by which a baby or adult is joined to the church, the mystical body of Christ. Many forms of Protestantism also practice infant baptism, but they vary in their understanding as to what this practice accomplishes. For example, the theology of traditional Lutheran churches is similar to the Catholic understanding: Baptism washes away original sin. Presbyterian churches reject this understanding, however, believing instead that baptism is the means by which children are included in the covenant God made with his people, similar to what circumcision signified in the Old Testament.

Other forms of Protestantism believe baptism is reserved for people who have made a personal decision to believe in and follow Jesus. Some groups perform this ordinance by pouring water on a believer's head, but most carry it out by immersing the person in water. Here, too, there is a variety of understandings. A few groups who practice adult baptism believe that baptism is God's means of remitting sin in a believer's life. Others hold to a more Presbyterian view, seeing it as the rite that publicly initiates a person into God's covenant. The most prevalent understanding among those who practice adult baptism, however, is that it is an outward public testimony of God's inward work. This is the most common view among Baptists.

All of these issues are debated within evangelicalism, but the issue most debated is whether baptism should be performed on children of believing parents or only on people who have made their own decision to believe in and follow Jesus. Hence, this is the issue the two essays in this section address.

Baptism and Christian Discipleship
(The Believer's Baptism View)

The Biblical Argument

Early on in church history, the church began to practice infant baptism. According to adherents of the believer's baptism view, this was a mistake.

Baptism is intended as the initiating rite into Christian discipleship and thus is intended only for people who are old enough to make a decision to believe in and obey Jesus Christ. Baptism is meaningless apart from a personal decision to follow Jesus. The New Testament supports this perspective.

In contrast to the Old Testament, in which God entered into a covenant with an entire nation, in the New Testament, God's covenant is with all *believers*. The class of those who are in covenant with God changed from a national class (the Jews) to a class of people who personally decide something (believers). Consequently, it made sense in the Old Testament to give the sign of the covenant (circumcision) to infants, since they were part of the nation with which God was covenanting. It makes no sense in regard to New Testament teaching, however, because God's covenant is with believers, and infants cannot believe.

Throughout the New Testament, salvation is offered to and baptism is commanded of only people who can meet the conditions of repenting, believing, and obeying Jesus Christ. We see this even in the ministry of John the Baptist, who was preparing the way for Jesus Christ. Mark writes: "People from the whole Judean countryside and all the people of Jerusalem were going out to him [John] and were baptized by him in the river Jordan, *confessing their sins*" (Mark 1:5, emphasis added). The ones who were baptized were the ones who confessed their sins. Infants, of course, cannot do this. Hence, there is no reason to suppose that infants were among those whom John baptized.

The same may be said about the ministry of Jesus. Though Jesus did not personally baptize people (John 4:2), his message was essentially the same as John's. "The kingdom of God has come near," he taught, so people must "repent, and believe in the good news" (Mark 1:15). What made a person a participant in the kingdom of God was his or her willingness to repent, believe, and obey the gospel. This is why Jesus' disciples baptized only people who were old enough to be made disciples (John 4:1–2).

The same point is reflected in Jesus' Great Commission when he says, "Go . . . and make disciples of all nations, baptizing them in the name of the Father and of the Son and of the Holy Spirit, and teaching them to obey everything that I have commanded you" (Matt. 28:19–20). Baptism was intended to be part of the process of making someone a disciple and makes sense only in the context of disciple-making. It was not intended for people too young to be taught and to decide whether they wanted to obey all that Jesus commanded.

The truth that baptism is a part of disciple-making becomes even more evident in the ministry of the earliest disciples. They obeyed Jesus' command to make disciples and therefore to baptize and teach them. In the first sermon preached after the Holy Spirit was poured out on the day of

Pentecost, Peter exclaimed: "Repent, and be baptized every one of you in the name of Jesus Christ so that your sins may be forgiven; and you will receive the gift of the Holy Spirit. For the promise is for you, for your children, and for all who are far away, everyone whom the Lord our God calls to him" (Acts 2:38–39).

Whereas in the Old Testament it meant something to be born a Jew, as opposed to a Gentile, in the New Testament, the only thing that mattered was whether a person repented and submitted to Jesus Christ. This is why the sign of the covenant was different. In the Old Testament, the sign was given to any male born a Jew. In the New Testament, it was given only to those who were born again into Jesus Christ (John 3:5). Only if one repents of sin does baptism into Jesus Christ mean anything.

It is true that in this passage Peter promises that the gift of the Holy Spirit is promised not only to adults but also to their children. Those who practice infant baptism argue on this basis that baptism must be administered to children of believing parents. This interpretation reads too much into the text, however. Peter goes on to say that the promise is "for all who are far away," but no one believes Peter was suggesting that we should baptize all Gentiles. The promise is *for* them in the sense that God *wants* to pour out his Spirit on them (Acts 2:17). But they become recipients of the promise—and we should baptize them—only when they make a personal decision to repent and believe in Jesus Christ. This is why Peter immediately adds that the promise is for "everyone whom the Lord our God calls to him." It is not for everyone in general. It is for everyone who will repent and believe and thus for everyone whom God calls. The same holds true for Peter's assertion that the promise is not only for adults but also for their children. God *wants* children to receive the Holy Spirit, but the promise is applied to them and we should baptize them only when they personally repent and believe.

Baptism is an act of discipleship that can be entered into only by people old enough to be disciples. This is why every example of baptism in the New Testament involves a person old enough to decide to follow Christ. Never do we read about infants being baptized.

For example, it was only after the Samaritans "believed Philip" as he preached the good news that "they were baptized, both men and women" (Acts 8:12). It was only after the Ethiopian eunuch embraced the good news about Jesus that he was baptized (Acts 8:35–38). The apostle Paul was baptized after he encountered Jesus and obeyed the heavenly vision (Acts 9:18). Peter commanded Cornelius and his household to be baptized only after he saw evidence of their faith in Jesus Christ (Acts 10:44–48). It was only after God opened Lydia's heart and she believed that she and her household were baptized (Acts 16:14–15). And it was only after the disciples of John the Baptist accepted Paul's teaching about Jesus that they were baptized "in the name of the Lord Jesus" and received the Holy Spirit (Acts 19:5–6). Without exception, baptism follows faith and constitutes the first act of discipleship made by a responsible person who has decided to follow Jesus.

Defenders of infant baptism argue that the references in Acts to households being baptized suggest that infants were baptized along with adults (Acts 11:13–14; 16:15, 30–34; 18:8). There is no reason to assume this, however. While all servants were included in a "household" in the ancient Roman world, children generally were not. This seems to be Luke's perspective, for in the same context in which he speaks about households being baptized, he speaks about households being taught, believing, and rejoicing (Acts 16:32, 34; 18:8).

Finally, some of the meanings given to baptism in the New Testament imply that it is intended only for people old enough to be disciples. For example, Paul says that baptism shows that "our old self was crucified with [Christ]" (Rom. 6:6) and that now we should "walk in newness of life" (Rom. 6:4). Infants can hardly do so. Similarly, Peter says that baptism "now saves you" not as a literal washing "of dirt from the body" but "as an appeal to God for a good conscience" (1 Pet. 3:21). But how can an infant have a good (or bad) conscience? Baptism should be administered only to those who are old enough to make a decision to die to sin, walk in a new life, and enjoy a good conscience before God.

Supporting Argument

The importance of discipleship. History testifies to the truth that infant baptism produces nominal, apathetic Christians. If someone is considered a Christian by virtue of being born to Christian parents (or in a Christian state), then the urgency of stepping out on one's own and making the radical decision to follow Jesus is compromised. This is not to suggest that all Christians baptized as infants are passionless or that the practice of infant baptism causes one to be passionless. But this practice invariably tends in that direction, and for obvious reasons. By contrast, the practice of adult baptism forces each individual to make his or her own decision to follow Christ.

Responding to Objections

1. *Scripture passages oppose this view.* **Paedobaptists** point to several clusters of texts that they believe support their practice. For example, they often point to the New Testament practice of "household" baptism. But as

already shown, these passages do not require or even suggest that infants were baptized. Some try to support infant baptism on the basis of Paul's statement that children are "sanctified" by believing parents (1 Cor. 7:14). But this passage says nothing about baptism. Paul is simply claiming that children are "set apart"—namely, for a unique godly influence—when their parents believe. Finally, some try to support infant baptism on the basis of Jesus' practice of accepting and blessing little children (e.g., Mark 10:14–16). But again, this passage says nothing about baptism. Of course Jesus loved and accepted children! But he never tried to make disciples out of them. Why should we suppose, therefore, that he would approve of baptizing them?

2. *This view ignores the continuity of the old and new covenants.* Some argue that believer's baptism ignores the continuity between the old and new covenants in general and their signs—circumcision and baptism—in particular. Admittedly, the covenant concept does connect the Old and New Testaments, and the Abrahamic covenant is fulfilled in the new covenant. However, those who baptize infants have failed to see the decisive shift in the new covenant as it relates to the fulfillment of Abraham's promise. It is no longer a genetic connection that determines a child of Abraham but rather the conscious act of faith. Paul makes this unequivocally clear:

> Just as Abraham "believed God, and it was reckoned to him as righteousness," so, you see, those *who believe* are the descendants of Abraham. And the scripture, foreseeing that God would justify the Gentiles by faith, declared the gospel beforehand to Abraham, saying, "All the Gentiles shall be blessed in you." For this reason, *those who believe* are blessed with Abraham who believed. (Gal. 3:6–9, emphasis added)

God's elect people are no longer a nationality. They are a people who do something, namely, believe. Hence, while the sign of belonging to the covenantal community could be given to physical newborns under the old covenant, it should be reserved for spiritual newborns under the new covenant.

3. *This view has been influenced by modern individualism.* Some argue that the practice of believer's baptism has been unduly influenced by Western individualism, which rejects the biblical view of familial corporateness within the saved community. In the Bible, it is argued, infants of covenant keepers were regarded as members of the covenant because people in biblical times, unlike people today, did not define individuals apart from their association with a community.

In reply, it is not Western individualism that drives the believer's baptism position. Rather, it is the New Testament's concept of personal salvation. Each individual must be "born from above" just as each individual must be born from the womb (John 3:3–6). Believers are to belong to and be mutually defined by their involvement in the community of God's covenantal people, but first they must individually decide to become disciples. According to New Testament teaching, the first act of obedience they perform as disciples is to be baptized.

4. *This view runs counter to church tradition.* Finally, the believer's baptism position is often rejected on the grounds that it runs counter to the majority view throughout church history. Two things must be said in response.

First, evangelicals cannot appeal to church tradition to settle an issue. The affirmation of *sola scriptura* means that Scripture is the sole authority on matters of faith and practice. Christians should not easily set aside traditional perspectives, but they can and must do so if traditional views disagree with Scripture.

Second, while it is true that the infant baptism view has been the primary perspective throughout church history, it is also true that there is no explicit evidence of infant baptism until the second century and no evidence that it was dominant until much later. This is plenty of time for an aberration of Christian practice and theology to take place. Indeed, most evangelicals would agree that the dominant theology of baptism was becoming aberrant by the mid-second century, because Christians at this time were increasingly holding that baptism literally washed away sin and was necessary for salvation, a view almost all evangelicals reject.

Covenanting with the Community of God (The Infant Baptism View)

The Biblical Argument

Throughout its history, the church has practiced infant baptism because the practice of infant baptism is firmly rooted in Scripture. Scripture's support for infant baptism falls under three motifs: children and the covenant, household baptisms, and baptism as New Testament circumcision.

First, throughout the Bible, children were included in God's covenant. For example, God's covenant with Abraham included his children. God said to Abraham, "I will establish my covenant between me and you, *and your offspring* after you throughout their generations, for an everlasting covenant, to be God to you *and to your offspring* after you" (Gen. 17:7, emphasis added). Both the stipulations and the promises of God's covenant applied to Abraham's offspring. The same was true of the Sinai covenant, which Joshua read to the Israelites. It was presented to and included everybody—even children. "There was not a word of all that Moses commanded that Joshua did not read before all the assembly of Israel, and the women, *and the little ones*, and the aliens who resided among them" (Josh. 8:35, emphasis added).

The assumption that children are included in God's covenant is carried over into the New Testament. When Jesus' disciples tried to restrict his ministry to adults, Jesus was "indignant" and said to them: "'Let the little children come to me; do not stop them; for it is to such as these that the kingdom of God belongs. Truly I tell you, whoever does not receive the kingdom of God as a little child will never enter it.' And he took them up in his arms, laid his hands on them, and blessed them" (Mark 10:14–16).

Those who practice adult baptism often defend this stance on the grounds that children cannot adequately understand what they are doing. But this clearly was no obstacle for Jesus. Though these children undoubtedly could not understand most of what Jesus taught, and though they could not make responsible decisions for themselves, Jesus accepted them and blessed them. In this light, how can the church withhold any blessing from children, including the blessing of baptism?

The same acceptance of children into God's covenant is seen in the early church. After the Holy Spirit had been poured out on the day of Pentecost, Peter preached to the crowd: "Repent, and be baptized every one of you in the name of Jesus Christ so that your sins may be forgiven; and you will receive the gift of the Holy Spirit. For the promise is for you, *for your children*, and for all who are far away, everyone whom the Lord our God calls to him" (Acts 2:38–39, emphasis added).

In this passage, Peter assumes that water baptism precedes the reception of the Holy Spirit, yet he says that the promise of the Holy Spirit is "for your children" as well as for "you"—namely, the adult audience who could understand what he was saying. Children are participants of the covenant of God and thus may receive the Holy Spirit when their parents enter into the covenant with God. The way this covenant is sealed in the New Testament is through baptism. Consequently, it is good and necessary that the church baptize children of believing parents.

Finally, the view that children are blessed by what their believing parents do is reflected in Paul's First Letter to the Corinthians: "For the unbelieving husband is made holy through his wife, and the unbelieving wife is made holy through her husband. Otherwise, your children would be unclean, but as it is, they are holy" (1 Cor. 7:14).

We Western people are intensely individualistic in our view of the world. We assume that people must make their own individual decisions and are responsible only for what they individually choose to do. The Bible agrees that individuals are responsible for what they choose to do, but it also stresses that no person stands or falls on his or her own. It does not define people individualistically but rather sees them as part of a community—a family, a nation, and ultimately the entire human race. This is why it makes perfect sense for Paul to teach that children are made holy by the faith of their parents, though the notion runs counter to the Western individualistic worldview. It is also why children are consistently included in their parents' covenant and why the church should baptize children of believing parents.

Second, the biblical understanding that people are intricately connected to and defined by their communities explains why the New Testament often speaks of salvation, and even of baptism, in terms of family units. From a biblical perspective, entering the covenant of God is not simply an individual affair. Indeed, as in the Old Testament, children are included within their parents' covenant.

For example, an angel announced to Cornelius that a man named Peter was going to show him how to be saved. The angel said, he will "give you a message by which you and your entire household will be saved" (Acts 11:13–14). When Lydia accepted Paul's teaching, Luke says, "She and her household were baptized" (Acts 16:14). When Paul preached to a despairing jailer, he promised him, "Believe on the Lord Jesus, and you will be saved, you and your household." Later, after Paul explained to them how to be saved more fully, the Bible says the jailer "and his entire family were baptized without delay" (Acts 16:31, 33). Similarly, Crispus "together with all his household" came to believe in Christ (Acts 18:8), and Paul testified that he baptized "the household of Stephanas" (1 Cor. 1:16).

It is true that none of these passages explicitly mentions that children were part of these households, but why should they need to mention this? The fact that no passage restricts baptism to adults suggests that whoever was in the household was baptized. Moreover, given the general biblical teaching concerning children and the covenant, those who believe in infant baptism are justified in assuming that children are included in these passages.

One final passage is significant in showing the corporate nature of salvation and of baptism. In the process of applying a lesson from the Old Testament for the Corinthian Christians, Paul writes, "I do not want you to be unaware, brothers and sisters, that our ancestors were all under the cloud, and all passed through the sea, and all were baptized into Moses in the cloud and in the sea" (1 Cor. 10:1–2). Despite this shared blessing, Paul continues, "God was not pleased with most of them" (1 Cor. 10:5), for they were disobedient. Being baptized and enjoying various religious experiences means little if a person gets involved in idolatry and/or immorality, as the Israelites did (1 Cor. 10:6–22). For our present purposes, it is significant that Paul begins his teaching by drawing a parallel between Christian baptism and the Israelite experience of being enveloped in the cloud and going through the Red Sea. This experience, of course, happened to all Israelites, including children, for all Israelites were part of God's covenant. Hence, the passage illustrates Paul's assumption that baptism is for all Christian adults who choose to follow Christ as well as for their children.

The third and final aspect of Scripture that supports infant baptism centers on the fact that Paul draws an analogy between baptism and circumcision as practiced in the Old Testament. Throughout the Old Testament, the practice of circumcision functioned as the sign that a person belonged to God's covenant (Gen. 17:10–27). This was ordinarily performed on all Jewish males eight days after birth. Whether they lived as faithful covenant keepers once they matured to adulthood was up to them, of course. But as already shown, God and the community of covenant keepers presumed the best for each child and graciously invited him into the covenant before he was able to understand or respond on his own.

This practice of circumcision—or receiving a sign that one belongs to the covenant—was carried over into the New Testament through baptism. Paul writes: "In him [Christ] also you were circumcised with a spiritual circumcision, by putting off the body of the flesh in the circumcision of Christ; when you were buried with him in baptism, you were also raised with him through faith in the power of God, who raised him from the dead" (Col. 2:11–12).

If water baptism is our "circumcision" under the new covenant, shouldn't we administer it to the same people circumcision was administered to in the Old Testament, namely, infants? Are we really to be less gracious toward parents and children than the community of believers under the old covenant who accepted children into the covenant their parents made on their behalf? Are we rather to presume that a child is outside the covenant until he or she chooses to enter it? Does such an attitude contradict the biblical teaching on God's acceptance of children? According to this view, it does.

Supporting Arguments

1. *Church tradition.* From at least the second century, infant baptism has been practiced by the majority of Christians throughout history. If infant baptism is wrong, then we must conclude that for nearly two thousand years there have been few legitimate baptisms in the church and that the majority continue to be invalid. Of course, evangelicals who affirm *sola scriptura* cannot deny the theoretical possibility that this may in fact be true. At the same time, it must be acknowledged that the dominance of the practice of infant baptism in church tradition counts strongly in its favor.

2. *God's initiative in salvation.* When people restrict baptism to adults, they give the impression that salvation is a matter of God responding to human choice. It suggests that the foundation of salvation is adult decision making. Infant baptism rather illustrates that God is always the initiator in salvation. It beautifully illustrates the truth that when a person is born, before he or she can understand or respond to moral choices, God is working in that person's life to incorporate him or her into the community of the redeemed.

Responding to Objections

1. *The Bible contains no explicit reference to infant baptism.* Some object to infant baptism on the grounds that there is no explicit teaching on or example of infant baptism in the New Testament. This cannot be denied. At the same time, this is an argument from silence and thus cannot carry much weight. Just because Scripture does not specifically mention infants in baptism texts does not mean that infants are excluded in these baptism texts. One could just as easily argue that physically challenged people should not be baptized because they are not explicitly mentioned in Scripture. Christians of course baptize physically challenged people (as well as all other kinds of believers) because Scripture teaches that baptism is for everyone and never qualifies it by restricting people according to gender, age, abilities, race, and so on. For this same reason, children of adult believers should be baptized.

2. *Scripture gives faith as a prerequisite to baptism.* Many who practice adult baptism argue that Scripture always specifies an adult decision (repentance, faith, etc.) as a prerequisite for baptism. For example, Peter told the crowd on the day of Pentecost to "*Repent,* and be baptized" (Acts 2:38, emphasis added). Jesus said his disciples were to "make disciples . . . baptizing *them* in the name of the Father and of the Son and of the Holy Spirit, and teaching *them* to obey everything" (Matt. 28:19–20, emphasis added). On this basis, only those who are old enough to repent, be taught, and become disciples should be baptized.

It is hardly surprising that all the commands to be baptized are given to adults and have repentance or belief as their prerequisites. Infants cannot understand commands, so of course the earliest disciples were not going to give them any. We must also remember that the New Testament concerns the first generation of the church in which all growth was the result of converting adult nonbelievers. Therefore, it is to be expected that the command to be baptized would be preceded by the commands to repent, believe, and obey the gospel. Adult baptism is meaningless without such personal decisions, but this observation has no implication as to whether children of believing parents should receive the sign of the covenant as they did in Old Testament times.

Further Reading

Booth, Robert R. *Children of Promise: The Biblical Case for Infant Baptism.* Phillipsburg, NJ: Presbyterian and Reformed, 1995.

Bridge, Donald, and David Phypers. *The Water That Divides: The Baptism Debate.* Downers Grove, IL: InterVarsity, 1977.

Bromiley, Geoffrey W. *Children of Promise: The Case for Baptizing Infants.* Grand Rapids: Eerdmans, 1979.

Brooks, Oscar S. *The Drama of Decision: Baptism in the New Testament.* Peabody, MA: Hendrickson, 1987.

Brownson, James V. *The Promise of Baptism: An Introduction to Baptism in Scripture and the Reformed Tradition.* Grand Rapids: Eerdmans, 2007.

Castelein, John, et al. *Understanding Four Views on Baptism.* Grand Rapids: Zondervan, 2007.

Dixon, Neil. *Troubled Waters.* London: Epworth, 1979.

Ferguson, Everett. *Baptism in the Early Church: History, Theology, and Liturgy in the First Five Centuries.* Grand Rapids: Eerdmans, 2008.

Green, Michael. *Baptism: Its Purpose, Practice, and Power.* Downers Grove, IL: InterVarsity, 1987.

Jewett, Paul K. *Infant Baptism and the Covenant of Grace.* Grand Rapids: Eerdmans, 1978.

Schreiner, Thomas R., and Shawn D. Wright. *Believer's Baptism: Sign of the New Covenant in Christ.* Nashville: Broadman and Holman, 2007.

Strawbridge, Gregg, ed. *The Case for Covenantal Infant Baptism.* Phillipsburg, NJ: Presbyterian and Reformed, 2003.

Vander Zee, Leonard J. *Christ, Baptism, and the Lord's Supper: Recovering the Sacraments for Evangelical Worship.* Downers Grove, IL: InterVarsity, 2004.

Witherington, Ben. *Troubled Waters: Rethinking the Theology of Baptism.* Waco: Baylor University Press, 2007.

13

The Lord's Supper Debate

"This Is My Body" (The Spiritual Presence View)
"In Remembrance of Me" (The Memorial View)

Posing the Question

Jordan was overjoyed when he noticed the Bible that the new employee, Gracie, had placed on her desk in the cubicle next to his. For months he had thought he was the only Christian working in the office. Soon Jordan and Gracie were eating lunch together and sharing their spiritual journeys with one another. In time, Jordan invited Gracie to visit his church. It happened to be the first weekend of the month, and therefore, it was communion Sunday at First Baptist Church—the one Sunday a month when they celebrated the Lord's Supper together.

As Jordan passed a tray containing tiny plastic cups of grape juice to Gracie, he couldn't help noticing the look of puzzlement on her face. Later that afternoon, as they were eating lunch, Gracie began to talk about the communion experience. She explained that she came from a Catholic background and that the service was a little strange for her. Her confusion was expressed in a string of questions: Why did Jordan's church celebrate communion only once a month? Why did they use grape juice and not wine? Why didn't the people go to the front of the church to receive the Eucharist from the pastor? And finally, why wasn't there more emphasis on the fact that the **communion elements** were the actual body and blood of Christ given as a sacrifice? Indeed, to Jordan's surprise, Gracie told him she found the entire service offensively casual.

Jordan didn't know what to say. "We're just remembering what Jesus did for us," he finally muttered. "What's the big deal?"

"The big deal?" Gracie retorted. "You're taking the body and blood of the Savior! That's the big deal!"

The Center and Its Contrasts

Virtually all Christians celebrate some form of the Lord's Supper (also known as communion or the Eucharist). Jesus himself established this important practice when, on the evening before his crucifixion, he gathered his disciples for a final meal together. The Gospel of Matthew recounts the event: "While they were eating, Jesus took a loaf of bread, and after blessing it he broke it, gave it to the disciples, and said, 'Take, eat; this is my body.' Then he took a cup, and after giving thanks he gave it to them, saying, 'Drink from it, all of you; for this is my blood of the covenant, which is poured out for many for the forgiveness of sins'" (Matt. 26:26–28; see also Mark 14:22–24; Luke 22:19–20; 1 Cor. 11:23–29).

Evangelicals, along with most Christians, agree on several aspects of the Lord's Supper. First, this practice is a celebratory rite to be shared within the **new covenant** community of Jesus Christ. Second, it is to be celebrated in some sort of regular fashion. Finally, whatever else it means, it allows the Christian church to remember and testify to Jesus' atoning death. As Paul writes, "For as often as you eat this bread and drink the cup, you proclaim the Lord's death until he comes" (1 Cor. 11:26).

The disagreements begin when one presses the question of the meaning and significance of communion. In particular, people hold differing perspectives on what Jesus meant when he said, "This is my body. . . . This is my blood." In other words, is Christ actually "present" in the Lord's Supper, and if so, how? This debate is connected to a wider debate on the nature of Christian religious rituals in general. Are practices such as baptism and the Lord's Supper sacramental in nature (see **sacrament**), or are they more accurately understood as **ordinances**? The difference is important. According to the sacramental view, these practices are gifts of God to his church by which he bestows grace and blessing. Those who understand these events as ordinances view them as practices that were ordained by Christ, by which the church demonstrates its loving obedience to God.

The contemporary debate about the nature of the Lord's Supper can be traced back to the Reformation era. With all Protestants, evangelicals reject the Roman Catholic view of the Lord's Supper, known as transubstantiation. According to this view, upon being blessed by a Catholic priest, the actual substance of the bread and wine is literally transformed into the body and blood of Christ. After breaking away from the Roman Catholic Church, Lutheranism, following Martin Luther's convictions, developed its own interpretation of the Lord's Supper that came to be known as **consubstantiation.** According to this view, there is no need for a priest to bless the elements in order for a transformation to take place. Rather, because he believed that Jesus is present everywhere, Luther claimed that Christ's body is literally "in, with, and under" the bread and wine. The bread and wine, however, are not themselves transformed into the body and blood of Christ.

In the evangelical world today, there are primarily two perspectives on the nature of the Lord's Supper. Those who hold to a **spiritual presence view** believe that, in a unique way, Christ is spiritually present in the Lord's Supper. There is therefore a sacramental aspect to communion in that the believer is sealed in Jesus Christ as a confirmation of God's saving promises. Those who hold to a **memorial view** claim that Christ is not literally present in the Lord's Supper. They affirm that a distinct spiritual blessing is involved in taking communion, for believers are remembering what Jesus did for them. But this blessing is due to their obedient response to Christ's instruction, not because Christ is uniquely present in the Lord's Supper itself.

The two essays that follow defend these positions.

"This Is My Body" (The Spiritual Presence View)

The Catholic Church has traditionally believed that the presence of Christ in the sacrament of communion results in a transformation of the communion elements. The bread and wine become the body and blood of Christ. Certain **radical Reformers** in the sixteenth century (e.g., Zwingli, the Anabaptists) reacted against this view and went to the opposite extreme. They denied that Christ was in any special sense present in the Lord's Supper. The Lord's Supper was thus reduced to a commemoration of Jesus' death. Hence, their view is sometimes referred to as the memorial view.

Though Martin Luther and John Calvin disagreed on this matter, they both held that the correct understanding of Christ's presence in the Lord's Supper was located between these two extremes. Against the radical Reformers they held that Christ *is* uniquely present in the communion elements, but against the Catholics they held that this presence does not result in a physical change in the elements. This is the position of many mainline Protestants today (e.g., some Lutherans, Presbyterians, and Episcopalians). It is sometimes labeled the spiritual presence understanding of communion and is the view defended in this essay.

The Biblical Argument

Three passages have traditionally been cited as important to the spiritual presence understanding of communion. The first and most important passage concerns Jesus' words when he administered the Last Supper. All three Synoptic Gospels as well as Paul's First Letter to the Corinthians record that Jesus referred to the bread *as his body* and the cup *as his blood* (Matt. 26:26–28; Mark 14:22–24; Luke 22:19–20; 1 Cor. 11:23–29). While adherents of the spiritual presence view do not accept the Catholic conclusion that the bread and wine actually become the body and blood of Christ, they do think that Jesus was claiming more than simply that the bread and wine symbolize his body and blood. He was promising to be spiritually present in the bread and wine.

Several aspects of the Corinthian passage emphasize this point. Paul writes:

> For I received from the Lord what I also handed on to you, that the Lord Jesus on the night when he was betrayed took a loaf of bread, and when he had given thanks, he broke it and said, "This is my body that is for you. Do this in remembrance of me." In the same way he took the cup also, after supper, saying, "This cup is the new covenant in my blood. Do this, as often as you drink it, in remembrance of me." . . . Whoever, therefore, eats the bread or drinks the cup of the Lord in an unworthy manner will be answerable for the body and blood of the Lord. . . . For all who eat and drink without discerning the body, eat and drink judgment against themselves. (1 Cor. 11:23–29)

Not only does Paul quote Jesus' words, identifying the communion elements as his body and blood, but on this basis he warns the Corinthians not to participate in communion in an unworthy manner. Because Christ is present in the bread and the cup, believers will be "answerable for the body and blood of the Lord" if they take them in an unworthy manner. It would be difficult to understand the severity of Paul's warning if he believed communion was simply a memorial meal.

Second, in John's Gospel, Jesus proclaims: "Very truly, I tell you, unless you eat the flesh of the Son of Man and drink his blood, you have no life in you. Those who eat my flesh and drink my blood have eternal life, and I will raise them up on the last day; for my flesh is true food and my blood is true drink. Those who eat my flesh and drink my blood abide in me, and I in them" (John 6:53–56).

The traditional interpretation of this passage is that Jesus was referring to communion. Again, these words do not imply that the bread and wine become the body and blood of Jesus, but at the same time, it certainly seems that Jesus' language was too strong simply to be interpreted symbolically. As Christ is present through his Spirit in every believer's life (Rom.

8:9–11)—that is, he is not *physically* present in the believer—so Christ is spiritually present in the communion elements. His physical body and blood are not present in communion, but his presence in the bread and cup are no less real because of this fact. In a spiritual sense, believers "eat the flesh" and "drink [the] blood" of the Son of God.

A third passage that conveys the reality of Christ's presence in the Lord's Supper is 1 Corinthians 10:16–17. Here Paul writes: "The cup of blessing that we bless, is it not a sharing in the blood of Christ? The bread that we break, is it not a sharing in the body of Christ? Because there is one bread, we who are many are one body, for we all partake of the one bread."

The memorial view that the bread and cup Christians share simply "commemorate" the Lord's death does not capture the force of what Paul says in this passage. Christians express the truth that they are one body when they take communion together, for in this celebration Christians are sharing in the body and blood of Christ.

This interpretation is confirmed several verses later, when Paul contrasts eating at "the table of the Lord" and eating at "the table of demons" (1 Cor. 10:21). Those who eat at "the table of demons" are "partners with demons" and "provoke the Lord to jealousy" (1 Cor. 10:20, 22). Paul seems to be suggesting that demons are spiritually present and that people partner with demons when they eat food that is dedicated to them. He is not simply talking about symbols. So, too, the Lord is spiritually present and believers partner with him when they eat the bread and drink the wine that is dedicated to him.

Supporting Argument

A traditional perspective. A view similar to the spiritual presence understanding of communion is evident in the writings of Ignatius of Antioch, Justin Martyr, and other second-century writers. The understanding of this unique presence became overly literalized in the medieval Catholic Church's doctrine of transubstantiation. Nevertheless, the teaching that Christ is present in the Lord's Supper is the traditional perspective. The view that the Lord's Supper simply commemorates the Lord's sacrificial death has no clear precedent before the sixteenth century. This provides significant support for the spiritual presence view.

Responding to an Objection

The language surrounding the Lord's Supper is metaphorical. The main objection to the spiritual presence understanding of the Lord's Supper is that it takes metaphorical language too literally. Defenders of the memorial view argue that the passages cited in support of the spiritual presence view contain textual clues that suggest the Lord was speaking metaphorically when he referred to bread and wine as his body and blood. For example, Paul cites Jesus' words, "This is my body that is for you. Do this in remembrance of me." He also teaches that "as often as you eat this bread and drink the cup, you proclaim the Lord's death until he comes" (1 Cor. 11:24, 26). Since the expressed purpose of communion is to "remember" and "proclaim" the death of the Lord, the teaching that the bread and wine are the body and blood of the Lord must be understood in this light: They help believers remember and proclaim the Lord's broken body and shed blood.

In response, mainline Protestants certainly do not want to deny that there is a symbolic element in the Lord's Supper. Indeed, a central aspect of the Reformed teaching on communion has been that it functions as a "sign." But this does not mean that the bread and wine cannot also function as a means by which Christ becomes uniquely present to believers as well. The memorial view objection poses a false dichotomy. Symbol and sacrament are not mutually exclusive. Believers best capture the entire teaching of Scripture on this matter if they accept that the communion elements function in both capacities, as God sees fit.

"In Remembrance of Me" (The Memorial View)

The Lord's Supper is an ordinance that Christ established to provide the church with a reminder of the love and grace he expressed on the cross at Calvary. Communion symbolizes and commemorates Christ's death and functions as a sign of the new covenant believers have with Christ. As such, it is an external reminder of Christ's act of redemption. Christ is of course present whenever believers celebrate the Lord's Supper but not in any sense different from the way he is present whenever believers are gathered in Jesus' name (Matt. 18:20). According to the memorial view, both the Catholic understanding that the communion elements become the body and blood of Christ and the mainline Protestant view that Christ is spiritually present in a unique way in the communion elements are unnecessary and unbiblical.

The Biblical Argument

Three biblical arguments support the memorial understanding of communion. The first concerns the words Jesus used when he established this ordinance. All three Synoptic Gospels as well as Paul's First Letter to the

Corinthians record that Jesus referred to the bread as his body and the cup as his blood (Matt. 26:26–28; Mark 14:22–24; Luke 22:19–20; 1 Cor. 11:23–29). There is no reason to think that Jesus was speaking literally here, as Catholics believe. If this were the case, we would have to accept that the cup Jesus held was literally the new covenant, for Jesus refers to it as such (Luke 22:20). But neither is there any reason to think that Jesus was referring to a unique presence in communion, as advocates of the spiritual presence view believe. The most natural understanding of Jesus' words is that he was simply saying, "This bread and wine *represent* my body and sacrificed blood," and "This cup *represents* the new covenant."

Second, as Paul records it, Jesus specifically told his disciples they were to celebrate communion "in remembrance" of him and to proclaim "the Lord's death until he comes" (1 Cor. 11:25–26). Remembrance language is used throughout the Bible in the context of covenant, usually indicating something that was to function as a sign of the covenant (e.g., Gen. 9:11–16; Exod. 2:24; 12:14). This is the sort of language Jesus' Jewish disciples would readily recognize as symbolic. Thus, it seems clear that the Lord's Supper was intended as a sign of the new covenant whose purpose was and is to help believers remember and commemorate the new covenant and its promises in Christ.

Along these same lines, it is important to notice that the metaphorical language Christ used at the Last Supper was hardly unique. Jesus frequently spoke nonliterally. For example, Jesus referred to himself as the vine, the shepherd, and the bridegroom, while his disciples were called the branches, the sheep, and the bride (John 15:5; 10:14–16; Matt. 9:14–15). No one interprets this language literally. So, too, in a passage that has great significance for the communion controversy, Jesus referred to himself as "the bread of life" that the Father sent down from heaven. He promised that any who ate this bread would never hunger again (John 6:32–36). Jesus was, of course, not advocating cannibalism. Believers should not interpret Jesus' teaching about the bread and the wine any more literally than they interpret these other statements of Jesus. They should assume that all such language is equally metaphorical.

Third, both the spiritual presence and the transubstantiation view of communion subtly contradict an important underlying theme of the New Testament: namely, that God is *always* present in a believer's life. Any belief that locates God's presence more in one place than another or more in one ritual than another is veering from New Testament teaching and tending toward magic. The New Testament view understands God's presence to be a matter of relationship, not ritual.

For example, Jesus taught his disciples, "Those who love me will keep my word, and my Father will love them, and we will come to them and make our home with them" (John 14:23). Jesus taught that he would "abide" in his disciples and his disciples would "abide" in him (John 15:4–5). And he promised to be with his disciples "always" (Matt. 28:20). In the power of the Spirit, both the Father and the Son permanently live in believers. Since this is the case, believers should not believe that they somehow receive more of God's presence in communion. To be sure, all believers can and should be reminded of the reality of God's gracious presence through communion, but the reminder is not the reality. It is important to keep the two distinct.

Supporting Argument

Communion and our relationship with God. The Reformers rediscovered the biblical truth that a believer's relationship with God is rooted in Christ's sacrificial death alone, based on faith alone, and informed by Scripture alone. Neither meritorious works nor rituals nor **ecclesiastical** authority are to define a believer's relationship with God. Neither Luther nor Calvin, however, fully developed these newly rediscovered truths. Both tried in different ways to retain a commonality with the traditional Catholic view of communion. A truly Reformed view of Christ's presence associates it only with the faith of the believer. This gracious presence is not funneled through the church, priests, or rituals.

Responding to an Objection

This view is not compatible with Scripture. Some object that the memorial view is not compatible with certain aspects of Paul's discussion of communion in his First Letter to the Corinthians. For example, at one point Paul writes: "The cup of blessing that we bless, is it not a sharing in the blood of Christ? The bread that we break, is it not a sharing in the body of Christ? Because there is one bread, we who are many are one body, for we all partake of the one bread" (1 Cor. 10:16–17).

People argue that Paul's claim that believers share in the body and blood of Christ cannot easily be interpreted metaphorically. This is especially true, they argue, considering the fact that Paul says when someone participates in communion in an unworthy manner, that person "will be answerable for the body and blood of the Lord." They "eat and drink judgment against themselves" (1 Cor. 11:27, 29). Such a severe warning suggests that communion is more than just a memorial meal.

But this reasoning overlooks the fact that Paul's main concern in 1 Corinthians 10 and 11 is not to teach on the nature of communion but to address the carnal immaturity and divisiveness of the Corinthians. Among other things, the way the Corinthians celebrated communion was almost barbaric. Some would hoard all the bread while others would consume all the wine. Consequently, Paul writes, "One goes hungry and another becomes drunk." This way of taking communion was unworthy of the Lord, for it showed "contempt for the church of God" (1 Cor. 11:20–22).

Against this carnal and divisive immaturity, Paul stressed that the purpose of celebrating the Lord's Supper was to remember that *we all share in the Lord's body and blood*. All who put their trust in Christ participate in the forgiveness and new life he purchased on Calvary. This is why the Corinthians were to share the one bread and the one cup. They brought judgment on themselves not because they violated the supposedly unique presence of Christ in the bread and wine, as advocates of the spiritual presence perspective sometimes argue, but because of the "contempt for the church of God" they demonstrated by turning a memorial meal that should have unified them into a carnal feast that further divided them.

Further Reading

Accola, Louis W. *Given for You: Reflections on the Meaning of the Lord's Supper*. Lutheran Voices. Minneapolis: Augsburg Fortress, 2007.

Bridge, Donald, and David Phypers. *Communion: The Meal That Unites?* Wheaton: Harold Shaw, 1981.

Gresham, Charles R., and Tom Lawson, eds. *The Lord's Supper: Historical Writings on Its Meaning to the Body of Christ*. Joplin, MO: College Press, 1993.

Henry, Jim. *In Remembrance of Me: A Manual on Observing the Lord's Supper*. Nashville: Broadman and Holman, 1998.

Hicks, John Mark. *Come to the Table: Revisioning the Lord's Supper*. Abilene, TX: Leafwood, 2002.

Jones, Paul H. *Christ's Eucharistic Presence: A History of the Doctrine*. New York: Peter Lang, 1994.

Marshall, I. Howard. *Last Supper and Lord's Supper*. Grand Rapids: Eerdmans, 1980.

Mathison, Keith A. *Given for You: Reclaiming Calvin's Doctrine of the Lord's Supper*. Phillipsburg, NJ: Presbyterian and Reformed, 2002.

Moore, Russell D., et al. *Understanding Four Views on the Lord's Supper*. Grand Rapids: Zondervan, 2007.

Schmidt, Dan. *Taken by Communion: How the Lord's Supper Nourishes the Soul*. Grand Rapids: Baker Books, 2004.

Smith, Gordon T. *The Lord's Supper: Five Views*. Downers Grove, IL: InterVarsity, 2008.

Stoffer, Dale R., ed. *The Lord's Supper: Believers Church Perspectives*. Scottdale, PA: Herald, 1997.

Vander Zee, Leonard J. *Christ, Baptism, and the Lord's Supper: Recovering the Sacraments for Evangelical Worship*. Downers Grove, IL: InterVarsity, 2004.

Witherington, Ben. *Making a Meal of It: Rethinking the Theology of the Lord's Supper*. Waco: Baylor University Press, 2007.

Wright, N. T. *The Meal Jesus Gave Us*. Louisville: Westminster John Knox, 2003.

14

The Charismatic Gifts Debate

The Gifts Are for Today (The Continuationist View)
"Tongues Shall Cease" (The Cessationist View)

Posing the Question

Sue had never been to a charismatic prayer gathering before. She had come this time only because a college friend had invited her, promising her she would experience the Holy Spirit as never before. Sue felt quite uncomfortable. During the two and a half hours of prayer, she frequently heard people **speaking in tongues.** She had heard of speaking in tongues, but she had never actually heard it done before. Not only this, but several times people claimed to get a "word" from the Lord for someone else in the group or for the group as a whole. A few people who were either sick or had disabilities were prayed over, and one claimed to be healed.

Then to top it off, there was a "prophecy" over her! Toward the end of the meeting, a middle-aged man came up to Sue and in front of the other thirty-five people who were present laid his hands on her and said, "The Lord loves you deeply. He knows your wound and your confusion. Do not be discouraged. Your healing and direction shall soon come to pass."

Sue did not know what to think or feel about this. On the one hand, it felt intensely awkward being put on the spot in front of strangers. On the other hand, Sue had indeed been going through some emotional pain and confusion, related mostly to a strained relationship. Was this really the Lord speaking to her? Or was it simply a person who *thought* he was speaking on behalf of God? The message was accurate about her being in pain and in a state of confusion. But then again, aren't many college students in at least a little bit of pain or confused about one matter or another much of the time? There was some biblical precedent (she later found out) for all the charismatic activity she had witnessed, but how could she be sure these activities were for the church today? Why had she never heard about them in her own church? Was charismatic experience something she should pursue or avoid?

The Center and Its Contrast

Over and against all forms of naturalism, all evangelicals believe the Holy Spirit is at work in the world. All believe the Holy Spirit supernaturally works in human hearts to bring people to the point of faith in Christ. All believe the Holy Spirit gives certain gifts to people to carry out ministry, such as teaching, preaching, administration, and hospitality. And all agree that God can and does at times miraculously intervene in the affairs of people. But evangelical Christians are divided on the issue of whether the **charismatic gifts** are for today and should be practiced today.

The charismatic gifts are a distinct class of gifts mentioned in 1 Corinthians 12:8–10. Paul writes:

> To one is given through the Spirit the utterance of wisdom, and to another the utterance of knowledge according to the same Spirit, to another faith by the same Spirit, to another gifts of healing by the one Spirit, to another the working of miracles, to another prophecy, to another the discernment of spirits, to another various kinds of tongues, to another the interpretation of tongues.

The central question in the charismatic debate is this: Were these gifts intended by God to be used throughout the entire church age until the Lord returns? **Continuationists** answer yes: The charismatic gifts were intended to continue throughout history. Therefore, contemporary believers should be open to them and, some would add, even aggressively seek them. **Cessationists** answer no: The charismatic gifts were intended to cease after the New Testament.

Three stages of development lead up to the present debate about the charismatic gifts. First, in the early twentieth century, a movement broke out that came to be called **Pentecostalism**. This movement generally taught that speaking in tongues (namely, an inspired foreign language one has not learned by natural means) was the **initial evidence** of receiving the baptism, or infilling, of the Holy Spirit. Members of this movement also emphasized that physical healing was available through Christ, and they practiced the other charismatic gifts as well. A number of Pentecostal denominations grew out of this movement, the largest being the Assemblies of God and the Church of God in Christ.

For the first fifty years of their existence, Pentecostals were mostly shunned by mainstream Christians. Then beginning in the early 1960s, some mainstream churches began to incorporate elements of Pentecostal thought and practice into their services. This movement soon became known as the **charismatic movement.** Unlike Pentecostals, charismatics did not generally leave their denominations, and therefore, they did not organize themselves into a distinct denomination. Charismatic Christians can be found in almost every denomination except those who have embraced a cessationist theology. While many charismatics do not embrace the Pentecostal doctrine that tongues is the necessary initial evidence of receiving the baptism of the Holy Spirit, they share the conviction that all the charismatic gifts are for today and thus should be pursued by believers.

A third stage leading up to the present debate began in the early 1980s. A movement began to sweep the Western world known as the **third wave** because it followed the Pentecostal (first wave) and charismatic (second wave) movements. This movement is characterized by a more aggressive theology of spiritual gifts and miraculous manifestations. "Signs and wonders," as adherents call them, are *normative* whenever the gospel is preached. More specifically, third wave Christians are convinced that Christians should expect healings and deliverances whenever the gospel goes forth, just as they did in the New Testament. The Vineyard Fellowship is a denomination that has formed around this theology.

Today, evangelical Christians can be roughly divided into three distinct groups. First, there are those who believe that the charismatic gifts ceased as soon as the New Testament was completed and disseminated to all the churches. Cessationists thus conclude that everything that passes as a charismatic experience today is in fact misguided emotionalism, at best, or demonic deception, at worst. On the other extreme are the Pentecostal, charismatic, and third wave Christians who believe that the charismatic gifts are for today and thus should be pursued and practiced.

In between the cessationists and the continuationists are Christians who are not theologically opposed to the exercise of charismatic gifts, but they are cautious. These people are often concerned with the extreme emphasis placed on the gifts in some Pentecostal, charismatic, or third wave circles as well as some of the unusual practices that at times accompany these gifts (e.g., being **slain in the Spirit, laughing in the Spirit,** etc.). This latter group is continuationist in theology but does not emphasize or pursue the charismatic gifts the way charismatic Christians do.

The following two essays contrast the cessationist and continuationist theologies.

The Gifts Are for Today (The Continuationist View)

The Bible mentions many gifts that are available to believers to use in ministry until the Lord returns. Some argue that one class of these gifts—the charismatic gifts—were intended only for the building of the early church and thus ceased in the first century. According to this view, people today should not, and in fact do not, speak in tongues, prophesy, get words of knowledge, and so on. Believers who *think* they exercise these gifts are either deceiving themselves or are being deceived by demons. This essay refutes the cessationist view and argues that the charismatic gifts are meant for today as much as any other gift mentioned in the New Testament.

The Biblical Argument

Five passages of Scripture list gifts given to the church by God. First Corinthians 12:8–10 lists nine charismatic gifts ("charismatic" comes from the Greek word *charismata*, which Paul uses to identify these gifts). They are an utterance of wisdom, an utterance of knowledge, faith, gifts of healing, miracles, prophecy, discernment of spirits, tongues, and the interpretation of tongues. First Corinthians 12:28–30 offers a slightly different list. God gives the church apostles, prophets, teachers, miracles, gifts of healings, helps, administrations, various kinds of tongues, and interpretations of tongues. In Romans 12:6–8, Paul offers a significantly different list consisting of prophecy, service, teaching, ministry, exhortation, giving, leadership, and showing mercy. Different still is the list in Ephesians 4:11, which consists of apostles, prophets, evangelists, and pastor-teachers. Peter's short list in 1 Peter 4:10–11 consists of speaking and serving.

The question we must ask is this: Where is it stated that God did not intend for these gifts to continue throughout history? Isn't it arbitrary to suppose, for example, that the gift of teaching is still valid but the gift of speaking in tongues is not? Isn't it arbitrary to allow for exhortation, giving, and showing mercy while excluding Spirit-inspired words of wisdom, prophecy, speaking in tongues, and healing?

Not only is disallowing an entire category of gifts arbitrary, but it is also unbiblical. At the beginning of his First Epistle to the Corinthians—the same epistle in which he incorporates his list of charismatic gifts—Paul writes:

> I give thanks to my God always for you because of the grace of God that has been given you in Christ Jesus, for in every way you have been enriched in him, in speech and knowledge of every kind—just as the testimony of Christ has been strengthened among you—so *that you are not lacking in*

any spiritual gift as you wait for the revealing of our Lord Jesus Christ. He will also strengthen you to the end, so that you may be blameless on the day of our Lord Jesus Christ. (1:4–8, emphasis added)

Paul affirms that Christians should not lack any spiritual gift as long as they "wait for the revealing of our Lord Jesus Christ." He uses the same word (*charisma*) in this passage to refer to spiritual gifts as he uses in 1 Corinthians 12:1 when discussing the charismatic gifts. The implication is that Paul believed the charismatic gifts would be in operation until the Lord's return.

Another passage that strongly suggests that all the gifts were intended for the entire church age is Ephesians 4:11–13. Here Paul writes:

The gifts [God] gave were that some would be apostles, some prophets, some evangelists, some pastors and teachers, to equip the saints for the work of ministry, for building up the body of Christ, until all of us come to the unity of the faith and of the knowledge of the Son of God, to maturity, to the measure of the full stature of Christ.

Until the body of Christ is fully built up into "the measure of the full stature of Christ"—until the Lord returns—the gifts are to remain in operation. In this passage, Paul explicitly mentions the charismatic gift of prophecy. This reveals the arbitrariness and unbiblical nature of the cessationist claim that prophecy along with the other charismatic gifts ceased in the first century.

Peter also suggests that the gifts are to operate until the Lord returns. After reminding his audience that "the end of all things is near," he instructs them to "serve one another with whatever gift each of you has received" (1 Pet. 4:7, 10). Along similar lines, John instructs his readers that "the anointing" they received "abides" in them and shall do so until the Lord returns. Hence, they "may have confidence and not be put to shame before him at his coming" (1 John 2:27–28). The assumption is that nothing substantially changes with the "anointing" the church receives until the Lord returns. Indeed, the New Testament generally depicts the work of the Spirit in believers' lives as unchanging throughout the church age (cf. e.g., Eph. 1:13–14; 4:30; Jude 20–21).

Other aspects of the New Testament confirm the view that all the gifts are intended for the entire church age. For example, Paul explicitly commands believers to "strive for the spiritual gifts" (speaking specifically of the charismatic gifts listed in 1 Corinthians 12). Believers are especially to "strive for" and be "eager" for the gift of prophecy (1 Cor. 14:1, 39). Paul specifically commands believers not to "quench the Spirit," "despise the words of prophets," or "forbid speaking in tongues" (1 Thess. 5:19–22; 1 Cor. 14:39)—the very thing cessationists do! Cessationists insist that these verses apply only to believers who lived before the New Testament was completed, but where is that doctrine taught in the New Testament? Paul gives his instruction in these passages without any temporal, cultural, or theological qualification. To the same audience and in the same context, he also gives his beautiful teaching on the supremacy of love (1 Cor. 13). If we believe he is talking to contemporary Christians about love, we have no reason to conclude he is not talking to contemporary Christians when he gives helpful instruction regarding the use of the charismatic gifts.

Supporting Arguments

1. *The weak biblical foundation for cessationism.* The exegesis used to support cessationism is dubious, and this itself is an argument in favor of continuationism. Three passages are most frequently cited in support of ceassationism.

First, Ephesians 2:20–22. In this passage, Paul says that "the household of God" is "built upon the foundation of the apostles and prophets, with Christ Jesus himself as the cornerstone." Cessationists use this passage to argue that the sole purpose of the charismatic gifts was to lay the foundation for the church. Once the foundation was laid, the gifts were to cease. However, Paul does not mention the charismatic gifts in this passage. The church is built on the foundation of the twelve apostles and the prophets he used to communicate his inspired Word. But this does not mean that no others will have the gift of being an apostle (meaning "sent one") or the gift of prophecy. And it certainly does not entail that other charismatic gifts such as speaking in tongues or receiving a word of knowledge have ceased.

Second, Hebrews 2:4–6. The author states that the apostles were validated by supernatural signs and wonders. Cessationists conclude that this was the primary purpose of the charismatic gifts. But the text does not suggest this. The New Testament also mentions other purposes for the charismatic gifts, such as strengthening the believer (1 Cor. 14:3), edifying the body (1 Cor. 12, 14), evangelism (e.g., Acts 9:32–43), glorifying God (e.g., John 11:4), and expressing compassion and love (e.g., Mark 1:40–41). Indeed, in 1 Corinthians 12 and 14, passages in which the charismatic gifts are most thoroughly discussed, no mention is made of their use in validating apostolic authority, of spreading the gospel, or of laying the foundation for the church.

Third, 1 Corinthians 13:8–13. In this passage, Paul mentions that tongues and prophecy shall cease when "the complete" arrives. Some cessationists argue that "the complete" refers to the New Testament and thus that the charismatic gifts were to cease once the New Testament was written and disseminated to all the churches. The majority of scholars, however, argue that "the complete" refers to the coming of Jesus Christ. Proof of this is found in the same epistle, when Paul tells the Corinthians that they should lack no gift as they "wait for the revealing of our Lord Jesus Christ" (1 Cor. 1:7). What is more, if all that is "partial" was done away with at the close of the New Testament, then "knowledge" must also have "come to an end" (1 Cor. 13:8). This clearly has not happened.

2. *Church history.* It is true that the exercise of the gifts gradually died down during the second to the fourth centuries. We should not read too much into this, however.

First, it is important to remember that the early post-apostolic church embraced a number of ideas and practices that most cessationists, and most Protestants in general, do not accept as biblical. For example, most believers during this time believed that baptism literally washed away sin and thus was necessary for salvation. Most Protestants today believe that salvation comes by faith alone. Hence, the fact that the exercise of the charismatic gifts waned during this period does not mean that it did so by God's design. Rather, it is an indication that the spiritual vibrancy of the church declined during this period.

Second, cessationists often exaggerate the extent to which the gifts waned during this time and the extent to which they were absent throughout history. From Tertullian, Origen, Irenaeus, and Hilary, we know that the charismatic gifts continued well into the third and fourth centuries. Moreover, no one disputes the fact that at different periods of church history, especially during revival movements, some of the gifts were manifested. There is no reason to refuse to identify the exercise of the charismatic gifts historically or today with the gifts spoken of in the New Testament.

3. *God's guidance today.* All evangelicals agree that the New Testament is the final, authoritative, written Word of God for the entire church age. All personal "revelations" received today—whether by prophecy or a word of knowledge—must conform to this standard. But it is as beneficial for believers today as it was in the first century to receive personalized words of direction, encouragement, and instruction from the Lord. These words do not add to the New Testament revelation, as cessationists sometimes argue. They simply help Christians *apply* the New Testament revelation to the particular situations they face.

Responding to Objections

1. *The pattern of God's miraculous activity does not support this view.* Cessationists sometimes argue that God provides signs and wonders at crucial turning points in history, usually to inaugurate a new era. Signs and wonders are not God's **modus operendi**, and hence, we should not

expect the supernaturalism of the New Testament church to continue throughout the church age.

This argument is misguided on several accounts. First, it may be that signs and wonders intensify when God inaugurates a new era in history, but the Bible does not teach that signs and wonders are *only* for these inaugurating times. On the contrary, while signs and wonders are more prevalent at times, they occur even when no new era is being inaugurated (e.g., the miracles of Samson, Elijah, and Elisha).

Second, the cessationist argument is an argument from silence that has no force. The relative absence of miracles in portions of the biblical narrative does not mean that there was an absence of miracles in biblical history. It may simply mean that authors were more inclined to mention miracles at turning points in human history than at other times. To illustrate, the prophet Jeremiah says, "You showed signs and wonders in the land of Egypt, and to this day in Israel and among all humankind, and have made yourself a name that continues to this very day" (Jer. 32:20). In Scripture, we read about the signs and wonders that the Lord performed in the land of Egypt, but we read nothing about the signs and wonders that were continuing in Jeremiah's day. The fact that something was not recorded clearly does not mean that it did not happen.

Finally, even if we grant that signs and wonders were largely absent throughout major periods of God's interaction with humans, this would not support the claim that God chose to cease performing signs and wonders. It may rather be due to the lack of faith and sometimes outright rebellion on the part of God's people. Even Jesus' power to perform miracles was hampered when people were hardened in unbelief (Mark 6:5–6).

2. *The continuation of charismatic gifts means the canon is open.* Cessationists often argue that continuationists presuppose an open canon, allowing for extra-biblical revelations of God's will today. Continuationists, however, deny this charge. They believe the canon of Scripture is closed and that it alone is the final authority for what Christians are to believe and how they are to live as kingdom people. New doctrines cannot be revealed through prophetic words, and no prophetic words of direction, guidance, or edification belong on the same level as Scripture.

Paul taught that Christians are not to "despise prophecy," but neither are they to uncritically accept it. Rather, they are to test it and hold fast to that which is good (1 Thess. 5:20–21). When prophets speak, people are to "weigh" what is said (1 Cor. 14:29). If anything does not conform to Scripture or is not confirmed by the inner witness of the Holy Spirit, people are not to subject themselves to the authority of the prophecy.

Admittedly, the gift of prophecy, as well as the other charismatic gifts, has at times been abused. This is unfortunate, but given fallen human nature, not at all surprising. Christians must not overreact against this abuse and violate clear scriptural teaching by dismissing the charismatic gifts altogether. Jeremiah and Ezekiel both had to confront people who imagined they were prophesying when they in fact were not (Jer. 5:30–31; 6:13–15; 14:13–16; Ezek. 13:1–11), but the prophets did not conclude from this that no one could prophesy. Rather, they took care to distinguish true prophecies from false ones (e.g., Jer. 28:5–9; cf. 25:4–11). So, too, Paul had to confront the abuse of various gifts in the church of Corinth, but thankfully, he did not draw the conclusion cessationists draw from the abuse of gifts today and argue that charismatic gifts should not be practiced. He rather encouraged believers to mature in the way they exercise and receive the charismatic gifts (1 Cor. 14:26–33; 1 Thess. 5:20–22). The charismatic gifts are for today and are of great benefit to the church when used and received according to biblical instruction.

"Tongues Shall Cease" (The Cessationist View)

The charismatic gifts spoken of in the New Testament were given to the church for three reasons: (1) They provided supernatural attestation to the apostolic authority of the early church; (2) they helped lay the foundation for the church; and (3) they provided divine guidance to early believers at a time when the New Testament, the final revelation of God, was not yet complete. The authority of the early church has now been attested; the New Testament is now complete; therefore, Christians do not need supernatural gifts to guide them in their faith walk. Hence, the charismatic gifts are no longer in operation today.

The Biblical Argument

The New Testament makes it clear that the charismatic gifts of the early church were intended to help build the church's foundation. An important passage in this regard is Ephesians 2:13, 18–22. Paul writes:

> But now in Christ Jesus you who once were far off have been brought near by the blood of Christ . . . for through him both of us [Jews and Gentiles] have access in one Spirit to the Father. So then you are no longer strangers and aliens, but you are citizens with the saints and also members of the household of God, built upon the foundation of the apostles and prophets, with Christ Jesus himself as the cornerstone. In him the whole structure is joined together and grows into a holy temple in the Lord; in whom you also are built together spiritually into a dwelling place for God.

With Jesus Christ as the "cornerstone" (namely, the point on which an edifice rests), the first generation of Christians were given apostles and prophets, who flourished in the revelational and miraculous gifts and were to build the foundation of the church. Upon this one foundation, "the whole structure is joined together and grows into a holy temple in the Lord." Clearly, Christians today are to build on the foundation already laid, not add to the foundation itself. Hence, there is no further need for apostles or prophets or the charismatic gifts that attested to their authority.

This temporary role of the charismatic gifts is expressed by the author of Hebrews. The author writes:

> For if the message declared through angels was valid, and every transgression or disobedience received a just penalty, how can we escape if we neglect so great a salvation? It was declared at first through the Lord, and it was attested to us by those who heard him, while God added his testimony by signs and wonders and various miracles, and by gifts of the Holy Spirit, distributed according to his will. (2:2–4)

The author is drawing a parallel between the attestation of the revelation given in the Old Testament and the attestation of the revelation given in the early church. The message in the Old Testament was "declared through angels," which is why people should have believed it was true and were punished if they disobeyed it. How much more should people in and after the first century accept the message given by Jesus and the apostles as true. Jesus' ministry was "attested to us by those who heard him" while God further confirmed his message by providing "signs and wonders and various miracles" and even by "gifts of the Holy Spirit."

This supernatural confirmation was specific to the anointed people who were initially giving the divine revelations. The signs and wonders in the New Testament were not intended for all time. They were used by those who declared the message first, those who were to become the one foundation of the church.

The fact that the charismatic gifts were given to attest to those who first declared the gospel is further demonstrated by Paul. In support of his own apostleship, he notes that "the signs of a true apostle were performed among you with utmost patience, signs and wonders and mighty works" (2 Cor. 12:12). If there are no "true apostles" today, then neither should there be charismatic gifts that attest to their authority. This perspective is further confirmed by the book of Acts, which notes that the preaching of the apostles was accompanied by supernatural signs and wonders. For example, Luke says that Paul and Barnabas remained in Iconium, "speaking boldly for the Lord, who testified to the word of his grace by granting signs and wonders to be done through them" (Acts 14:3; cf. 2:22, 43; 4:30;

5:12; 7:36; 8:13). The signs and wonders were God's way of showing the audiences that his hand was upon these preachers as they spoke the Word of the Lord and laid the foundation for the future church.

The fact that charismatic gifts were intended to cease with the completion of the New Testament is further suggested by Paul in 1 Corinthians 13. Here Paul writes:

> Love never ends. But as for prophecies, they will come to an end; as for tongues, they will cease; as for knowledge, it will come to an end. For we know only in part, and we prophesy only in part; but when the complete comes, the partial will come to an end. When I was a child, I spoke like a child, I thought like a child, I reasoned like a child; when I became an adult, I put an end to childish ways. For now we see in a mirror, dimly, but then we will see face to face. Now I know only in part; then I will know fully, even as I have been fully known. And now faith, hope, and love abide, these three; and the greatest of these is love. (vv. 8–13)

Some argue that "the complete" refers to the second coming of Jesus. But nowhere else does Paul use this term in this way. The contrast is rather between the partial revelation the Corinthians had and the complete revelation that was coming with the New Testament. At the time Paul was writing to the Corinthians, the foundation was still in the process of being laid. This is why the Corinthians needed the charismatic gifts. They were getting overly enthusiastic about these gifts, however, so Paul reminded them that there would soon come a time when "the partial will come to an end." Indeed, compared to the full revelation given in the New Testament, Paul is saying, reliance on the charismatic gifts is childish. If the Corinthians were more mature in their faith, they would emphasize love, for love shall abide even after God's full revelation is given.

Supporting Arguments

1. *Church history.* It is an indisputable historical fact that the exercise of charismatic gifts significantly decreased shortly after the first century and eventually ceased altogether in the early church. Moreover, it is likely that the few references to charismatic gifts we find in the second, third, and fourth centuries refer not to genuine New Testament gifts but to counterfeits. The group that tried to hang on to the use of charismatic gifts—a group called the **Montanists**—was clearly heretical in aspects of its theology. The primary reason the early church opposed them was because they were purporting to give new revelations and end-times prophecies. There was no place for such revelations and prophecies, the church rightly saw, because all the church needed was found in the completed New Testament.

In any event, whether the exercise of charismatic gifts ceased altogether in the first century or lingered for a period before finally coming to an end, the fact that it ceased in the early church is good evidence that this was God's will. If God had wanted the gifts to continue, he would have ensured that they did so.

2. *The canon is closed.* If continuationism is correct, then God is still speaking directly to his church through various people who supposedly have revelational gifts such as the gift of prophecy or words of knowledge. If that is the case, we should adhere to the word of these people as though it were the Word of God. But this assumes that the canon of the New Testament is still open. It assumes that we can still contribute to the foundation of the church. Not only does this contradict the New Testament's teaching that the foundation has already been laid by the apostles and prophets, but it also directly contradicts the closing words of the New Testament.

> I warn everyone who hears the words of the prophecy of this book: if any-one adds to them, God will add to that person the plagues described in this book; if anyone takes away from the words of the book of this prophecy, God will take away that person's share in the tree of life and in the holy city, which are described in this book. (Rev. 22:18–19)

The immediate context of this passage, of course, applies these words to the book of Revelation. But the church has historically discerned the sovereign hand of God in placing these words at the end of the New Testament as a whole. Therefore, the historic orthodox church has always applied these warnings to any who would seek to add to or take away from the collection of works that constitute the New Testament.

3. *Practical considerations.* Three practical considerations also favor the cessationist understanding of the charismatic gifts.

First, as happened in the second century with the Montanist controversy, the theology that encourages people to use what they think are the charismatic gifts tends to be divisive. Few movements have divided churches in modern times as has the charismatic movement.

Second, when Christians allow that a person can speak a word from God that has the same authority as the New Testament, they are vulnerable and can easily be led astray. None can dispute the fact that large numbers of people have adopted erroneous theologies and made tragic decisions because someone supposedly spoke to them in the name of the Lord. If we commit ourselves to the Bible as the sole, divinely inspired Word of God, we shall never be led astray.

Third, an emphasis on the charismatic gifts of the Spirit has in many quarters led to an underemphasis on the fruit of the Spirit. This is not co-incidental. It is easier to rely on subjective experiences and follow exciting signs and wonders than it is to engage in discipleship and cultivate the fruit of the Spirit. This is precisely why Paul pronounced that the charismatic gifts were childish in comparison to the full revelation that was coming. It is not surprising, then, that many of those who try to experience the gifts today remain in rather childish forms of spirituality.

Responding to Objections

1. *This view has a naturalistic bias.* Charismatic and Pentecostal Christians frequently assert that cessationists are driven by naturalistic and **ratio-nalistic** presuppositions. On the contrary, cessationists are not prejudiced against genuine miracles, though they are justifiably weary of fraudulent miraculous claims. They firmly believe that the Holy Spirit is still super-naturally active in the world. Nothing is more miraculous than the Holy Spirit bringing spiritual life to a person formerly dead in sin! Cessationists also generally hold that God still occasionally heals people supernaturally in response to prayer (cf. James 5:14–16). They simply deny, however, that the charismatic gifts, including the gift of healing, have an *ongoing* role in the church today. They served their purpose in building the church's one foundation and guiding the earliest Christians while the New Testament was being written and collected.

2. *This view contradicts Scripture.* Some argue that the cessationist position contradicts certain verses of Scripture. Doesn't Paul say believ-ers should "strive for the spiritual gifts" (1 Cor. 14:1)? Doesn't he insist that believers not "quench the Spirit" or "despise the words of prophets" (1 Thess. 5:19–20)? Does he not rather command that believers "be eager to prophesy" and "do not forbid speaking in tongues" (1 Cor. 14:39)?

These passages are frequently quoted by continuationists, but they are actually irrelevant to the issue at hand. These passages were all addressed to Christians prior to the completion of the New Testament. They no more apply to post–New Testament era believers than do, say, those passages that depict the early church picking leaders by drawing straws (Acts 1:23–26) or healing people by sending out prayer clothes (Acts 19:11–12).

3. *This view cannot explain contemporary charismatic experiences.* Perhaps the most passionate objection to the cessationist position comes from believers who regularly experience what they believe are the charis-matic gifts. No one can claim the charismatic gifts have ceased, they argue, when thousands of people personally experience them all the time. How can anyone refute another person's personal experience?

The answer is, by appealing to the Word of God. The Bible itself teaches that if an experience is not consistent with God's Word, we must reject it, regardless of how impressive the experience may seem (Gal. 1:8). Demons are capable of mimicking authentic spiritual experiences and masquerading as angels of light. Even on its own, the fallen mind is capable of deceiving itself and imagining things. Thus believers must always be willing to subject experience to the light of Scripture. The contemporary charismatic gifts are not consistent with the New Testament and on this basis must be ruled out, however impressive they seem to some who practice them.

Several other considerations support this position. First, many who supposedly experience charismatic gifts do so in environments that are emotionally charged and in which there is a social pressure to manifest such gifts. Second, the so-called charismatic gifts are occasionally found in non-Christian religions as well as in Christianity. For example, some form of *glossolalia* ("speaking in tongues") has been found in ancient Greek religions, the early Mormons, and certain primordial African tribes. As with contemporary charismatic practices, such religious experiences have little in common with the charismatic gifts of which Paul speaks. These nonbiblical "gifts" are merely psychological phenomenon, at best, or demonic mimicking of the true gifts, at worst.

Further Reading

Baxter, Ronald E. *Charismatic Gift of Tongues*. Grand Rapids: Kregel, 2000.

Carson, D. A. *Showing the Spirit: A Theological Exposition of 1 Corinthians 12–14*. Grand Rapids: Baker Academic, 1987.

Deere, Jack. *Surprised by the Power of the Spirit*. Grand Rapids: Zondervan, 1993.

Del Colle, Ralph, et al. *Perspectives on Spirit Baptism: Five Views*. Nashville: Broadman and Holman, 2004.

Fee, Gordon D. *God's Empowering Presence: The Holy Spirit in the Letters of Paul*. Peabody, MA: Hendrickson, 1994.

Gaffin, Richard B. *Perspectives on Pentecost: Studies in New Testament Teaching on the Gifts of the Holy Spirit*. Phillipsburg, NJ: Presbyterian and Reformed, 1979.

Geisler, Norman. *Signs and Wonders*. Wheaton: Tyndale, 1988.

Grudem, Wayne A., ed. *Are Miraculous Gifts for Today? Four Views*. Grand Rapids: Zondervan, 1996.

Kydd, Ronald A. N. *Charismatic Gifts in the Early Church*. Peabody, MA: Hendrickson, 1984.

Menzies, Robert P., and William W. Menzies. *Spirit and Power*. Grand Rapids: Zondervan, 2000.

Robertson, O. Palmer. *The Final Word: A Biblical Response to the Case for Tongues and Prophecy Today*. Carlisle, PA: Banner of Truth Trust, 1993.

Turner, Max. *The Holy Spirit and Spiritual Gifts: In the New Testament Church and Today*. Rev. ed. Peabody, MA: Hendrickson, 1998.

Warfield, Benjamin B. *Counterfeit Miracles*. Edinburgh: Banner of Truth Trust, 1983.

15

The Women in Ministry Debate

Created Equal, with Complementary Roles (The Complementarian View)
The Irrelevance of Gender for Spiritual Authority (The Egalitarian View)

Posing the Question

Christina knew the evening's conversation would be interesting, to say the least. Recently graduated from a Christian liberal arts college and home for the summer, Christina had asked her pastor to stop by that evening. Tonight was the night she would tell her parents and her pastor just what God had been doing in her heart with regard to future ministry. Tonight was the night she would tell them that she had a strong sense of calling to the pastoral ministry and that she planned to start seminary in the fall. Her dream was to fulfill the role of senior pastor in a church one day.

They all listened intently as she shared her pilgrimage with them. When she finally asked for their feedback, the responses were far from unanimous. Her pastor began: "Christina, I have watched you grow as a Christian from the time you were a little girl. Your heart for God and your passion for his kingdom have always been evident in your life. I am so excited that you want to minister within the church in a full-time capacity. However, the Bible teaches that the particular role you are aspiring to—that of senior pastor—is to be reserved for male ministers.

In passages such as 1 Timothy 2:12–15, the apostle Paul is very clear about this matter."

At this point, Christina's mother could not contain herself any longer. "But as I read through the Bible, I find women fulfilling leadership roles in both Testaments. In the Old Testament, there are women leaders such as Miriam and Deborah. In the New Testament, Paul mentions women leaders such as Priscilla and Phoebe. How can you tell my daughter that God isn't calling her to pastoral ministry when we have these clear examples of women leaders in the Bible?" As Christina turned to her father, the confused look on his face was evidence enough that he had no idea where he stood on the issue. "Now what?" she thought to herself.

The Center and Its Contrasts

When it comes to the issue of gender in regard to the church, evangelical Christians agree on a number of foundational convictions. First, there is the acknowledgment that both genders are created in the "image of God" (Gen. 1:26–27) and thus that both males and females are of equal dignity, value, and worth. Second, there is the shared belief that since all Christians—male and female—have the Holy Spirit within them, all believers are gifted by God for ministry within the body of Christ. With this diversity of giftings come numerous possible ministry callings. The question that divides evangelicals is this: Is it appropriate for women to aspire to leadership roles within the church that will place them in positions of authority over men?

This question emerged in many sectors of the twentieth-century church. The Roman Catholic Church, continuing its tradition, allows only males to be ordained to the priesthood. In the 1990s, however, the Church of England opened the door to women's ordination. Evangelical denominations remain divided on this issue. Throughout the twentieth century, Pentecostal churches tended to support the idea of women in pastoral roles. A number of conservative denominations, however, have retained the idea that ordained pastors should be men.

Two evangelical organizations dedicated to these issues have emerged in recent years. The Council on Biblical Manhood and Womanhood champions the **complementarian view**. Males and females have different, complementary roles in the church (and at home), and leadership roles in the church are reserved for males only. Christians for Biblical Equality, on the other hand, holds to an **egalitarian view**. Church leadership roles and roles in the home are determined by gifting rather than by gender.

The following two essays defend each of these two perspectives.

Created Equal, with Complementary Roles
(The Complementarian View)

In sharp contrast with the thinking and practices of most cultures through-out history, the Bible emphasizes that men and women are equal in God's eyes. Both are made "in the image of God" (Gen. 1:27). The Bible proclaims that men and women have equal dignity, worth, and responsibility before God. This is why historically the status of women has almost always im-proved wherever Christianity has been received.

However, this is not to claim that men and women have identical func-tions, according to Scripture. God created the male-female distinction for a reason: They are to complement, not to replicate, one another. This functional differentiation is obvious biologically, but it is also taught in Scripture. Among other things, Scripture teaches that God's design is for men to have primary spiritual authority in the church.

The Biblical Argument

The Bible declares that God created woman to be a "helper" and "partner" of man (Gen. 2:18). It is important to notice that Adam was given the mandate to care for the Garden *before* Eve was created (Gen. 2:15). Eve was to share in this mandate (Gen. 1:28), but she was to do so as a comple-mentary helper to Adam (Gen. 2:18). Adam alone was directly commanded by God to rule the earth. Hence, Adam bore primary responsibility for carrying out the mandate (Gen. 2:15–17; 3:17–19; cf. Rom. 5:12, 17–19). This functional differentiation between man and woman was reiterated even more intensely after the fall, for the Lord said that Eve shall "desire" Adam, and he shall "rule" over her (Gen. 3:16).

The leadership role of man is assumed throughout the Old Testament. For example, only males were permitted to appear before the Lord at the three great feasts each year (Deut. 16:16–17), and only males were allowed to serve as priests before the Lord (Exod. 28–29; Lev. 8–9). Since only priests were allowed to teach the law (Lev. 10:11), it is clear that this restriction implied that only males were allowed to give spiritual instruction.

Some suggest that this restriction was merely part of the law of the Old Testament, which was done away with after the coming of Christ. As a matter of fact, however, the restriction is applied and explicitly reiter-ated throughout the New Testament. It is not without significance that Jesus chose twelve men to be the foundational spiritual leaders of the new community of God's people. When Jesus sent out seventy people to fur-ther his ministry, he sent all men (Luke 10:1–16). When he gave his Great

Commission to "teach" all that he had commanded, he was speaking to his male apostles (Matt. 28:16–20). Some suggest that Jesus was simply acquiescing to the culture of his day by retaining this restriction, but the suggestion carries little weight. Jesus was perfectly willing to be radically countercultural when he wanted to be (e.g., Matt. 5:21–48; Mark 3:1–6).

The teaching that men alone are to be spiritual leaders is strongly reiterated by the apostle Paul on a number of occasions. Like Jesus, Paul restricts leadership roles to men. An overseer, Paul says, must be "the husband of but one wife" and must "manage his own family well" (1 Tim. 3:2, 4 NIV). Deacons also must be "men worthy of respect" who are "the husband of but one wife" (1 Tim. 3:8, 12 NIV).

Paul's convictions are expressed even more explicitly in other passages. One of the strongest is 1 Corinthians 11:3–16. In this context, Paul confronts certain women who apparently had mistakenly concluded that "freedom in Christ" meant freedom to do away with the functional difference between men and women. The proof of this, for Paul, was that Corinthian women were praying and prophesying with their heads uncovered (v. 5). To counter this, Paul appeals to God's pre-fallen, creational design.

> I want you to understand that Christ is the head of every man, and the husband is the head of his wife, and God is the head of Christ. Any man who prays or prophesies with something on his head disgraces his head, but any woman who prays or prophesies with her head unveiled disgraces her head—it is one and the same thing as having her head shaved. . . . For a man ought not to have his head veiled, since he is the image and reflection of God; but woman is the reflection of man. Indeed, man was not made from woman, but woman from man. Neither was man created for the sake of woman, but woman for the sake of man. For this reason a woman ought to have a symbol of authority on her head. (vv. 3–5, 7–10a)

We may agree that the issue of covering or not covering one's head is cultural. An uncovered head is no longer a sign of headship for men, nor is a covered head a sign of submission for women. But the teaching that men are to be spiritual leaders and that women are to submit to their leadership is not cultural in this passage, for Paul grounds it in how God originally created men and women. "Man was not made from woman, but woman from man. Neither was man created for the sake of woman, but woman for the sake of man." He concludes, "*For this reason* a woman ought to have a symbol of authority on her head." *How* female submission is expressed is cultural. *That* it needs to be expressed, however, is not.

Several chapters later Paul makes another application of this same principle when he instructs the Corinthians that "women should be silent in the churches. For they are not permitted to speak, but should be subordinate, as the law also says" (1 Cor. 14:34). Whatever else Paul meant in this passage, it cannot be denied that he explicitly validates the teaching of the Old Testament that men alone are to be spiritual teachers. He makes this very connection when he adds, "as the law also says."

This teaching is repeated, just as explicitly, in Paul's First Letter to Timothy. As in Corinth, it seems that certain women in Timothy's congregation were mistakenly drawing the conclusion that freedom in Christ meant overturning the functional differentiation between men and women concerning spiritual headship. As a result, Paul writes: "Let a woman learn in silence with full submission. I permit no woman to teach or to have authority over a man; she is to keep silent. For Adam was formed first, then Eve; and Adam was not deceived, but the woman was deceived and became a transgressor" (1 Tim. 2:11–14).

Again, it is clear that Paul is not giving a culturally relative teaching in this passage, for he appeals to God's creational design to ground his teaching. "Adam was formed first." This implies that his instruction was intended for all Christians, in all cultures, at all times.

The sum of the matter is that while men and women are equal in terms of their worth and dignity, they are gifted and called by God to carry out different roles. Men are called to be spiritual leaders; women are not. There is no value judgment in this differentiation. Men are in no respect superior because they are called to be spiritual leaders, any more than women are superior because they are able to bear children. The different roles are to complement, not compete with, one another. Nevertheless, the differentiation is important, as is evidenced by the fact that Scripture reiterates it frequently and in strong terms.

Supporting Arguments

1. *The Trinity.* The concept of complementary differences between equals is rooted in God himself. The Bible teaches that God is a Trinity—Father, Son, and Holy Spirit. Each person is eternally distinct from the others but equal to the others, for each is fully God. Yet there is a natural hierarchy within the Godhead. The Father commands the Son and the Spirit (e.g., John 5:19, 30; 16:13). The Father sends the Son and the Spirit (e.g., John 7:28–29; 14:16–17, 26). They willingly and lovingly submit to the Father's will (e.g., Matt. 26:39–42). Never does the Father receive commands from the Son or the Spirit. Never is the Father sent by the Son or the Spirit. And never does the Father submit to the will of the Son or the Spirit. Still, the Father is not better than the Son or the Spirit, for each is fully and completely God. The Father is simply different. The three work in perfect harmony with each other, because their roles are complementary.

2. *Church history.* The complementarian view has been the dominant view throughout church history. The church has always encouraged and valued the significant contributions of women in many areas of ministry, but the church has almost always forbidden women leaders until recent times.

3. *Social disorder.* One contributing factor to the problems our society presently faces is the loss of traditional male and female roles. Both in families and in churches, order and stability are compromised when God's design for the different roles for men and women is tossed aside for the sake of a more "modern" egalitarian perspective.

Responding to Objections

1. *This view is culturally conditioned.* The most frequent objection to the view that males alone should be spiritual heads is that the New Testament texts that support this view are culturally conditioned. It is argued that Paul was dealing with new female converts, most of whom were Gentiles, who lacked formal education. Indeed, it seems evident that some of these women were coming directly out of pagan contexts (including temple prostitution in Ephesus, where Timothy was pastoring). Therefore, it makes sense for Paul to forbid women teachers *in these contexts*. But his words should not be universally applied to all times and places.

Admittedly, there are culturally specific elements in Paul's teaching. The issue of head coverings in 1 Corinthians 11 and the issue of women wearing jewelry or braided hair in 1 Timothy 2:9 are obviously culturally relative. However, every culturally specific issue has an underlying universally relevant principle. In both passages, the underlying principle concerns women forsaking their God-given place. Evidence of this is that in both passages Paul grounds his teaching in God's design for creation (Adam was created first) and in historical fact (Eve was deceived first) (1 Cor. 11:7–9; 1 Tim. 2:13–14). Neither God's design nor historical facts are culturally conditioned.

2. *Women make effective leaders.* While it cannot be denied that at times God has used women to preach the gospel and even to pastor churches, three considerations caution against interpreting this fact as evidence that the biblical ideal for male headship has been overturned.

First, experience should never be used to override the teachings of Scripture. Scripture must be used to interpret experience, not vice versa. Therefore, the fact that women have at times been used by God in positions of spiritual authority over men should not alter the meaning of biblical texts that clearly teach this is not God's ideal will.

Second, and closely related to this, throughout biblical history God has demonstrated his willingness to accommodate his will to imperfect circumstances when necessary. God was at times willing to use pagan kings, false prophets, even donkeys to speak his Word and further his purposes when other more appropriate means were not available. So, too, God has at times acquiesced to using women as spiritual leaders when men were unwilling to fulfill the task.

Finally, while there is a diversity of opinion about this matter, many complementarians interpret the New Testament prohibitions regarding women in leadership to mean only that women should not function as the top spiritual leader and teacher of a congregation. There are many other contexts in which they can teach, preach, or evangelize. Many of the outstanding achievements of women throughout church history fall within what many complementarians consider to be biblical parameters.

The Irrelevance of Gender for Spiritual Authority (The Egalitarian View)

Like a missionary going to a foreign culture, God must temporarily acquiesce to many things he does not approve of in order to gradually move the world in a direction he does approve of. For example, God's ideal from the moment of creation was monogamy. But throughout history, God has tolerated and worked within polygamous (see **polygamy**) cultures in order to transform them over time (e.g., Gen. 29). Similarly, God's ideal has always been freedom for all people made in his image. Yet for centuries God tolerated and worked within systems of slavery in order to eventually overthrow them (e.g., Eph. 6:5–9).

The subservient role of women to men, especially in regard to spiritual leadership, is another aspect of fallen culture that God wants to overthrow. God tolerated and worked within the **patriarchal** cultures of both the Old and the New Testaments, but his ideal—and thus the ideal the church should be striving for—is for leadership to be based on gifts, not gender.

The Biblical Argument

Admittedly, some verses teach that women are to submit to men and expressly forbid women to exercise spiritual authority over men (e.g., 1 Tim. 2:11–14). But these passages do not express God's will for all time. If this teaching constituted part of the created order and God's ideal, the Bible would not contain counterexamples. As matters stand, however, the Bible contains many examples of women exercising spiritual authority over men. Following are ten such examples.

1. It often goes unnoticed, but God incorporated the songs and statements of a number of women into his inspired authoritative Scripture (e.g., Exod. 15:21; Judges 5; Luke 1:46–55). In as much as the whole Word of God has authority over believers, these passages constitute examples of women having spiritual authority over all (including men) who read them.

2. Women were given the same command to "rule" over creation as were men. "So God created humankind in his image . . . male and female he created them. God blessed them, and God said to *them*, 'Be frutiful and multiply, and fill the earth and subdue it'" (Gen. 1:27–28, emphasis added).

3. God commanded Abraham to obey his wife, Sarah (Gen. 21:12). If female submission was part of God's creational design, this command would constitute a violation of nature.

4. Miriam is mentioned as a leader of Israel alongside Moses and Aaron (Mic. 6:4). Miriam was also a noted worship leader (Exod. 15:20–21).

5. Deborah served as an admirable judge and leader over Israel (Judg. 4–5). This example shows that it is acceptable for a woman who is so gifted to exercise strong leadership over men and women alike.

6. Huldah was a prophetess consulted by both men and women (2 Kings 22:14). Noadiah and Anna are also depicted as prophetesses who could teach (Neh. 6:14; Luke 2:36–38). Indeed, a portion of Anna's teaching about Christ is found in Scripture (hence, it has authority over all who read it). More generally, one evidence of the outpouring of the Spirit was that "your sons and . . . daughters [would] prophesy. . . . Even . . . slaves, both men and women . . . shall prophesy" (Acts 2:16–18). It is not surprising, therefore, that Philip's four daughters each possessed the "gift of prophecy" (Acts 21:8–9). Nor is it surprising to find that Paul allowed women to prophesy in church, as long as they kept their heads covered (1 Cor. 11:4–5).

7. God used women as the first Christian evangelists, proclaiming (to the male apostles) the truth that Jesus had risen from the tomb (John 20:16–18).

8. Both Priscilla and Aquila taught the man Apollos (Acts 18:26).

9. In Romans 16:1–12, Paul lists a number of women involved in Christian service. Phoebe is called a "deacon" (vv. 1–2); Priscilla is given equal status to her husband, Aquila, in their kingdom work (vv. 3–4); Mary is described as a hard worker among believers (v. 6); Andronicus and Junia are said to be "prominent among the apostles" (v. 7); and Tryphosa and Persis are described as "workers" in the Lord (v. 12).

10. Paul refers to Euodia and Syntyche as coworkers—as much so as Clement or any man (Phil. 4:2–3).

Again, if it were part of God's creational ideal that women never exercise spiritual authority over men, Scripture would not contain these counter-examples. The wealth of examples proves that the prohibition against women serving as spiritual leaders is cultural, not timeless.

While God's willingness to accommodate himself temporarily to fallen culture is expressed in the prohibition passages, God's ideal will is expressed in passages such as Galatians 3:28. Here Paul writes, "There is no longer Jew or Greek, there is no longer slave or free, there is no longer male and female; for all of you are one in Christ Jesus." It seems evident that restricting roles on the basis of gender is no more justified in the body of Christ than restricting roles on the basis of race or class. There are cultural situations—the first century, for example—in which such restrictions must in fact be tolerated. But they must always be what the church works *against* as it strives to realize God's *ideal* in the world.

Related to this, it is important to note that whenever Paul or anyone else discusses ministry in the church, he speaks of gift-based roles, not gender-based roles. Indeed, the New Testament passages that list gifts do not imply that certain gifts are inextricably connected to a person's gender—including the gifts of pastoring, teaching, and evangelizing (e.g., 1 Cor. 12:4–31; Eph. 4:11). This absence of gender specification is hardly what one would expect if indeed the leadership gifts were restricted to men, for the issue of women in leadership was certainly present in New Testament churches (e.g., 1 Cor. 11:1–16; 1 Tim. 2:11–14). Instead, there is the straightforward declaration that "there are varieties of gifts . . . varieties of services . . . varieties of activities, but it is the same God who activates all of them *in everyone*" (1 Cor. 12:4–6, emphasis added). Again, the Spirit "allots [gifts] to each one individually just as the Spirit chooses" (1 Cor. 12:11). There is no hint that gender has anything to do with the Spirit's choosing.

While fallen cultures have consistently pigeonholed people according to gender, race, or class, the Spirit of God frees people from these arbitrary restrictions and liberates people to exercise their God-given gifts. As Peter declared so powerfully on the day of Pentecost, the Spirit is now being poured out on "*all* flesh"—with the result that surprising people are going to be used by God in surprising ways. Women and even slave girls, among others, will be used to declare authoritatively and prophetically the wonders of God (Acts 2:16–18).

We are guilty of idolizing fallen culture and quenching the Spirit if we canonize first-century restrictions against women and construe them as part of God's ideal for all time. It is no different than certain Christians in the past trying to use the Bible's acceptance of slavery as a justification for its ongoing practice.

Supporting Arguments

1. *Reason and experience.* Neither reason nor experience support the notion that women cannot be gifted to exercise the highest levels of spiritual authority. There is simply no rationally discernable connection between a person's gender and his or her natural ability to preach, teach, or lead others. Indeed, the last 150 years have indisputably demonstrated that women can be used by God as outstanding preachers, teachers, evangelists, and pastors.

2. *Subordinate by nature?* Despite claims to the contrary by complementarians, denying that women have the capacity to exercise spiritual headship presupposes a view of women as essentially inferior to men. A female, by virtue of being female, is deemed to be incapable of carrying out a role that men can carry out. This is not functional subordination but subordination rooted in nature.

Responding to Objections

1. *Jesus selected male disciples.* Opponents of the egalitarian view often cite Jesus' selection of twelve men as evidence that the highest level of spiritual authority belongs to men. In response, Jesus' choice of twelve men was based on cultural expediency and religious symbolism, not a deficiency in the nature of females. That is, in first-century Jewish culture, a woman would have found it impossible to gain widespread respect as a spiritual authority. Not only this, but Jesus was reconstituting the "New Israel" and as such would naturally have chosen twelve men to represent the twelve sons of Jacob (viz., the twelve tribes of Israel). Hence, Jesus' choice says nothing about his views of the inherent capacities of women.

2. *What about Paul's prohibitions?* The main objection against the egalitarian position is that Paul explicitly prohibits women to teach or have authority over men (1 Tim. 2:11–14) or even to speak in church (1 Cor. 14:34). Since Scripture provides examples of women violating these prohibitions (see above), there must be cultural reasons why Paul made these statements.

Concerning the Corinthian passage, Paul's prohibition against women speaking in church cannot be taken as absolute for the simple reason that Paul earlier taught that women could pray and prophesy in church, as long as they covered their heads (1 Cor. 11:5). How do we reconcile these statements? It is significant that immediately after instructing women to keep silent, Paul adds, "If there is anything they [women] desire to know, let them ask their husbands at home" (1 Cor. 14:35). While at the synagogue, women (who were usually denied an education) would have questions about the message. They would disrupt services by asking their more educated husbands (usually sitting across the aisle, as was the custom) what the teacher meant. It seems likely that Paul is addressing this problem at Corinth. His instruction has no application in a cultural situation in which women have the same educational opportunities as men.

Regarding the Timothy passage, two things need to be said. First, the context of this instruction offers clues that it is culturally conditioned. Paul says that women should "dress themselves modestly . . . not with their hair braided, or with gold, pearls, or expensive clothes" (1 Tim. 2:9). Few today consider these instructions to be timeless commands. Why then do some assume he is speaking timeless truth in the next sentence when he says women should "learn with full submission" (1 Tim. 2:11)?

Second, the context in which Timothy is pastoring his new church gives further clues to the culturally conditioned nature of Paul's prohibition. We know that women had prominent leadership roles in a religious cult that permeated Ephesus. The center of this cult was the temple of Diana, an enormous structure that was considered one of the seven wonders of the world. Part of the religious function of some of these female spiritual leaders was to engage in ritualistic prostitution. In this context, having newly converted pagan women in leadership positions would have been unwise and would have formed a barrier to the furthering of the gospel. (This is also why Paul restricts the offices of overseers and deacons to men [1 Tim. 3:2, 4, 12].)

But doesn't Paul base his teaching on the fact that "Adam was formed first, then Eve" as well as on the fact that "Adam was not deceived, but the woman was deceived" (1 Tim. 2:14)? On the surface, this instruction is puzzling. What difference does it make that Adam came before Eve? Wouldn't this same logic require that the animals have authority over humans, since they were created before us? And wasn't Adam deceived as much as the woman? Indeed, doesn't Paul elsewhere place the onus of responsibility for the deception on Adam (Rom. 5:12, 17–19)?

The puzzle is removed when Paul's instruction is seen in the light of a common rabbinic understanding of what happened in the Garden. According to this tradition, Adam was at fault for not properly instructing Eve about the dangers and consequences of eating from the forbidden tree. Adam had been created first and had received instruction directly from God. Eve had been created second and was dependent on Adam for this information. This is why she was more vulnerable and also why Adam bore the brunt of responsibility for the fall.

If read in this light, Paul's instruction to Timothy begins to make sense. Paul is appealing to this rabbinic understanding as a rationale for telling Timothy not to allow women in his church to teach. They are in the same position as Eve was and are therefore vulnerable (cf. 1 Tim. 5:11–15, where

Paul expands on this vulnerability). This warning would have no application in cultural contexts in which women are afforded as much opportunity to learn as men are and in which there are no negative religious connotations associated with women in leadership.

Further Reading

Bilezikian, Gilbert. *Beyond Sex Roles: What the Bible Says about a Woman's Place in Church and Family*. 3rd ed. Grand Rapids: Baker Academic, 2006.

Blomberg, Craig L., and James R. Beck, eds. *Two Views on Women in Ministry*. Grand Rapids: Zondervan, 2001.

Clouse, B., and R. G. Clouse, eds. *Women in Ministry: Four Views*. Downers Grove, IL: InterVarsity, 1989.

Hurley, James B. *Man and Woman in Biblical Perspective*. Downers Grove, IL: InterVarsity, 1981.

Husbands, Mark, and Timothy Larsen, eds. *Women, Ministry, and the Gospel: Exploring New Paradigms*. Downers Grove, IL: InterVarsity, 2007.

Kostenberger, A. J., T. R. Schreiner, and H. S. Baldwin, eds. *Women in the Church: A Fresh Analysis of 1 Timothy 2:9–15*. Grand Rapids: Baker Academic, 1995.

Kroeger, Richard Clark, and Catherine Clark Kroeger. *I Suffer Not a Woman: Rethinking 1 Timothy 2:11–15 in Light of Ancient Evidence*. Grand Rapids: Baker Academic, 1992.

Mickelsen, Alvera, ed. *Women, Authority, and the Bible*. Downers Grove, IL: InterVarsity, 1986.

Pawson, J. David. *Leadership Is Male*. Nashville: Thomas Nelson, 1988.

Pierce, Ronald W., Rebecca Merrill Groothuis, and Gordon D. Fee, eds. *Discovering Biblical Equality: Complementarity without Hierarchy*. 2nd ed. Downers Grove, IL: InterVarsity, 2005.

Piper, John, and Wayne Grudem, eds. *Recovering Biblical Manhood and Womanhood: A Response to Evangelical Feminism*. Wheaton: Crossway, 1991.

Sumner, Sarah. *Men and Women in the Church: Building Consensus on Christian Leadership*. Downers Grove, IL: InterVarsity, 2003.

Witherington, Ben. *Women and the Genesis of Christianity*. New York: Cambridge University Press, 1990.

16

The Millennium Debate

The Return before the Reign (The Premillennial View)
Working toward and Waiting for a Coming Reign of Peace
(The Postmillennial View)
The Symbolic Thousand-Year Conquest of Satan (The Amillennial View)

Posing the Question

The book had all the makings of a bestseller. Adventure, drama, action, mystery, even a touch of horror; it was all there. Paul finished reading the final few pages, put the book down, and reflected on the author's dramatized account of the events recorded in the last book of the Bible, the book of Revelation. The author had a gift for bringing the biblical ideas to life.

Kelly, a friend from church, had recommended the book to Paul. She had told him the book was not only an excellent read—it had changed her life. With a new understanding of the way in which the end-times would unravel, Kelly again felt excited to be a Christian. She had explained to him how the book had enabled her to figure out the mysterious symbolism of Revelation. With this understanding, she was now able to see that the end-times scenario was unfolding right before her eyes!

Paul had to admit the book had held his attention from cover to cover. And he too felt a new urgency regarding the end-times. He was especially intrigued by the author's view that Christ would soon come and take Christians out of the world, wage war against his enemies, and then embark on a thousand-year period, which he called the millennium—the period when Christ and his church would rule the world.

Just then the phone rang. It was Bob, a close friend of Paul's and a member of his Bible study group. The timing was perfect. Bob had majored in biblical studies in college and loved to discuss theological subjects. Paul explained the basic story line of the book and then asked Bob what he thought.

Bob hesitated before finally saying, "Actually, Paul, I've looked through that book. I'll agree that it seems to be an exciting book. But to be honest, I think the author's interpretation of the book of Revelation is way off base, and I'm worried about its impact on people. The author treats the book of Revelation as though it's a snapshot of the future when in fact it is intended to be symbolic. The apostle John wasn't writing about events that will take place at the end of history. He was writing about events that were going to take place in the lives of the people he was writing to. He tells us this at the very beginning of the book. I'm afraid Christians will read this book and waste time trying to interpret current events through this book the same way some people use horoscopes."

After their conversation, Paul was left with many questions. How should Christians interpret the book of Revelation? Literally or symbolically? Does it speak about events in the first century or about events in the twenty-first century? And what about this idea of the millennium? Will Christ return soon and set up a thousand-year reign on the earth?

The Center and Its Contrasts

Some of the most controversial questions in evangelical theology are related to the end-times in general and the book of Revelation in particular (see the appendix for evangelical interpretations of this book). One of the central issues in this general debate involves the millennium, the thousand-year period mentioned in Revelation 20:1–10, during which Christ is said to rule the world. What is the nature of the millennium, and when will it take place?

The millennium debate, however, is simply one issue within the wider debate about the end-times in general. It is safe to say that there is no more complicated and confusing topic in theology than **eschatology**—the study of the end-times.

Despite the complex debates about these matters, evangelical Christians can agree on several things. First, all evangelicals affirm that Jesus Christ will return to earth one day. This event is known as the second coming or the *parousia*. At his return, Christ will finally and fully defeat all evil. A second point of agreement is that there will be a bodily resurrection of all people who have ever lived, followed by a final judgment. Finally, all evangelicals affirm that believers will reign with Christ forever while non-believers will be separated from God's presence. These areas of agreement reveal that evangelicals take issue with any understanding of the end-times that interprets Christ's return in merely figurative or mythological terms. Evangelicals unanimously agree that with the return of Christ, God will intervene in human history in a decisive and undeniable way.

While most evangelicals agree on this basic outline of end-times events, any number of differences surface when it comes to filling in the details. The question of the nature of the millennium has been one area of perpetual debate throughout church history. The majority view in the first few centuries of the early church was a form of what today is called **premillennialism**. Premillennialism holds that the millennium is a literal thousand-year period, following Christ's return, during which he will reign on earth. It is important to note that there are at least two significantly different models of premillennialism—historic premillennialism and **dispensational premillennialism**. (See the appendix for more on this distinction.)

With Augustine in the early fifth century, a new perspective came to the forefront: **amillennialism**. Amillennialism views the millennium not as a literal thousand-year period but rather as a symbol of Christ's reign in general. It remained the dominant view throughout the Middle Ages. After the Reformation, a third view arose (though it had predecessors). Many Protestants came to believe that a thousand-year reign of peace was coming but that it would not be preceded by Christ's return, as premillennialists hold. Rather, the church itself would usher in this thousand-year reign of peace by evangelizing and transforming the world. Christ's return would culminate this millennial period. This view is known as **postmillennialism**.

While a majority of evangelicals today embrace a form of premillennialism, the other two views have defenders as well. The three essays in this chapter argue for each of these perspectives.

The Return before the Reign (The Premillennial View)

Despite some noteworthy differences (see "The Rapture Debate," issue 13 in the appendix), all premillennialists agree that a literal thousand-year reign of peace is coming in the future that will not begin until Jesus physically returns to earth. Premillennialists are so named because they believe that Jesus' return will take place *before* the millennium.

The Biblical Argument

The only passage that explicitly mentions the millennium is found in Revelation 20. John writes:

> Then I saw an angel coming down from heaven, holding in his hand the key to the bottomless pit and a great chain. He seized the dragon, that ancient serpent, who is the Devil and Satan, and bound him for a thousand years, and threw him into the pit, and locked and sealed it over him, so that he would deceive the nations no more, until the thousand years were ended. After that he must be let out for a little while. Then I saw . . . the souls of those who had been beheaded for their testimony to Jesus. . . . They came to life and reigned with Christ a thousand years. (The rest of the dead did not come to life until the thousand years were ended.) This is the first resurrection. Blessed and holy are those who share in the first resurrection. Over these the second death has no power, but they will be priests of God and of Christ, and they will reign with him a thousand years. When the thousand years are ended, Satan will be released from his prison and will come out to deceive the nations. (vv. 1–8)

Amillennialists dismiss the notion that a literal thousand-year reign of peace is coming on the grounds that the book of Revelation is an **apocalyptic** book. Admittedly, Revelation is largely apocalyptic, and apocalyptic literature is largely symbolic. But this is no reason to assume that apocalyptic literature in general, or the book of Revelation in particular, cannot communicate *anything* literally. Revelation 20 reads like a straightforward depiction of a future event. Four times this passage mentions, in a matter-of-fact way, that a thousand-year period is coming when Satan will be bound and the Lord will reign. There is no compelling reason to interpret this symbolically.

Nor is there a compelling reason to interpret as symbolic the clear distinction between a first and second resurrection. This is crucial to the premillennial perspective, for the view is rooted in the belief that the future holds two resurrections. The first will be a resurrection of saints, who will rule with Christ during the millennium. The second will be a resurrection of all others to eternal judgment. This distinction is not found only in Revelation 20. A host of other passages suggest it as well.

For example, in Luke 14:14, Jesus refers to "the resurrection of the righteous." This phrase implies that there is also a distinct "resurrection of the unrighteous." Similarly, Paul tells the Philippian Christians, "I want to know Christ and the power of his resurrection and the sharing of his sufferings by becoming like him in his death, if somehow I may attain the resurrection from the dead" (Phil. 3:10–11). Paul is not speaking of a general resurrection, otherwise he would have no need to strive to attain it. He can be referring to a resurrection intended only for saints, one that separates saints from unredeemed sinners. The original Greek supports this, for it literally states that Paul longs to attain a "resurrection out from among dead-ones." Paul clearly envisaged a first resurrection that was selective. This would later be followed by a general resurrection of all "dead-ones."

Another passage that strongly supports the idea of two resurrections is 1 Corinthians 15. Paul says that all will be resurrected: "but each in his own order: Christ the first fruits, then at his coming those who belong to Christ. Then comes the end, when he hands over the kingdom to God the Father, after he has destroyed every ruler and every authority and power. For he must reign until he has put all his enemies under his feet" (vv. 23–25). Note the distinctions Paul makes in this passage. First, Christ is raised. Then Christ returns and resurrects "those who belong to [him]." Finally, "the end" comes when he is victorious over all his foes. This agrees with what Paul says in 1 Thessalonians:

> For the Lord himself, with a cry of command, with the archangel's call and with the sound of God's trumpet, will descend from heaven, and the dead in Christ will rise first. Then we who are alive, who are left, will be caught up in the clouds together with them to meet the Lord in the air; and so we will be with the Lord forever. (4:16–17)

When Christ returns, those who are "in Christ," whether dead or alive, will be "caught up in the clouds together." This is the "resurrection of life," for the resurrected will dwell with the Lord forever (cf. John 5:28–29). It is distinct from the "resurrection of condemnation" in which all nonbelievers are raised and then judged according to their works (cf. Dan. 12:2). Since only the premillennial view affirms two distinct resurrections, this evidence for two resurrections supports the premillennial perspective.

Although premillennialists disagree amongst themselves about the timing of the great and final **tribulation** in relationship to Christ's return, they agree that his return will immediately lead to a thousand-year "Sabbath" on the earth. Many passages refer to this thousand-year Sabbath.

The Old Testament as a whole envisions God's kingdom established on the earth. The Son of Man is portrayed as ruling over "all people, nations, and languages." Indeed, with his "holy ones"—the saints of God—the Son of Man will rule over all the earth's kings and kingdoms (Dan. 7:14, 18). So, too, Isaiah prophesies of a time when

> the mountain of the LORD's house shall be established as the highest of the mountains, and shall be raised above the hills; all the nations shall stream to it. Many peoples shall come and say, "Come, let us go up to the mountain of the LORD, to the house of the God of Jacob; that he may teach us his ways

and that we may walk in his paths." For out of Zion shall go forth instruction, and the word of the LORD from Jerusalem. He shall judge between the nations, and shall arbitrate for many peoples; they shall beat their swords into plowshares, and their spears into pruning hooks; nation shall not lift up sword against nation, neither shall they learn war any more. (2:1–4)

This is the time when "the wolf shall live with the lamb, the leopard shall lie down with the kid, the calf and the lion and the fatling together, and a little child shall lead them." During this time of peace, "the lion shall eat straw like the ox. The nursing child shall play over the hole of the asp, and the weaned child shall put its hand on the adder's den" (Isa. 11:6–8). Other passages describe similar visions (e.g., Ezek. 36–48; Mic. 4:1–8). These promises all apply to and are explained by the earthly millennium.

The New Testament also suggests a future reign of Christ on the earth. The author of Hebrews draws a direct parallel between the Sabbath in the Old Testament that God wanted the Jews to enter into and the Sabbath God has in store for Christians (Heb. 3:7–4:13). The parallel suggests that the "rest" for the church is on the earth, just as the "rest" for the Jews was intended to be. Relatedly, Jesus promised that the "meek . . . will inherit the earth" (Matt. 5:5). He also taught us to pray to the Father that his will would "be done, on earth as it is in heaven" (Matt. 6:10). Such passages make it clear that Jesus knew the Father had not given up on the earth. Rather, he was going to win it back, bind Satan, and have his earthly church rule with him over it. The millennium will be the time when the "new earth" is established (Isa. 65:17–22; 2 Pet. 3:13; Rev. 21:1).

Supporting Arguments

1. *Church tradition.* While the early post-apostolic fathers did not seem to have a clear understanding of the **rapture** of the church, they nevertheless generally held to a premillennialist eschatology. It was unequivocally the view of Justin Martyr, Tertullian, Irenaeus, and Lactantius. Unfortunately, some pushed this premilliennial perspective in a crassly materialistic direction, creating a version that came to be called **chiliasm.** In the fourth century, Augustine and several others reacted against chiliasm, ultimately rejecting premillennialism altogether in favor of an amillennial position. Nevertheless, the fact that this view was dominant in the early post-apostolic church supports the view that the apostles taught a premillennial position.

2. *The deteriorating state of the world.* Christians sometimes get discouraged because it often does not look as though "God is winning." While Christianity is growing remarkably in many parts of the world, the

same is true of Islam and some other non-Christian religions. In some parts of the world, such as America and Europe, Christianity is actually losing ground. In terms of the number of people accepting Christ and the impact the church is having on the culture as a whole, the church is not heading in the right direction.

This state of affairs is not easy for a postmillennialist or an amillennialist to explain, for according to their accounts the world is supposed to become increasingly Christian. The premillennialist has no such hope, however. Most premillennialists accept that prior to the Lord's second coming things will generally get worse and worse. They are of course saddened by the deteriorating state of the world and of Western culture in particular, but it only confirms their faith that the Lord is returning soon.

Responding to Objections

1. *This view has an inadequate foundation.* Amillennialists object to the premillennial position on the grounds that the millennium is mentioned in only one passage, which happens to be apocalyptic. It is true that the millennium is mentioned only in Revelation 20, but it is mentioned four times. That is four times more than the number of times the word "Trinity" is mentioned! Moreover, as noted above, simply because Revelation is an apocalyptic text does not justify the conclusion that nothing in it can be taken literally. Almost all scholars interpret the seven churches and the messages that were recorded to them literally (Rev. 2–3). Thus, one must examine each passage independently to determine its literal or symbolic nature. Finally, while the term *millennium* is not mentioned explicitly anywhere else, numerous passages allude to it, as shown above.

2. *This view runs counter to the "mustard seed" pattern of kingdom expansion.* Some postmillennialists object to the premillennial position on the grounds that it is not consistent with the way God generally operates in world history. God usually expands his kingdom progressively. Jesus talks of the kingdom growing and taking over as a mustard seed—not as a single and momentary power play, as the premillennial perspective supposes (cf. Matt. 13:31–32).

Granted, there is a season in which God expands his kingdom in a slow and subtle mustard seed fashion. This is the church age we are now in. But there is no reason to assume this pattern will continue indefinitely. Sometimes the ordinary is suspended for the extraordinary. Noah's flood and the plagues of Egypt are examples of this. So shall it be at the end of time. On a day known only to the Father, Jesus will return, gather his bride to himself, bring judgment on the world, bind Satan, and set up his millennial rule. This time can be described as anything but business as usual.

Working toward and Waiting for a Coming Reign of Peace (The Postmillennial View)

The view defended in this essay is called postmillennialism, for, among other things, it advocates that the Lord will return and judge the living and the dead *after* he reigns on earth through his church for a millennium. In contrast to both the premillennial and amillennial positions, postmillennialists believe that Christ will return after the Christianization of the entire world.

As with the other views, there are a few significant differences of opinion among postmillennialists. Classical postmillennialists such as the Puritans and many evangelicals in the nineteenth century interpreted the thousand-year reign spoken of in Revelation 20 literally. However, some contemporary postmillennialists maintain that the millennium is symbolic for a complete and total epoch when the Lord will rest from his labor of winning back the world. Postmillennialists also disagree as to when this millennial period will begin. Classical postmillennialists believed this period of time was in the future, though not usually the distant future. They were optimistic that the mission of the church to win back the world to God was going to be completed soon. Their optimism is surpassed by other postmillennialists, however, who maintain that we are already in the millennial age. Satan is in principle already bound and Christ is in principle already enthroned, though neither is yet perfectly manifested.

In spite of these differences, however, postmillennialists agree on the central point of the position: The church must expect and work for the Christianization of the world before it can expect the Lord to return physically and bring a cataclysmic end to world history.

The Biblical Argument

In the midst of the craze of premillennialism sweeping the evangelical masses (as evidenced, for example, by the Left Behind novel series and movies), many sincere evangelicals expect the Lord to return physically at any moment. The fear of being caught off guard and "left behind" is one of the selling points of this doctrine. Until the Lord returns, these Christians expect sin and suffering to increase in the world. Through the work of the church, individuals will be saved, but the world as a whole is a lost cause.

Postmillennialists consider this outlook pessimistic and biblically misguided. The prevalence of this attitude explains why the evangelical church of the twentieth century, in which premillennialism has been dominant, has been passionate about personal evangelism but apathetic and impotent in addressing social evil. In this respect, contemporary evangelicalism contrasts sharply with the evangelicalism of the nineteenth century, in which postmillennialism was dominant. For postmillennial preachers such as Charles Finney, the idea that Christians can bear witness to Christ by winning souls without transforming culture was unthinkable.

The premillennial mind-set stands in contrast to the attitude about the coming of the kingdom that Jesus advocated. When people asked Jesus when the kingdom of God was coming, Jesus did not answer the way premillennialists answer this sort of question. "The kingdom of God is not coming with things that can be observed," Jesus said. "Nor will they say, 'Look, here it is!' or 'There it is!' For, in fact, the kingdom of God is among you" (Luke 17:20–21). Jesus in essence taught that we will not be able to tell when the kingdom of God comes. He was not looking for a cataclysmic occurrence to mark the arrival of the kingdom.

Just as significantly, in this passage, Jesus taught that in one sense the kingdom of God had already arrived! The kingdom was already "among" the people who asked the question. It seems evident that the verse presupposes a strong continuity between the kingdom of God as it is growing *now* and the kingdom of God as it will be when it is brought to completion *then*. Jesus did not envision a cataclysmic discontinuity between the now and the then. This teaching contradicts the popular twentieth-century premillennial notion that before God's kingdom can be set up on earth, Christians first have to be raptured and those who are left behind have to go through a tribulation period. If *that* wouldn't evoke the response, "Look, here it is" or "There it is," what would?

Jesus stressed the continuity between the kingdom of God *now* and the kingdom of God *then* in many of his teachings. For example, at one point Jesus taught: "The kingdom of heaven is like a mustard seed that someone took and sowed in his field; it is the smallest of all the seeds, but when it has grown it is the greatest of shrubs and becomes a tree, so that the birds of the air come and make nests in its branches" (Matt. 13:31–32).

Immediately following this teaching, Jesus said, "The kingdom of heaven is like yeast that a woman took and mixed in with three measures of flour until all of it was leavened" (Matt. 13:33). The point of both teachings is that the kingdom of God begins in a small way, but gradually and subtly it grows until it eventually takes over the entire field or lump of dough— namely, until it takes over the world. In this light, the church should faithfully expect and work for nothing less than the gradual expansion of the kingdom of God over the entire world. The defeatist notion that there is nothing Christians can do to stem the tide of corruption in the world denies the kingdom authority the Lord has given to Christians and undermines the church's motivation to advance the kingdom of God.

The central goal of God's activity throughout world history, from his election of the nation of Israel to his sending of his Son into the world, has been to reclaim the world and its people as his own. He established humans as his **viceregents** over the world, but they tragically surrendered their authority to Satan. The Lord is in the process of defeating his archenemy, freeing his people, and thereby regaining the world. The millennium is that time in world history when the Lord's objective will be attained.

This millennium is anticipated throughout the Bible as the goal to which history is moving. Scripture looks forward to a time when "every knee shall bow, every tongue shall swear" to the Lord (Isa. 45:23–24). In New Testament terms, "every knee [shall] bend, in heaven and on earth and under the earth, and every tongue [shall] confess that Jesus Christ is Lord, to the glory of God the Father" (Phil. 2:10–11). This is the time when the Messiah, the Lord's anointed ("Christ"), will reign supreme. Satan will be put in prison for an extended period of time (Rev. 20:1–10). Peace will reign throughout the world—expressed symbolically as the lion lying down with the lamb (see Isa. 11:6–9). All who oppose God will be vanquished, while all who accept his reign will be united as one under him (e.g., Isa. 55:1–9; 66:18–24). The entire world will finally be united in the love and lordship of the Creator.

So, for example, Psalm 72 says of God's anointed:

> May he be like rain that falls on the mown grass,
>   like showers that water the earth.
> In his days may righteousness flourish
>   and peace abound, until the moon is no more.
> May he have dominion from sea to sea,
>   and from the River to the ends of the earth.
> May his foes bow down before him,
>   and his enemies lick the dust. . . .
> May all kings fall down before him,
>   all nations give him service. (vv. 6–9, 11)

Psalm 110 expands on the theme.

> The Lord says to my lord,
>   "Sit at my right hand
> until I make your enemies your footstool."
> The Lord sends out from Zion
>   your mighty scepter.
>   Rule in the midst of your foes.
> Your people will offer themselves willingly
>   on the day you lead your forces
>   on the holy mountains.

From the womb of the morning,
  like dew, your youth will come to you.
The Lord has sworn and will not change his mind,
  "You are a priest forever according to the order of Melchizedek."
(vv. 1–4; cf. Isa. 2:1–4)

The promise of Scripture is that the Messiah will eventually defeat all his enemies and rule over the entire world. This rule in principle began when Jesus was resurrected from the dead. The only remaining task is for the church to apply in practice, by the power of the Spirit, what God has already established in principle. Christians are called to be the means by which God increasingly manifests Christ's rightful rule throughout the world. They are commanded to go into all the world and make disciples of all nations (Matt. 28:18–20), recognizing that the Lord will not return until all nations have been evangelized, with multitudes accepting the Good News of salvation (Matt. 24:14). Already, Jesus assures us, Satan has been "driven out" of the world. Therefore, Christians may be assured that when they lift him up, he "will draw all people" to himself (John 12:31–32). The mustard seed has been planted. Christians must allow it to grow in them and through them until it takes over the entire world.

The wonderful promise of Scripture is that despite occasional setbacks, the church will be successful in fulfilling its task, for its success depends not on the efforts of humans but of God. Postmillennialists do not deny that there are still serious battles to fight and that Christians may be called on to undergo suffering. Nor do they deny that there will be an ultimate battle between God and the forces of evil, a time when the world will undergo tribulation. This will take place after an epoch of Christ's reign, not before (Rev. 20:3, 7). According to this view, nothing justifies believers having anything but an optimistic stance toward the world and a passionate motivation to see God's will done in every area of society.

Supporting Arguments

1. *Confidence for the future.* Because the postmillennial view embodies the New Testament's confidence that the kingdom will continue to expand, and because it understands that the church is the primary means by which this expansion will occur, the postmillennial view motivates believers in a way that premillennialism and amillennialism do not. Fueled by an optimistic postmillennial vision as to how the future will unfold, believers are motivated to engage passionately in social action, as the postmillennial evangelicals of the nineteenth century did. They are inspired to work to bring culture into conformity with God's will. They are not concerned

only with leading individuals to Christ while leaving the society to the devil. They are inspired to seek to demonstrate the truth that Jesus is Lord by confronting and overcoming racism, genderism, hunger, homelessness, and all other forms of social injustice throughout the world. The premillennial and amillennial positions do not offer this motivation and hope to believers.

2. *A credible eschatology*. It can be argued that the premillennial craze that has gripped contemporary evangelicalism has encumbered the church's mission of credibly communicating its faith to a lost world. Instead of embracing an eschatological vision that would inspire Christians to witness to the world by demonstrating Christ's love in radical social action, many evangelicals have embraced an eschatological vision that leads them to demand that unbelievers accept that Christians shall soon disappear in the clouds (the rapture) and to warn them that if they do not accept Christ, they will be left behind. Apart from the issue of whether we should interpret the rapture literally or symbolically, it is ill-advised to wager the credibility of Christianity on a highly unusual concept that is opaquely referred to in only one verse in the New Testament (1 Thess. 4:17). With postmillennialism, eschatology becomes an asset to evangelism rather than a liability.

Responding to Objections

1. *This view runs counter to church tradition.* Some argue that postmillennialism is not adequately rooted in church tradition, which must count against it. If it is true that considerations of church tradition are never decisive for evangelicals in settling doctrinal disputes, then the consideration of church tradition on matters of eschatology can carry little weight indeed, for there has never been a consensus of opinion on such matters.

Various forms of premillennialism were popular in the early church, but not exclusively so. Amillennialism was most popular during the Middle Ages, but again, not exclusively so. And postmillennialism was most popular among the Puritans and evangelicals of the nineteenth century, but again, other views were entertained by these groups and by others as well. Hence, the criticism that postmillennialism is without adequate grounding in church tradition has little force.

2. *How does this view explain evidence of a decaying world?* Critics of the postmillennial position point out that as a matter of **empirical** fact the church does not seem to be winning the battle for the world. In some geographical regions, non-Christian movements are growing faster than Christianity. In some areas, Christianity is actually losing ground. It is understandable why European and American evangelicals in previous cen-

turies may have been optimistic about Christianity taking over the globe, they argue, for at the time there were positive indications that Christianity was moving in that direction. It seemed that Christianity was advancing steadily and that society was improving. But the twentieth century reversed many of these trends.

Postmillennialists acknowledge that the world goes through various ebbs and flows of evil and that Christianity experienced some setbacks in the twentieth century. They deny, however, that this constitutes a valid reason to abandon the optimism of Scripture that Christ's rule will eventually extend to the entire world and that this expansion can be accomplished through the work of the church. Two things may be said in response to this erroneous conclusion.

First, hope must be based on the Lord's promise that the mustard seed will continue to grow, not on human ability to observe its progress. Much of the growth of a mustard seed occurs underground, where no one can observe it.

Second, Christians must not become pessimistic by focusing too much on recent setbacks of kingdom expansion, thus magnifying them out of proportion. They must recall that the kingdom of God also experienced significant advances in the twentieth century. Though some ground was lost, overall, Christian missions advanced steadily throughout the last century, to the point at which many missiologists predict that in several more decades there will be no remaining unreached people groups! While many Islamic regions remained resistant to the gospel, Christianity made remarkable progress in other regions, especially in Two-Thirds World regions where various forms of ancient paganism previously held people in bondage. The Bible, or at least portions of the Bible, is being made available to people around the globe in a manner that could hardly be imagined a hundred years ago. Television, radio, and more recently the Internet have increased the availability of the gospel. Moreover, despite the incredible waste of human life that occurred in the twentieth century through wars, and despite the persistence of hunger, poverty, and disease, it must be acknowledged that overall humanity experienced unprecedented advances in health and human rights awareness throughout the twentieth century.

Christians must not minimize the reality of setbacks, but neither should they allow these setbacks to dim the hope that the Lord's kingdom will steadily advance in the world and the clear indications that this hope is in the process of being fulfilled.

3. *There are scriptural problems with this view.* Some argue that certain passages of Scripture contradict the postmillennial understanding of the end-times. For example, in Matthew 24, Jesus taught that before the end there would be false messiahs (vv. 4–5, 10), wars (vv. 6–7), famines and earthquakes (vv. 7–8), persecution (v. 9), and increased lawlessness and

apathy (v. 12). Does this not imply that we should expect things to get worse, not better, as we approach the end?

Some postmillennialists interpret this passage in a **preterist** fashion, concluding that Jesus was not talking about the end of the world as such, but the end of the world as the Jews of the time understood it. This "world" came to an end with the Jewish-Roman war between AD 66 and 70, resulting in the destruction of the temple and the banishment of the Jews from Jerusalem. In support of this view, these postmillennialists point out that the question Jesus was answering throughout Matthew 24 concerned when the temple would be destroyed (vv. 1–2). Moreover, Jesus ended this discourse by promising them, "Truly, I tell you, this generation will not pass away until all these things have taken place" (v. 34).

Other postmillennialists believe this passage refers to the actual end of world history but do not agree that it means the world will get increasingly worse until the Lord returns. There will be increased wars and the like, but Jesus also promises in this very discourse that "this good news of the kingdom will be proclaimed throughout the world, as a testimony to all the nations; and then the end will come" (v. 14). The optimism of the postmillennial vision of the future is not that things will get easier and easier but that the kingdom will continually advance—despite resistance from human and spiritual opponents of the gospel.

The Symbolic Thousand-Year Conquest of Satan (The Amillennial View)

Amillennialists deny that there is a literal millennium, either before or after the return of Jesus Christ. Indeed, they reject the notion that there are two future resurrections or two stages in the Lord's return, which premillennialism is largely based on. Once the symbols are recognized for what they are, New Testament eschatology is actually remarkably simple. In the fullness of time, the Lord will return, the dead will be resurrected, and all will be judged. The complex eschatological schemes of many contemporary evangelicals are at best unnecessarily complex if not misleading.

The Biblical Argument

First, there is no compelling reason to conclude that a literal thousand-year period of peace is coming upon the earth. True, the book of Revelation says that Christ will reign with martyred saints for a thousand years while Satan is "in prison" (Rev. 20:1–16). But why should we interpret this literally? The genre of Revelation is apocalyptic, which by definition means it is filled with metaphorical and symbolic images. There is no more reason to take this thousand-year reign literally than there is to interpret as literal the twenty-four elders who wear gold crowns and flash forth lightning while surrounded by four creatures who "are full of eyes all around and inside" (Rev. 4:4–8). Indeed, when considering Revelation 20, are we to believe that an angel will literally hold a "key" and "lock and seal" Satan into a "bottomless pit" (vv. 1–3)? Are we to believe that after a thousand years Satan will "deceive the nations at the four corners of the earth" (v. 8)? Will "the earth and the heaven" literally flee from God's presence as he sits on a literal "great white throne" (v. 11)? Will he literally open a "book of life" and read it before "the dead" who have come up from a "sea" (vv. 12–13)? Will the wicked then go into a literal "lake of fire" and "sulphur" (v. 14)? Most readers and all scholars of apocalyptic literature understand these concepts to be symbolic. There are no grounds for holding that the thousand-year reign spoken of in this chapter should be taken literally.

Second, according to premillennialism, there will be two resurrections in the future, separated by the thousand-year reign of Christ and the church. Not only is the thousand-year reign not mentioned outside of Revelation, but nowhere outside of this passage is there any clear reference to two distinct resurrections. This is fatal to the premillennial position.

Jesus referred to a future time "when all who are in their graves will hear his voice and will come out—those who have done good, to the resurrection of life, and those who have done evil, to the resurrection of condemnation" (John 5:28–29). The passage depicts the righteous and the unrighteous responding with different outcomes *to one and the same call*. There is no thousand-year gap. Similarly, Paul taught that there will "be a resurrection of both the righteous and the unrighteous" (Acts 24:15)—*one* resurrection that includes both the righteous and the unrighteous.

The consistent depiction of the end-times in the New Testament is of one multifaceted, interconnected event. It includes the Lord's return, his victory over evil, the general resurrection from the dead, and the final judgment. Hence, for example, Paul speaks of the Lord relieving those who suffer and judging those who are rebellious as one future event. When "the Lord Jesus is revealed from heaven with his mighty angels in flaming fire," Paul says, he will "repay with affliction those who afflict you, and . . . give relief to the afflicted as well as to us." When Jesus "comes to be glorified by his saints and to be marveled at on that day among all who have believed," the wicked "will suffer the punishment of eternal destruction, separated from the presence of the Lord and from the glory of his might" (2 Thess. 1:5–10). The reward and the punishment are given at the same time. There is no thousand-year interval.

Peter speaks in the same way about the end-times. "The day of the Lord will come like a thief," at which time "the heavens will pass away with a loud noise, and the elements will be dissolved with fire, and the earth and everything that is done on it will be disclosed" (2 Pet. 3:10). At this juncture "the heavens will be set ablaze and dissolved, and the elements will melt with fire" (2 Pet. 3:12) so the righteous will be "at home" in a "new heavens and a new earth" (2 Pet. 3:13). According to standard premillennial eschatology, a seven-year tribulation period followed by a thousand-year epoch will separate the Lord's coming from the final judgment, when "the elements will be dissolved." Nothing like this is suggested in this passage.

Similarly, Paul links the final restoration of the entire creation with the redemption of the sons of God (Rom. 8:18–23). He never mentions a redemption followed by a thousand years followed by a renewed Satanic assault after Satan is released from prison. In 1 Corinthians 15, Paul links the resurrection with the handing over of all things to God the Father after Christ has "destroyed every ruler and every authority and power" (1 Cor. 15:24; cf. vv. 20–28).

Since there is clear teaching neither of a thousand-year reign nor of two distinct resurrections or returns of Christ, and since the book of Revelation is an apocalyptic book that is thoroughly symbolic, there is no reason to expect a literal thousand-year period of peace sometime in the future.

Third, many postmillennialists agree, against the premillennialists, that the thousand years spoken of in Revelation 20 are symbolic. And all postmillennialists agree in rejecting the premillennial view that there will be two resurrections and two judgments separated by a thousand years. The end-times events referred to in the New Testament occur roughly at the same time. But postmillennialists disagree with the amillennial view that there is no coming millennium at all. They rather believe that the thousand-year reign spoken of in Revelation refers to some future time when the devil will be imprisoned and Christ will reign through his church on the earth. At the end of this period of time, all the end-times events spoken of in the New Testament will take place.

There are three problems with postmillennialism, however. First, this view presumes that the church will make consistent headway in advancing the kingdom and fighting the devil until it reaches the millennial period. But as premillennialists have always insisted, the Bible does not support this optimistic conclusion. Many passages suggest that as the end approaches, things are going to get worse.

For example, in Matthew 24 the disciples asked Jesus, "What will be the sign of your coming and of the end of the age?" (v. 3). Jesus answered by first warning them that the number of false messiahs and false prophets will increase (vv. 4–5, 11). He said that wars (vv. 6–7) and famines and earthquakes (vv. 7–8) will increase as well. He then said his disciples will be "tortured and . . . put to death" as they are "hated by all nations" (v. 9). There will be widespread apostasy, and former disciples will hate and betray one another (v. 10). Not only this, but people in general will become loveless, lawless, and brutally wicked (v. 12). Those who want to be saved will simply have to "endure" it (v. 13). This hardly sounds like a positive crescendo as the church works to apply Christ's rule to the entire world.

Paul and Peter express a similar pessimism toward the future of this world. Paul says that as the end approaches

> people will be lovers of themselves, lovers of money, boasters, arrogant, abusive, disobedient to their parents, ungrateful, unholy, inhuman, implacable, slanderers, profligates, brutes, haters of good, treacherous, reckless, swollen with conceit, lovers of pleasure rather than lovers of God, holding to the outward form of godliness but denying its power. (2 Tim. 3:2–5)

Similarly, Peter says that in the final days, "scoffers will come, scoffing and indulging their own lusts and saying, 'Where is the promise of his coming? For ever since our ancestors died, all things continue as they were from the beginning of creation!'" (2 Pet. 3:3–4).

The point is that the hope the New Testament offers is not associated with an expectation that the world will increasingly be won over for Jesus Christ. It is rather centered on the certainty that Christ will return and rescue us from a world that is increasingly moving away from God.

Second, and closely related to this, it is clear that the earliest disciples expected the Lord to return at any moment. This is impossible to square with the view that they expected a thousand-year period of peace to take place prior to the Lord's return. Paul notes how the Thessalonians "turned to God from idols" as they "wait for his Son from heaven" who "rescues us from the wrath that is coming" (1 Thess. 1:9–10). So, too, he instructs his disciple Titus to teach people to "live lives that are self-controlled, upright, and godly, while we wait for the blessed hope and the manifestation of the glory of our great God and Savior, Jesus Christ" (Titus 2:12–13). The early Christians were not waiting or even working for a millennium of peace. They were waiting for Jesus to return and rescue them from a decaying world (Heb. 9:28; James 5:7; 1 Pet. 1:13; 2 Pet. 3:11–12).

Third, while the church is making great gains in some parts of the world, there is no evidence that the church is taking over, or ever will gradually take over, the world, as postmillennialists maintain. If the Lord is going to regain lordship of the earth—and he certainly will—it will take a radical supernatural act, such as his second coming, to bring it about.

In sum, then, amillennialists agree with premillennialists, over against postmillennialists, that the Lord will return at any time and that we cannot expect the world to improve significantly until he does so. But amillennialists agree with postmillenialists, over and against premillennialists, that the attempt to reconcile Revelation 20 with the rest of the New Testament's thinking on eschatology by positing two resurrections and two judgments, separated by a thousand years, is convoluted and unnecessary.

A Supporting Argument

Church tradition. While it seems that a type of premillennialism was popular in the early church, we know that amillennialism was present as well. Its acceptance increased after being endorsed by Augustine in the fifth century. Indeed, amillennialism has arguably been the most commonly held position throughout church history, if not explicitly, then implicitly. Since Augustine, relatively few theologians have interpreted Revelation 20 literally (the premillennial view) or held out hope that the church will gradually evangelize the entire world prior to the Lord's return (the postmillennial view).

Responding to Objections

1. *The amillennial position spiritualizes Scripture.* Some conservative Christians argue that the "spiritualizing" heremenuetic of amillennialism is dangerous. Not only do amillennialists interpret the thousand-year reign spoken of in Revelation 20 symbolically, but they also interpret the multitude of Old Testament prophecies about a future world peace symbolically. This approach, it is argued, allows people to interpret anything symbolically that does not fit their theological system if interpreted literally.

In response, no one takes everything in the Bible literally, for all recognize that portions of Scripture are not meant to be taken literally. This means that all Christians must discern which portions of Scripture are and are not literal. Amillennialists cannot be criticized for seeing some things as literal and other things as symbolic any more than any other Bible interpreter.

The issue is not whether someone understands some portions of Scripture to be symbolic—for all do—but whether someone decides what is and is not symbolic for good reasons. Amillennial advocates make this decision in line with established principles of exegesis and only as a particular genre of Scripture calls for it (e.g., apocalyptic, certain Old Testament prophetic texts, etc.).

2. *This view offers a weak defense.* Some argue that the amillennial position is unwarranted on the grounds that the case for it is largely a negative one. Its defense largely consists of a refutation of postmillennialism and premillennialism.

This approach is to be expected, however, given the nature of the controversy. After all, the other two views make a positive claim for a literal millennium, while amillennialism is, by definition, a denial that this claim is adequately grounded in Scripture. However, this does not mean that the amillennial position does not offer a constructive case for its own interpretation of biblical eschatology. Amillennialists affirm all that the New Testament teaches about the Lord's return. They simply deny that this affirmation needs to be complicated by the insertion of a literal period of peace, either after the Lord's return (as premillennialists hold) or before the Lord returns (as postmillennialists hold).

Further Reading

Bock, Darrell L., ed. *Three Views on the Millennium and Beyond*. Grand Rapids: Zondervan, 1999.

Boettner, Loraine. *The Millennium*. Philadelphia: Presbyterian and Reformed, 1957.

Clouse, Robert G., ed. *The Meaning of the Millennium: Four Views*. Downers Grove, IL: InterVarsity, 1977.

Erickson, Millard J. *A Basic Guide to Eschatology: Making Sense of the Millennium*. Rev. ed. Grand Rapids: Baker Academic, 1998.

Gentry, Kenneth L., Jr. *He Shall Have Dominion: A Postmillennial Eschatology*. 2nd ed. Tyler, TX: Institute for Christian Economics, 1997.

Grenz, Stanley. *The Millennial Maze*. Downers Grove, IL: InterVarsity, 1992.

Hoekema, Anthony. *The Bible and the Future*. Grand Rapids: Eerdmans, 1979.

Ladd, George E. *The Presence of the Future*. Grand Rapids: Eerdmans, 1974.

Lewis, Arthur. *The Dark Side of the Millennium: The Problem of Evil in Revelation 20:1–10*. Grand Rapids: Baker Academic, 1980.

Mathison, Keith A. *Postmillennialism: An Eschatology of Hope*. Phillipsburg, NJ: Presbyterian and Reformed, 1999.

17

The Hell Debate

The Unending Torment of the Wicked (The Classical View)
The Wicked Shall Be No More (The Annihilationist View)

Posing the Question

While attending a get-together, you befriend a young man named Brandon. It turns out that Brandon was raised in a nonreligious home. Thanks to a number of caring Christian acquaintances, however, Brandon has recently been considering acknowledging Christ as Lord and Savior. He eventually opens up to you about the one remaining obstacle: He cannot accept the Christian view of hell. "I've come to understand why God can't allow people in heaven who don't want to be there," he explains. "But I can't see why or how an all-loving God would torture people in hell forever!" You explain that God is not torturing them so much as he is simply letting rebels have their own way. Brandon is not convinced. "But the Creator has to intentionally keep people existing in this tormented state. Why doesn't he simply punish them and then let them go into nonexistence? What's the point of keeping people in existence simply for the purpose of having them suffer hopelessly?"

The Center and Its Contrasts

For the last decade, there has been a significant debate surrounding this very topic within evangelical circles. With the historic-orthodox Christian church, almost all evangelicals agree that those who resist God's plan of salvation to the bitter end will be eternally damned. This belief contrasts with universalism, which holds that eventually everyone will be saved. It also contrasts with the doctrine of reincarnation, which denies that there is a final judgment, holding instead that we pay for the wrongs we have done in this life by the things we go through in future lives. The Christian view also clearly contrasts with the naturalistic view, which holds that there is no ultimate standard of morality against which actions are judged. Therefore, there are no eternal consequences for wrong actions.

Christians believe that all people will stand before their Creator and answer for everything they have done. Those who have placed their trust in Jesus Christ will be saved (though their "works" will be judged, 1 Cor. 3:11–15). Those who have refused to place their trust in Christ will be judged according to their works and will consequently suffer eternal punishment (Rev. 20:11–13).

Evangelical Christians disagree over whether this punishment is eternal in *duration* or in *consequence*. That is, when the Bible speaks of "eternal destruction," does it mean that rebels will eternally suffer a process of destruction, or does it mean that once rebels are destroyed, it is eternal (namely, permanent, irreversible)? The traditional view is that rebels will consciously suffer eternally, but some within church history and an increasing number of evangelicals today argue that rebels are eternally annihilated.

The following two essays defend these two perspectives. The first argues for the classical view of hell as eternal, conscious torment. The second argues for the annihilationist view that hell is eternal in consequence, not duration.

The Unending Torment of the Wicked (The Classical View)

The church has traditionally held that the wicked will be cast into hell, where they will experience unending suffering. The doctrine is admittedly a difficult one. Among other things, it challenges ideas about the inherent goodness of people and the kindness of God. Not surprisingly, it has been increasingly replaced by a milder doctrine that the wicked will be annihilated rather than suffer endless torment. This essay defends the traditional doctrine and attempts to show that annihilationism is simply not grounded in Scripture.

The Biblical Argument

In the Old Testament, little was explicitly revealed about the afterlife. While Old Testament authors sometimes expressed an awareness of rewards and punishments (e.g., Isa. 25:8–9; Dan. 12:1–3), they were much more concerned with God's justice being administered in the present age. Still, several texts make it clear that even at this stage of biblical revelation, some were aware of the unending joy of the righteous and the unending suffering of the wicked.

In Daniel 12:2, the author proclaims that there will be a resurrection of the dead in which some will be granted "everlasting life" while others will be condemned to "shame and everlasting contempt." Annihilationists teach that the punishment of the wicked is everlasting in consequence, not duration. That is, the effect (but not the experience) of the judgment of the wicked is unending or irreversible. This passage refutes this conception, however. How could the wicked experience shame and contempt if they had been annihilated? And why would the author contrast the everlasting shame of the wicked with the everlasting joy of the righteous unless the shame was as much an ongoing experience as the joy? Not only this, but it seems odd that God would resurrect people from the dead only to annihilate them.

Another Old Testament passage that supports the traditional view of hell as unending torment is Isaiah 66:24. The prophet offers an eschatological vision in which the righteous "shall go out and look at the dead bodies of the people who have rebelled against me; for their worm shall not die, their fire shall not be quenched, and they shall be an abhorrence to all flesh."

In Old Testament times, the ultimate disgrace was for a person's corpse to be left above ground, where it would be eaten by maggots or burned with fire. The prophet uses this imagery to communicate the intense disgrace in the afterlife of those who oppose the Lord. When people suffered this terrible fate in history, the maggots or fire eventually consumed their corpses. In the final judgment, however, the maggots will never die and the fire will never go out! To enter into eternity in opposition to the sovereign Creator is to enter into unending suffering.

The New Testament has much more to say about the nature of hell. One of the clearest passages on the unending nature of hell is Matthew 25:31–46. Here Jesus acts as "King" on the day of judgment. Those who know Christ will be given eternal life (v. 34), while those who do not know him will be condemned to eternal punishment (v. 46). The fact that Jesus contrasts the "eternal punishment" of the wicked with the "eternal life" of the righteous suggests that the wicked will endure punishment forever (vv. 41, 46; cf. John 5:28–29). If the state of eternal life is an eternal state of consciousness, the state of punishment must also be one of eternal consciousness. In other words, hell cannot simply be eternal in consequence, as annihilationists teach. The fact that Jesus explicitly refers to the fire of this punishment as an "eternal fire" seems to confirm this (v. 41).

The parable of the greedy rich man who would not care for Lazarus supports the traditional view of hell as well. After death, the rich man finds himself "in Hades . . . being tormented" (Luke 16:23). In this state, he begs Abraham to send Lazarus to "dip the tip of his finger in water and cool my tongue; for I am in agony in these flames" (Luke 16:24). Despite the figurative language, the passage certainly teaches that the wicked continue to exist in a tormented state after death. So does Jesus' teaching that the sin against the Holy Spirit is "an eternal sin" (Mark 3:29), which "will not be forgiven, either in this age or in the age to come" (Matt. 12:32). Scholars debate what this sin against the Holy Spirit consists of, but this debate does not affect the passage's implications for our understanding of hell. Why would Jesus say that certain people will not be forgiven in the age to come if these same people will be annihilated?

The unending nature of hell is also evident in Jude's reference to fallen angels who are kept in "eternal chains" (Jude 6). If the chains are eternal, what the chains hold must be eternal as well. A similar argument can be made of Paul's teaching that the Lord will be revealed "in flaming fire, inflicting vengeance on those who do not know God. . . . These will suffer the punishment of eternal destruction." This destruction cannot be annihilation, for the punishment includes being "separated from the presence of the Lord and from the glory of his might" (2 Thess. 1:8–9). One can be separated from someone else only if one continues to exist. In addition, in the preceding verses, Paul draws a parallel between the affliction that the Thessalonians innocently suffered at the hands of persecutors and the affliction the persecutors will justly suffer at the hands of God (2 Thess. 1:6–7). If the affliction the Thessalonians suffered was conscious—and it obviously was—the affliction of the persecutors must also be conscious. Along the same lines, Paul teaches that there will be "wrath and fury" to all who reject God, adding that this fury will cause "anguish and distress" (Rom. 2:8–9). The fact that people must be conscious to suffer anguish and distress implies that hell is a conscious state.

Other teachings of Jesus suggest that hell is conscious in nature and unending in duration. For example, when the wicked are cast into "outer darkness" or "into the furnace," Jesus says, "there will be weeping and gnashing of teeth" (Matt. 13:42; 22:13). People must be conscious in order to weep and gnash their teeth. Following Isaiah, Jesus teaches that in this horrid place of torment the worm that devours will never die and the fire will never go out (Mark 9:48), which, as we have already seen, implies that the wicked will suffer eternally.

Along the same lines, Jesus' teaching that it would be better to be "drowned in the depth of the sea" than to be cast into hell for being a stumbling block makes sense only if the wicked consciously suffer throughout eternity (Matt. 18:6). If hell is annihilation, then its consequence is the same as being drowned. So, too, only if hell is eternal in duration does it make sense for Jesus to say that it would have been better for Judas if he had never been born (Mark 14:21). If hell is annihilation, then Judas' fate would in fact be as though he had never been born. But in this case how could Jesus describe his fate as *worse* than nonbirth? And how could Jesus describe the fate of some as being worse than others on the day of judgment if indeed all the wicked are annihilated (Matt. 11:20–24)?

The most explicit statements on the unending nature of hell, however, are found in the book of Revelation. Here an angel proclaims that anyone who worships the beast and its image will "be tormented with fire and sulfur in the presence of the holy angels and in the presence of the Lamb" (Rev. 14:10). Then he adds, "The smoke of their torment goes up forever and ever. There is no rest day or night for those who worship the beast and its image and for anyone who receives the mark of its name" (Rev. 14:11).

Annihilationists argue that the "smoke of their torment," not the torment itself, goes on forever. But lest there be any doubt, Revelation 20 explicitly states that the devil, the beast, and the false prophet were all thrown "into the lake of fire and sulfur," where "they will be tormented day and night forever and ever" (v. 10). Later it is said that "anyone whose name was not found written in the book of life was thrown into the lake of fire," apparently to suffer the same eternal fate as the devil they followed (v. 15). It is not just the smoke that goes on forever. It is the torment that gives rise to the smoke.

Supporting Arguments

1. *Church tradition*. The teaching that the wicked suffer unending torment has been the dominant teaching of the church throughout its history, and this must count in its favor.

2. *Sin against an infinite God*. As Anselm taught, sin against an infinite God is an infinite crime exacting an infinite punishment. We have difficulty fathoming the justice of an infinite punishment only because we have difficulty fathoming the glory of an infinite God.

3. *Criminals must pay*. Even apart from the infinite glory of God, it does not seem as though annihilation is an adequate punishment for the wicked. We instinctively want criminals to pay for their crimes. If criminals simply cease to exist, however, their crimes are not atoned for. Justice is not

served. True, they miss out on eternal joy in heaven, but what punishment is this if the wicked are not around to experience their loss?

4. *No fear of hell.* Many nonbelievers do not expect to live on after death. The threat of annihilation is thus no incentive to trust God for salvation. Yet Jesus and New Testament authors used warnings about hell to convince people they should get right with God. This implies that hell is not annihilation.

Responding to Objections

1. *Eternal hell is cruel.* The main objection to the traditional view of hell has always been that it is cruel. How could an all-loving God send anyone to a place of unending pain? Three things may be said in response to this objection.

First, God is not cruel if this punishment is just. It may be difficult to fathom the justice of unending punishment, for, as noted above, we have difficulty fathoming the infinite glory of God. But if we agree that God's glory is infinite and that sin is therefore an infinite crime, we cannot accuse God of being cruel for meting out this unending punishment.

Second, while the Bible at times portrays God as sending people to hell, other passages suggest that it is a state that the wicked actually choose for themselves. As C. S. Lewis noted, hell is simply the result of God letting obstinate people have their own way.[1] Along these same lines, Lewis suggested that if hell is locked for all eternity, it is "locked from the inside."[2] In other words, it is not that God keeps people in hell throughout eternity against their will. Rather, people refuse to accept God's love and submit to God's will throughout eternity. In the words of John, "This is the judgment, that the light has come into the world, and people *loved darkness* rather than light" (John 3:19, emphasis added).

Third, the charge of cruelty on God's part is somewhat mitigated if we consider that the images used throughout Scripture to describe hell are not literal. They are meant to convey the truth that to fall under the judgment of God and to miss out on the joy of heaven are the worst things imaginable. But there is no reason to suppose that the images of fire or worms are literal. Indeed, if taken literally, they seem to contradict each other. For example, how can hell be a place of "outer darkness" (Matt. 22:13) if it is also a place of perpetual fire (Matt. 18:8)?

2. *Scripture teaches annihilation.* Annihilationists argue that some passages of Scripture suggest that the wicked are annihilated. These passages can be accounted for in two ways.

First, as noted above, Old Testament authors are primarily interested in how God's justice gets played out in history. The majority of passages that speak of the wicked being utterly destroyed are taken from the Old Testament and refer not to the ultimate destiny of the wicked but to the earthly fate of the wicked (e.g., Ps. 37:38; Isa. 1:28, 30–31).

Second, when the New Testament speaks about the judgment of the wicked as "death," "corruption," or "destruction," it is contrasting the fate of the wicked with the destiny of those who belong to Jesus Christ (e.g., Rom. 6:23; 1 Thess. 5:3). Those who are in Christ will eternally experience life as God intended it to be lived. Those who reject Christ eternally exist in antithesis to this. Their life can be described only as a kind of death. What God intended humans to be is corrupted and destroyed in hell. But we read too much into these terms and contradict other teachings of Scripture if we interpret them to mean that the wicked are completely annihilated.

The Wicked Shall Be No More
(The Annihilationist View)

This essay defends the annihilationist view of hell and argues that the traditional view resulted from people reading the Bible with pagan philosophical presuppositions.

The Biblical Argument

While the Hellenistic philosophical tradition generally viewed the human soul as inherently immortal, Scripture sees immortality as something that belongs to God alone (1 Tim. 6:16). God graciously offers immortality as a gift to people who align themselves with his will (e.g., John 3:15–16; 10:28; 17:2; Rom. 2:7; 6:23; 1 Cor. 15:53–54; Gal. 6:8; 1 John 5:11). Those who choose to reject God's will are denied this gift, following the pattern of Adam and Eve when God denied them access to "the tree of life" (Gen. 3:22–24). Unfortunately, early church fathers accepted the Hellenistic view and consequently read into Scripture the belief that the wicked suffer unending torment. If we read Scripture without this Hellenistic assumption, we see that God justly and mercifully annihilates the wicked. He does not subject them to eternal torment.

Scripture certainly teaches that the wicked are punished eternally, but it does not teach that the wicked *endure* eternal punishment. The wicked suffer "eternal punishment" (Matt. 25:46), "eternal judgment" (Heb. 6:2), and "eternal destruction" (2 Thess. 1:9) the same way the elect experience "eternal redemption" (Heb. 5:9; 9:12). The elect do not undergo an eternal process of redemption. Their redemption is eternal in the sense that once the elect are redeemed, it is forever. So, too, the damned do not undergo an eternal process of punishment or destruction. But once they are punished and destroyed, it is forever. Hell is eternal in consequence, not duration.

Along the same lines, Scripture's references to an "unquenchable fire" and "undying worm" refer to the finality of judgment, not its duration (Isa. 66:24; cf. 2 Kings 22:17; Isa. 17:27; 51:8; Jer. 4:4; 7:20; 21:12; Ezek. 20:47–48). If these passages are read in context, it becomes clear that the fire is unquenchable in the sense that it cannot be put out before it consumes those thrown into it. And the worm is undying in the sense that there is no hope for the condemned that it will be prevented from devouring their corpses. These passages teach that the wicked will justly suffer for their sins, but the end result will be their destruction (cf. Luke 16:19–31; Rom. 2:8; 2 Thess. 1:6).

The traditional view that the wicked suffer eternally makes little use of the Old Testament. Adherents of this view justify this on the grounds that Old Testament authors were not concerned with the afterlife. This is mistaken. The Old Testament has a good deal to say about the ultimate destiny of those who resist God. Peter specifically cites the destruction of Sodom and Gomorrah as a pattern of how God judges the wicked. The Lord turned the inhabitants of these cities "to ashes" and "condemned them to extinction," thus making "them an example of what is coming to the ungodly" (2 Pet. 2:6). Conversely, the Lord's rescue of Lot sets a pattern for how the Lord will "rescue the godly from trial" (2 Pet. 2:9). There is thus a precedent in the New Testament for learning about the fate of the wicked in the Old Testament: The wicked are "condemned . . . to extinction."

Throughout the Old Testament, the Lord threatens the wicked with annihilation. To all who refuse to comply with the covenant God had established, for example, the Lord vows to "blot out their names from under heaven" (Deut. 29:20). Indeed, he vows to destroy them and the land "like the destruction of Sodom and Gomorrah . . . which the LORD destroyed in his fierce anger" (Deut. 29:23). So, too, through the prophet Isaiah the Lord warns that:

> rebels and sinners shall be destroyed together,
>   and those who forsake the LORD shall be consumed.
> For you shall be like an oak
>   whose leaf withers,
>   and like a garden without water.
> The strong shall become like tinder,
>   and their work like a spark;
> they and their work shall burn together,
>   with no one to quench them. (1:28, 30–31)

Again:

> as the tongue of fire devours the stubble,
>> and as dry grass sinks down in the flame,
> so their root will become rotten,
>> and their blossom go up like dust,
> for they have rejected the instruction of the LORD of hosts. (5:24)

The theme that the Lord will annihilate the wicked is especially prominent in the Psalms. The psalmist says that whereas those who take delight
in the Lord will be "like trees planted by streams of water" (Ps. 1:3), the
wicked will be "like chaff that the wind drives away. . . . The wicked will
perish" (Ps. 1:4, 6). They will be dashed "in pieces like a potter's vessel" (Ps.
2:9), torn into fragments (Ps. 50:22), and "blotted out of the book of the
living" (Ps. 69:28; cf. Deut. 29:20). Each metaphor depicts annihilation.

Similarly, the Lord's plan for evildoers is to "cut off the remembrance
of them from the earth. . . . Evil brings death to the wicked" (Ps. 34:16,
21). The wicked will be so thoroughly destroyed that they will not even be
remembered (Ps. 9:6; 34:16). In the powerful words of a later author, the
wicked "shall be as though they had never been" (Obad. 16).

With the same force, Psalm 37 proclaims that the wicked "will soon fade
like the grass, and wither like the green herb" (v. 2). They "shall be cut off
. . . and . . . will be no more; though you look diligently for their place, they
will not be there" (vv. 9–10). While the righteous "abide forever" (v. 27),
"the wicked perish . . . like smoke they vanish away" (v. 20); they "vanish like water that runs away; like grass [they will] be trodden down and
wither . . . like the snail that dissolves into slime; like the untimely birth
that never sees the sun" (Ps. 58:7–8). And again, "transgressors shall be
altogether destroyed" (Ps. 37:38; cf. v. 34). In short, the fate of the wicked
is disintegration into nothing.

The psalmist's emphasis on the total destruction of the wicked has
parallels throughout the Old Testament. Daniel, for example, speaks of
all who will be crushed by the rock of God's judgment as being "broken."
They become "like the chaff of the summer threshing floors," blown away
by the wind "so that not a trace of them [can] be found" (Dan. 2:35).
Nahum says that in the judgment the wicked "are consumed like dry
straw" (Nah. 1:10). Malachi tells us that the judgment day will come
"burning like an oven," and "all the arrogant and all evildoers will be
stubble." The judgment thus "shall burn them up" (Mal. 4:1). Proverbs
tells us that all who hate the Lord "love death" (Prov. 8:36) and that when
"the tempest" of God's judgment passes, "the wicked are no more" (Prov.
10:25). Again, when God's fury rises, "the wicked are overthrown and are
no more" (Prov. 12:7). And finally, "the evil have no future; the lamp of

the wicked will go out" (Prov. 24:20). It is impossible to accept that the wicked have no future if in fact they never cease to experience an eternal future in hell.

The teaching that the wicked will be completely destroyed is even stronger in the New Testament. As in the Old Testament, they are frequently depicted as being destroyed or consumed by fire (Heb. 6:8; 10:27; Jude 7; cf. Isa. 33:11). John the Baptist proclaims that "every tree . . . that does not bear good fruit is cut down and thrown into the fire" (Matt. 3:10). He says that the Messiah "will clear his threshing floor and will gather his wheat into the granary; but the chaff he will burn with unquenchable fire" (Matt. 3:12). Jesus himself several times describes hell as a consuming fire (Matt. 7:19; 13:40; John 15:6).

The New Testament describes the fate of the wicked in other ways as well, all directly or indirectly speaking of annihilation. Jesus contrasts the wide gate that "leads to destruction" with the narrow gate that "leads to life" (Matt. 7:13). Destruction clearly contrasts with life in this passage, implying cessation of consciousness such as when a person is dead. Along similar lines, Jesus tells his disciples not to fear those who kill the body but cannot kill the soul; rather "fear him who can destroy both soul and body in hell" (Matt. 10:28). The implication is that God will do to the souls of the wicked what humans do to the body when they kill it, implying that the souls of the wicked will not go on existing in a conscious state after they have been destroyed.

James teaches that God alone is able to both "save and destroy" (James 4:12). Peter teaches that "destruction" awaits false, greedy teachers (2 Pet. 2:3). Paul teaches that the quest for riches can plunge people into "ruin and destruction" (1 Tim. 6:9). Moreover, all who are "enemies of the cross" have "destruction" as their final end (Phil. 3:18–19; cf. 1:28). So, too, if anyone "destroys God's temple, God will destroy that person" (1 Cor. 3:17). With the same force the apostle teaches that "sudden destruction" will come upon the wicked in the last days (1 Thess. 5:3). This day is elsewhere described as a day for "the destruction of the godless" (2 Pet. 3:7). These passages clearly contradict the traditional view that the souls of the wicked are in fact never destroyed but rather endure endless torment.

The New Testament also frequently expresses the destiny of the wicked by depicting them as dying or perishing (*apollymi*). John proclaims the good news that God sent Jesus so that "everyone who believes in him may not perish but may have eternal life" (John 3:16). Paul utilizes this same contrast when he states that while those who proclaim the gospel are a "fragrance from life to life" to those "who are being saved," it is "a fragrance from death to death" to those "who are perishing" (2 Cor. 2:15–16). So, too, Paul teaches that "the wages of sin is death, but the free gift of God is eternal life" (Rom. 6:23; cf. 1:32; 6:21). This is consistent with Jesus' teaching that those who try to find life apart from God end up losing it (Matt. 10:39).

Along the same lines, James writes that "sin, when it is fully grown, gives birth to death" (James 1:15) and so the person who "brings back a sinner from wandering will save the sinner's soul from death" (James 5:20). So, too, Christ is said to have come to "[abolish] death and [bring] life and immortality to light through the gospel" (2 Tim. 1:10). Indeed, he came to "destroy the one who has the power of death, that is, the devil" (Heb. 2:14). Life and immortality are connected with following God, death with following Satan. The contrast in these passages between death, losing life, and perishing, on the one hand, and life, on the other, is incompatible with the contrast between eternal bliss and eternal pain, which the traditional teaching on hell presupposes. Death, losing life, and perishing do not signify another kind of life, namely, a life of eternal conscious pain.

When all the biblical evidence is assessed apart from the Hellenistic philosophical assumption that the soul is innately immortal, it becomes clear that the fate of the wicked is annihilation, not unending torment.

Supporting Arguments

1. *Unending suffering is inconsistent with the love of God.* The central revelation of God in the New Testament is that God is love (1 John 4:8, 16). His anger endures for a moment, but his mercy endures forever (Ps. 103:8–14). How is this consistent with the view that God's wrath burns eternally toward the wicked? Would we call a human being good or merciful—or anything other than cruel—who retaliated on his foes with this sort of unmitigated, insatiable vengeance?

From the annihilationist perspective, God's justice and mercy unite in condemning the wicked to extinction. He justly punishes their sin and forbids them a place within the kingdom. Yet he mercifully annihilates them precisely so they will not endlessly endure what the traditional view says they will endure.

2. *Unending torment is inconsistent with God's victory.* The teaching that people and fallen angels will be tormented throughout eternity contradicts the Bible's teaching that God is altogether victorious at the end of history. How can we affirm that Christ will be over all (Eph. 1:10, 21–22) and that God will be "all in all" (1 Cor. 15:28) when a dimension of reality will perpetually oppose God? How can we accept the scriptural affirmation that all creatures in heaven and on earth will bow before the throne (Phil. 2:10–11; cf. Rom. 14:10–11) and that all things will be reconciled to God (Col. 1:20; cf. Acts 3:21) if in fact many creatures will forever exist

in hostile rebellion to God? How can we affirm the final and ultimate victory of God's joy and peace and accept that there will be no more tears, sorrow, or death (Rev. 21:4) if throughout eternity there will be "weeping and gnashing of teeth" as multitudes suffer an endless second death? If the traditional view of hell is correct, God remains nonvictorious. Instead of a glorious universal kingdom unblemished by stain, an ugly dualism will reign throughout eternity.

Responding to Objections

1. *Scripture states that the wicked will be tormented day and night.* The most difficult passages for annihilationists to explain are Revelation 14:10–11 and 20:10, which speak of the wicked being tormented "day and night forever and ever." These passages are not as problematic for the annihilationist view as they might initially seem. The phrase "forever and ever" can be translated "for ages upon ages," which implies an indefinite but not necessarily unending period of time. Even more fundamentally, it is important to keep in mind that Revelation is a highly symbolic book. Its apocalyptic images should not be interpreted literally. This is particularly true of the phrase "forever and ever," since phrases similar to this are used elsewhere in Scripture in contexts in which they clearly cannot literally mean unending (e.g., Gen. 49:26; Exod. 40:15; Num. 25:13; Ps. 24:7).

Perhaps the most significant example of this is Isaiah 34:9–10, for it closely parallels the two passages in Revelation. In this passage, Isaiah says that the fire that shall consume Edom will burn "night and day" and "shall not be quenched." Its smoke "shall go up forever," and no one shall pass through this land again "forever and ever." Obviously, this is symbolic, for the fire and smoke of Edom's judgment are not still ascending today. If Isaiah contains symbolic meaning, we should be less inclined to interpret similar expressions in the book of Revelation literally.

2. *This view undermines fear of hell.* Some argue that if annihilationism is true, fear of hell is undermined. Two things may be said in response.

First, most annihilationists do not deny that the wicked will suffer, perhaps for long periods of time, prior to being annihilated. God's justice will be severe and ought to be dreaded.

Second, it is questionable that the traditional teaching on hell generally instills fear in the hearts of unbelievers. It rather seems that this teaching often has the opposite effect. The notion of unending punishment is so out of sync with people's ordinary sense of justice that it is easily rejected as preposterous. There is certainly a need to warn unbelievers of the impending judgment of God. The warning that the annihilationist gives is both biblical and believable.

292

Further Reading

Brower, Kent E., and Mark W. Elliott, eds. *Eschatology in Bible and Theology: Evangelical Essays at the Dawn of a New Millennium*. Downers Grove, IL: InterVarsity, 1997.

Cameron, Nigel M. de S., ed. *Universalism and the Doctrine of Hell*. Grand Rapids: Baker Academic, 1992.

Crockett, William, ed. *Four Views on Hell*. Grand Rapids: Zondervan, 1992.

Dixon, Larry. *The Other Side of the Good News: Confronting the Contemporary Challenges to Jesus' Teaching on Hell*. Wheaton: BridgePoint, 1992.

Fudge, Edward W. *The Fire That Consumes: A Biblical and Historical Study of Final Punishment*. Houston: Providential Press, 1982.

Fudge, Edward W., and Robert A. Peterson. *Two Views of Hell: A Biblical and Theological Dialogue*. Downers Grove, IL: InterVarsity, 2000.

Hilborn, David, et al. *The Nature of Hell*. Carlisle: Paternoster, 2000.

Kvanvig, Jonathan L. *The Problem of Hell*. New York: Oxford University Press, 1993.

Morgan, Christopher W., and Robert A. Peterson, eds. *Hell under Fire: Modern Scholarship Reinvents Eternal Punishment*. Grand Rapids: Zondervan, 2004.

Peterson, Robert A. *Hell on Trial: The Case for Eternal Punishment*. Phillipsburg, NJ: Presbyterian and Reformed, 1995.

Walls, Jerry. *Hell: The Logic of Damnation*. Notre Dame: University of Notre Dame Press, 1992.

Appendix

Issue 1: How Should Evangelicals "Do" Theology? The Theological Method Debate

A central debate among evangelical theologians concerns the question of theological method. In other words, how should we "do" theology?

All evangelical Christians believe the Bible is God-inspired revelation. Thus, evangelicals agree that Scripture must form the foundation for theological thought. But Scripture is not the only factor to consider when doing theology. Many evangelicals have adopted the Wesleyan quadrilateral (named after the eighteenth-century British revivalist and founder of Methodism, John Wesley) as a way to explain the various sources of theology and how they relate to each other. The quadrilateral, as the name suggests, presents theology as rooted in four sources: Scripture, church tradition, reason, and experience. Scripture is viewed as the foundation of theology, with each of the other three aspects helping to clarify and interpret Scripture in a faithful manner for the purpose of doing theology.

The debate arises when the question is asked, How are we to balance the four aspects of the quadrilateral, and to what degree do tradition, reason, and experience shape and determine our understanding of the Bible? Although there is a spectrum of views on the question of evangelical theological method, the two basic models can be described as follows.

According to the traditional evangelical model, the task of theology is to systematize and articulate the doctrinal truths found in the Bible. The emphasis is on the Bible as the unchanging, transcultural revelation of God. In the words of Carl F. H. Henry, "Divine revelation is the source of all truth, the truth of Christianity included. . . . The task of Christian theology is to exhibit the content of biblical revelation as an orderly whole."[1] This view of the theological task is rooted in an understanding of the Bible known as propositionalism. For those who hold to a propositionalist understanding, the Bible is seen primarily as containing and offering information about God. In Henry's words, "Scriptures contain a body of divinely given information actually expressed or capable of being expressed in propositions."[2]

In contrast to the traditional view is the postfoundationalist evangelical model of theological method. Like other expressions of the postmodern perspective, the postfoundationalist approach emphasizes the culturally conditioned nature of all human intellectual enterprises—theology included. Simply put, the postfoundationalist method, while still recognizing the Bible as the primary theological norm, places greater emphasis on the way human reason and experience structure and shape any given theology. Stanley Grenz expresses this conviction when he writes that "the categories we employ in our theology are by necessity culturally and historically conditioned, and as theologians each of us is both 'a child of the times' and a communicator to those times."[3]

While the fundamental Christian faith-commitment does not change, the conceptualization and articulation of this faith-commitment does change over time and across cultures. Thus, there is no expectation of ever arriving at a single evangelical "theology"; there will always be a number of diverse evangelical "theologies." This is true both because God, the primary object of theology, is beyond any human system of thought, and because every human theological system will always be conditioned by its cultural context.

From a postfoundationalist perspective, the Bible is the inspired *narrative* of the saving acts and message of God. This means that the central locus of revelation is the narrative itself, not a set of propositions that can be distilled from and expressed outside of that narrative. The truths of God and his character are expressed in the unchanging story of Christian faith. A systematic theology, then, being necessarily and dramatically shaped by the components of human reason and experience, is always a culturally conditioned conceptualization and articulation of the implications of the unchanging biblical narrative for a particular people at a particular time and place.

Further Reading

Clark, David K. *To Know and Love God: Method for Theology*. Wheaton: Crossway, 2003.

Erickson, Millard J. *The Evangelical Left: Encountering Postconservative Evangelical Theology*. Grand Rapids: Baker Academic, 1997.

Franke, John R. *The Character of Theology: An Introduction to Its Nature, Task, and Purpose*. Grand Rapids: Baker Academic, 2005.

Grenz, Stanley. *Renewing the Center: Evangelical Theology in a Post-Theological Era*. 2nd ed. Grand Rapids: Baker Academic, 2006.

———. *Revisioning Evangelical Theology: A Fresh Agenda for the Twenty-first Century*. Downers Grove, IL: InterVarsity, 1993.

Grenz, Stanley, and John R. Franke. *Beyond Foundationalism: Shaping Theology in a Postmodern Context*. Louisville: Westminster John Knox, 2001.

Henry, Carl F. H. *God, Revelation, and Authority*. 6 vols. Waco: Word, 1976–83.

Lints, Richard. *The Fabric of Theology: A Prolegomena to Evangelical Theology*. Grand Rapids: Eerdmans, 1993.

McGrath, Alister E. *Understanding Doctrine: Its Relevance and Purpose for Today*. Grand Rapids: Zondervan, 1990.

Pinnock, Clark. "New Dimensions in Theological Method." In *New Dimensions in Evangelical Thought: Essays in Honor of Millard J. Erickson*, edited by David S. Dockery, 197–208. Downers Grove, IL: InterVarsity, 1998.

Schults, F. LeRon. *The Postfoundationalist Task of Theology: Wolfhart Pannenberg and the New Theological Rationality*. Grand Rapids: Eerdmans, 1999.

Stackhouse, John G., Jr., ed. *Evangelical Futures: A Conversation on Theological Method*. Grand Rapids: Baker Academic, 2000.

Thorsen, Donald A. D. *The Wesleyan Quadrilateral: Scripture, Tradition, Reason, and Experience*. Grand Rapids: Zondervan, 1990.

Wells, David F. *No Place for Truth, or, Whatever Happened to Evangelical Theology?* Grand Rapids: Eerdmans, 1993.

Issue 2: The Psychological and Social Models of the Trinity

The Bible teaches that there is only one God. At the same time, it teaches that the Father, Son, and Holy Spirit are each fully God. For this reason the church has always affirmed the doctrine of the Trinity, which teaches that God has one substance (*ousia*) but eternally and fully exists as three distinct Persons (*hypostases personae*).

The question left unanswered is how we are to understand the relationship between the substantial unity and personal plurality within the Godhead. Throughout church history, two distinct models have been proposed.

The first model goes back to the second-century apologists and was made famous by Augustine. It is usually called the psychological model of the Trinity, for it likens the unity and diversity of the Godhead to the unity and diversity of the human self. According to Augustine, the unity of the Father, Son, and Holy Spirit is like the unity of the mind (thoughts), heart (emotions), and volition (will) of a person. A different version was put forth by Jonathan Edwards in the eighteenth century. He argued that as the human psyche consists of a self, a self-image, and a relationship between the self and the self-image, so the Godhead consists of a self (Father), a perfect self-image (Son), and a perfect loving relationship (Spirit) between the self and the self-image.

   While many have found the psychological model helpful, others have objected to it on the grounds that it is not faithful to the biblical data. The Bible depicts the Father, Son, and Holy Spirit as three distinct Persons, they argue, not three distinct aspects of one Person. Hence, they have proposed that we should think of the unity of the Trinity more like the unity of mind, heart, and will of three people. This has been labeled the social model of the Trinity.

   To some defenders of the psychological model, the social model borders on tri-theism (the belief in three separate gods). To some defenders of the social model, the psychological model borders on modalism (reducing the three Persons to modes of one person). Still others argue that since models are only models, not exact replicas of reality, we may affirm both models as valid in capturing distinct perspectives on a God whose full reality defies exhaustive description.

Further Reading

Augustine. *The Trinity*. Translated by Edmund Hill. New York: New City, 1991.

Brown, David. *The Divine Trinity*. LaSalle, IL: Open Court, 1985.

Feenstra, Ronald J., and Cornelius Plantinga Jr., eds. *Trinity, Incarnation, and Atonement: Philosophical and Theological Essays*. Notre Dame: University of Notre Dame Press, 1989.

Gregory of Nyssa. *One Not Three Gods*. In *The Trinitarian Controversy*, edited and translated by William G. Rusch. Philadelphia: Fortress, 1980.

Grenz, Stanley J. *Rediscovering the Triune God: The Trinity in Contemporary Theology*. Minneapolis: Augsburg Fortress, 2004.

Hodgson, Leonard. *The Doctrine of the Trinity*. London: Nisbet, 1943.

Kärkkäinen, Veli-Matti. *The Trinity: Global Perspectives*. Louisville: Westminster John Knox, 2007.

Moltmann, Jürgen. *The Trinity and the Kingdom*. Minneapolis: Augsburg Fortress, 1993.

Pinnock, Clark, and Robert C. Brow. *Unbounded Love*. Downers Grove, IL: InterVarsity, 1994.

Rea, Michael C. "Polytheism and Christian Belief." *Journal of Theological Studies* 57 (2006): 133–48.

Toon, Peter. *Our Triune God: A Biblical Portrayal of the Trinity*. Wheaton: BridgePoint, 1996.

Volf, Miroslav, and Michael Welker, eds. *God's Life in Trinity*. Minneapolis: Augsburg Fortress, 2006.

Warfield, B. B. "Calvin's Doctrine of the Trinity." In *Calvin and Augustine*, edited by Samuel G. Craig, 189–284. Philadelphia: Presbyterian and Reformed, 1956.

Welch, Claude. *In This Name: The Trinity in Contemporary Theology*. New York: Scribner's, 1952.

Issue 3: Was Noah's Flood Global or Local?

Though many regard the biblical story of a great flood in the days of Noah to be an ancient legend, evangelical Christians affirm it as historical fact because Scripture presents it as such. However, a debate has arisen during the last two hundred years as to whether the flood was global or local. Those who defend the traditional position that the flood was global argue that the language used in the Genesis narrative requires this interpretation. For example, the narrative says, "All the high mountains under the whole heaven were covered" with water (Gen. 7:19). When one considers the height of the Himalayas or Mount Everest, it is clear that the flood was global. The Bible even names the mountain the ark came to rest on (Mount Ararat), and it alone is high enough to require a global flood (Gen. 8:4).

Defenders of the traditional view also point out that if the flood were only local, it would have been unnecessary for Noah to build a gigantic ark and house all species of animals for a year (Gen. 7:2–4). Not only this, but Scripture says the flood was intended to destroy all humanity. A local flood could not have accomplished this (Gen. 6:7, 13). Besides, the New Testament cites the flood episode as an example of the judgment *upon the whole earth* that is yet to come (2 Pet. 2:5).

Not all are convinced by these arguments, however. Some evangelicals argue that the language of the flood narrative may be interpreted phenomenologically (in terms of appearance) and hyperbolically (exaggeration for emphasis) rather than literally. In this case, the "high mountains" (Gen. 7:19) that were covered by the flood may be understood as the hills in Noah's region—probably the low-lying hills of Shinar or Babylon (cf. Gen. 11:2)—not as the mile-high mountains of the Himalayas. Moreover, there is no evidence that the mountain presently named Mount Ararat is the mountain referred to in Genesis, since this mountain received its name in recent times. Defenders of a local flood also argue that the purpose for the ark need not have been that there was no other way to save a remnant of animals or humans. It may have served as a warning for and witness against the generation that was to undergo judgment.

The main driving force behind the local flood theory, however, is the problems some find with the global flood theory. Local flood defenders customarily point to six major problems with the idea of a global flood. (1) Water high enough to cover the Himalayas and Mount Everest would have nowhere to run off. Yet the Bible describes the flood as abating with wind over several hundred days (Gen. 8:1). (2) A global flood in the recent past (10,000 years or less) would have left easily discernible evidence. Local flood defenders argue that while there is indisputable evidence for a mass local flood in the Mesopotamian region, there is no evidence for a global flood. (3) The mingling of freshwater and salt water produced by a global flood would have killed all freshwater life. Yet freshwater life, including freshwater fish, still exists. (4) A blanket of water thick enough to cover all mountains would have destroyed dry land vegetation. Where did the dove find a "freshly plucked olive leaf" (Gen. 8:11)? (5) There is no way a pair of every species of animal could have traveled around the globe to the ark. (6) As large as the ark was, there is no way that tens of thousands of different species of animals could have fit on it—along with food sufficient to feed them (Gen. 6:21). Nor could this variety of animals have survived in closed quarters without sunlight for a year, according to local flood advocates.

Defenders of the traditional view argue that the reinterpretation of the Genesis narrative required by local flood theorists is unnatural. They also insist that the six objections to the traditional view are answerable, especially when one allows for the reality of a miracle-working God. It may in fact be, for example, that there is no way to account for the disappearance of all the water that once blanketed the earth on a strictly natural basis, but this would be a small feat for the omnipotent Creator to accomplish. Something similar may be said of the transportation of the animals to the ark and their survival on the ark.

Further Reading

Brown, Walter T. *In the Beginning: Compelling Evidence for Creation and the Flood*. 7th ed. Phoenix: Center for Scientific Creation, 2001.

Filby, Frederick A. *The Flood Reconsidered*. Grand Rapids: Zondervan, 1970.

Ryan, William, and Walter Pitman. *Noah's Flood: New Scientific Discoveries about the Event That Changed History*. New York: Simon and Schuster, 2000.

Vardiman, Larry. *Climates before and after the Genesis Flood: Numerical Models and Their Implications*. Dallas: Institute for Creation Research, 2001.

Whitcomb, John C., and Henry M. Morris. *The Genesis Flood: The Biblical Record and Its Scientific Implications*. Philadelphia: Presbyterian and Reformed, 1961.

Young, Davis A. *The Biblical Flood: A Case Study of the Church's Response to Extrabiblical Evidence*. Grand Rapids: Eerdmans, 1995.

———. *Creation and the Flood: An Alternative to Flood Geology and Theistic Evolution*. Grand Rapids: Baker Books, 1977.

Youngblood, Ronald, ed. *The Genesis Debate: Persistent Questions about Creation and the Flood*. Nashville: Nelson, 1986.

Issue 4: According to the Bible, Are Humans Made Up of One, Two, or Three Parts?

Christians have always affirmed that humans are made in "the image of God" (Gen. 1:27). There has, however, been a debate about the actual "constitution" of human beings throughout history. The Bible uses a wide variety of terms to refer to various aspects of a human self, including "soul," "spirit," "body," "flesh," "heart," "mind," and "will." The issue at hand is: What do these terms mean and how do they relate to one another? Are humans made of one, two, or three "parts"? When the body dies, does another part of the person continue to exist in a conscious state?

The most commonly held view throughout history is called the **dichotomist** or **dualistic view of the self**, for it holds that the human self is composed of two basic parts: the body and the soul (or spirit). This view became the predominant view in the early church, particularly after the Council of Constantinople in AD 381. Advocates of this position throughout church history have included such noted theologians as John Calvin, Charles Hodge, and A. H. Strong.

Dichotomists point out that, while Scripture consistently distinguishes between the body, on the one hand, and the soul or spirit, on the other, it almost never distinguishes between soul, on the one hand, and spirit, on the other. Related to this, Scripture usually mentions body and soul (or spirit) without mentioning a third thing.

To illustrate, Scripture says that God "formed man from the dust of the ground, and breathed into his nostrils the breath of life; and the man became a living being [i.e., soul]" (Gen. 2:7). The passage says nothing about a third thing that was given to Adam over and above his body and soul. Similarly, Jesus teaches us not to worry about those who "kill the body but cannot kill the soul." Rather, we should fear [reverence] God "who can destroy both soul and body in hell" (Matt. 10:28). Jesus elsewhere notes that the "spirit" of the disciples was "willing" to pray with him, but "the flesh [was] weak" (Matt. 26:41).

With the same distinction in mind, Paul writes that one reason it is advantageous to remain unmarried is that the unmarried person can give their undivided attention to being "holy in body and spirit" (1 Cor. 7:34). James says that "just as the body without the spirit is dead, so faith without works is also dead" (James 2:26). And John prays for all to go well with his readers so "that [they] may be in good health [i.e., body], just as it is well with [their] soul[s]" (3 John 2). Passages such as these suggest that the physical and spiritual aspects of human beings are two fundamentally distinct realities and that the terms "soul" and "spirit" are really just synonyms, different words referring to the same spiritual part of the human self.

According to the dichotomist view, the "soul" or "spirit" remains alive and conscious after the body dies. For example, Paul tells his readers he is not sure whether it is better for him to live or die. "My desire is to depart and be with Christ," he confesses, "for that is far better." At the same time, "to remain in the flesh is more necessary for you" (Phil. 1:23–24). So too,

Paul describes the body as an "earthly tent" that the soul leaves to be with the Lord when we die (2 Cor. 5:1–8). It seems evident Paul believes that when he dies physically his soul (spirit) goes on to be with the Lord.

The second perspective held throughout history and today is the **trichotomist view of the self.** Unlike dichotomists, trichotomists hold that the human self is composed of three fundamentally distinct parts, for they distinguish not only between the body and soul, but between the soul and the spirit. This view, in various forms, was espoused by such early church fathers as Clement of Alexandria, Origen, Gregory of Nyssa, and Didymus the Blind.

Trichotomists have various ways of describing the difference between the soul and spirit. For example, the term "soul" refers to the self we experience—our personality, reason, emotions, and will. The term "spirit," however, refers to something more fundamental than our conscious experience. Spirit is the center of our being, the seat of the self that determines whether we are fundamentally open or closed to God. Ultimately, all that we do in our soul and body, thought and action, is a working out of what we become in our spirit.

Trichotomists admit that biblical authors usually use "soul" and "spirit" interchangeably, for they weren't trying to teach a particular theory about the constitution of the self. In conventional, everyday language, there's no point to distinguishing between the two. But there are two passages that make it clear that soul and spirit are not identical.

The first is found in a prayer by the apostle Paul: "May the God of peace himself sanctify you entirely; and may your spirit and soul and body be kept sound and blameless at the coming of our Lord Jesus Christ" (1 Thess. 5:23). While "soul" and "spirit" are used interchangeably in conventional language, here Paul distinguishes between "soul" and "spirit" just as strongly as he does "body" and "soul," for he is praying for the *total* sanctification of his reading audience.

A second passage that distinguishes between "spirit" and "soul" is Hebrews 4:12. As a way of stressing how important it is to walk circumspectly before God, both in what we think and in what we do, the author says, "the word of God is living and active, sharper than any two-edged sword, piercing until it divides soul from spirit, joints from marrow; it is able to judge the thoughts and intentions of the heart." As with the previous passage, in this context the author has a reason to go beyond conventional usage and distinguish between the "spirit" and "soul." He wants to stress how deeply God knows us and how profoundly he examines us (cf. Heb. 4:13). The word of God, the author teaches, is so sharp and so precise it is able to divide "soul" from "spirit" just as a master surgeon might hypothetically divide "joints" from "marrow." If "joints" are distinct from "marrow," then "soul" must be distinct from "spirit."

In fact, the analogy of joints and marrow reveals something about what the distinction between "soul" and "spirit" amounts to. A joint is what holds bones together while marrow is what makes a bone a bone. So too, the author seems to be suggesting that what holds the human self together is its "soul." The experienced togetherness of our mind, emotions, and will gives us our united self-identity and personality. What makes humans *human*, however, is their spirit. This is the very essence—the "marrow," if you will—of the human self. It constitutes the center out of which all the issues of life are decided.

A third, less common, view has become increasingly popular in modern times, partly as a result of advances in neuroscience. It is called the **monistic** (or unitary) **view of the self**, for it maintains that humans are composed of *one* substance, not two or three. In this view, the various terms used to describe the human self—"body," "soul," "spirit," "heart," etc.—refer not to different parts of the human constitution but to different aspects of a single, indivisible, human self.

Monists stress the fact that the Bible often refers to the deceased as sleeping (e.g., Acts 13:36; 1 Cor. 15:6) and sometimes explicitly denies that people remain conscious after death (e.g., Job 17:13–16; Ps. 6:5; 30:9; 88:3–5; Isa. 38:18). Related to this, monists emphasize the fact that the hope given to people in the Bible is not an immediate life after death for their disembodied soul but the bodily resurrection from the dead at the end of the age (1 Thess. 4:16–17). For monists, this suggests that the Bible does not share the view of the majority of Christians throughout history, namely, that humans are composite beings and that one part of their constitution survives death. When the body dies, the monist argues, the soul and spirit (and heart and mind, etc.) cease to exist as well, for these simply reflect the multifaceted nature of the **holistic** human self.

Monists argue that the composite view of humans—whether dichotomist or trichotomist—originated in Greek philosophy, not the Bible. The Greeks generally downplayed the value of the physical realm and considered the "rational" and "spiritual" aspects of the self to be superior to the body. For this reason most Greeks believed the superior part of a person—the rational spirit—survived the decay of the inferior part, the body. The Hebraic view of the self and of the world was much more holistic, they argue. God created the material body along with the material cosmos and declared it all to be very good. It is this body that God will resurrect at the end of the age, and, at the same time, it is this material cosmos that he shall redeem. Monists argue it is time to abandon the Greek view of the self and world and recover the original holistic, integrated Hebraic view.

Further Reading

Brown, Warren S., Nancey Murphy, and H. Newton Maloney, eds. *Whatever Happened to the Soul? Scientific and Theological Portraits of Human Nature*. Minneapolis: Augsburg Fortress, 1998.

Cooper, John W. *Body, Soul, and Life Everlasting: Biblical Anthropology and the Monism-Dualism Debate*. Grand Rapids: Eerdmans, 1989.

Delitzsch, Franz. *A System of Biblical Psychology*. 2nd ed. Grand Rapids: Baker Academic, 1977.

Green, Joel B., and Stuart L. Palmer, eds. *In Search of the Soul: Four Views of the Mind-Body Problem*. Downers Grove, IL: InterVarsity, 2005.

Jewett, Paul K. *Who We Are: Our Dignity as Human*. Edited by Marguerite Shuster. Grand Rapids: Eerdmans, 1996.

McDonald, H. D. *The Christian View of Man*. Westchester, IL: Crossway, 1981.

Moreland, J. P., and Scott B. Rae. *Body and Soul: Human Nature and the Crisis in Ethics*. Downers Grove, IL: InterVarsity, 2000.

Murphy, Nancey. *Bodies and Souls, or Spirited Bodies?* New York: Cambridge University Press, 2006.

Reichenbach, Bruce R. *Is Man the Phoenix? A Study of Immortality*. Grand Rapids: Eerdmans, 1978.

Sherlock, Charles. *The Doctrine of Humanity*. Contours of Christian Theology. Downers Grove, IL: InterVarsity, 1996.

Issue 5: Must Wives Submit to Their Husbands?

In the New Testament, Paul writes: "Wives, be subject to your husbands as you are to the Lord. For the husband is the head of the wife just as Christ is the head of the church, the body of which he is the Savior. Just as the church is subject to Christ, so also wives ought to be, in everything, to their husbands" (Eph. 5:22–24).

Along similar lines, Peter writes: "Wives . . . accept the authority of your husbands. . . . It was in this way long ago that the holy women who hoped in God used to adorn themselves by accepting the authority of their husbands. Thus Sarah obeyed Abraham and called him lord. You have become her daughters as long as you do what is good and never let fears alarm you" (1 Pet. 3:1, 5–6).

Many evangelicals (labeled complementarians) maintain that these words are as applicable today as they were in the first century. Male headship is part of God's timeless design for creation (Gen. 2:21–24; 3:16; Eph. 5:22). Much of the trouble modern families are experiencing, they argue, is due to the confusion that now exists concerning this very issue.

This, of course, does not mean that husbands are allowed to tyrannize their wives. On the contrary, Scripture commands that they lead with a gentle, self-sacrificial spirit. Indeed, though they have authority over their wives, as

Christ does over the church, husbands must be willing to lay down their lives for their wives, as Christ did for the church (Eph. 5:25–28). Male headship without male sacrifice is no closer to God's ideal than no headship at all.

Other evangelicals (labeled egalitarians) disagree with this view, however. In their view, these passages represent God working within a non-ideal culture to change it from the inside out. The instruction of wives to submit to their husbands is thus on the same level as Paul's instruction to Philemon to take back his slave Onesimus (Philem. 12–16). Though God's desire was to do away with slavery, in this culture, at this time, the most he could do was "Christianize" it, as it were. Hence, God transformed the master-slave relationship by having Paul command the one who holds the power (Philemon) to use it in a Christlike way. In the same way, adherents of this view argue, God's desire was to do away with gender-based authority and replace it with gift-based authority. But in this culture, at this time, the most he could do was "Christianize" the gender-based authority. Hence, Paul tells the one in power (the husband) to use his power in a Christlike way. He is to subject himself to his wife (Eph. 5:21) and be willing to give himself sacrificially for his wife, even as Christ did for the church (Eph. 5:25–28). As with all relationships among believers, husbands and wives should not be concerned with who is boss but should rather seek to serve and defer to one another (Luke 22:24–27; Phil. 2:5–8).

Further Reading

Bilezikian, Gilbert. *Beyond Sex Roles: What the Bible Says about a Woman's Place in Church and Family*. Grand Rapids: Baker Academic, 2006. (egalitarian)

Clark, Stephen B. *Man and Woman in Christ: An Examination of the Roles of Men and Women in Light of Scripture and the Social Sciences*. Ann Arbor, MI: Servant, 1980. (complementarian)

Foh, Susan T. *Women and the Word of God: A Response to Biblical Feminism*. Phillipsburg, NJ: Presbyterian and Reformed, 1979. (complementarian)

Groothuis, Rebecca M. *Good News for Women: A Biblical Picture of Gender Equality*. Grand Rapids: Baker Academic, 1997. (egalitarian)

Hull, Gretchen Gaebelein. *Equal to Serve*. Tarrytown, NY: Revell, 1991. (egalitarian)

Hurley, James B. *Man and Woman in Biblical Perspective*. Downers Grove, IL: InterVarsity, 1981. (complementarian)

Jewett, Paul K. *Man as Male and Female: A Study in Sexual Relationships from a Theological Point of View*. Grand Rapids: Eerdmans, 1975. (egalitarian)

Kassian, Mary. *Women, Creation, and the Fall*. Westchester, IL: Crossway, 1990. (complementarian)

Keener, Craig S. *Paul, Women, and Wives: Marriage and Women's Ministry in the Letters of Paul*. Peabody, MA: Hendrickson, 1992. (egalitarian)

MacArthur, John A. *Different by Design*. Wheaton: Victor Books, 1994. (complementarian)

Neuer, Werner. *Man and Woman in Christian Perspective*. Translated by Gordon Wenham. Wheaton: Crossway, 1990. (complementarian)

Pierce, Ronald W., Rebecca Merrill Groothuis, and Gordon D. Fee, eds. *Discovering Biblical Equality: Complementarity without Hierarchy*. Downers Grove, IL: InterVarsity, 2004. (egalitarian)

Piper, John, and Wayne Grudem, eds. *Recovering Biblical Manhood and Womanhood: A Response to Evangelical Feminism*. Wheaton: Crossway, 1991. (complementarian)

Issue 6: Christians and Politics: Three Views

Cal Thomas and Ed Dobson were leaders in the Moral Majority, a conservative evangelical social and political movement in the 1980s that attempted to rally "moral" people to change public policy on a number of issues. The movement died out in the 1990s. In 1999, Thomas and Dobson wrote a book entitled *Blinded by Might* in which they declare that they now believe Christians should not try to change culture primarily by influencing the political system. They should rather rely on the power of the gospel to change lives, one at a time. Christianity becomes corrupted, they argue, when it becomes overly involved in the politics of the world.

How involved should Christians be in secular politics? Throughout history, Christians have embraced a number of perspectives on this issue. These perspectives can be broken down into three groups.

First, some Christians believe that one of the church's jobs is to transform and ultimately control politics. This view has often been labeled the transformational model and has been the dominant model among Calvinists. It was also popular with most nineteenth-century revivalists (e.g., Charles Finney, Dwight Moody) and the church throughout the Middle Ages. Since God is Lord of everything, Christians should seek to manifest this lordship in everything, including politics. They should therefore use any righteous means possible to sanctify the political system and seek to pass laws that reflect God's will for people as revealed in Scripture.

At the opposite end of the spectrum are Christians who believe that Christians should not involve themselves at all in secular politics or at least should be wary of doing so. This oppositional model has been the traditional view among Anabaptists and is embraced by a number of noteworthy evangelical leaders today, including Cal Thomas. Christ said his kingdom was not of this world, and he never involved himself in the political debates of his day (John 18:36). Christians are called to be loyal to Christ's kingdom alone and to see themselves as citizens and ambassadors of the kingdom of God living in a "foreign" land (e.g., Phil. 3:20). This present world, including its political systems, is under the control of Satan. Therefore, trying to conform it to God's will is futile and even dangerous. The power of the gospel is found in evangelism and prayer, not in influencing the political process.

In between these two positions is the two-kingdoms model of church and state. This has been the dominant view of Lutherans and arguably the dominant view among American Christians. Unlike the oppositional model, this model holds that "secular" politics are under God's authority. Unlike the transformational model, however, it does not hold that the politics of the world should be or can be transformed into a Christian system. Rather, secular government and the church are two ways that God works in the world, and they accomplish different purposes. The purpose of secular government is to keep sin in check and rule over sinners by force. The purpose of the church is to transform sinners into saints who do not need to be ruled by law, and to do so by the power of the gospel and prayer. Christians may or may not get involved in government, depending on their calling from God. But they should not think that any alterations they make in government, however laudable, will further the purpose of transforming lives the way God wants to transform them.

Further Reading

Bornkamm, Heinrich. *Luther's Doctrine of the Two Kingdoms in the Context of His Theology*. Philadelphia: Fortress, 1966.

Boyd, Gregory A. *The Myth of a Christian Nation: How the Quest for Political Power is Destroying the Church*. Grand Rapids: Zondervan, 2005.

Budziszewski, J. *Evangelicals in the Public Square: Four Formative Voices on Political Thought and Action*. Grand Rapids: Baker Academic, 2006.

Carson, D. A. *Christ and Culture Revisited*. Grand Rapids: Eerdmans, 2008.

Carter, Craig A. *Rethinking Christ and Culture: A Post-Christendom Perspective*. Grand Rapids: Brazos, 2006.

Claiborne, Shane, and Chris Haw. *Jesus for President: Politics for Ordinary Radicals*. Grand Rapids: Zondervan, 2008.

Clapp, Rodney. *A Peculiar People: The Church as Culture in a Post-Christian Society*. Downers Grove, IL: InterVarsity, 1996.

Colson, Charles. *Kingdoms in Conflict*. Grand Rapids: Zondervan, 1987.

Geisler, Norman, and Frank Turek. *Legislating Morality*. Minneapolis: Bethany, 1998.

Niebuhr, H. Richard. *Christ and Culture*. New York: Harper, 1951.

Noll, Mark A., et al. *Adding Cross to Crown: The Political Significance of Christ's Passion*. Grand Rapids: Baker Academic, 1996.

Stassen, Glen H., D. M. Yeager, and John Howard Yoder. *Authentic Transformation: A New Vision of Christ and Culture*. Nashville: Abingdon, 1996.

Thomas, Cal, and Ed Dobson. *Blinded by Might*. Grand Rapids: Zondervan, 1999.

Webber, Robert E. *The Church in the World: Opposition, Tension, or Transformation?* Grand Rapids: Academie/Zondervan, 1986.

———. *The Secular Saint: The Role of the Christian in the Western World*. Grand Rapids: Zondervan, 1979.

Issue 7: What Happens to Babies Who Die?

The Bible does not directly address the issue of what happens to babies who die before being able to make a decision for or against Christ. People have thus had to arrive at conclusions about this matter on the basis of other beliefs they hold to be true.

The majority of evangelicals today assume that all who die before "the age of accountability" automatically go to heaven. (The same holds true for severely mentally incapacitated adults, though historically this topic has rarely been addressed.) What drives this view is the conviction that babies are not guilty of any explicit sin, and therefore, it would be unjust for God not to save them. The view is so self-evident to some today that they are surprised to learn that few church spokespersons throughout history have shared this assumption.

The prevailing opinion from Augustine through the medieval period was that all babies who had received Christian baptism went to heaven, but all others went to hell. This view was driven by a particular understanding of inherited original sin and the belief that baptism washed away this sin. The difficulty of accepting this conclusion led to the qualification that the level of hell babies go to (limbo) was devoid of pain. Some evangelicals within liturgical traditions hold a form of this belief.

Some Christians in the late Middle Ages and Reformation period, focusing on the importance of family covenants in Scripture, maintained that the fate of babies was directly connected to the faith or unbelief of their parents. This view is embraced by some evangelicals today.

Yet another view has traditionally been espoused by Reformed theologians. Rooted in a particular understanding of divine election, this view maintains that the fate of babies is decided in the same way as the fate of adults. As spelled out in the Westminster Confession of Faith, elect babies are predestined to salvation; nonelect babies are not. Often this view is combined with the above mentioned covenantal theology, assuring Christian parents that their deceased babies are indeed elect.

Finally, evangelicals who are convinced that love must be freely chosen suggest that perhaps babies who die are somehow allowed to mature in the afterlife, at which point they, like the rest of us, decide for themselves whether they want to submit to Christ.

Further Reading

Boors, L. *The Mystery of Death*. Translated by G. Bainbridge. New York: Herder & Herder, 1965.

Buswell, J. O. *A Systematic Theology of the Christian Religion*. Grand Rapids: Zondervan, 1962.

Dyer, G. J. "The Unbaptized Infant in Eternity," *Chicago Studies* 2 (1963): 147.

Gumpel, P. "Unbaptized Infants: May They Be Saved?" *Downside Review* 72 (1954): 342–458.

Hastings, Adrian. "The Salvation of Unbaptized Infants." *Downside Review* 77 (1958–59): 172–78.

Sanders, J. *No Other Name: An Investigation into the Destiny of the Unevangelized.* Grand Rapids: Eerdmans, 1992.

Warfield, B. B. "The Development of the Doctrine of Infant Salvation." In *Studies in Theology*, edited by E. D. Warfield, 411–44. New York: Oxford University Press, 1932.

Issue 8: The Debate over the Baptism in the Holy Spirit

Evangelicals believe that all believers are *indwelt* by the Holy Spirit, but there is debate over whether all believers are *baptized* in the Holy Spirit. John the Baptist prophesied that while he baptized with water, the one who would come after him (Jesus) would "baptize . . . with the Holy Spirit and fire" (Matt. 3:11). Jesus reminded his disciples of this prophecy before he ascended, telling them to wait for this baptism in Jerusalem (Acts 1:4–8). This occurred on the day of Pentecost (Acts 2:1–4). The question is, Do all believers now receive this Spirit baptism when they believe, or should believers seek to be baptized in the Spirit as an experience subsequent to salvation?

The classic Protestant position, embraced by a majority of evangelicals, is that people are baptized with the Spirit when they believe. This position argues that the New Testament does not distinguish between the act of receiving the Holy Spirit and being baptized in the Spirit. All believers are "marked with the seal of the promised Holy Spirit," which is "the pledge of our inheritance towards redemption" (Eph. 1:13–14). All who believe are "baptized into one body" by "one Spirit" and are "made to drink of one Spirit" (1 Cor. 12:13). If one is not baptized by the Spirit, this view maintains, that person is not part of Christ's body and does not drink of the Spirit. Either a person has the Holy Spirit, in which case he or she is saved, or a person does not have the Holy Spirit, in which case "Christ does not belong to [him]" (Rom. 8:9).

This position argues that the equating of Spirit baptism with conversion is found throughout Acts. True, the disciples had to wait for the baptism of the Holy Spirit for forty days, even though they already believed in Jesus. But this is only because the Holy Spirit had not yet been given (cf. John 7:38–39). Since Pentecost, this position maintains, the Holy Spirit comes immediately when a person believes. On the day of Pentecost, Peter promised his audience that all who would repent and be baptized would receive what they had just witnessed the disciples receive: They would "receive the gift of the Holy Spirit" (Acts 2:38). When Cornelius and his household heard the gospel for the first time, they believed and "the Holy Spirit fell upon all who heard the word" (Acts 10:44). Similarly, when the disciples of John the Baptist first heard Paul preach the gospel, "the Holy Spirit came upon them" (Acts 19:6). The fact that there is no interval in these episodes between believing and receiving the Holy Spirit, and the fact that the Holy Spirit falls on everyone at the same time (none were left out who were not yet "ready" for the full baptism) demonstrate that being baptized in the Spirit is not an experience subsequent to salvation.

The only time there is an apparent interval between people believing and receiving the Spirit occurs when Philip preaches to the Samaritans in Acts 8. Luke says that many Samaritans "believed Philip," including the sorcerer Simon (vv. 11–13). Yet they did not receive the Holy Spirit until John and Peter came from Jerusalem and prayed over them (v. 17).

According to adherents of the classic Protestant position, the Acts 8 episode should not be taken as normative for all believers. The interval took place because God wanted to demonstrate that the Samaritan mission had apostolic authority behind it. Hence, God wanted the Spirit to come as Peter and John laid their hands on the Samaritans (v. 17). Others argue that the interval took place because there was something defective about the Samaritans' faith. It is significant, they argue, that Luke says the Samaritans "believed Philip," not that they believed in Jesus (v. 12). It is also significant that Luke says the Samaritans believed Philip immediately, after noting that they previously were amazed at Simon's magic, to the point of calling him "the power of God that is called Great" (vv. 9–10). This suggests that the Samaritans simply transferred their carnal allegiance from Simon to Philip. Most importantly, it is significant that Luke says Simon himself also "believed" (v. 13), while also recording that Simon wanted to buy the apostles' power to dispense the Holy Spirit through the laying on of hands (vv. 18–19). Peter replied to him, "May your silver perish with you, because you thought you could obtain God's gift with money!" (v. 20). As in the case of the other Samaritans, Simon's belief was not a genuine faith in Christ but an external infatuation with power. In any event, the apparent interval between belief and Spirit baptism in this narrative should not be taken as normative for Christians, according to the classic Protestant position.

Other evangelicals disagree, however, and maintain that the New Testament distinguishes between receiving the Holy Spirit and being baptized in the Spirit. The baptism of the Spirit occurs at some point subsequent to salvation and is for the purpose of empowering believers for ministry. Hence, Jesus told his disciples that they would "receive power when the Holy Spirit" came upon them and that they would be his "witnesses in Jerusalem, in all Judea and Samaria, and to the ends of the earth" (Acts 1:8). The disciples already believed in Jesus and thus already had the Holy

Spirit present in their lives, for no one can authentically confess Jesus as Lord without the Holy Spirit (1 Cor. 12:3). But they were not yet empowered for ministry.

This position argues that the distinction is found throughout Acts as well as in some of Paul's epistles. For example, in his first sermon on the day of Pentecost, Peter commands his audience to "repent, and be baptized" and then "you will receive the gift of the Holy Spirit" (Acts 2:38). The gift is promised *after* repentance and obedience. In Acts 6, the apostles tell the Christians in Jerusalem to find "seven men of good standing, full of the Spirit and of wisdom," to help with some of the tasks of ministry (6:3). According to advocates of this position, this implies a distinction between those who are "full of the Spirit" and others who are not. The distinction is further shown in Paul's dialogue with the disciples of John the Baptist at Ephesus. Before he knew that these disciples had not received the full gospel, Paul asked them, "Did you receive the Holy Spirit when you became believers?" (Acts 19:2). The question does not make sense, defenders of this position argue, if all who believe automatically receive the full empowering of the Holy Spirit. Paul later wrote to the church at Ephesus, encouraging them not to "get drunk with wine . . . but be filled with the Spirit" (Eph. 5:18). How could Paul command this if all believers are automatically filled with the Spirit?

The distinctiveness of Spirit baptism is also clearly evidenced in Acts 8, according to advocates of this position. They argue that the attempts to explain away the interval between faith and Holy Spirit baptism in this passage are forced. More to the point, advocates of the view that Spirit baptism is subsequent to salvation ask, How could Philip or the apostles have considered the possibility that the Samaritans had not been filled with the Spirit if being filled with the Spirit is synonymous with conversion?

For all these reasons, advocates of the view that Holy Spirit baptism is subsequent to salvation encourage all believers to seek to be filled with or baptized with the Holy Spirit. Only when this occurs will they be fully empowered to carry out the work of the kingdom.

Further Reading

Del Colle, Ralph, et al. *Perspectives on Spirit Baptism: Five Views*. Nashville: Broadman and Holman, 2004.

Dunn, James D. G. *Baptism in the Holy Spirit: A Re-examination of the New Testament Teaching on the Gift of the Spirit in Relation to Pentecostalism Today*. Naperville, IL: Allenson, 1970.

Ervin, Howard M. *Conversion-Initiation and the Baptism in the Holy Spirit: A Critique of James D. G. Dunn,* Baptism in the Holy Spirit. Peabody, MA: Hendrickson, 1984.

Hoekema, Anthony A. *Tongues and Spirit-Baptism: A Biblical and Theological Evaluation.* Grand Rapids: Baker Academic, 1981.

Lederle, Henry I. *Treasures Old and New: Interpretations of "Spirit-Baptism" in the Charismatic Renewal Movement.* Peabody, MA: Hendrickson, 1988.

Menzies, Robert P., and William W. Menzies. *Spirit and Power.* Grand Rapids: Zondervan, 2000.

Pinnock, Clark H. *Flame of Love: A Theology of the Holy Spirit.* Downers Grove, IL: InterVarsity, 1996.

Issue 9: Is Speaking in Tongues the Initial Evidence of Receiving the Baptism of the Holy Spirit?

Some Christians (called cessationists) believe that all the charismatic gifts ceased when the New Testament was completed and disseminated to all Christian churches (namely, in the second and third centuries). Other Christians (called continuationists) believe that the charismatic gifts are still available today. There is much debate among continuationists regarding the role of speaking in tongues, however. Pentecostals have traditionally taught that speaking in tongues is evidence that a person is filled with the Holy Spirit. If a person has not spoken in tongues, he or she cannot claim to be filled with or baptized in the Spirit. This is usually labeled the initial evidence doctrine. Most non-Pentecostal continuationists deny this doctrine, stating that as with the other charismatic gifts, some people may be given the gift of speaking in tongues and others not. It is not a special indication that a person has been filled with or baptized in the Spirit.

Those who defend the classic Pentecostal position do so primarily on the basis of a pattern they discern in Acts. They note that when the disciples were first baptized in the Spirit on the day of Pentecost, "all of them . . . began to speak in other languages, as the Spirit gave them ability" (Acts 2:4). Similarly, when the Gentiles were initially filled with the Holy Spirit, Peter and the other Jewish Christians recognized it, "for they heard them speaking in tongues and extolling God" (Acts 10:46). And when the disciples of John the Baptist first received this blessing from God after Paul preached to them and prayed with them, they all "spoke in tongues and prophesied" (Acts 19:6).

The only other explicit account in Acts of an initial in-filling of the Spirit concerns Samaritan believers who were prayed over by Peter and John. Speaking in tongues is not mentioned, but something remarkable obviously happened, for "Simon saw that the Spirit was given through the laying on of the apostles' hands," and he foolishly "offered them money" to get this ability (Acts 8:18). What he saw could not have been joy or even miracles, for Simon had himself already witnessed this among the Samaritan believers (Acts 8:6, 13). Defenders of the initial evidence doctrine argue that it is reasonable to assume that what Simon saw was Pentecost repeated: The Samaritans must have spoken in tongues when they received the Holy Spirit by the laying on of the apostles' hands.

On the basis of these four accounts, defenders of the initial evidence doctrine say that believers should expect the same initial evidence as that witnessed by the earliest disciples. All should seek to be filled with the Holy Spirit (Eph. 5:18), and they will know they are filled when they speak in tongues.

Most evangelicals reject this line of argumentation on a number of grounds. First and foremost, detractors of the initial evidence doctrine argue that it is illegitimate hermeneutics to base a doctrine on historical narrative. As a historian, Luke reported what happened; he did not teach what should always happen. His narrative is descriptive, not prescriptive. If we took everything Luke recorded as a prescription for how the church is always supposed to believe and behave, we would have to insist that all congregations be communistic (Acts 2:44–45) and that prayer clothes be sent out to heal people (Acts 19:11–12).

Defenders of the initial evidence doctrine reply that in certain cases historical precedent can form the foundation for a doctrine. For example, Christian theology of communion is rooted more in the example given in the Gospels than in any explicit New Testament teaching.

Second, non-Pentecostal evangelicals believe that the Bible provides a good amount of explicit teaching about the evidence of being filled with the Spirit, and none of it centers on speaking in tongues. As people are filled with the Holy Spirit, they exhibit the fruit of the Spirit, especially love (Rom. 5:5; 1 Cor. 13; Gal. 5:22–23). Their lives are characterized by a zeal for the Lord, a boldness to proclaim truth, and holiness (Acts 1:8; Rom. 8:2–6; 2 Cor. 3:17–18; Gal. 5:16–18). If any charismatic phenomenon is to be associated with being filled with the Spirit, it is prophecy—to speak the word of the Lord with a powerful anointing—and revelatory visions, for Peter *taught* that these would follow the outpouring of the Spirit (Acts 2:17–18). It is worth noting that even based on the New Testament, it does not seem that speaking in tongues requires a unique spiritual maturity or presence. The Corinthians spoke in tongues a great deal, but Paul chastises them for being spiritual babies (1 Cor. 3:1–4).

Defenders of the initial evidence doctrine reply that things such as love, holiness, and boldness are indeed evidence of the Spirit's presence in a believer's life, but they are not to be confused with the distinct initial evidence of the baptism or in-filling of the Holy Spirit that Luke talks about in Acts.

Third, to those who deny the initial evidence doctrine, it seems clear from Paul's First Epistle to the Corinthians that he did not assume that all believers spoke in tongues at some point. Paul asks, "Are all apostles?

Are all prophets? Are all teachers? . . . Do all possess gifts of healing? Do all speak in tongues?" (1 Cor. 12:29–30). The answer, of course, is no. Yet Paul encourages all believers continually to seek to be "filled with the Spirit" (Eph. 5:18). This clearly demonstrates that Paul did not associate tongues with being filled with the Spirit.

Defenders of the initial evidence doctrine reply that Paul is talking about the use of charismatic gifts here, not the initial evidence of the baptism of the Holy Spirit. All who are filled with the Spirit will evidence this by speaking in tongues, though they may not have the gift of speaking in tongues after this time.

Finally, on a more practical note, those who oppose the initial evidence doctrine argue that it sets up a two-class Christianity between those who have spoken in tongues and those who have not. The New Testament knows of no such classification. Those in Pentecostal circles who have not spoken in tongues are encouraged to seek this initial evidence. Yet the New Testament contains no accounts of believers seeking the experience of speaking in tongues. Even in the episodes in Acts that Pentecostals cite in support of their position, the act of speaking in tongues just happens. No one is looking for it.

Defenders of the initial evidence doctrine reply that the New Testament recognizes that not all believers are filled with the Holy Spirit. For example, the apostles told the Jerusalem Christians to find "seven men of good standing, full of the Spirit and of wisdom" (Acts 6:3). This clearly implies that not everyone was full of the Spirit. So, too, the fact that the apostles recognized that the Holy Spirit "had not yet come upon any of [the Samaritan believers]"—which is why they went down to pray with them (Acts 8:16–17)—presupposes that not all believers are baptized with the Spirit and that others can recognize this. This distinction results in a two-class Christianity only when Christians violate the biblical prohibition of judging one another (Matt. 7:1; Rom. 14:4).

Further Reading

Cartledge, Mark J. *Speaking in Tongues*. Tyrone, GA: Paternoster, 2006.

Del Colle, Ralph, et al. *Perspectives on Spirit Baptism: Five Views*. Nashville: Broadman and Holman, 2004.

Dunn, James D. G. *Baptism in the Holy Spirit: A Re-examination of the New Testament Teaching on the Gift of the Spirit in Relation to Pentecostalism Today*. Naperville, IL: Allenson, 1970.

Ervin, Howard M. *Conversion-Initiation and the Baptism in the Holy Spirit: A Critique of James D. G. Dunn*, Baptism in the Holy Spirit. Peabody, MA: Hendrickson, 1984.

Hoekema, Anthony A. *Tongues and Spirit-Baptism: A Biblical and Theological Evaluation*. Grand Rapids: Baker Academic, 1981.

Lederle, Henry I. *Treasures Old and New: Interpretations of "Spirit-Baptism" in the Charismatic Renewal Movement*. Peabody, MA: Hendrickson, 1988.

Menzies, Robert P., and William W. Menzies. *Spirit and Power*. Grand Rapids: Zondervan, 2000.

Pinnock, Clark H. *Flame of Love: A Theology of the Holy Spirit*. Downers Grove, IL: InterVarsity, 1996.

Issue 10: Can a Christian Be Demonized?

Because the Bible teaches that spirits exist—both good and evil, angelic and demonic—evangelical Christians across the board acknowledge the reality of Satan and demons (e.g., Matt. 4:1–11; Mark 5:1–20; Luke 11:14–26; Eph. 6:10–18). However, a number of issues connected to the demonic—including the nature of spiritual warfare, methods of deliverance, the question of territorial spirits and spiritual mapping, and the degree to which demons can influence Christians—have caused vigorous debate within evangelicalism. All parties agree that every human being, even the most mature Christian, is subject to temptations from the enemy—just as Jesus was (Matt. 4:1–11). As a result, Jesus taught his followers to pray, "Lead us not into temptation, but deliver us from the evil one" (Matt. 6:13 NIV). But when it comes to the question of the degree to which the demonic can influence a Christian, there is significant disagreement.

On the one hand, some believe that while it is possible for non-Christians to be demon possessed, Christians never have to fear this condition. Biblical support for this view comes from those passages that proclaim the defeat of Satan and the victory of Christians through Jesus Christ (e.g., John 12:31; Col. 2:13–15; 2 Thess. 3:3; Heb. 2:14–15; 1 John 5:18). Colossians 1:13 assures believers that God "has rescued us from the power of darkness and transferred us into the kingdom of his beloved Son." If we are delivered from Satan's kingdom, we certainly cannot be possessed by the evil spirits of that kingdom. In 1 Corinthians 10:21, the apostle Paul emphasizes that a person is either in one kingdom or the other: "You cannot drink the cup of the Lord and the cup of demons. You cannot partake of the table of the Lord and the table of demons."

Finally, 1 John 4:4 tells us that "the one who is in you is greater than the one who is in the world." Christians have been redeemed from the power of the evil one and are now "possessed" by the Holy Spirit of God. How could they be owned by God and yet at the same time be "possessed" by a demon? Evil cannot dwell in the presence of God. Since we know that a Christian is one in whom the presence of God dwells by the Holy Spirit, we can be assured that no demon would be able to inhabit the body of a believer at the same time. Each believer's body is a temple of God, and God does not share his temple with demons (1 Cor. 6:19–20). Thus, while acknowledging that believers can be tempted, harassed, and even oppressed at times by demons, this view states that no true Christian can be indwelt by a demon such that he or she would need spiritual deliverance (exorcism).

On the other hand, some evangelicals claim that Christians can have a demonic presence in their lives to such a degree that deliverance ministry is required. This view typically clarifies its position by pointing out that the Greek word usually translated "demon possessed" in the New Testament (*daimonizomai*) is actually best translated "demonized"—which simply means to be under the influence of a demon. Thus, there is no connotation of possession or ownership. Demonized Christians are saved and redeemed members of Christ's body. However, either through evil done to them or through their own choices, a doorway has been opened to the demonic.

For scriptural support, adherents of this view point to passages that indicate the possibility of demonic influence and attack in the lives of individual Christians and the church in general (e.g., 2 Cor. 2:11; Eph. 4:26–27; 6:10–12; 1 Thess. 2:18; 1 Tim. 4:1; 2 Tim. 2:26; 1 Pet. 5:6–8). Specific biblical examples of the demonization of believers include King Saul (1 Sam. 16:14–23), Ananias and Sapphira (Acts 5:1–3), the Corinthian believer involved in an incestuous relationship (1 Cor. 5:1–13), and Judas Iscariot (John 13:27). Perhaps the strongest case is that of the woman in Luke 13:11–16. This woman had been ill for eighteen years with an ailment caused by a demon. Jesus prayed for her, and she was healed. In verse 16, Jesus explains the situation: "And ought not this woman, a daughter of Abraham whom Satan bound for eighteen long years, be set free from this bondage?" By referring to her as a "daughter of Abraham," Jesus indicates her authentic faith—she is a true believer. And yet she was afflicted with a demon until Jesus prayed for her healing and deliverance. Those who hold to this view point out that many of the great saints in church history, including Martin Luther, John Wesley, Jesse Penn-Lewis, V. Raymond Edman, and Chuck Swindoll, acknowledged that Christians could be demonized and in need of deliverance prayer.

Further Reading

Arnold, Clinton E. *3 Crucial Questions about Spiritual Warfare*. Grand Rapids: Baker Academic, 1997.

Basham, Don. *Can a Christian Have a Demon?* Monroeville, PA: Whitaker, 1971.

Dickason, C. Fred. *Demon Possession and the Christian: A New Perspective*. Chicago: Moody, 1987.

Miller, Paul M. *The Devil Did Not Make Me Do It*. Scottdale, PA: Herald, 1977.

Powlison, David. *Power Encounters: Reclaiming Spiritual Warfare*. Grand Rapids: Baker Academic, 1995.

Unger, Merrill F. *Biblical Demonology: A Study of the Spiritual Forces behind the Present World Unrest*. Wheaton: Scripture, 1952.

————. *What Demons Can Do to Saints*. Chicago: Moody, 1977.

Issue 11: The Debate over the Book of Revelation

Few biblical topics have captured the imagination of contemporary evangelicals like the book of Revelation. The recent unprecedented success of the Left Behind series is evidence of this popular fascination. Many evangelicals do not realize that the futuristic interpretation of Revelation advocated in this popular novel series is only one of several interpretations evangelicals espouse. This section looks at the three major evangelical options as well as some alternative perspectives.

The Preterist View

The term *preterist* comes from the Latin word *praeteritus,* which means "gone by." The preterist interpretation of Revelation holds that the events spoken of in this book were all specifically fulfilled in the first century. This view has precedent in the early church, but it did not become widespread until the nineteenth century. With the advent of the historical-critical method of biblical interpretation, it became the dominant interpretation among New Testament scholars, though it has been less popular among evangelical scholars.

According to preterism, Revelation is a heavily symbolic, apocalyptic, and prophetic book that was written primarily to warn readers of impending persecution, to encourage them to persevere in the face of suffering, and to reassure them that God is in control and will overcome evil in the end. Preterists argue that most of the symbolic events in this book can be correlated with first-century figures and events. For example, "the beast" refers to Nero, whose "number" is 666 (the numerical value of "Nero Caesar" in Hebrew [*NRWN QSR*]). Similarly, the forty-two months of his horrifying reign (Rev. 13:5) happen to be the exact duration of the Roman siege on Jerusalem beginning in AD 66.

In defense of their position, preterists contend that we must not abandon sound hermenuetical principles when we consider Revelation. As with every book in the Bible, we must attempt to read Revelation from the perspective of the first-century Christians to whom it was originally written. Revelation was written to "the seven churches that are in Asia" (Rev. 1:4) about matters that "must soon take place" (Rev. 1:1) because "the time is near" (Rev. 1:3, cf. 22:6, 10). Throughout the book, there is an urgency for the readers to respond quickly (e.g., Rev. 2:16; 3:10–11; 22:6, 7, 12, 20). According to preterists, these statements require that we look for fulfillments in the lifetime of the original audience. The spiritual themes of Revelation are timeless, but the specific events of which this book speaks were all fulfilled in the first century.

The Idealist View

Many Christians throughout history held to the idealist (sometimes called the spiritualist) interpretation of the book of Revelation, and many evangelicals today continue to support this view. What is most distinctive about the idealist interpretation is that it denies that the events and figures recorded in this book have a direct correlation either with events and figures in the past (as the preterist believes) or the future (as the futurist believes). To search for such specific fulfillments, they argue, is to fundamentally misunderstand the apocalyptic genre of this book. Revelation should be read as a heavily symbolic dramatization of the ongoing battle between God and evil.

According to the idealist view, Revelation is a spiritual paradigmatic work that summons Christians to faithful living in the face of persecution and reassures believers that, however dire their circumstances, God will win in the end and their perseverance will be rewarded. Hence, the multitude of symbols employed in this book, most of which are drawn directly from the Old Testament, are in various ways "fulfilled" whenever Christians find themselves in spiritual conflict.

Idealists defend their interpretation on a number of fronts. Most emphasize that the nature of the apocalyptic genre does not require and may actually rule out locating specific correlations with the symbols it employs. They frequently point out that attempts to find such fulfillments in the past, and even more so in the future, are guesses at best. They often argue that absurdity results from attempts to interpret Revelation literally (e.g., Rev. 6:13; 8:12; 12:4). Perhaps most importantly, they emphasize that the spiritual application of this book's message does not hinge on and may even be compromised by trying to locate specific fulfillments for the dramatizations it presents.

The Futurist View

By far, the view that is most popular among the evangelical masses today is the futurist view (sometimes called the dispensational view). According to this view, almost all of Revelation (chaps. 4–22) records events that will take place at the end of time. While many early church fathers believed segments of Revelation concerned the end of history, the understanding that the bulk of this book concerns the end of history is almost without precedent until the nineteenth century.

A key verse for the futurist interpretation is Revelation 1:19, in which the Lord tells John, "Now write what you have seen, what is, and what is to take place after this." According to most futurists, "what you have seen" refers to the vision recorded in chapter 1. "What is" refers to the seven letters written to the seven churches in Asia Minor in his day, recorded in chapters 2 and 3. "What is to take place after this" refers to all the end-times events recorded throughout the rest of the book (chaps. 4–22). While there is disagreement about this matter, the fact that the church is not mentioned in these chapters leads many futurists to conclude that these events will occur after the rapture, when the church is literally taken out of the world (1 Thess. 4:16–17).

Futurists usually grant that there are apocalyptic elements in Revelation that cannot be interpreted literally, but they insist that Revelation is first and foremost a prophecy (Rev. 1:3). The things that will take place are literal events that have yet to be fulfilled. Indeed, futurists argue that many of the events prophetically recorded in this book are such that they could not have taken place before modern times (e.g., the reference to an army numbering two hundred million in Rev. 9:16).

Alternative Interpretations

These three options do not exhaust the possible interpretations of Revelation. In the late Middle Ages, for example, a number of leaders entertained what is sometimes called a historicist interpretation of Revelation. According to this view, Revelation records the gradual unfolding of God's plan for history up to the present. The majority of Protestant Reformers held to a version of this view. They viewed Revelation as a prophetic survey of church history and used this interpretation to argue that the pope of their day was the Antichrist. While one finds occasional popular commentaries yet espousing some version of this approach, it has fallen far out of favor with evangelicals.

Some contemporary scholars combine preterist and idealist interpretations. The symbolic dramatizations of Revelation may have first-century correlations, but they are written with paradigmatic significance. For example, Nero may in fact have been the specific Antichrist referred to in Revelation 13:8, but the reference to him is cosmic in significance, covering all Antichrist movements that resist God's purposes in the world. Other scholars have sought to combine elements of all three views. They say that the dramatic events of Revelation have been fulfilled, are continuing to be fulfilled, and will at the end of time be climactically fulfilled as the Lord concludes history and ushers in his reign as king.

Further Reading

Caringola, Robert. *The Present Reign of Christ: A Historical Interpretation of the Book of Revelation*. Springfield, MO: Abundant Life Ministries Reformed Press, 1995. (historicist)

Chilton, David. *The Days of Vengeance: An Exposition of the Book of Revelation*. Fort Worth: Dominion, 1987. (preterist)

Gentry, Kenneth. *Before Jerusalem Fell: The Dating of the Book of Revelation*. Tyler, TX: Institute for Christian Economics, 1989. (preterist)

Gregg, Steven, ed. *Revelation: Four Views. A Parallel Commentary*. Nashville: Nelson, 1997.

Ladd, George Eldon. *A Commentary on the Revelation of John*. Grand Rapids: Eerdmans, 1972. (futurist)

Miller, Fred P. *Revelation: A Panorama of the Gospel Age*. Clermont, FL: Moellerhaus, 1991. (historicist)

Morris, Leon. *The Revelation of St. John*. Grand Rapids: Eerdmans, 1969. (spiritualist)

Mounce, Robert H. *The Book of Revelation*. New International Commentary on the New Testament. Grand Rapids: Eerdmans, 1977. (futurist)

Pate, C. Marvin, ed. *Four Views on the Book of Revelation*. Grand Rapids: Zondervan, 1998.

Wilcock, Michael. *I Saw Heaven Opened: The Message of Revelation*. Downers Grove, IL: InterVarsity, 1975. (spiritualist)

Issue 12: Has Jesus Already Returned? The Preterist Debate

Almost all Christians throughout history have believed that the Lord is coming back some time in the future to finish the work of building his kingdom. They have disagreed about the details of this return but not about the fact of the return. Recently, however, a small group of evangelicals has argued that all the teachings and prophecies about the Lord's return were fulfilled in the first century. They are usually labeled preterists. However, they do not merely hold to a preterist interpretation of the book of Revelation, a view shared by a number of evangelicals. (See issue 11: "The Debate over the Book of Revelation.") These Christians believe that *everything* the New Testament has to say about the end-times—including Jesus' return, the resurrection of the dead, and God's ultimate victory over Satan—was fulfilled in the first century.

Three fundamental convictions drive the preterist perspective. First, preterists are impressed by the repeated statements in the New Testament that "the end is near" (e.g., 1 Pet. 4:7). First-century disciples seemed to believe that Jesus would return and that all the end-times predictions they had been given would come to pass in their lifetime. Indeed, Jesus explicitly taught that "this generation will not pass away until all these things have taken place" (Matt. 24:34)—referring, it seems, to all the apocalyptic events he spoke of in his Olivet discourse (Matt. 24:1–33). If it is impossible either for Jesus or his inspired disciples to err, preterists argue, then we must look to the fulfillment of the end-times in the lifetime of the disciples.

Second, preterists argue that the apocalyptic imagery used throughout the Bible to describe the end-times is figurative. None of it should be taken literally. For example, language about cosmic disturbances (e.g., earthquakes, sun darkening, etc.) and about the Son coming in "the clouds of glory" must be interpreted as typical biblical symbolic depictions of judgment (e.g., Matt. 24:29–31; cf. Isa. 13:6–13; 34:2–15; Ezek. 32:1–10; Mic. 1:3–5). The nonliteral nature of these apocalyptic images is clearly seen in the simple fact that Peter understood them to be fulfilled on the day of Pentecost, when God poured out his Spirit "upon all flesh" (Acts 2:17–21)!

Third, preterists believe that all end-times predictions were ultimately fulfilled in the destruction of Jerusalem in AD 70. It was at this point that Israel ceased to be a distinct nation and that Old Testament Judaism came to an end. In their view, the Lord returned at this time, judged Israel, defeated Satan, and established his permanent presence in the world through the church. Therefore, according to preterists, there is no future return of the Lord to look forward to. There are no future battles for him to fight. He has already returned and has already won.

The majority of evangelicals reject the preterist interpretation of the New Testament for a variety of reasons. First, they argue that the New Testament teaches that Jesus will return in a visible, indeed bodily form. For example, after Jesus' bodily ascension, two angels announced to the disciples, "This Jesus, who has been taken up from you into heaven, will come *in the same way as you saw him go into heaven*" (Acts 1:11, emphasis added). It is difficult to reconcile this teaching with the preterist view that Jesus returned in AD 70.

Second, preterists make too much out of the disciples' belief that Jesus would return in their lifetime. The disciples' zeal, which flowed from their expectation that the Lord could return at any moment, was godly and should be imitated by all believers. This, most evangelicals argue, is the point of these passages. But we do not need to conclude that the disciples were wrong because Jesus has not yet returned. Some in the early church apparently were drawing this very conclusion, for Peter corrected them by reminding them that "with the Lord one day is like a thousand years, and a thousand years are like one day" (2 Pet. 3:8). We must live as though today were our last day, all the while knowing that the Lord might not bring history to a close for another thousand years (or more).

Third, most evangelicals believe that preterists stretch apocalyptic imagery too far. While most scholars agree that the imagery of cosmic cataclysms is symbolic, this cannot be applied to, say, New Testament talk about people rising from the dead (e.g., John 5:28–29; Rom. 6:5; 8:11; 1 Cor. 15:35–52; 1 Thess. 4:13–18). When the New Testament speaks of a future resurrection of the dead, it clearly means what most Jews of the time took it to mean: namely, a literal, bodily resurrection. The preterists' attempt to spiritualize the resurrection is often regarded as one of the weakest points of their theological system.

   Finally, the majority of evangelical scholars argue that preterists make too much of the destruction of Jerusalem in AD 70 and too little of the ongoing battle with evil that has characterized the world since that time. True, the destruction of Jerusalem and especially the desecration and obliteration of the temple were earth-shattering events. Everything about Judaism changed at that time. Much of the apocalyptic imagery Jesus uses in his Olivet discourse, and perhaps (some would argue) much of the book of Revelation, is about this monumentally important event. But it requires an enormous stretch of the imagination to suppose that the kingdom of God was established at that time. Though we may concede that there are symbolic elements in the New Testament vision of a "new heaven and a new earth" (Rev. 21:1), the fact that evil still reigns with intensity throughout the world suggests that Satan is still "the god of this world" and "the ruler of the power of the air" (2 Cor. 4:4; Eph. 2:2). The kingdom of God has in principle been established on the earth through the church. Satan was in principle defeated at Calvary. But this victory is clearly not yet perfectly manifested. Hence, the vast majority of evangelicals yet look forward to the time when Christ will unambiguously reign victorious over all his foes.

Further Reading

Caringola, Robert. *The Present Reign of Christ: A Historical Interpretation of the Book of Revelation*. Springfield, MO: Abundant Life Ministries Reformed Press, 1995. (historicist)

Chilton, David. *The Days of Vengeance: An Exposition of the Book of Revelation*. Fort Worth: Dominion, 1987. (preterist)

Gentry, Kenneth. *Before Jerusalem Fell: The Dating of the Book of Revelation*. Tyler, TX: Institute for Christian Economics, 1989. (preterist)

Gregg, Steven, ed. *Revelation: Four Views. A Parallel Commentary*. Nashville: Nelson, 1997.

Ladd, George Eldon. *A Commentary on the Revelation of John*. Grand Rapids: Eerdmans, 1972. (futurist)

Miller, Fred P. *Revelation: A Panorama of the Gospel Age*. Clermont, FL: Moellerhaus, 1991. (historicist)

Morris, Leon. *The Revelation of St. John*. Grand Rapids: Eerdmans, 1969. (spiritualist)

Mounce, Robert H. *The Book of Revelation*. New International Commentary on the New Testament. Grand Rapids: Eerdmans, 1977. (futurist)

Noe, John R. *Beyond the End Times: The Rest of the Greatest Story Ever Told*. Bradford, PA: Preterist Resources, 1999. (preterist)

Pate, C. Marvin, ed. *Four Views on the Book of Revelation*. Grand Rapids: Zondervan, 1998.

Wilcock, Michael. *I Saw Heaven Opened: The Message of Revelation*. Downers Grove, IL: InterVarsity, 1975. (spiritualist)

Issue 13: When Will Jesus Return? The Rapture Debate

When it comes to the issue of the end-times, most evangelical believers wholeheartedly agree on at least one thing: Jesus Christ is going to return one day! Jesus himself promised his return (Matt. 24:30; 26:64; John 14:3). At Jesus' ascension, two angels proclaimed, "Men of Galilee, why do you stand looking up toward heaven? This Jesus, who has been taken up from you into heaven, will come in the same way as you saw him go into heaven" (Acts 1:11). This hope is consistently witnessed to throughout the New Testament (e.g., Acts 3:19–21; Phil. 3:20–21; 1 Thess. 4:15–16; Titus 2:13).

It is when we turn to the question of when in the course of end-times events Jesus will return that we find an array of differing perspectives. One central debate, especially among premillennialists, is whether Christ will return before or after the tribulation period. Many believe this future period was prophesied by Jesus when he said: "For at that time there will be great suffering, such as has not been from the beginning of the world until now, no, and never will be. And if those days had not been cut short, no one would be saved; but for the sake of the elect those days will be cut short" (Matt. 24:21–22).

The two major views held by premillennialists are pre-tribulationism and post-tribulationism. Pre-tribulationists have several core convictions. First, they have a two-stage understanding of Christ's return. They believe that Christ will return to remove (or "rapture") his church out of the world before the tribulation. He will then return with his saints to judge the world after the tribulation. In the first stage, Christ will not be seen by the world, though the world will of course notice the miraculous and instantaneous disappearance of every Christian. In the second stage, everyone will behold the Lord returning in glory. Pre-tribulationists find support for their belief in a literal rapture, prior to the tribulation period, in the words of Paul: "For the Lord himself, with a cry of command, with the archangel's call and with the sound of God's trumpet, will descend from heaven, and the dead in Christ will rise first. Then we who are alive, who are left, will be caught up in the clouds together with them to meet the Lord in the air; and so we will be with the Lord forever" (1 Thess. 4:16–17).

Pre-tribulationists emphasize the difference between passages they believe refer to the rapture (e.g., Matt. 24:40) and those that all agree refer to the *final* coming of Christ (Rev. 19). The rapture passages speak of a secret, instantaneous snatching-away of believers—one shall be "taken" and one "left behind"—while other passages speak of an event that everyone will see.

Second, pre-tribulationists point to passages in the Bible that they believe teach that believers will be kept from having to endure the wrath of God.

For example, Paul states that Jesus will "[rescue] us from the wrath that is coming" (1 Thess. 1:10; see also 5:9; Rev. 3:10). Since the tribulation period is a time when God's wrath will be poured out in judgment on the wicked, they believe the rapture must take place before this time.

Finally, pre-tribulationists highlight the fact that many texts clearly state that Christ's return could happen at any moment and that Christians are not to be caught off guard (e.g., Matt. 24:42–51; 25:1–30; 1 Cor. 1:7; Phil. 4:5; Titus 2:13). But if Christ will not return until after the tribulation period, as post-tribulationists maintain, how could his return be imminent or surprising? If the post-tribulationists are correct, we should not expect Christ to return until after the rather obvious events of Christ's prophecy are fulfilled.

Post-tribulationists, on the other hand, deny that there are two stages to Christ's return. He will return once, after a final tribulation period, at which time he will set up his millennial kingdom. Post-tribulationists support their view with several lines of argument.

First, many passages of Scripture tell believers to expect persecution (e.g., Acts 14:22; Rom. 5:3; 1 Thess. 3:3). Jesus told his disciples, "In the world you face persecution. But take courage; I have conquered the world!" (John 16:33). What is more, post-tribulationists emphasize the fact that Jesus explicitly prayed that his Father would *not* take his church out of the world. He asked that he protect them from the enemy in the midst of a hostile world (John 17:15). Indeed, according to post-tribulationists, Jesus explicitly taught that the church would endure the tribulation period, for he said, "at that time there will be great suffering. . . . And if those days had not been cut short, no one would be saved; but *for the sake of the elect* those days will be cut short" (Matt. 24:21–22, emphasis added). The elect are clearly present during the tribulation period.

Second, post-tribulationists argue that the passages cited in support of a pre-tribulation rapture do not teach what the pre-tribulationists suggest. For example, Paul's teaching that the church will meet "the Lord in the air" (1 Thess. 4:17) does not mean that Christians will literally ascend into the clouds. The passage rather refers to the common ancient practice of people going outside the gates of their city to welcome home a victorious general with triumphant jubilation. The imagery of the Lord coming in clouds was frequently used to speak of the Lord coming in glory and power (e.g., Ps. 68:4; Jer. 4:13; Dan. 7:13). What is more, if the passage is taken literally, it can hardly refer to an unnoticed coming. Paul says the Lord will descend with "a cry of command, with the archangel's call and with the sound of God's trumpet" (1 Thess. 4:16). The images suggest that the return will be loud—like the call of a general returning home.

Finally, passages that speak of one being taken while another is left behind (e.g., Matt. 24:40) do not refer to a secret rapture. If read in context, post-tributionists argue, the one taken is likened to those who were judged in Noah's flood, not to one who is rescued from judgment (Matt. 24:38–39). Jesus is speaking about how suddenly people will disappear under persecution during the tribulation period, not how they will be raptured away from persecution before the tribulation. Hence, post-tribulationists argue that Christ will return only once, and he will come after the world has gone through a final tribulation period.

Further Reading

Blomberg, Craig L., and Sung Wook Chung, eds. *A Case for Historic Premillennialism: An Alternative to "Left Behind" Eschatology*. Grand Rapids: Baker Academic, 2009.

Brower, Kent E., and Mark W. Elliott, eds. *Eschatology in Bible and Theology: Evangelical Essays at the Dawn of a New Millennium*. Downers Grove, IL: InterVarsity, 1997.

Erickson, Millard J. *A Basic Guide to Eschatology: Making Sense of the Millennium*. Grand Rapids: Baker Academic, 1998.

Ladd, George E. *The Last Things*. Grand Rapids: Eerdmans, 1978.

Lewis, Daniel J. *Three Crucial Questions about the Last Days*. Grand Rapids: Baker Academic, 1998.

MacPherson, Dave. *The Great Rapture Hoax*. Fletcher, NC: New Puritan Library, 1983.

Reiter, Richard R., Paul D. Feinberg, Gleason L. Archer, and Douglas J. Moo. *The Rapture: Pre-, Mid-, or Post-Tribulational?* Grand Rapids: Zondervan, 1984.

Walvrood, John F. *The Blessed Hope and the Tribulation*. Grand Rapids: Zondervan, 1976.

Notes

Chapter 1

1. Augustine, *Epistle* 82.1, in *Letters of Augustine*, trans. Wilfrid Parsons, 5 vols. (Washington, DC: Catholic University of America Press, 1951), 1:285.

2. Martin Luther, *Works*, ed. Jaroslav Pelikan and Helmut T. Lehmann, 55 vols. (St. Louis: Concordia, 1955–73), 14:1073.

3. John Calvin, *Institutes of the Christian Religion*, ed. John T. McNeill, trans. Ford L. Battles, Library of Christian Classics, 2 vols. (Philadelphia: Westminster, 1960), 1:149.

4. Speech act theory, associated with J. L. Austin and John Searle, flows from the "ordinary language" wing of analytic philosophy. Evangelical theologians like Kevin Vanhoozer and Nancey Murphy, and Christian philosophers like William Alston and Richard Swinburne, have used speech act theory to understand religious language.

Chapter 2

1. Augustine, *Enchiridion*, ed. J. Baille, J. McNeill, and H. P. Van Duren, trans. A. C. Outler, Library of Christian Classics 7 (Philadelphia: Westminster, 1955), 389. See also 395, 400.

2. C. S. Lewis, *The Problem of Pain* (New York: Macmillan, 1962), 127.

Chapter 6

1. See T. V. Morris, *The Logic of God Incarnate* (Ithaca, NY: Cornell University Press, 1986).

2. Ibid., 106.

Chapter 8

1. Calvin, *Institutes*, 2:921.

Chapter 9

1. Sinclair B. Ferguson, "The Reformed Perspective," in *Christian Spirituality*, ed. Don Alexander (Downers Grove, IL: InterVarsity, 1988), 49.

2. John Murray, *Collected Writings*, 2 vols. (Carlisle, PA: Banner of Truth Trust, 1976), 1:82.

3. Ibid.

4. Calvin, *Institutes*, 1:527–28.

5. Heidelberg Catechism, Q86.

. 6. J. Robert McQuilkin, "The Keswick Perspective," in Melvin E. Dieter et al., *Five Views on Sanctification* (Grand Rapids: Zondervan, 1987), 153–54.

7. J. I. Packer, *Keeping Step with the Spirit* (Downers Grove, IL: InterVarsity, 1984), 157.

8. Charles W. Carter, ed., *A Contemporary Wesleyan Theology* (Grand Rapids: Francis Asbury, 1983), 529.

9. Laurence W. Wood, "The Wesleyan Perspective," in Alexander, *Christian Spirituality*, 99.

10. John Wesley, *The Works of John Wesley*, ed. Thomas Jackson, 14 vols. (1831; reprint, Kansas City, MO: Beacon Hill, 1978), 11:84.

11. John Wesley, *Standard Sermons*, ed. E. H. Sugden, 2 vols. (London: Epworth, 1951), 1:267–68. See Wood, "Wesleyan Perspective," 109.

Chapter 17

1. Lewis, *Problem of Pain*, 122–23, 128.

2. Ibid., 127. See also his *Great Divorce* (New York: Collier, 1984).

Appendix

1. Carl F. H. Henry, *God, Revelation, and Authority*, 6 vols. (Waco: Word, 1976), 1:215.

2. Ibid., 3:457.

3. Stanley Grenz, *Revisioning Evangelical Theology: A Fresh Agenda for the Twenty-first Century* (Downers Grove, IL: InterVarsity, 1993), 83.

Glossary

amillennialism. In contrast to the literal understanding of the millennium as a future thousand-year epoch, this view of the end-times understands the millennium to be a symbolic reference to the present reign of Christ through the church. It has been argued that this position is the one most commonly held throughout church history.

anachronistic. Out of proper chronological order. For example, if someone reports that a computer crash caused the great depression in 1929, they are speaking anachronistically, for computers were not yet invented in 1929.

anthropomorphism. To ascribe human characteristics to God, as when biblical authors refer to "the right hand of God" or "the arms of God." Such phrases are not to be taken literally. One major issue within evangelicalism is whether biblical passages that talk about God "changing his mind" or "regretting" decisions should be interpreted anthropomorphically or taken as literal descriptions of God's activity and emotions.

antithesis. The direct opposite, contrast, or contradiction.

apocalyptic. Revelatory writings dealing with the end-times largely by way of visions, rich metaphors, and symbolism. This literary genre was popular in the two centuries preceding and following the life of Christ. The book of Revelation is the clearest example in the Bible of an apocalyptic book.

apollinarianism. This view sees the humanity of Christ as a mere shell for the divine person of God. This view was pronounced heretical at the Council of Chalcedon (AD 451) because it denies the full humanity of Christ.

apostasy. Abandonment of the faith.

a priori. Deductive reasoning from an assumed premise to a necessary conclusion.

Arianism. This view holds that Christ was God's first and greatest creation, but he was not God. Arianism rivaled trinitarianism in the early church but was finally pronounced heretical, beginning at the Council of Nicea (AD 325).

autographs. The original handwritten documents.

Bhagavad Gita. A central sacred text of Hinduism that contains philosophical dialogue between the god Krishna and the warrior Arjuna. Matters pertaining to Hindu ethics, philosophy, and personal devotion are discussed.

bibliolatry. Literally, making the Bible an idol. Many argue that bibliolatry takes place whenever faith in the Bible is placed over faith in Christ.

big bang theory. The dominant scientific theory for explaining the origin of the universe whereby it is understood that all the mass of the universe exploded forth from a single point roughly fifteen to sixteen billion years ago.

Book of Mormon. A central sacred text of the members of the Church of Jesus Christ of Latter-Day Saints. The claim is that the Bible was a record of God's dealings with people in one region of the world, while the Book of Mormon is a record of God's dealings with the people of the Americas. Joseph Smith is said to have received a visit from the angel Moroni, who led Smith to an ancient record preserved on gold plates buried in a hill near Smith's home. The plates were then said to be supernaturally translated (from "reformed Egyptian") into English by Smith and published in 1830.

cessationists. Those who believe that the charismatic gifts were intended to cease after the completion of the New Testament.

charismatic gifts. The distinct class of spiritual gifts identified in 1 Corinthians 12:8–10 that includes word of wisdom, word of knowledge, faith, healing, miracle-working, prophecy, discernment of spirits, tongues, and interpretation of tongues. *See also* **Pentecostalism.**

charismatic movement. Designated "second wave," following the "first wave" (**Pentecostalism**), the charismatic movement consists of people who emphasize the charismatic gifts of the Spirit but who remain in their own denominations (unlike Pentecostals). The movement began in the 1960s and now finds adherents in most established denominations that do not hold to a cessationist theology.

cheap grace. Whereas the biblical concept of grace requires a person to die to himself in order to be alive in Christ, cheap grace denotes the sort of forgiveness that does not involve the believer in a relationship with God that transforms the individual. Grace is thus understood as little more than a license to do whatever one wants. *See also* **judgment seat.**

chiliasm. A belief in the millennium of Christian prophecy, or a belief in a coming ideal society, especially one created by revolutionary action. *See also* **premillennialism.**

Christus Victor view of the atonement. According to this view of the atonement, Christ's act on the cross delivered the death blow to sin, death, and especially the devil. The Latin "Christus Victor" means "Christ is victorious." This view was widely held by the early church fathers. The main text for this view is Colossians 2:14–15, though the theme is pervasive throughout the New Testament.

communion elements. The bread and wine (or juice) used in a communion service.

compatibilism. The belief that freedom of the human will is compatible with the all-determining power of God.

complementarian view. The view that women are complementary "helpers" of men (Gen. 2:18). Men and women are indeed created equal, but their functions as prescribed by God differ. Most significantly, leadership roles in the church and the family are reserved for males.

conditional security. The Arminian view that salvation is conditioned on the ongoing willingness of the believer to remain in relationship with God. Salvation, in other words, is not an unconditional gift and is thus not eternally secure.

consubstantiation. The view of the Lord's Supper associated with Martin Luther and Lutheranism. It emphasizes the real (physical) presence of Christ "in, with, and under" the elements of bread and wine.

continuationists. People who believe that the charismatic gifts mentioned in 1 Corinthians 12:8–10 are as much for the church today as they were for the early church.

covenant. An oath or promise binding two or more parties to agreed upon terms, often with certain conditions involved. Some covenants that God entered into with humanity were binding only upon God (i.e., the promise not to destroy the world again by flood). Other covenants that God entered into with humanity required the fidelity of humans (i.e., the covenant with Israel).

day-age view. This reading of Genesis 1 states that the word *day* in this passage need not be interpreted as one literal twenty-four-hour period. Rather, the Hebrew word for day in this case (*yom*) refers to extended ages, which better correlates with what we know to be the case from modern science.

Deism. The view that God set the universe in motion and does not interfere with it. A common illustration used to explain this view is that of the watchmaker and the watch. God is the watchmaker who sets the gears, arms, and so on in place, winds up the watch, and allows things to take their natural course from that point forward.

dichotomist view of the self. A view of the self that states that the human person is composed of two fundamental substances: body and soul.

dispensational premillennialism. A form of premillennialism created by John Nelson Darby in the 1830s. This way of organizing history recognizes a number of distinct "economies," or ways in which God relates to humanity and tests humans according to different criteria for each period. Dispensationalists view this doctrine as a return to a biblical theology after nearly eighteen hundred years of darkness and error.

docetism. A heresy that denies the full humanity of Christ. Docetists asserted that Jesus Christ was purely divine and merely appeared human.

dominion. Responsibility and authority to govern, cultivate, and provide leadership for.

dualist view of the self. *See* **dichotomist view of the self.**

ecclesiastical. Having to do with the church.

ecumenical. Belonging to the one universal church. An ecumenical creed is one that has been affirmed by the historic orthodox church and/or is now affirmed by all branches of Christianity.

egalitarian view. The belief that women and men are, in principle, fully equal in regard to authority in all aspects of Christian life, including leadership in the church and the family. This view is grounded in Galatians 3:28, in regard to public life, and Ephesians 5:21, in regard to family life. This view maintains that gender is irrelevant in regard to spiritual authority.

election. The common Christian belief that God elects who will be saved. This can be understood either corporately, as in the case of Israel and the church, and/or individually. Election also refers to the belief that God elected Christ to save humans, and those who are "in Christ" are thus saved.

empirical. Evidence based on information gathered from experience.

Enuma Elish. An ancient Babylonian creation myth dated to the second millennium BC that parallels the creation story of Genesis 1 in several important ways.

epistemology. Having to do with how we know what we know.

eschatology. The study of the "last things" or the end-times.

eschaton. The end of this age.

eternal security. The belief that the gift of salvation is unconditional. Once a person has been saved, God will not let that person permanently fall away from faith. *See also* **perseverance of the saints.**

evolution. The biological theory that groups of organisms change over time. Microevolution recognizes small changes within a species. Macroevolution maintains that the changes can be from one kind of organism (species) to another, usually progressing to greater levels of complexity. Evangelicals who hold to a literal reading of Genesis 1 and believe that the earth is relatively young acknowledge microevolution but deny macroevolution. Other evangelicals affirm both micro- and macroevolution but insist that God is the creative mind and force behind the process.

exclusivism. The belief that Jesus Christ is the only Savior for all humanity and that it is not possible to attain salvation apart from explicit knowledge of Jesus Christ.

exegesis. To draw meaning out of a text. This method of study attempts to answer the question, What did this text mean to its original author and hearer? Great attention is paid to linguistic issues as appropriate to the original social setting and context.

existentialism. A philosophical movement that emphasizes subjectivity, individuality, and the freedom and responsibility of the self.

ex nihilo. A Latin phrase meaning "out of nothing." This phrase is used to assert that creation is not "co-eternal" with God (in opposition to pantheism and panentheism). Rather, God created the universe out of nothing.

faith. As used in the New Testament, faith can refer to either a person's assent and trust in another or the content that a person assents to and trusts in.

fate. The pagan notion that the future is fixed by impersonal forces. Christians have always affirmed that God, not fate, governs the flow of history. (Whether humans and/or angels by use of their free will have the power to affect this flow in ways God may not desire is disputed.)

finitude. All that is definable. That which is capable of being described, measured, and contained. The direct opposite of infinitude.

flood geology. Geological studies that operate on the assumption that a worldwide flood occurred as described in Genesis 6–8. Many creationists account for the geological strata in this way rather than accepting that the earth is billions of years old, as most contemporary geologists believe.

foreknowledge. As applied to God, the classical confession that God knows with certainty all that shall come to pass. Open Theists modify this definition by maintaining that because God made humans free, God's foreknowledge includes possibilities. Some of God's foreknowledge consists of maybes.

freewill defense. The belief that explains the presence of evil in the world by appealing to the free will of humans and angels. Because agents are free, they sometimes make decisions that are against God's will and are thus evil.

functional view of the *imago Dei*. The view that the image of God is to be understood as our God-given authority. In "having dominion" over the earth (Gen. 1:26–28), humans reflect God's dominion over all creation.

gap theory. A way of reading Genesis 1 that suggests there is a "gap" between verses 1 and 2. In the interval between these verses, angels rebelled against God and corrupted his creation, causing the world to become "formless and void" as described in verse 2. Gap theorists argue that their interpretation allows for a more literal reading of Genesis 1 while affirming the prevailing opinion among scientists that the earth is billions of years old. *See also* **restoration view.**

glossolalia. The Greek word that is translated "speaking in tongues." Most scholars believe the term, as used in 1 Corinthians, referred to people speaking in a God-inspired language they did not know. Cessationists maintain that this ability to speak in tongues ended in the first century. Continuationists maintain that the gift is still operative today.

grace. Undeserved favor.

Great Commission. The command of Christ to the church that we must spread the Good News to all people in all places (Matt. 28:19). The command includes the mandate to baptize and make disciples.

Hebraic. Having to do with Hebrew language, culture, or people.

Heilsgeschichte. A German word meaning "salvation history." Some contemporary theologians argue that the locus of revelation is found in God's mighty deeds in history, centered on the resurrection of Jesus Christ, not in the words of the Bible.

Hellenistic. Having to do with Greek language, culture, or people.

heretic. One condemned as unorthodox—or incorrect in belief or practice of faith—to the point of being dangerous to the fidelity of the church.

higher biblical criticism. The use of historical-critical methods on the Bible. These methods are employed by literary and historical scholars to assess the reliability and meaning of texts.

historical Jesus. The view of Jesus arrived at by historical-critical means. Evangelical historians argue that the view arrived at by this means supports the view of Jesus portrayed in the Gospels. Other more skeptical historians often argue that in varying degrees the real historical Jesus is different from the Jesus portrayed in the Gospels.

holistic. Pertinent to the entirety of something rather than to only some aspect(s).

imago Dei. Latin for "image of God."

inclusivism. The belief that Jesus is the only Savior for all humanity but that it is possible to attain salvation apart from explicit knowledge of him. One can be saved by expressing faith in God based on the general knowledge of him that is available to everyone. Thus, Jesus is ontologically but not epistemologically necessary for salvation.

incompatibilism. The belief that true human freedom is not consistent with the belief that God determines all things.

individualism. The modern Western emphasis on the individual as the ultimate bearer of value rather than the people groups to which an individual belongs.

inerrancy. The belief that the Bible contains no errors of any kind. *See also* **infallible.**

infallible. The belief that, while the Bible may contain errors regarding irrelevant matters when judged by modern standards, it cannot fail to accomplish what God intends it to accomplish. *See also* **inerrancy.**

initial evidence. The classical Pentecostal view that speaking in tongues is the initial sign that one has received the baptism of the Holy Spirit.

irresistible grace. The Calvinist belief that a person whom God has chosen cannot resist the work of the Holy Spirit in his or her life in bringing him or her to a faith-filled saving relationship with God.

Jesus Seminar. A controversial group of mostly liberal New Testament scholars who, since the early 1980s, have been voting on what aspects of the Gospels are and are not historical. Their goal is to influence public opinion by effectively disseminating their views to the general public.

judgment seat. Mentioned in Romans 14:10 and 2 Corinthians 5:10. Most scholars believe this is where the works of believers will be judged (cf. 1 Cor. 3:12–13). The concept has been emphasized by moral government theorists who are concerned with a common Protestant attitude that since believers are saved by grace, their actual lifestyles are largely irrelevant. *See also* **cheap grace.**

justification. To be declared righteous. In classical Protestant theology, people are declared righteous by God when they place their trust in Jesus Christ. Sanctification—the process of growing into a holier lifestyle—is understood to arise on the basis of, and subsequent to, justification.

kenotic Christology. The belief that when the Son of God became incarnate as Jesus of Nazareth, he emptied himself of all divine attributes that would have been inconsistent with his ability to be a full human being. He took on the limitations of finitude and humanity. Hence, Jesus was not, for example, omniscient or omnipotent while on earth. *See also* **two minds Christology.**

laughing in the Spirit. Also described as "holy laughter," this is one of the manifestations that some of the more extreme continuationists (some Pentecostal, charismatic, or third wave Christians) experience during worship when the joy of the Lord is expressed among the believers in the form of overwhelming public laughter.

Leviathan. A mythological monster that ancient Near Eastern people (including the Israelites) believed inhabited the waters that circled the earth (though a minority of evangelical scholars think it refers to an actual creature). This is a way ancient people depicted forces of evil that threatened the earth. Old Testament authors emphasized that Yahweh was able to be victorious over Leviathan (e.g., Job 41; Ps. 74:14; 104:26; Isa. 27:1). *See also* **Rahab.**

limited atonement. The Calvinist belief that Jesus died only for the elect.

literary framework view. In contrast to all views that believe Genesis 1 depicts the actual creation of the world, this theory suggests that the author was interested only in expressing the significance of God as Creator. It is God, not some other deity, who brings order out of chaos.

Manichaeism. A popular religious movement in the fourth and fifth centuries that taught that there were two equal but opposite gods in the world, one good, the other evil. Before converting to Christianity, St. Augustine, arguably the most influential theologian in church history, was a Manichaean.

materialism. The belief that matter is all that exists. Hence, this view holds that all events are ultimately explainable on the basis of physical ("matter") cause-effect relations. Chemistry, physics, biology, and the other hard sciences are looked to for the most adequate explanation for any given problem.

memorial view. This view of communion centers on Christ's words, "Do this in remembrance of me." Rather than speculating on the nature of Christ's presence in the physical elements of communion, this view finds meaning in obedience to the command and reflection on the person of Jesus Christ.

meritorious works. Behaviors or actions that gain divine favor for the one who does them.

metaphysical. Literally, beyond physics. Metaphysics is the speculative attempt to conceive of all things together in a grand explanatory scheme.

modus operendi. Latin for "mode of operation," meaning, the usual way in which one works.

monism. The belief that all events are part of one single, timeless, divine reality. In the philosophical problem of the one and the many, this view resolves "the many" completely into the "One."

monistic view of the self. This view of the human asserts that there can be no final distinction between the body, soul, and spirit of a human being. A human being is fundamentally one unitary entity.

Montanists. A heretical group in the early church who claimed to have new revelations and end-times prophecies. This group was also notable for its emphasis on the charismatic gifts, which the orthodox church dismissed as counterfeit in this particular instance.

moral government view of the atonement. According to this view, the atonement is not a transference of guilt from sinful humans to Jesus (as per penal substitution) but rather a vivid presentation of God's wrath against sin for all to see. This message should inspire believers to flee from sin because there will indeed be a judgment, even for believers, in the **eschaton**.

Muslim. One who believes in the Islamic faith. Muslims regard Muhammad as Allah's (God's) final prophet and the Qur'an as Allah's final and perfect revelation.

mythologized. The end result of the process of weaving mythology in and around a historical person and event.

naturalism. The belief that all events can be explained by appealing to laws and forces of nature. Therefore, adherents of naturalism deny that God (if he exists) exercises any discernable influence in the world.

neo-orthodoxy. Beginning with Karl Barth in the early twentieth century, this school of thought saw itself as a mediating response to the modern split between liberals and fundamentalists. Neo-orthodox theologians affirmed that the Word of God is an event that takes place when Jesus Christ, as witnessed to in the Bible, is proclaimed. But unlike evangelicals, they denied that the Bible is the Word of God in and of itself.

Nestorianism. The heresy that states there were two persons—with two minds—present in Jesus Christ, one divine person and one human person. Nestorianism was condemned at the Council of Chalcedon in AD 451.

New Age. A contemporary movement that incorporates elements of Eastern mysticism, superstition, as well as pagan and occult beliefs. *See also* **pantheism**.

new covenant. Another term for the New Testament. The new covenant is the covenant or promise of grace given to believers through the death and resurrection of Christ. In Christ, believers enter a new relationship of trust, faith, and faithfulness that is based on God's holiness rather than their own.

omnipotent. Literally, all-powerful. All evangelicals affirm that God is all-powerful. Some evangelicals (Calvinists) interpret this to mean that God exercises all power. Others (Arminians) interpret this to mean that all power comes from God.

omnipresent. Literally, present in all places. All evangelicals affirm that God is everywhere.

omniscient. Literally, all-knowing. All evangelicals affirm that God knows everything. Traditionally, evangelicals have interpreted this to mean that God knows all that shall take place in the future. More recently, however, Open Theists have held that the "everything" God perfectly knows includes future possibilities.

ontology. The study of what it is to exist or to "be."

ordinance. A command. Some see the Lord's Supper and baptism as ordinances, as opposed to sacraments, believing that their meaning lies in the simple fact that the people who engage in them are obeying God. *See also* **sacrament.**

paedobaptist. Literally, one who baptizes children or infants. Paedobaptists believe that because children are part of the covenant community of God, they ought to bear the sign of the promise—baptism.

panentheism. Literally, all is in God. All that exists has its being within the being of God, but God transcends the universe itself. God is not identical with the universe (as in pantheism) because God is more than the universe, but the universe is coeternal with God. The most prevalent form of panentheism today is found in process philosophy.

pantheism. Literally, all is God. This view identifies the cosmos completely with God. All that is, is divine. This view was common in Eastern cultures but has now become popular in the West because of the New Age movement. *See also* **New Age.**

parousia. A term that refers to the future return of Christ.

patriarchal. Male dominated.

Pelagianism. A movement based on the teachings of a fifth-century monk named Pelagius. As Augustine recounts it, Pelagius denied that the fall affects human nature and thus held that even in the fallen world humans possess the power on their own to live free from sin. Grace helps people live for God, but Pelagians deny that people are saved by grace alone. For this reason, evangelicals are in agreement that Pelagianism is an unbiblical belief system.

penal substitution view of the atonement. Christ frees humans from the penalty of sin (hell) by accepting the punishment for sin in their place. *See also* **substitutionary view of the atonement.**

Pentecostalism. A movement that began in the early twentieth century that recovered and emphasized the charismatic gifts. These gifts include speaking in tongues, interpretation of tongues, healing, words of knowledge, etc. Pentecostals also hold that all people baptized in the Spirit initially manifest this indwelling by speaking in tongues. *See also* **charismatic gifts.**

perichoresis. A term that refers to the mutual indwelling or interpenetration of the three Persons of the Trinity. Each Person makes "room" for the other within his own being.

perseverance of the saints. The Calvinist belief that true believers can never permanently fall away from the faith and thereby lose their salvation. *See also* **eternal security.**

phenomenology. A way of thinking that proceeds from the basis of descriptions of actual events and scientific observations. This approach is inherently dependent on experience.

pluralism. The belief that there are many roads to God. According to this view, it is presumptuous for anyone to claim that Jesus (or any other "savior" figure) is the one true way to God for all people.

polygamy. Having more than one spouse. While God, for a variety of reasons, at times permitted the Israelite men to have more than one wife, God's ideal has always been monogamy (having only one spouse).

polytheism. The acknowledgment and worship of more than one god.

postmillennialism. The belief that Christ will return after a thousand-year period of peace occurs on earth.

postmodernism. A broad cultural movement that is in various ways critical of modernity. Postmodernists are intensely aware of the large roles experience and culture play in shaping a person's belief system. They are thus suspicious of absolute truth claims that supposedly arise from an indisputable foundation, whether this be empirical evidence, reason, or a religious authority. Hence, postmodernism is sometimes called post-foundationalism.

postmortem evangelism. Some evangelicals believe in a postmortem (after death) opportunity for people, who had no chance to do so in life, to develop or reject faith in Christ.

predestination. To determine ahead of time. God "destines" events ahead of time. The term is usually used in the context of discussing the salvation or eternal destiny of individuals or groups of people. Calvinists believe God predestines all things, including who will and who will not be saved. Arminians and Open Theists believe that God predestines some things but leaves other things, including the salvation or damnation of individuals, to be determined by human free will.

premillennialism. The belief that Christ will return before inaugurating a thousand-year reign of peace on earth. *See also* **chiliasm.**

presupposition. An assumed belief that is not argued for but is related to the argument as a necessary condition for its validity or coherence.

preterist. Literally, already. A preterist interpretation of the book of Revelation holds that the events it speaks of have already taken place. A few evangelicals hold to a broader preterist theology, believing that all end-times predictions were fulfilled in the first century.

prevenient grace. Grace that "goes before" any participation of a person in the process of salvation. Arminian Christians usually hold that God gives prevenient grace to everybody, thereby enabling them to choose freely to accept or reject the message of salvation.

probationary. A trial period. Some Arminian and Open Theists argue that we are currently in a probationary period in which we each have an opportunity to choose freely for or against God. How we respond to God's call in this probationary period will determine our eternal destiny when God brings this probationary period to a close.

problem of evil. The problem of reconciling the fact of evil in the world with faith that the Creator is all-good and all-powerful.

process theology. Traceable to A. N. Whitehead and C. Hartshorne, this school of philosophical theology holds that God and the world are two coeternal realities that are eternally in the process of enriching each other. Process theology denies many of the classical attributes of God. Most problematic for evangelicals is its denial of omnipotence, creation out of nothing, and a final consummation of all things in the end-times.

propitiation. Literally, appeasement. In regard to atonement theory, Christ appeased God's wrath toward humanity, and as a result, God did not take out his wrath on humanity directly.

providence. God's governing of the universe. Some evangelicals hold that God's providence is meticulous—he governs each and every detail. Others hold that it is more general—he controls the "big picture" but gives humans freedom to make their own choices.

Qur'an. The sacred text of Islam, containing the teachings and commands for those of the Muslim faith. It purportedly contains the teachings of Muhammad, the founding prophet of Islam. Muslims consider the Qur'an to be the perfect word of Allah (God).

radical Reformers. Protestants who during the Reformation felt they had to go further than Martin Luther and John Calvin in reforming the church.

Rahab. Like Leviathan, Rahab is an ancient way in which the Bible portrays evil and chaos as cosmic forces against God. *See also* **Leviathan.**

rapture. The act of Christ literally taking the church out of the world before he judges the world and then sets up his millennial kingdom.

rationalistic. To focus on the rational, cognitive, or deductive element of a proposal or problem. Having to do with reason.

reincarnation. The Eastern belief that upon death, a person will be born again in better or worse circumstances based on the status of that person's karma in his or her most recent life. The belief has become popular in the West as a part of the New Age movement. *See also* **New Age.**

relational view of the *imago Dei*. This view asserts that because God exists in the eternal loving community of Father, Son, and Spirit, the essence of the *imago Dei* is the ability of humans to enter into relationships with God and other people.

relativism. The conviction that humans are so conditioned by their social experiences and biological makeup that they can never know absolute truth. All truth claims are relative to the person making them.

restoration view. The belief that Genesis 1:2ff. tells the story not of the original creation but of the restoration of creation after the initial angelic fall. *See also* **gap theory.**

restrictivism. The belief that only those who have consciously responded to the proclamation of the gospel of Jesus Christ are saved.

sacrament. Traditionally understood as a means of grace. Something is sacramental when it is said to "bear the divine." Some evangelicals see the Lord's Supper and baptism as sacraments in that God uses them as a means of dispensing grace to those who participate in them. *See also* **ordinance.**

sanctification. The process of growing into a Christlike person.

satisfaction view of the atonement. A medieval view that relied heavily on the metaphor of "debt and payment" or the reparation that is due someone after that person has been wronged. Because our sin is against God, the debt is infinite. Either we can repay this debt through eternal punishment, or God, who is infinite, can pay the debt on our behalf. The latter is what Christ did on the cross. This payment by God (the Son) to God (the Father) satisfied the infinite nature of the debt humans owed to God for sin.

secular humanists. People who believe that human welfare is the ultimate good and that humans have the power and responsibility to determine their own future.

self-determination. The ability of a person to determine freely his or her own course of action and to move toward becoming a certain kind of person. Arminians hold that people are self-determining. Calvinists hold that God ultimately determines all things.

***sensus divinitatus*.** A Latin phrase meaning "sense of the divine."

slain in the Spirit. This is one of the manifestations of the Spirit that some of the more extreme continuationists (some Pentecostal, charismatic, or third wave Christians) experience during prayer or worship. People typically describe the experience as one of being so overwhelmed by God that they are unable to stand in God's presence.

Socinianism. A heretical movement that denied the divinity of Jesus and the redeeming power of his death.

sola scriptura. Latin phrase meaning "the Scripture alone." This is the reformational conviction, embraced by all evangelicals, that the Bible is the final authority on all matters of faith and practice.

soteriological. Having to do with salvation.

speaking in tongues. *See glossolalia.*

spiritual presence view. This is a moderating view of the Lord's Supper that sees the elements as more than merely symbolic (Anabaptist view) but not necessarily the literal physical flesh and blood of Christ (transubstantiation and consubstantiation views). This view prefers to speak sacramentally of Christ's spiritual presence in the Lord's Supper, an intensified presence that is more than what is assumed by the mere fact of God's omnipresence.

stewardship mandate. In Genesis 1:26–28, after God creates humans in his image, he gives them the stewardship mandate, which is the command to multiply and have dominion over the earth.

subjective view of the atonement. This view emphasizes the example that Christ's life provides more than the objective effect that Christ's death and resurrection accomplished. Jesus is seen as a role model of perfect love and self-sacrifice, and believers are to emulate that character in their own lives.

substantival view of the *imago Dei*. The view that the soul is the image of God in humans—the capacity to reason, feel, love, choose, and live forever.

substitutionary view of the atonement. The view that Jesus died in the place of humans and that this is what allows them to be reconciled with the Father. *See also* **penal substitution view of the atonement.**

supernaturalism. The belief that God can and does miraculously intervene in the world.

Synoptic Gospels. Matthew, Mark, and Luke are referred to as the Synoptic Gospels because they each provide similar summaries (or synopses) of the life of Christ.

textual criticism. As applied to Scripture, this is the discipline of critically examining existing copies of the Bible to determine the most likely original wording of the biblical authors.

theists. People who believe in a personal God.

third wave. Following the Pentecostal movement in the early twentieth century and the charismatic movement in the 1960s, there arose what came to be called the third wave of spiritual revival. Since the early 1980s, an increasing number of leaders have been teaching that Christians can and should expect signs and wonders whenever the gospel is preached, just as the early apostles did. The movement is controversial to many evangelicals.

total depravity. The conviction that all humans are dead in their sins and completely unable to rectify their separation from God on their own.

transubstantiation. The traditional Roman Catholic doctrine that the bread and wine are transformed into the physical body and blood of Christ during Mass.

tribulation. A period of terrible suffering, loss, and destruction worldwide when God's wrath is poured out in judgment. This period of time is related to the ominous prophecies about eschatological events and is expected at various times according to particular schemes.

trichotomist view of the self. The belief that the human self is composed of three distinct constitutive elements: body, soul, and spirit.

two minds Christology. The belief that Jesus Christ had both a human and a divine mind. The divine mind had full access to the human mind but not vice versa. This is a common view of many who hold to classical Christology, which affirms that Christ exercised both human and divine attributes while on earth. This view contrasts with kenotic Christology, which holds that Christ set aside many of his divine attributes—including his omniscience—in order to become a full human being. *See also* **kenotic Christology.**

typology. A parallel occurrence. An element of a story calls to mind another incident with a similar element. Typical comparisons are made in Scripture between Adam and Christ, the Exodus and the passion story, or even the flood and baptism.

Ugaritic. An ancient Semitic language with affinities to Hebrew. Documents written in this language have shed light on ancient Canaanite language, history, and culture in the late second millennium BC.

unconditional election. The Calvinist belief that God's selection of who will be saved is not dependent in any way on what humans do.

universalism. The belief that ultimately all will be saved. Hell is not eternal but rather eventually serves to turn sinners toward God. Very few people throughout church history and very few evangelicals today affirm this perspective.

universal opportunity. The view that God finds some means of giving every person who would believe in Christ the chance to do so. If it is not possible to reach a person through evangelism, God may use dreams, visions, or even angelic visitations.

viceregent. One who governs in place of another. A delegated authority.

young earth view. According to this view, the six days of creation were six literal twenty-four-hour periods of time. This belief, combined with a literalist reading of the genealogies in the Old Testament, leads young earth theorists to conclude that the earth is less than ten thousand years old.

Scripture Index